The Nationalization of American Political Parties, 1880–1896

This book investigates the creation of the first truly nationalized party organizations in the United States in the late nineteenth century, an innovation that reversed the parties' traditional privileging of state and local interests in presidential nominations and the conduct of national campaigns. Between 1880 and 1896, party elites crafted a defense of these national organizations that charted the theoretical parameters of American party development into the twentieth century. With empowered national committees and a new understanding of the parties' role in the political system, national party leaders dominated American politics in new ways, renewed the parties' legitimacy in an increasingly pluralistic and nationalized political environment, and thus maintained their relevance throughout the twentieth century. The new organizations particularly served the interests of presidents and presidential candidates, and the presidencies of the late nineteenth century demonstrate the first stirrings of modern presidential party leadership.

Daniel Klinghard is Assistant Professor of Political Science at the College of the Holy Cross in Worcester, Massachusetts.

For Cheri

The Nationalization of American Political Parties, 1880–1896

DANIEL KLINGHARD

College of the Holy Cross
Worcester, Massachusetts

CAMBRIDGE
UNIVERSITY PRESS

CAMBRIDGE UNIVERSITY PRESS
Cambridge, New York, Melbourne, Madrid, Cape Town, Singapore,
São Paulo, Delhi, Dubai, Tokyo

Cambridge University Press
32 Avenue of the Americas, New York, NY 10013-2473, USA

www.cambridge.org
Information on this title: www.cambridge.org/9780521192811

First published 2010

Printed in the United States of America

A catalog record for this publication is available from the British Library.

Library of Congress Cataloging in Publication data

Klinghard, Daniel, 1974–
The nationalization of American political parties, 1880–1896 / Daniel Klinghard.
   p.   cm.
Includes bibliographical references and index.
ISBN 978-0-521-19281-1 (hardback)
   1. Political parties – United States – History – 19th century.   2. Political parties –
United States – States – History – 19th century.   3. United States – Politics and
government – 19th century.   I. Title.
JK2261.K58   2010
324.27309′034–dc22   2009053441

ISBN 978-0-521-19281-1 Hardback

Contents

Preface	*page* vii
Acknowledgments	xi
	Introduction	1
1	Localism and the Jacksonian Mode	25
2	The Nineteenth-Century Associational Explosion and the Challenge to the Jacksonian Mode	66
3	Organizational Transformation and the National Parties	98
4	National Campaign Clubs and the Party-in-the-Electorate	124
5	Grover Cleveland and the Emergence of Presidential Party Leadership	144
6	Party Transformation in the Republican Party	191
	Conclusion	235
Selected Bibliography	259
Index	263

Preface

This study began as a search for remedies for the familiar disease of party decline. It made sense to look for such remedies in the late nineteenth century, the period of American parties' supposed peak performance. Perhaps, I supposed, by better understanding the parties' defense of methods that have since come to be mistrusted, today's parties could be strengthened. This original purpose quickly collapsed. As I pursued the public and private writings of party leaders of the time, I was struck by just how willing they were to jettison much of what political scientists believe made the parties strong, and just how willing they were to adopt practices that presaged twentieth-century party politics. Instead of a ringing defense of traditional methods – along the lines of George Washington Plunkitt's famous series of very plain talks on very practical politics – I found a raging debate over the need to renew party organizations in America. This is odd. Why would party leaders be experiencing a crisis of confidence in parties at precisely the time that many political scientists believe parties to have been operating at optimal productivity?

This book is an account of their collective wondering, their struggle to preserve institutions that held great emotional and practical value to them, while adjusting them to a new political environment. It is a story of changing ideas and changing institutions, but it is also a story of what it is that allows institutions as loosely constructed as parties to perpetuate themselves. In an age in which partisan politics was viewed as suspiciously as any (except perhaps in the Founding era or our own), these elites struggled to force the parties to adapt without abandoning their commitment to the two-party system. Despite the frequent charge that the parties have done little but weaken since the dawn of the twentieth century, their work made the two-party system stronger. It effectively silenced a generation of third-party challenges, made peace with a flurry of extra-partisan citizen associations, updated parochial and dysfunctional party methods to meet the emergent demands of a newly nationalized political environment, and fashioned a new style of campaigning that was particularly well suited to this new mode of organizing. This is a reminder that party organizations are not just about facilitating participation on a particular scale – an activity with high normative but variable practical value – but about ordering political conflict – an activity with ambiguous normative and enormous practical value.

Throughout the late 1800s, the parties were challenged by a variety of entities (third parties, national interest associations, reform organizations) that suggested the parties had lost their relevance to the conditions faced by most voters. These entities did not succeed in displacing the Republican and Democratic parties from their preeminent place in American public life; but by exploiting some of the parties' weaknesses (and the period's tight electoral competition), they did arouse national party leaders to new openings for popular leadership. For all the zeal of the late-nineteenth-century reform movement, party leaders were not forced to accept reform; they were persuaded that the newly nationalized political environment provided opportunities as well as threats. Thus, the two-party system survived – and emerged stronger from – the late nineteenth century because it served the purpose it was established to serve: helping ambitious politicians obtain power.

In particular, national party leaders became aware of the potential for expanding the parties' national campaign operations to craft a truly national party-in-the-electorate. The parties had originally been organized to resist just this kind of nationalization. Although party competition as an abstract concept had become widely accepted by the mid-nineteenth century, it was party competition of a particular sort – distinctively republican in structure and style, presuming the proper and safest form of political organizing to be grounded in local communities. A national party organization that reached a national party-in-the-electorate could not simply be asserted; a national party politics had to be defined and defended.

Others are left to decide whether or not this is a positive development (the thrust of much of the decline of party literature). This work is limited to two chief contentions. First, the nineteenth-century opposition to party did not have the effect of neutering the parties but provided a new intellectual heritage for the parties that shaped them during the twentieth century. Second, this new idea of party triggered constitutional potentials that had lain dormant under the republican revolution of the Jacksonian organizational mode. Without revising the Constitution, the Jacksonian party system grafted republican political practices onto the American regime that diminished its liberal elements; especially its fostering of a national community of conflicting interests (as articulated by James Madison in *The Federalist*), and its endorsement of positive presidential leadership (as articulated by Alexander Hamilton in *The Federalist*). To prevent the salience of national communities of interest, the Jacksonian mode rigorously enforced geographic communities as the sole means of entry into the national party organization and subordinated the presidency to a nominating system dominated by state and local party organizations. The late-nineteenth-century idea of party, however, envisioned a party-in-the-electorate that transcended geographic boundaries (some of which, it should be noted, were also supplied by the Constitution), a special role for national interest associations in party politics, and a presidency that could mobilize mass publics independently of local partisan communities.

This transformation in the fundamental idea of party did not effectively remake the party organizations by 1896 – the end point of this study. Not until the solidification of the presidential direct primary in the 1970s did the new idea of party achieve something like full institutionalization. In the meantime, the new idea underwrote the emergence of the direct primary in the early 1900s, an emergent style of national presidential leadership, and an increasingly confident public interest association sector, even as the first half of the twentieth century saw the reassertion of state and local organizational power. Although most previous studies of these twentieth-century developments have emphasized the creation of institutions and laws that have formalized these changes, this study makes the case for the formative role of party leaders' ideas of how political conflict should be ordered. Those ideas coalesced into broad agreement among a critical cadre of national elites between 1880 and 1896; and this consensus formed the parameters of the ways their successors – in politics, the media, and the social sciences – evaluated the parties. Concurring with Richard Hofstadter, I do not describe this as anything as systemic as a "theory," nor as pleasing as an "ideal" of party. It was a political thing, crafted by practical politicians (who, like Plunkitt, were more concerned with what worked than with reconciling their practice to democratic theory). It was used to promote individual politicians' competencies and to legitimate party politics to the public. The idea was shaped by a variety of insights into the ways in which political life changed in the late nineteenth century and the ways in which parties would continue to order political affairs despite these changes. It was not written in any textbook; but it became part of the language politicians used to communicate with one another – sometimes openly, sometimes in a kind of insider shorthand. It told politicians how to behave, how to win votes, and where to concentrate resources. In short, it envisioned a distinct mode of party operations. If this idea did not achieve immediate organizational transformation from within the parties, it provides a powerful explanation of the source of the long process of party transformation in the twentieth century.

Acknowledgments

I owe more debts in the writing of this book than I can satisfactorily discharge. They began to accrue in the office of my dissertation advisor, Sidney M. Milkis, who demonstrated to me the value of a historical approach to political science, convinced me of the causes for concern about the state of American political parties, and urged me to take the late-nineteenth-century parties seriously; his influence on my thinking, style, and inclinations is apparent throughout. I was fortunate that Morton Keller, whom I have come to know as a superb advisor as well as a superb historian, agreed to serve on my committee; and even more fortunate that he generously agreed to give more time to guiding me than I thought I deserved (especially after he read a draft of my proposal, which provoked his first piece of advice to me: "If you're going to study the nineteenth century, you have to learn how to spell 'tariff' and 'gilded.'"). Marc Landy's careful reading and thoughtful comments continue to influence the way I think about the period. Steve Teles, my bighearted counselor in all things academic, the long-suffering reader of my lengthening prose, and as faithful a dissertation reader as ever there was, deserves special credit for making this possible.

I could not have completed the archival research for this book without the financial support I received from a number of sources. Brandeis University funded my earliest trips to the Library of Congress. A "We the People" grant from the National Endowment for the Humanities enabled me to spend a valuable year at the Library of Congress and at the Pennsylvania Historical Society. The College of the Holy Cross generously granted me leave that year, as well as funding for another archival trip. At those archives, as well as at the Massachusetts Historical Society and the American Antiquarian Society, I had the benefit of the assistance of archivists and staff who not only fulfilled my requests for materials, but alerted me to new materials of interest; in going above the call of duty, they have helped me fill in a number of gaps in my research. Sharon Matys of Holy Cross provided much-needed assistance with the graphics in Chapters 1 and 6.

Portions of Chapters 5 and 6 were published as "Presidential Party Leadership and the Emergence of the President as Party Leader: Grover Cleveland, William McKinley, and Presidential Politics in the Post-Jacksonian Organizational Mode," in *Presidential Studies Quarterly* (December 2005). That piece, and my subsequent reworking of some of the material, benefited from the editorship of George C. Edwards III and two helpful anonymous reviewers.

Since the dissertation stage, I have pressed this work on more colleagues than I can recall. I first began thinking about party development when working on an undergraduate thesis advised by Mike Nelson (I never print a page without thinking of his editorship or his approach to the presidency), along with Daniel Cullen and Stephen Wirls. Dennis Hale first alerted me that there might be something interesting to say about Grover Cleveland. David Mayhew and David Art kindly read drafts that were much longer than what appears here. My colleagues at Holy Cross, B. Jeffrey Reno, Dustin Gish, and Loren Cass, have all provided helpful advice, thoughts, and ideas; Donald Brand has been an especially inspiring mentor, an exemplar of what academic life should be. Brian Cook not only led me to some helpful thoughts on Cleveland and Woodrow Wilson but was a cheerleader in times of stress. At various conference panels along the way, I received helpful comments from John Berg, Daniel Carpenter, Joseph Cooper, Graham Dodds, Brian Glenn, Timothy Nokken, Howard Reiter, and John Reynolds; in many ways that I hope they recognize, I have integrated their suggestions into my argument. I have also been blessed to have had good friends who have tolerated a lot of talk about the minutiae of nineteenth-century politics, including Jeremy Bailey, Andrew Bove, Nicole Hales, Daniel Kenney, Mark Miller, and Andrew Veprek. At Cambridge University Press, Lewis Bateman nurtured the manuscript from a very early stage, and Emily Spangler graciously walked me through the details of publication. My two anonymous reviewers were a model of constructive scholarly criticism – they engaged me honestly and genuinely, and this is a better book because of them.

My mother, my father, my brother David, and my sister Mary Elizabeth gave me moral support from the beginning; and I am forever grateful for that. My grandmother, Martha Sue Mills, gave me an appreciation of the importance of history that continues to influence my work. This book is dedicated to my wife Cheri, because she gave me more to love in life than my work. Her encouragement makes the completion of this book a sweeter accomplishment than it could ever have been alone; as does the prospect of repaying my patient children, Amsden and Jocelyn Mae, for all of the time I spent with it rather than with them.

Worcester, Massachusetts
September 2009

Introduction

Between 1880 and 1896, national party leaders in both major American parties discarded the basic organizational preferences that had guided them since the formulation of the Jacksonian party organization in the 1830s and 1840s, and adopted new ones that informed the parties' development throughout the twentieth century. The purpose of this book is to bring this late-nineteenth-century transformation back into scholars' understanding of the development of American parties. These changes were legitimated by a new idea of party that was as portentous as that of the late 1790s described by Richard Hofstadter as the rise of "the idea of a party system."[1]

Rejecting the traditional understanding of the national party organizations as a congeries of independent, local organizations, national party leaders reconfigured the conduct of national campaigns to reach voters directly with nationally printed material and with direct presidential campaigning. Contrary to the traditional parties' insistence on local control of campaigns, they centralized control of presidential campaigns in the national committees, which became more capable than ever before of transposing national politics into national electoral mandates. Combating the traditional insistence on restraining the independence of the national committees, they empowered them to raise money independently of state party organizations, expanding the national organizations' ability to fund their own operations. They broke through the traditional geographic boundaries of party regularity to found party clubs designed to nationalize the party-in-the-electorate. Republicans rejected the ability of state party organizations to control the votes of national convention delegates, affirming the national character of their nominees. Finally, presidents and presidential candidates used these new methods to free themselves from the party system's traditional restraints on presidential party leadership. Together, these practices undermined the fundamental tenets of the Jacksonian era idea of party

---

[1] Richard Hofstadter, *The Idea of a Party System: The Rise of Legitimate Opposition in the United States, 1780–1840* (Berkeley: University of California Press, 1969).

and the Jacksonian mode of party organization that it implied. State and local organizations were not dissolved, but they ceased to play the determinative role that they once had in nominations and campaigns. National conventions were not disbanded, but they never again performed the same way in shaping presidential candidacies.

Although Hofstadter portrayed the Jacksonian idea of party as constituting a modern party politics fitted to the new constitutional regime, I argue that this Jacksonian organizational mode (referred to as such because it was founded in the Jacksonian era, not because it was contiguous with that period) aimed to institutionalize what Marvin Meyers calls "an ideal of a chaste republican order" that predated the Constitution, one that John F. Reynolds argues "flourished amid traditions grounded in the ideology of republicanism." In this sense, the Jacksonian party organization displaced the liberal, national politics of interest depicted in *The Federalist* by enforcing an older republican tradition that Jacksonians believed would enable the common man to achieve self-governance in the face of powerful tendencies to oligarchy.[2] As Moisei Ostrogorski put it, the Jacksonian party system "had made its way into the government behind the back of the Constitution."[3] Whereas Hamilton, Madison, and Jay conceived of a national political order that could "refine and enlarge the public view" by filtering it through an extended national republic, the Jacksonian mode subordinated the ambitions of national politicians to the political power of state and local political communities.[4] As Sidney Milkis argues, "the confederative form of parties seemed to defy the 'more perfect union' created by the Constitution of 1787."[5] Indeed, the attempt of Martin Van Buren – the Jacksonians' most thoughtful party organizer – to use the party system to contain presidential ambition leads James Ceaser to suggest that he "turned his back on the Founders and showed himself to be a thoroughgoing Republican, being concerned first and foremost with restraining power."[6]

[2] Marvin Meyers, *The Jacksonian Persuasion: Politics and Belief* (Stanford, CA: Stanford University Press, 1957), 12; John F. Reynolds, *The Demise of the American Convention System, 1880–1911* (Cambridge: Cambridge University Press, 2006), 20–1.

[3] Moisei Ostrogorski, *Democracy and the Organization of Political Parties: Volume II: The United States*, ed., Seymour Martin Lipset (Chicago: Anchor Books, 1964, originally published in 1903), 76.

[4] Alexander Hamilton, James Madison, and John Jay, *The Federalist*, edited by Robert Scigliano (New York: Random House, 2000), 58–9.

[5] Sidney M. Milkis, *Political Parties and Constitutional Government: Remaking American Democracy* (Baltimore: Johns Hopkins University Press, 1999), 15.

[6] James W. Ceaser, *Presidential Selection: Theory and Development* (Princeton, NJ: Princeton University Press, 1979), 136. Ceaser goes on to conclude that "Van Buren might well have countered that the Founders' system, which was designed both to restrain popular leadership and to promote excellence, had not worked. . . . who is to say that the Founders, faced with the same choice, would not have resolved the issue in the same way?" I argue that the continuity between his party organization and the Founders' version of liberal republicanism is not as strong as Ceaser suggests.

In the late nineteenth century, this republican idea of party was rejected in favor of a renewed vision of national, liberal democratic politics, one that informed a distinctively nineteenth-century organizational mode. It was not fully implemented by 1896, just as the party system was not formalized by the emergence of two-party conflict in the 1790s. Nonetheless, it provided intellectual justification for the trends of party development into the twentieth century, particularly the move to direct primaries, closer relationships between the major party organizations and interest groups, and presidential dominance of party politics.

In rethinking the party organizations, national party leaders were responding to new conditions, most notably an electorate that was more focused on national politics and less attached to community interests, more open to persuasion by independent interest associations and less susceptible to partisan appeals, more concerned about substantive policy issues and less attracted to party harmony. As Richard McCormick observes, this process of accommodating new conditions "undermined the old political system and the party organizations that had dominated it."[7] The result was not a completely new party organization but a new party mode designed to conduct party politics (especially the politics of nominating presidential candidates, clarifying party principles, and conducting campaigns) differently from the way the Jacksonian mode operated; the new mode was grounded in a different view of the relation of individuals to the party and worked to establish a new balance of power between national and subnational political elites. The old mode was not destroyed; it persisted in tension with the new mode for some time, shaping the parameters of the early and mid-twentieth century. National conventions still selected the parties' nominees for president; the presidency, which was the prize around which the first stirrings of organized partisanship in America occurred, remained the focal point of U.S. party politics; parties still issued platforms; the same party labels were used, along with their nineteenth-century iconography; and a commitment to a two – and only two – party system continued to define the parameters of mainstream partisanship. As Karen Orren and Stephen Skowronek argue, "all political change ... is accompanied by the accumulation and persistence of competing controls within the institutions of government, [and so] the normal condition of the polity will be that of multiple, incongruous authorities operating simultaneously." The tension between these multiple orders generated the distinctive characteristics of the American party system as it passed through time.[8]

It is common to fold these changes into a longer process of party development or to argue that parties have simply "declined." This book contends something

---

[7] Richard L. McCormick, *From Realignment to Reform: Political Change in New York State, 1893–1910* (Ithaca, NY: Cornell University Press, 1981), 36–7; Alan Ware, *The Democratic Party Heads North, 1877–1962* (Cambridge: Cambridge University Press, 2006), 118–19.

[8] Karen Orren and Stephen Skowronek, *The Search for American Political Development* (New York: Cambridge University Press, 2004), 108.

different: that the Jacksonian organizational mode, established in the party battles of the 1830s and 1840s and long heralded by political scientists as a model of strong parties, was not, in fact, dominant throughout the nineteenth century but was subverted at the end of the century by persistent liberal and nationalizing features of the American regime. This is not occasion to celebrate the old mode or to praise a return to Founding intent, but to recognize that too often the rubric of party decline masks a normative preference for a particular way of engaging in politics that practical politicians have questioned for more than a hundred years. This book argues that what others label "party decline" has, in many cases, been the recurrence of persistent patterns of American politics triggered by the confluence of social change and the muscular force of persistent features of the American polity. Although this argument runs counter to the (small-p) progressive view of history that suggests a one-way directionality to the course of political development, it is not a prescription for a "return to Founding intent" that often derives from taking the Founders seriously. Instead, it proposes that the American constitutional order has had a conservative impact on the course of party development, reversing trends that challenge it, regardless of individuals' reverence for Founding principles. The Jacksonian party mode and the Founders' constitutional order existed in tension with one another; party politics in the late nineteenth century replaced the Jacksonian mode with a new, mixed organizational mode that, although a new departure in many ways, was invited by the original constitutional framework.

Republican and Liberal Organizational Values

As the past few decades of historiography on the political thought of the Founding have fully established, the Founders blended a variety of sometimes-contradictory intellectual traditions, including those that have come to be identified as liberalism and republicanism; Jacksonians most certainly did the same.[9] Yet although it is problematic to simplify either the Founders or the Jacksonians as monolithically liberal or republican, it is helpful to understand the Jacksonian party organizations as reinforcing the distinctively republican elements of the American tradition and as deemphasizing the effects of the Founders' national liberalism. Republicanism and liberalism define the values of a regime as a whole, not just a component part of that regime, such as parties. However, Jacksonian party organizations supplemented Americans' commitment to republican values, channeling behavior in ways that colored the practice of politics generally. As Joel Silbey argues, "powerful partisan perspectives . . . were adopted as the nation's norm with important behavioral consequences," as party politics institutionalized "a set of rules and understandings, and the internalizing of a number of habits, perceptions, and customs, that

---

[9] James T. Kloppenberg, "The Virtues of Liberalism: Christianity, Republicanism, and Ethics in Early American Political Discourse," *The Journal of American History* (June 1987), 9–33.

all together added up to 'the common law of democracy.'"[10] Richard Bensel similarly argues that "these rituals, rules, and the physical setting constitute the structure of the political site in which decisions are made and alternatives chosen."[11] Thus, party organizations not only participated in the regime, they consciously and selectively structured their routines according to the regime's values, thereby both absorbing some of the legitimacy of those values and reinforcing the legitimacy of some of the regime's values over others.

It would be short-sighted not to characterize the Jacksonian party organization as democratic. As James Stanton Chase argues, the Jacksonian convention system was "democracy applied to party government."[12] In the United States, however, "democracy" alone is a vague term, and in the Jacksonian era, Americans were struggling to define exactly what kind of democracy the Constitution countenanced. The Jacksonians' opponents envisioned a national, economically diverse democracy that was best guided by a beneficent central government, a "positive liberal state."[13] Jacksonians mistrusted a government that was distant from the people, believing that democracy at its purest was practiced at a level at which the people could participate; although they recognized the usefulness of a national government in preserving this kind of democratic republican practice, they were wary of its tendency to overwhelm the common man.[14]

Characterizing the Jacksonian mode as republican follows Rogers Smith's description of American republicanism as being "said to present citizens as persons who have contracted with those whom they can regard as civic siblings to create institutions of collective self-governance."[15] As Thomas Pangle notes, this notion of mutual duty tends to exert "pressure toward conformity or homogeneity," including "the need to stifle the internecine factions that were endemic to the fiercely ambitious and restless citizenry" and the drive to "instill a sense of kinship by imbuing all citizens with similar tastes, opinions, and property holdings."[16] In the face of a constitutional regime that encouraged nationalism and the representation of a diverse array of interests, the Jacksonian organization "was intended to preserve the integrity of local

---

[10] Joel Silbey, *The American Political Nation, 1838–1893* (Stanford: Stanford University Press, 1991), 34, 35, 65.

[11] Richard Franklin Bensel, *Passion and Preferences: William Jennings Bryan and the 1896 Democratic National Convention* (Cambridge: Cambridge University Press, 2008), 125.

[12] James S. Chase, "Jacksonian Democracy and the Rise of the Nominating Convention," in Otto Gatell, ed., *Essays on Jacksonian America* (New York: Holt, Rinehart and Winston, 1970), 89.

[13] Daniel Walker Howe, *The Political Culture of the American Whigs* (Chicago: University of Chicago Press, 1979), 16, 20.

[14] Wilson Carey McWilliams, "Parties as Civic Associations," in Gerald M. Pomper, ed., *Party Renewal in America: Theory and Practice* (New York: Praeger, 1980).

[15] Rogers M. Smith, *Stories of Peoplehood: The Politics and Morals of Political Membership* (New York: Cambridge University Press, 2003), 75.

[16] Thomas Pangle, "The Federalist Papers' Vision of Civic Health and the Tradition out of Which That Vision Emerges," *The Western Political Quarterly* (December 1986), 584.

communities" in which "all potentially disruptive influences be cast aside."[17] It drew from a pre-Revolutionary republican heritage in which "a locally validated elite shielded local customs from... outside interference."[18] Wilson Carey McWilliams explains that this reintroduced the republican notion of civic brotherhood into the practice of American national democracy, because through the operation of political parties, politics

> would begin... with the localities where popular judgment is sound and public control is possible.... local partisan groups were to choose their natural leaders. Natural leaders from several localities, united in a face-to-face society of their own, would select their natural leaders. Ideally, an hierarchy of face-to-face societies, connected by relations of personal trust, would connect the locality and the central state.[19]

In the midst of cross-cutting foundational commitments to republicanism and liberalism, the Jacksonian mode, by institutionalizing republican-oriented political practices, reminded voters of their commitment to local communities, emphasized popular cooperation as a bulwark against despotism, and reinforced party loyalties as a form of public kinship that reinforced "the longstanding notions of deference, the mistrust of ambition, and the craving for harmony" that were part of the nation's republican tradition.[20] In this way, as Hofstadter argues, the republican construction of party politics reconciled Americans' republican mistrust of parties between 1789 and 1840.

This idea of party was not merely grounded in philosophical prescriptions; it reinforced the political position of its founders, a generation of "new men" coming out of the lower and middle classes who emerged as the Founding generation faded away. They had been "previously overshadowed in the establishment politics of the colonial era, [but]... began to assume a much more forceful role in government," especially at the state level.[21] Nationalization threatened to subvert the gains they had made in state politics by concentrating power in the national government; the Jacksonian-republican idea of party insulated these subnational political elites from the challenge of a national elite that would be empowered by either the perpetuation of the national caucus or the emergence of a nonpartisan national political sphere.[22] These "new men" did not build conventions merely to suit democratic principles; they had their own political power first and foremost in their minds and utilized political

---

[17] Milkis, *Political Parties and Constitutional Government*, 27; Reynolds, *The Demise of the American Convention System*, 60.

[18] Robert E. Shalhope, *The Roots of Democracy: American Thought and Culture, 1760–1800* (Boston: Twayne, 1990), 25.

[19] McWilliams, "Parties as Civic Associations," 59.

[20] Reynolds, *The Demise of the American Convention System*, 20–1.

[21] Hofstadter, *The Idea of a Party System*, 214; William E. Nelson, "Officeholding and Power-wielding: An Analysis of the Relationship between Structure and Style in American Administrative History," *Law and Society Review* (Winter 1976), 206; Lee Benson, *The Concept of Jacksonian Democracy: New York as a Test Case* (Princeton: Princeton University Press, 1961).

[22] Ceaser, *Presidential Selection*, 149–50.

forms they believed best suited to perpetuate that power.[23] The convention model had the advantage of lending democratic pretenses to what had been an elite-centered activity and thus "prevailed over other nominating methods because it satisfied the ideological demands of the Jacksonian era." Conventions also had strategic advantages. The earliest conventions grew out of caucuses; because not every legislative seat was held by any party, the caucus inevitably excluded a number of locales. Gradually, the parties allowed unrepresented districts to send representatives to caucuses, for the purpose of better aggregating coalitions over a broader array of locales and uniting the ambitions of a wider array of local politicians. Conventions also provided more effective campaign coordination in an era of limited travel options.[24] The first national organizations were thus, built out of an alliance of extant, independent state and local party organizations, which had become tools of the new men in state and local politics. Such groups were not willing to sacrifice their hard-won state and local independence simply to empower national majorities.[25]

The aspirations for national collective action that the Jacksonian mode was designed to promote were therefore quite modest. Jacksonianism was not premised on the leadership of an enlightened vanguard; unlike European working-class radicals, Jacksonians did not require the elaboration of an ideology that promised to rebuild the state to serve the interests of their constituents, so their new party organization was designed neither to elaborate a popular ideology nor to direct the state positively to serve the interests of the people. Instead, it mobilized the people into politics in numbers that would make their assent necessary to any who would rule them in a political system that was already designed to receive popular input; the republican ideology of the Revolution was ideology enough. New principles, in fact, were believed to divide the people, confusing their permanent interests with conflicts over temporary issues.[26] The results were legitimate: "from everything we know," Richard L. McCormick concludes, "the American people got roughly the economic policies they wanted."[27] Jacksonian parties assembled quadrennially to nominate presidents, and they provided some semblance of unity on political matters in Congress, but their ability to use national majorities to direct government to accomplish national governing objectives was limited.

Characterizing the late-nineteenth-century party mode that replaced the Jacksonian mode as liberal follows Smith's explanation that liberals understand society as "an artificially, consensually created instrument of a diverse range

---

[23] Benson, *The Concept of Jacksonian Democracy*, 9.

[24] Chase, "Jacksonian Democracy and the Rise of the Nominating Convention," 87, 89; Richard P. McCormick, *The Second American Party System: Party Formation in the Jacksonian Era* (Chapel Hill: University of North Carolina Press, 1966), 349–50.

[25] John Aldrich, *Why Parties? The Origin and Transformation of Political Parties in America* (Chicago: University of Chicago Press, 1995), 124.

[26] Hofstadter, *The Idea of a Party System*, 245.

[27] Richard L. McCormick, "The Party Period and Public Policy: An Exploratory Hypothesis," *The Journal of American History* (September 1979), 287, 285.

of self-interested personal life plans, with the emphasis generally on seeking economic, religious, and familial fulfillment."[28] Pangle argues that liberalism is defined by the absence of strong mutual duties and "the liberty to remain in a private station, the right to refuse most of the burdens and responsibilities of republicanism," and to instead pursue the satisfactions of private interest, over which the claims of the community have less power.[29] In the new party idea, the claims of local community homogeneity, deference to fellow partisans, even duty to the partisan community, were subordinated to an organizational mode that promised to service national communities of interest, which were decreasingly likely to identify themselves geographically.

Rather than assuming voters to be embedded in communal contexts that defined their partisan affiliation, the new idea presumed narrow communities to be insufficient in articulating the interests of a diverse society. The national party's job was to more effectively inform partisan citizens about their distinctive individual interests, thus perfecting their capacity to maintain those interests. Abandoning the pretense of consistent party identities, the new idea of party presumed party principles to be in constant flux as new issues and new publics rose to prominence, forcing the parties continuously to revise their public appeals. A definitive feature of this new idea was a new means of mobilizing national publics called the educational campaign, the premise of which was that local prejudices had to be enlarged and replaced by "educated" views on questions of public policy.

This new organizational mode and the idea that legitimated it were also sponsored by a new generation of political elites. Not coincidentally, many of these men – like John Wanamaker, William Whitney, and Mark Hanna – built careers in the emergent national economic order and saw the value of a coherent national politics that could rationalize an unwieldy system. Unlike the Jacksonian mode's founders, they advocated an active national policy agenda and were frustrated when the Jacksonian mode empowered subnational elites who were willing to sacrifice coherent national politics to maintain the local basis of power that was the source of their position in the national organization itself.[30] Although many of these individuals pursued political power through the parties, an increasing number worked through extra-partisan channels such as interest groups or civic associations. These associations became testing grounds for collective action tactics eventually absorbed by the parties. Neither localism nor republicanism was eradicated by the new idea of party any more than nationalism was eradicated by the Jacksonian idea. The American Constitution ensures powerful tendencies toward localism by grounding

---

[28] Smith, *Stories of Peoplehood*, 75.

[29] Pangle, "The Federalist Papers' Vision of Civic Health," 597.

[30] This is not to suggest that these new national publics were advancing the policy recommendations of either traditional Whigs or twentieth-century liberals. As Chapter 2 makes clear, the new methods were not defined by the policy objectives they sought. See Howe, *The Political Culture of the American Whigs*, 20.

national constituencies in subnational geographic jurisdictions and the federal division of power. As a vision of the component parts of national politics, however, the new idea of party enabled the parties to explain themselves, and the new organizational mode enabled them to comport themselves, in ways that reflected the new kind of popular demands being made on the national political system.

Change and Learning in Party Organizations

Change happened rapidly between the Civil War and 1880, challenging the Jacksonian organizations' republican foundations and inviting a reconsideration of party methods. Railroads lowered transportation costs dramatically, opening the full breadth of the nation to travelers, producers, consumers, and political organizers. They allowed cheaper and more reliable mail delivery, facilitating the mass distribution of newspapers, circular letters, and politically themed literature. The telegraph became more popularly available, and to the thousands who crowded telegraph offices on election day, something akin to a national culture emerged over the shortened distances of the wire. Both technologies facilitated the organization of interstate associations, enabling the proliferation of the kind of mass national constituencies that had once been unique to the parties. They also integrated what had been largely "a collection of regional economies" because the railroad linked labor, product, and capital markets and broadened the availability of economic information.[31] A Philadelphia editor enthused in 1878 that, given the rapid advance of technology, "at no distant day is it more than likely that the phonograph and the telephone will come in to take the place of the patriot and the orator." Perhaps he misjudged the direction in which campaigning would evolve, but he was correct in asserting that with technological change, "our present system of political campaigns is susceptible of great modification and improvement in the future."[32]

Business enterprises inflated and infiltrated the lives of citizens in new ways. National corporations increasingly consumed the means of production in ways that took decisions about pricing, investment of capital, and terms of credit out of the hands of local businessmen and handed them to faraway bureaucracies beyond the control of local governments. It was an expression of hopefulness that "great numbers of Americans came to believe that a new United States, stretched from ocean to ocean, filled out, and bound together, had miraculously appeared," but it came with a sinister side, the sense that economic "power lay elsewhere, in alien hands."[33]

---

[31] Ronald N. Johnson and Gary D. Libecap, *The Federal Civil Service System and the Problem of Bureaucracy: The Economics and Politics of Institutional Change* (Chicago: University of Chicago Press, 1994), 22. See also Howard Reiter, *Selecting the President: The Nominating Process in Transition* (Philadelphia: University of Pennsylvania Press, 1985), 134.

[32] No title, (Philadelphia) *Evening Bulletin*, July 15, 1878, 4.

[33] Robert H. Wiebe, *The Search for Order, 1877–1920* (New York: Hill and Wang, 1967), 11, 7.

The public's awareness of national economic and political issues shifted. Popular demands for government intervention increased. As Morton Keller notes, "a variety of spokesmen insisted that new social realities required new approaches to governance," including a range of government policies designed to do everything from imposing order on a culturally diverse society to reconciling the inequalities of industrial capitalism.[34] Insurgent politicians in the South and West ridiculed mainstream politicians for their failure to respond to perceived crises and attributed their intransigence to corruption. Reformers publicized government misdeeds, finding a form of political power in shocking exposes of official corruption. As a result, trust in the national government declined in the years following the Civil War; in fact, mistrust of the federal government's and the parties' capacities to harness the forces of expansion produced retrenchment.[35]

The role of government in the people's lives also became inflated during the war, and the effects reverberated throughout the following decades. Conscription and other privations were over relatively quickly, but the federal government had turned to novel measures to finance the war, and these became enduring sites of national political conflict. Republicans imposed a high tariff to fund wartime operations and maintained its popularity afterward under the banner of protection for American industry. The government inflated the currency with paper money to stave off wartime depression but afterward followed a deflationary policy as the country returned to the gold standard over the next two decades.[36] Arguments used to defend or assail the tariff and the gold standard demonstrated the extent to which the federal government had come to touch citizens' lives. High tariffs raised the cost of consumer goods but secured the wages of those who worked in protected industries. The gold standard strengthened the dollar and benefited economic growth but was a reminder that politicians chose to shrink the money supply when, by fiat, they could expand it.

Finally, the extended republic inflated. The addition of new states to the electoral college (and to the national nominating conventions) and accompanying western population growth complicated the realm of compromise within the parties and made the localistic and republican basis of organization less tenable.

---

[34] Morton Keller, *Affairs of State: Public Life in Late Nineteenth Century America* (Cambridge, MA: Harvard University Press, 1977), 290–4.

[35] On the trend toward retrenchment generally, see Keller, *Affairs of State*; on loss of confidence among business elites, see Richard Franklin Bensel, *Yankee Leviathan: The Origins of Central State Authority in America, 1859–1877* (Cambridge: Cambridge University Press, 1990). Theda Skocpol, *Protecting Soldiers and Mothers: The Political Origins of Social Policy in the United States* (Cambridge, MA: Belknap Press, 1992), documents how mistrust of the parties' use of government power for political gain discouraged the growth of federal social welfare programs.

[36] Richard Franklin Bensel, *The Political Economy of American Industrialization, 1877–1900* (New York: Cambridge University Press, 2000), chap. 6; Elizabeth Sanders, *Roots of Reform: Farmers, Workers, and the American State, 1877–1917* (Chicago: University of Chicago Press, 1999), 109.

It was increasingly difficult not only to select broadly acceptable candidates but also to mount effective campaigns with the Jacksonian mode's localistic style of campaigning. The West's distinct political proclivities also destabilized the parties' coalitions by making it difficult for either to both satisfy western insurgents and maintain or make inroads into the vital Northeast.[37] Further, because of the relatively unformed state of party organizations in newly settled western states, traditional party loyalties took looser hold, rendering voter behavior less predictable and more likely to veer from party regularity.[38]

An essential feature of this modernizing society was the emergence of a newly nationalized citizen. There had long been national political movements and associations, and although the war did not thoroughly or completely nationalize American politics, the experience of it broke through barriers of ideology and praxis that had limited the scope of national politics in the early republic, transforming the political horizons of many voters.[39] If conscription, suspension of habeas corpus, and increased economic intervention characterized the expansion of governing authority, the experience of marching in the Union Army, serving in the United States Sanitary Commission, contracting to provide military goods or services, or merely following national fortunes during the war characterized the newly expansive experience of citizens. After the war, these experiences channeled citizens into national civic associations such as the Grand Army of the Republic, the Grange, the American Red Cross, and the Women's Christian Temperance Union that reworked the civic landscape.

These developments produced new "values, attitudes, and expectations" as social and economic groups not effectively represented in traditional party politics "became increasingly aware of themselves as groups and of their interests and claims in relation to other groups."[40] These new national citizens viewed the Jacksonian mode's organizational framework with skepticism. Even as party leaders – at all levels, but especially the national party leaders, whose job it was to execute national electoral campaigns – recognized and responded to these new citizen impulses, the organizations that they served failed to empower them fully to act. They were mired in an organizational mode that limited their ability to formulate national public mandates. The widespread outpouring of condemnation against the parties during the late nineteenth century is a testament to this tension, as is the growth of advocacy associations, including interest groups, reform clubs, and third-party movements. As Margaret Susan Thompson explains in her study of the growth of the lobby during Grant's

[37] Ware, *The Democratic Party Heads North*, 64–6, 74–5; Paul Kleppner, *The Third Electoral System, 1853–1892* (Chapel Hill: University of North Carolina Press, 1979), 130–4; Bensel, *Political Economy of American Industrialization*, 435.

[38] Wiebe, *The Search for Order*, 86; Martin Shefter, "Regional Receptivity to Reform: The Legacy of the Progressive Era," *Political Science Quarterly* (Autumn 1983), 459–83.

[39] Keller, *Affairs of State*; Robert Higgs, *Crisis and Leviathan: Critical Episodes in the Growth of American Government* (New York: Oxford University Press, 1987).

[40] Samuel P. Huntington, *Political Order in Changing Societies* (New Haven, CT: Yale University Press, 1968), 32, 37, 397–8.

administration, "there was a time . . . when groups seemed logical frameworks to neither petitioners of government nor most officials: when practically no one saw groups (other than parties) as especially effective, desirable, or necessary to the presentation or advocacy of substantive interests." This outlook evaporated in the late nineteenth century, because "as the scope of policy grew, more and more interests were affected by it and therefore felt a need to be represented actively in public affairs."[41] Joel Silbey concludes that "people's perspective on political matters shifted toward highly individual and/or group economic determinants that cut across community loyalties,"[42] and this required the parties to develop different forms of political persuasion to retain their control of the ordering of political conflict.[43]

Stephen Skowronek argues that the American state could not simply adapt to these new governing expectations without fundamentally restructuring the national governing apparatus, and that the parties faced a similar challenge in adjusting their early-nineteenth-century structure to late-nineteenth-century expectations. Skowronek contends that the parties were not up to this task of effecting the necessary restructuring of government because they were unable to effect their own reconstruction, which required that they "transform the loose, segmented structure of the constituent party organization from within." But the creative efforts of late-nineteenth-century party leaders suggests that though it is true that party leaders were unable to respond to new expectations without significantly revising the parties' organizational design, they proved themselves up to the transformative task.[44] Under incredible pressure to achieve "a greater fit with environmental demands over time," politicians proved willing to experiment,[45] which gradually led to a nationalist, liberal party mode that rejected the particularism of local politics and looked instead to unleash the nationalizing tendencies of the extended republic. In this mode, the parties were not regulators of national ambitions but instigators and abettors of them. The presidency – under the Jacksonian mode, a force to be restrained – was the particular patron and beneficiary of this new mode; its capacity to focus an otherwise distracted electorate provided the political capital on which the new organizational mode was built.

Implementing the new mode required that party leaders resolve two connected tactical problems. First, the parties had to revive their connections with a social order that had grown more nationalistic and diversified than the Jacksonian mode could accommodate. This required convincing voters of the parties' continued ability to comprehend the relevant political divisions into which

[41] Margaret Susan Thompson, *The "Spider Web": Congress and Lobbying in the Age of Grant* (Ithaca, NY: Cornell University Press, 1985), 254, 120.
[42] Silbey, *The American Political Nation*, 245.
[43] Ware, *The Democratic Party Heads North*, 110, 120.
[44] Stephen Skowronek, *Building a New American State: The Expansion of National Administrative Capacities, 1877–1920* (Cambridge: Cambridge University Press, 1982), 10–12, 60.
[45] Elisabeth S. Clemens and James M. Cook, "Politics and Institutionalism: Explaining Durability and Change," *Annual Review of Sociology* (1999), 451–2.

voters were grouping themselves. Here, mimicking the style of the new national associations was helpful; it demonstrated an awareness of popular concerns and acceptance of forms of organizing that appeared to spring from public enthusiasms. Second, the parties had to enable the new national citizen to develop and expand political capital inside the two major parties rather than through interest associations or minor parties, both of which tended to emphasize the incapacity of the parties to respond to popular demands. This required opening the party apparatus to new avenues of influence and weakening the hold of traditional subnational party elites, whose concerns centered on maintaining political control within their local jurisdictions. Given the deep roots of the Jacksonian party mode, changing its operations involved uncertainty, and resolving that uncertainty required a great deal of political learning, or "a relatively enduring alteration in behavior that results from experience."[46] As they did so, they honed new methods in national organization and tested new kinds of public appeals.

This openness to organizational tinkering made possible a learning process heavily influenced by examples set outside of the parties and experimenting with novel tactics within the parties. The men involved in effecting the change were not philosophers (indeed, practitioners like Theodore Roosevelt and James Clarkson scorned the philosophical pretensions of more academically inclined reformers), and, befitting their status as politicians, they explained themselves through a language of political expediency, strategy, and campaign devices. They did not often explicitly mobilize the language of liberalism and republicanism, nor were they guided by a carefully articulated political theory, because the basic structure of the constitutional order provided them with ready-at-hand strategic opportunities to exploit. The independence of the presidency and the unifying tendency of presidential elections provided convenient tools for concentrating national attention. The breadth of the extended republic worked as Madison said it would – supplying a range of interests that could be marshaled against the existing party leadership. The organization of political authority into congressional districts as well as states provided cross-cutting political divisions that were used by the Republican party to break down the state-centeredness of party politics.

This lack of philosophical trappings was an essential element of the new idea of a party's success. By keeping the discussion at the level of expediency and legitimacy, party leaders did not turn the new methods into a partisan debate – which is what happened in the early 1800s as party methods became a topic of dispute between Federalists and Republicans and then Democrats and Whigs. The result was an astonishingly broad pattern of borrowing across partisan and organizational lines, as Republicans and Democrats alike embraced elements of the new idea. Victories on both sides reinforced it, and defeats failed to produce longstanding setbacks. Even methods adopted by groups such as

46 Hugh Heclo, *Modern Social Politics in Britain and Sweden: From Relief to Income Maintenance* (New Haven, CT: Yale University Press, 1974), 306.

the Mugwumps and the Farmers' Alliance were drained of their radical connotations as regular politicians scrambled to adopt any strategy that worked. The new idea took on a sort of political caché; politicians who mastered it gained the respect of their peers and the public at large. Much as twenty-first-century politics has seen excitement generated around politicians who are believed to have successfully used the Internet,[47] late-nineteenth-century politicians who mastered the new methods of party politics were perceived to be modern and effective. In the presidential campaigns of Grover Cleveland, William Jennings Bryan, and William McKinley, mastery of these new methods was held up as a demonstration of fitness for office.

Revising the Reformist Account

Many accounts of party decline begin in the late nineteenth century, in some cases identifying the same changes that I document here as evidence of the waning legitimacy of party in American politics. Political scientists and historians have frequently described this decline as instigated by nonpartisan reformers who resented the parties' influence in American politics.[48] Reformers played a large role in generating attention for such change and as such are part of the story of so-called party decline. In too many accounts of party change, this part is taken to be the whole. The reality is that the most pivotal role reformers played was mobilizing the newly nationalized citizens and in doing so demonstrating new methods of national organization that served as models for national party leaders.

Reformers acted as carriers of new ideas that were eventually absorbed into the parties, facilitating the process of political learning and contributing to the creation of the late-nineteenth-century's new idea of party, but party leaders themselves played the determinative role in achieving the necessary transformations in party organization and political practice. Reconceptualizing these reforms as party-based change reminds scholars that party elites were at the center of the developmental events of the nineteenth century. Indeed, not only were party leaders willing to accept reforms, their vision for transforming the parties were much more far-reaching than the more familiar legal reforms advocated by party outsiders. Reformers, after all, were often more concerned with restraining the role of parties in public affairs; party leaders wanted to renew their parties' legitimacy and so were forced to reenvision a new, positive role for parties in American life.

---

[47] Matthew Hindman, "The Real Lessons of Howard Dean: Reflections on the First Digital Campaign," *Perspectives on Politics* (March 2005), 121–8.

[48] As Gary Orren notes, "there is remarkable agreement among the political science profession on the proposition that the strength of American political parties has declined significantly over the past several decades." "The Changing Styles of American Party Politics," in *The Future of American Political Parties: The Challenge of Governance*, Joel L. Fleishman, ed. (Englewood Cliffs, NJ: Prentice-Hall, 1982), 31.

Another element of the Reformist Account is the tendency to celebrate the early and mid-nineteenth century as a "Golden Age of Party," emphasizing high voter turnout rates in the 1800s and the dramatic decline in participation during the early 1900s. Notably, historian Michael McGerr takes on some of the same evidence I present to suggest that at the end of the nineteenth century, liberal reformers brought about "the decline of popular politics," and thus this was "the end of a system that confined people but still gave them a means of political liberation." In McGerr's interpretation, the vibrant parades, rallies, and packed convention halls of the traditional party organizations constructed a politics that "required the visible endorsement of the people." The erosion of this traditional form of politics gave way to upper-class reformers who "rejected the popular politics and formulated a new, less partisan, and less democratic conception of political life."[49] In this view, the elitism of the reformers (many Mugwumps and Progressives mistrusted the poor and immigrants, and southern Populists excluded blacks from political participation) serves as a convenient foil for traditional party leaders, who positioned themselves as men of the people and invited widespread popular participation. This celebration of the Golden Age of party politics has had a significant effect on political scientists' views of twentieth-century parties; as J. P. Monroe argues, "much of the criticism of contemporary parties stems from comparing them to this glorified standard."[50]

Recent research has been chipping away at the familiar prejudices of the Reformist Account, pointing to the decisive role played by party politicians in party reform and addressing "the problem of party transformation from the perspective of whether the disappearance of certain party structures might mean that the parties have opted for superior forms of organization."[51] Ronald M. Johnson and Gary D. Libecap argue that presidents and members of Congress achieved the reform goal of professionalizing the civil service for political reasons, not out of antipartisan passion for civil service reform, a phenomenon that they rightly describe as "a major institutional change" in which "federal politicians play a central, leading role, rather than a peripheral or reluctant one."[52] Scott James similarly argues that as the nineteenth century waned, patronage increasingly became a tool for national policy making rather than the maintenance of personal or local power, pointing "the way toward an understanding of patronage party leaders as skilled professionals (as well as self-interested politicians), individuals who undertook sustained efforts to reform (as well

49 Michael McGerr, *The Decline of Popular Politics: The American North, 1865–1928* (New York: Oxford University Press, 1986), 218, 5, 9.

50 J. P. Monroe, *The Political Party Matrix: The Persistence of Organization* (Albany: State University of New York Press, 2001), 36. Austin Ranney, "The Political Parties: Reform and Decline," in *The New American Political System*, Anthony King, ed. (Washington, DC: American Enterprise Institute, 1978). Everett Carl Ladd, Jr., *Where Have All the Voters Gone* (New York: W.W. Norton, 1978).

51 Monroe, *The Political Party Matrix*, 1.

52 Johnson and Libecap, *The Federal Civil Service System*, 13.

as preserve) 19th-century party organizations as they confronted the political challenges wrought by a modernizing America."[53] Alan Ware's study of direct primary legislation reveals that party leaders willingly adopted reforms that limited traditional powers to confer rationality on an often chaotic nominating process. "Institutionalization in a democracy," Ware concludes, "is not something that happens to politicians, it is something they do."[54] Questioning the Golden Age component of the account, Glenn Altschuler and Stuart Blumin have examined participation in Jacksonian era party affairs and found a number of troubling indices that party organizations tended to be managed by small cliques of elites, leaving most citizens "disengaged from political affairs." Indeed, they point to "the failure of political parties in all sections of the country to organize fully at the grass roots, to attract many voters to or widespread interest in local nominating caucuses and conventions, or even to assure that the elected delegates participated in conventions closer to the apex of the party pyramid."[55]

This book pursues this less celebratory approach to nineteenth-century party democracy, along the following lines. First, it complicates the nature of party democracy, asking whether the parades, rallies, and conventions of the Jacksonian mode really produced a government broadly representative of the people; on the basis of contemporary complaints, I conclude that it did not. Nineteenth-century voters frequently engaged in popular displays of enthusiasm, but in doing so, they were celebrating the selection of candidates and the writing of platforms with which they had very little to do, and the powerful incentives of party loyalty made the "visible endorsement of the people" relatively easy to achieve for the regular party organizations. As Ostrogorski observed long before the decline in turnout and party loyalty registered in the election returns, the parties left behind a "long line of systematically eliminated minorities," meaning white males who were legally permitted to vote and who participated in the lower levels of the parties' delegate-selection process, not only those groups legally prohibited from voting. These "minorities" were shut out of the process of intraparty democracy, even if they turned out to vote.[56]

Second, it questions the claim that the undemocratic pretensions of antiparty reformers (and there were many reformers who were deeply uncomfortable with democracy) was effectively translated into the actions of party leaders. I conclude, to the contrary, that national party leaders looked to the methods of the reformers – democratic and undemocratic alike – and saw a means of

---

[53] Scott James, "Building a New American Party: Patronage Discipline and the Emergence of Strong Party Government in the U.S. Congress." Paper presented at the annual meeting of the Midwest Political Science Association, Chicago, IL, April 25–28, 2002, 24.

[54] Ware, *The American Direct Primary*, 22.

[55] Glen C. Altschuler and Stuart M. Blumin, "Limits of Political Engagement in Antebellum America: A New Look at the Golden Age of Participatory Democracy," *The Journal of American History* (December 1997), 857, 859.

[56] Ostrogorski, *Democracy and the Organization of Political Parties: Volume II*, 17. See also McCormick, *The Second American Party System*, 349.

revitalizing party democracy. With these new methods, they not only preserved the partisan quality of the American political system, they enhanced its capacity for ensuring the practice, rather than merely the appearance, of democracy. Indeed, a chief concern of late-nineteenth-century party leaders was making the party organization accessible to those "systematically eliminated minorities" who were shut out of the traditional convention system.

Third, as a matter of historical accuracy, it questions the charge that blame for the "decline of popular politics" rests on the shoulders of conservative political forces, namely, "the conservative William McKinley, aided by his canny manager Mark Hanna." This is not a charge unique to McGerr; he draws on a seminal essay by Walter Dean Burnham, which similarly charges that the rise of the business-oriented wing of the Republican party in 1896 was an unapologetic advantage to the rise of corporate capitalism, "insulating American elites from mass pressures without formally disrupting the pre-existing democratic-pluralist political structure," by stunting popular participation and therefore the potential for popular economic disruption.[57] My goal is not to provide an apology for McKinley or his policies – indeed, other than an account of how his campaign strategy shaped his policies, I offer no evaluation of those policies or their merit, and none is central to the broader argument made in this book. Rather, the point is to disentangle the political ideologies of the 1896 campaign from the organizational tools with which it was fought to better understand those tools.[58] McKinley and Hanna did exhibit new forms of party leadership, but they were forms that had been pioneered in the Democratic and Republican parties for some time and that were themselves inspired by alternative forms of political organization including the radical Farmers' Alliance. In fact, Bryan's party in 1896 was grounded in an organizational structure similar to McKinley's. It is true that Bryan's policy proposals were more radical than McKinley's, and his ideas might have made American society more democratic. Nonetheless, the change in political style alone cannot be attributed to the dominance of a conservative policy regime.

Further, as Richard Bensel has demonstrated, it was during the period in which the parties maintained their highest levels of turnout that the American political economy was most friendly to capitalist economic development and least friendly to popular claims either on private wealth or for government regulation.[59] The decline of voter turnout may have made for a more friendly atmosphere for corporate power, but in his masterful work on urban machines,

---

[57] Walter Dean Burnham, "The Changing Shape of the American Political Universe," *The American Political Science Review* (March 1965), 25.

[58] McGerr, *The Decline of Popular Politics*, on McKinley, 7; on the Jacksonian model as an alternative, 6; on traditional politics and third parties, 214.

[59] Bensel, *The Political Economy of American Industrialization*. Bensel's conclusions do not acquit the charges, but they degrade claims that the pre-1896 parties were better at representing the interests of the common man. In *Yankee Leviathan*, Bensel's analysis of the trajectory of state development between 1859 and 1877 provides little reason to suspect that Burnham's hopes for party politics were more likely in earlier years.

Stephen Erie establishes that even those nineteenth-century party organizations that relied most heavily on mobilizing the urban working poor (and thus should have been subject to the popular influences Burnham said were missing after 1896) accomplished less for their constituents than is often implied.[60] High turnout and the kinds of "mass pressures" Burnham had in mind are simply not as closely related in history as advocates of the Reformist Account suggest. More dramatic claims on wealth, more decisive expansions of state authority, and more powerful exercises of that authority in the name of economic equality took place in the twentieth century, under the auspices of the party organizations that Burnham claims were eviscerated by 1896.

The Presidency and Party Change

Among the practical politicians who took part in the transformation of parties in the late nineteenth century, presidents and presidential candidates were central, and they play a large role in the following narrative. This is not to say that the transformation of national party organizations was an artifact of modernizing changes in the presidency. Instead, I argue that most of the elements of what has come to be called modern presidential leadership were present at the office's constitutional founding, that the Jacksonian mode weakened the potential for executive branch power embedded in the Constitution of 1787, and that the disruption of the Jacksonian mode was an essential precondition for modern presidential leadership. Between 1836 and 1880, the tension between the requirements of presidential power and the practice of Jacksonian party politics increased, and it grew tremulous in the years 1880 to 1896. An understanding of the contours of this tension and the events that enabled presidents to weaken the Jacksonian mode's restraints is essential to an understanding of what happened to American parties in the late nineteenth century.

That the party system shaped presidential power (and vice versa) should come as no surprise. Jesse Macy observed in his classic work on American parties that the party system "has grown up around the Presidency, and its most manifest, most spectacular, and, in the general public view, most important purpose is that connected with the choice of the Chief Magistrate." Indeed, presidential elections "may be regarded as the culmination of [the party system's] activities and that upon which all others have an ultimate bearing."[61] The creation of the Jacksonian mode in the 1830s and 1840s turned explicitly on the need to achieve coordination in the electoral college (as had the first party system in the 1790s),[62] and although American parties are shaped by politics at all levels of government, they have retained the spirit of this original

---

[60] Steven Erie, *Rainbow's End: Irish-Americans and the Dilemmas of Urban Machine Politics, 1840–1985* (Berkeley: University of California Press, 1988).

[61] Jesse Macy, *Party Organization and Machinery* (New York: The Century Co., 1912), 3.

[62] James Sterling Young, *The Washington Community, 1800–1828* (New York: Columbia University Press, 1966).

purpose. Nonetheless, even as they organized to attain the presidency, the Jacksonian mode diminished the potential for political leadership that the Founders had implanted in the executive.

There are generally two components of most modern presidency arguments: administrative control and agenda setting. The former ranges from the growth of the White House support staff to the assertion of presidential control over executive branch agencies during and after the New Deal.[63] Presidential administrative control was diminished by the Jacksonian mode, as explained in Chapter 1, as the parties absorbed the prerogative of staffing executive branch offices. This argument for the centrality of administrative control includes a variety of developments that have expanded presidents' ability to set the legislative agenda, personalize presidential campaigns, and build political support through popular appeals.[64] The Jacksonian mode's effect was felt most acutely in this context. It was geared specifically to limiting the executive's independent agenda-setting power. This, argues James Ceaser, was the central goal of the Jacksonian view of party: to prevent the rise of presidential aspirants who staked out distinctive policy positions as a means of boosting their own political careers – and in the process raised divisive issues. Instead, "under the convention system the power of choosing the nominees came increasingly into the hands of state and local politicians, men who may have been less inclined than Congressmen to view problems from a national perspective" and who were therefore less likely to empower their nominees with national mandates for party leadership.[65]

These diminutions of presidential power did not reflect the Founders' intent. As David Brian Robertson argues, the Founders created a presidential office capable of directing national political affairs. The presidential veto power, the power to convene Congress, the appointment power, and the duty to report on the state of the union all conspire toward presidential control over the political agenda – even apart from the president's initiative in foreign and national security affairs. Coupled with the Founders' refusal to make the president responsible to an executive council or to allow members of the legislature to serve in the executive departments, Robertson identifies a predilection to presidential

---

[63] Lewis Gould suggests that key elements of the modern presidency include a significant increase in White House staff, a chief of staff, a press office, formalized relations with Congress, greater power for the president as commander in chief, expanded travel in and out of the United States, and continuous campaigning. Louis Gould, *The Modern American Presidency* (Lawrence: University Press of Kansas, 2004), xi. Sidney M. Milkis, *The President and the Parties: The Transformation of the American Party System since the New Deal* (New York: Oxford University Press, 1993).

[64] Samuel Kernell, *Going Public: New Strategies of Presidential Leadership* (Washington, DC: CQ Press, 2006).

[65] Ceaser, *Presidential Selection*, 131–49. Marc Landy and Sidney Milkis argue to the contrary that political parties have been an essential means by which presidents achieve effective leadership. *Presidential Greatness* (Lawrence: University Press of Kansas, 2000). It is notable that of the five presidents they examine, only Abraham Lincoln served under the Jacksonian mode – Jackson cannot be said to have counted because he was not elevated through the convention system.

initiative that has not always been fully exploited but that provided a constitutional basis for the political development of characteristically "modern"
presidential power.[66] Nineteenth-century party organizations obscured presidential power by reducing opportunities for presidents to take advantage of this
intrinsic potential. Nevertheless, endowed by the Constitution with significant
agenda-setting power, presidents perpetually resisted the parties' constraints
on these abilities, with varying degrees of success.

In the late nineteenth century, this perennial presidential struggle coincided
profitably with the emergence of a newly nationalized party mode and the new,
liberal idea of party, as collusion between presidents and national party leaders
reshaped popular expectations of presidential power and laid the groundwork
for the activist presidency of the twentieth century. Grover Cleveland's attempts
to force his party to take up tariff reform – initiated by a constitutionally
mandated State of the Union Address – led to his unprecedented three popular
vote victories (only the electoral college denied him reelection in 1888). His
successor William McKinley's reconstruction of the Republican coalition in
1896 was grounded in a convention strategy designed to undermine old norms
and culminated in a first inaugural that took advantage of his constitutional
authority to call a special session of Congress. Even Benjamin Harrison's oft-
derided "front porch Campaign" stands out as an audacious recognition of
the ability of presidential candidates to capture the attention of the national
electorate.

The impulse to presidential assertion of power goes back further. As
explained in Chapter 1, President Rutherford B. Hayes crafted strategies
designed to overcome the Jacksonian mode; Hayes's strategy mimicked James
K. Polk's of more than thirty years earlier, as each sought to master his party
by foreswearing a second term in office. David Nichols argues that Andrew
Jackson's (Polk's personal hero) use of the veto power represented a preco-
cious injection of presidential influence into legislative affairs, that his turn
to the spoils system presages later presidents' attempts to control the administrative apparatus, and that his campaign tactics enabled him to claim that
"he acted by virtue of a mandate granted to him by the people."[67] In arguing
that Thomas Jefferson demonstrated essentially modern presidential leadership, Jeremy Bailey suggests that the third president's idea of executive power
"requires a president who will use declarations to articulate the principles of
his administration in order to direct national aspirations, present a standard by
which administration can be judged, and, most important, bring the opinions of
citizens together under a single head"[68] – a position that betokened the modern

[66] David Brian Robertson, *The Constitution and America's Destiny* (Cambridge: Cambridge University Press, 2005), 214–27.
[67] David Nichols, *The Myth of the Modern Presidency* (University Park, PA: The Pennsylvania State University Press, 1994), 26–7. See also Robert Remini, *The Revolutionary Age of Andrew Jackson* (New York: Harper and Row, 1976), 123.
[68] Jeremy D. Bailey, *Thomas Jefferson and Executive Power* (Cambridge: Cambridge University Press, 2007), 225.

presidency, if it did not initiate it. Nichols goes so far as to argue that George Washington demonstrated the essential features of modern presidential power, shaping the legislative agenda, establishing precedents for presidential control over the administration, and modeling the kind of personalistic presidential politics often associated with the modern presidency.[69]

The point here is not to press presidential modernity backward administration-by-administration – an exercise in historical trivialization that does nothing to clarify the decreasingly useful concept of the modern presidency. However, viewing events from this long-term perspective reveals that the solidification of the Jacksonian mode of party organization began a presidential interregnum interposed between a Founding tradition of quite strong presidential party leadership and the late nineteenth century, when the executive branch experienced a renaissance as presidents turned the inherent strengths of their office to their advantage. This consistency in presidential politics suggests that there is little reason to distinguish the "modern" from the "classical" presidency of the Founding period, except insofar as its passage through the Jacksonian organization's dark age altered it.[70] The Jacksonian mode was a prominent step toward present-day presidential power, but if the Jacksonian party mode encouraged a perception of the appropriateness of a presidency-centered party system, it failed to provide presidents with a source of power that made that perception politically actionable. As explained in Chapter 5, the Jacksonian mode largely succeeded in clearing and holding institutional space, foreclosing non-presidentialist alternatives at the national level without activating the Constitution's provisions for presidential power.

The success of later presidents stemmed from the fact that by the 1880s, attempts at presidential leadership reinforced changes that were under way in the national party organizations. For instance, after the Republican party decentralized its nominating process, Republican presidents broke the hold of subnational party leaders and launched national campaigns designed to appeal directly to the party-in-the-electorate. Presidents in both parties benefited from the emergence of a national party elite that consolidated power in the parties' national committees and began conducting coherent national campaigns that transcended the traditional parties' politics of evasion and compromise. In this way, presidents positioned themselves to assert popular mandates for policies they desired, enabling them to bypass traditional subnational party leaders and reach voters directly, which in turn forced party conventions to respond. Contrary to the perspective that blames the direct primary for the increasing personalization of the presidency, this interpretation shares John Reynold's conclusion that the emergence of the "hustling candidate" created the conditions

---

[69] Nichols, *The Myth of the Modern Presidency*, 29–30.

[70] As Stephen Skowronek's pivotal study of the presidency points out, it is more useful to think about the presidency in terms of consistencies in the office over time rather than of disjunctions between the past and the present. *The Politics Presidents Make: Leadership from John Adams to George Bush* (Cambridge, MA: Belknap Press, 1993), 9.

that made primaries attractive, rather than the other way around.[71] That late-nineteenth-century presidents started something new is indicated by the fact that Cleveland was the first president to use the term "mandate" in an inaugural address (in his second inaugural).[72] He began a short-lived trend; McKinley, Harding, Coolidge, Hoover, and Franklin Roosevelt all used some form of the word in theirs. That no president has used the word in an inaugural since speaks more to the pervasiveness of the assumption that presidents come to office with political capital earned in the election than to the fading away of the concept.

Sources

That this tension between traditional operating procedures and emergent pressures existed is reinforced by a broad public and private dialogue among party elites in the late nineteenth century. Analysis of this discourse takes seriously Paul Kleppner's admonition that analysis of elite writings and correspondence "is to glimpse the type of belief systems characteristic of those *at one level* of the political structure" without proving linkages to other components of the political system, especially voting behavior.[73] Yet if electoral returns can best be explained by recourse to voting analysis, the type of organizational change documented in this text is best understood as an elite-driven response. As Alan Ware argues, parties turned out to be "much better at managing change than is usually claimed," although "it is not voters, acting as an exogenous variable, whose changed behavior transforms the party system; it is the actors in political parties, whose decisions about strategy . . . shape the likely responses from voters."[74] In evaluating period sources, I pay attention both to individuals' explanations of their actions and to indications of responses by party elites, the press, and the public to politicians' methods. Where these explanations or responses comport with their actions, I take them at face value. This is not because I assume that politicians are always open about their intent or that period observers are always correct in their analysis; rather, the assumption is that politicians communicated to the attentive public and to their fellow politicians through their writings and speech – both private and public. I have evaluated period sources on these grounds, but beyond using them to understand party leaders' policy preferences, I understand party leaders as appealing to voters and to one another to demonstrate their political competence, especially their ability to understand and master political activities that are seen as forward-thinking and helpful to the party's cause. Then as now, politicians

---

[71] Reynolds, *The Demise of the American Convention System.*

[72] Jefferson used the word "mandates" in his second inaugural but in reference to those who follow the mandates of habit, not a popular mandate. *Inaugural Addresses of the Presidents of the United States From George Washington, 1789, to George Bush, 1989* (Washington, DC: U.S. Government Printing Office, 1989).

[73] Kleppner, *The Third Electoral System,* 7.

[74] Ware, *The Democratic Party Heads North,* xvi; see also pp. 22–3.

paid attention to conventional wisdom and attempted to demonstrate their command of it, even when they disagreed or secretly plotted different strategies. The ways in which they spoke to one another thus tell scholars something about popular and elite perceptions – they rarely spoke just for the sake of speaking, and successful politicians were rarely oblivious to the ways in which they telegraphed messages about their competence. As historian Lee Benson notes, "aside from the principles and policies it adopts and advocates, a party radiates an aura that influences the way the electorate appraises and responds to its principles and policies."[75] Politicians not only promoted popular policies, they also cultivated an aura (or character) for their party and themselves by discussing the ways in which they gained the public's trust. That aura was never an end but always a means, and when conditions made the parties appear to be out of touch, they deliberately reconstructed their organizations to generate a more appropriate form of self-presentation.

This new idea thus emerged from politicians struggling to find solutions to problems that the electorate presented them. To root out the sources of this strategizing and the resultant new idea of party, I have probed the residue of this "collective wondering,"[76] particularly the correspondence of party leaders and newspaper accounts of party affairs, which are "barometers of orthodoxy."[77] Again, Benson is helpful in demarcating newspaper accounts and editorials (which, although hardly official party mouthpieces, "could not be considered free agents") as well as speeches and "day-to-day informal conversations and associations" as elements of a "semi-official" and "unofficial" party image. Saturation in primary sources

can serve two related but separate functions: 1.) They permit analysts to ascertain the grounds on which political parties appealed for support and they help them to draw inferences about why men voted as they did. 2.) They also permit analysts to draw inferences about the arguments and appeals that practicing politicians believed would win support from certain groups of voters.[78]

Richard Bensel similarly notes that "newspaper accounts and reporters were as much a part of the public sphere" as were politicians, and that politicians often used the press to communicate with one another, making the press "a medium for transmitting information and coordinating action."[79] For example, in the final chapters, I focus on the words of presidents and presidential candidates – both written and spoken – to demonstrate their use of the new idea of party to explain their actions and demonstrate their competence. In the late nineteenth century, presidents became more visible to the electorate and more vocal about their views on the nature of party politics. This can best be understood as an attempt to legitimate their efforts to seize control of the

---

75 Benson, *The Concept of Jacksonian Democracy*, 216.
76 Heclo, *Modern Social Politics in Britain and Sweden*, 305.
77 Silbey, *The American Political Nation*, 54.
78 Benson, *The Concept of Jacksonian Democracy*, 217–18.
79 Bensel, *Passion and Preferences*, 10, 62.

partisan agenda and exert pressure on their partisan colleagues in Congress. As Benson argues, however, the language of presidential candidates reveals party leaders' perceptions of public opinion, because "the selection of candidates is usually influenced by the party's assessment of the kind of image most likely to please the electorate," just as platforms and presidential addresses (even if they substitute rhetoric for reality) "usually reflect what their architects think the voters want to hear.[80] Presidential candidates reflected their parties' collective decisions about how parties could legitimate themselves with voters, and so their rhetoric should be parsed with care. The prominence of the new idea of party in the rhetoric of presidential nominees thus not only reveals the sense that candidates had of the potentialities of that idea, it also suggests that they believed the idea resonated with their audiences. Presidents tend not to adopt language that makes them appear out of step or old-fashioned, but language that they believe will make them appear relevant, informed, and powerful. The new idea of party served this purpose well in the late nineteenth century.

The growing chorus of concern with organizational transformation within these sources reveals a significant reworking of the party image, as newspaper editors, elected officials, and members of the party organization struggled to come to grips with the problems of understanding how these traditional party organizations could serve immediate needs. They are imperfect sources; newspaper editors were partisan and opinionated, party leaders' have left behind only fragmentary collections of letters, and politicians' letters themselves were composed with mixed motives. Nonetheless, they are helpful in re-creating party leaders' efforts to formulate a new idea of party. This meant devising strategies to make new methods work within the extant party organization, evolving a defense of those new methods, and understanding how the new methods encouraged new ways of thinking about individuals' attachments to parties. Part of what made this transformation so successful was the broad dispersion of the new idea of party across the political system; by the 1880s, the new idea had become positively trendy, and politicians across the country echoed elements of it. To demonstrate this breadth, I draw from sources in a variety of locations and from a range of individuals, rather than delving deeply into a single location or identifying a single pivotal actor.

[80] Benson, *The Concept of Jacksonian Democracy*, 216, 217.

I

Localism and the Jacksonian Mode

The Jacksonian organizational mode emerged in the 1830s, as the congressional caucus method of presidential nominations was supplanted by the national nominating convention method. Along with this change came an entire organizational and cultural apparatus, including a network of institutional relationships linking local party organizations with state and national party organizations, standard assumptions about how campaigns should be conducted, and a view of partisanship and two-party competition as not only acceptable but a valuable supplement to republican political culture.[1] This party mode passed through the realignment of the 1850s virtually unscathed. In fact, the Jacksonian party mode emerged from the ruins of the second party system stronger than before because of the Republican party's replication of the Democratic party's organizational framework.[2] So close was its mimicry that, as explained in Chapter 6, when Republicans sought to abolish the Democrat-inspired unit rule in the 1880s, they had to specifically defend deviation from the Democrats' standard operating procedures despite the absence of a formal unit rule in the Republican party. The legitimacy of the party of Jackson's organizational structure, shaping both major party organizations, compelling broad public legitimacy, and enduring with little change over time, suggests that Martin Van Buren founded more than a single organization but an organizational mode that provided American politics with rules of appropriateness in partisan behavior that applied outside of his party.

---

[1] Joel Silbey dates the solidification of the new party mode to 1838 in *The American Political Nation*.

[2] Paul Kleppner's study of nineteenth-century voting confirms that the basic electoral coalitions that underlay the Democratic–Whig conflict in the Jacksonian era were continued in the Democratic–Republican conflict after the Civil War, suggesting that the institutional continuity was also reflected in the electorate. *The Third Electoral System*; on the Republican replication of Democratic Party organization, see Robert D. Marcus, *Grand Old Party: Political Structure in the Gilded Age, 1880–1896* (New York: Oxford University Press, 1971), 22.

These rules told the parties how to select delegates, select nominees, and create platforms. They had broader impacts beyond the nominating process; they also reflected a series of priorities within party life, four of which are highlighted in this chapter. First, they established expectations of how individuals and factions would behave within the realm of intraparty conflict; both were encouraged to place particular policy preferences aside in favor of party unity, to believe that "the... party was greater and nobler than any man or any organization in it, and its success was of vastly more importance than the gratification of the spites and revenges and passions of factions or individuals."[3] Second, they enshrined a balance of power between national and subnational communities; the delegate selection process was especially designed to strengthen local political forces in national politics. Convention delegations were "made up of men who will, it is to be assumed, represent the dominant political opinions of the States by which they were chosen," specifically the dominant state party organizations.[4] Third, they proffered particular campaign strategies and dismissed others; national campaigns were left largely to state and local party organizations, which often subordinated national campaign themes to local political prejudices. Finally, they invited particular types of candidates and discouraged others. Candidates deemed to be "available" were those who were least offensive to the greatest number of localities, and so aspirants to national office avoided committing themselves on the controversial issues of the day, believing that nominees should "not be able to ride into office on a hobby constructed of questions on which wide differences of opinion are allowable within the party."[5] These rules of appropriateness were grounded in a vision of republicanism that held local communities to be central to public life, encouraging a public spiritedness that protected the common man from a fractionalized politics of narrow self-interest.

In the late nineteenth century, this institutional framework continued to serve the political imperatives of the era in which it was created, an era in which broadly dispersed publics sought to find some narrow common ground on which to seize control of the national political apparatus and use it to protect local prerogatives. This played an important role in the development of American parties. It foreclosed the legislative caucus model and spread partisan identities across the nation – if not evenly, at least in a way that approximated decentralized democratic control over the national governmental apparatus. It forged the ideal of a national party with a base in a broad national electorate, even if it never quite achieved that ideal. Conventions appeared to embrace the public value of popular sovereignty and so "countered the image of closed, restricted, elite-dominated decision making associated with the legislative nominating caucus that had been dominant till then."[6] In doing so, however, they

---

[3] "The Democratic Problem," *New York Times*, September 22, 1882, 5.
[4] "Sound Money Will Win," *New York Times*, May 6, 1895, 1.
[5] Untitled article, *Arkansas Gazette*, March 18, 1882, 2.
[6] Silbey, *The American Political Nation*, 60.

made popular input more apparent than real, clearing institutional space that was revised in the twentieth century by the adoption of the direct primary system.

The Jacksonian Mode's Persistence

The realignment synthesis has distracted political scientists from the long-term persistence of this Jacksonian party mode.[7] Although there is much to be gained from the electoral periodization scheme that demarcates the Jacksonian electoral era from the Civil War electoral era, and that from the "System of 1896," an undue focus on the distinctiveness of different parts of the nineteenth century obscures much of what there is to learn from its institutional continuities. It also obscures the persistent tensions that defined the parties during this period. The Jacksonian mode was so successful that, although the Jacksonians built their organization to contest Federalist party resurgence, the heirs of the Federalists – both Whigs and Republicans – adopted the Jacksonians' organizational framework for their own partisan ends.[8] The Whig and Republican adoption of the localistic Jacksonian organization was somewhat ironic, because both parties advocated the kind of nationalist policies that Jacksonian Democrats opposed. The adaptation was not absolute: neither Whigs nor Republicans adopted the Democratic party's two-thirds rule, which prevented the nomination of any candidate without the support of two-thirds of national convention delegates and gave slaveholding states a veto over abolitionist candidates. The localistic bias of the Jacksonian organization ran deeper than the two-thirds rule, however; institutional concepts such as a pyramidal network of nominating conventions, party regularity as a nonideological tool to define members and nonmembers, loosely empowered national committees dominated by state party organizations, a mobilizing apparatus that relied on subnational party franchises to conduct national campaigns, and geographically based patronage distribution systems all skewed the parties toward localistic political forces. As John Aldrich explains, "the reality of the agreement was the same in both parties – forbearance of extremists and a principled rather than an institutional commitment to moderation, intersectional alliance, and national unity."[9]

The Jacksonian mode persisted for the same reasons that other institutions persist: it shaped the habits and expectations of the politicians who staffed it and the political culture of the people who watched it. It "was in such common use that it commanded acceptance almost like a natural phenomenon."[10] Career paths for politicians became regularized, as individuals established their

[7] David R. Mayhew, *Electoral Realignments: A Critique of an American Genre* (New Haven: Yale University Press, 2002).
[8] Silbey, *The American Political Nation*, 34; Kleppner, *The Third Electoral System*, 78.
[9] Aldrich, *Why Parties?*, 134.
[10] Ostrogorski, *Democracy and the Organization of Political Parties: Volume II*, 69.

political prowess by demonstrating their mastery of Jacksonian mode forms. The popular press covered political events as if the average reader had a complex grasp of how the Jacksonian mode worked, reporting violations of party regularity, "treacherous" acts that failed to observe intraparty courtesy, conflicts over patronage, and the minutiae of credentials contests in nominating conventions. A complex array of operational precedents, strategic assumptions, conventional wisdom, and behavioral norms all reinforced its republican orientation. As presented to popular audiences, its procedures were imminently fair and democratic.[11]

This view of a long Jacksonian period – stretching across two political alignments into the late nineteenth century – complicates standard political science analyses of the Jacksonians' formative role in U.S. politics. In particular, the realignment synthesis's tendency to look for proximate rather than systemic causes tends to obscure consistencies created by institutional structure; for instance, it has suggested a greater connection between the 1896 realignment and the emergence of the Progressive movement than between the Jacksonian organization's formation in the 1830s and the emergence of serious dissatisfaction with that organization 50 years later.[12] Nineteenth-century observers saw the connection; taking centennial stock of U.S. parties in 1876, William Graham Sumner concluded that "the political party system which had been developed previous to the war underwent no change during the heroic period."[13] Moisei Ostrogorski similarly argued that "in the crisis brought on by the slavery question the old parties foundered, but the system of organization survived them . . . it even took a fresh start under cover of the distress and the perils of the fratricidal struggle."[14]

Historians have been less willing than political scientists to ignore these long-term continuities, recognizing that although much that the Jacksonians established had been washed away by the Civil War, the influence of their practice continued to be felt long afterward. Thus, Joel Silbey charts the long-standing influence of the party structure they created on political behavior in the American political nation from 1838 (when party organizational norms were solidified) until 1893 (when industrialism raised questions about the parties' effectiveness in a new socioeconomic order). Richard McCormick notes that "it would be misleading to exaggerate the disruption in the party period's electoral style caused by either the realignment of the 1850s or the Civil War. . . . The basic structure of party organizations persisted, as did their techniques for mobilizing the voters."[15] Ronald Formisano cautions against a sharp division between pre- and postwar parties, insisting that "while their power to reward

---

[11] Reynolds, *The Demise of the American Convention System*, 4.

[12] Martin Shefter, *Political Parties and the State: The American Historical Experience* (Princeton: Princeton University Press, 1994), 72–7.

[13] William Graham Sumner, "Politics in America, 1776–1876," *North American Review*, January 1876, 82.

[14] Ostrogorski, *Democracy and the Organization of Political Parties, Volume II*, 69.

[15] McCormick, "The Party Period and Public Policy," 283.

loyal workers with government jobs no doubt increased after the Civil War, from the 1830s on political parties' sway in elections and voting was fairly continuous."[16] Furthermore, Kleppner's study of the nineteenth-century electorate finds continuity in voting alignments and suggests that the stark division between the second and third party systems implied by the realignment synthesis creates an unnatural division around the 1860 election.[17] The Jacksonian mode was so resilient that it carved out a specific location on the American political landscape for local party organizations that persisted across time and place – from the 1830s to the 1890s and in most towns, cities, counties, and states. There were some changes in the way parties did business over time. Examining subtle shifts in patronage distribution, Martin Shefter and Scott James have identified distinct patronage regimes that vary as constituencies, governing capacities, and popular demands changed, but these were merely changes in technique that left the underlying organizational structure virtually unchanged.[18]

The Troublesome Operation of the Jacksonian Mode

Some conceptual clarity is in order. First, as illustrated in Figure 1, the definition of party organization used here distinguishes the representative decision-making assemblies that select candidates (party conventions and the delegates who attend them), the mechanisms that link these entities and the electorate (primaries or caucuses and the membership rules that allow participation in them), and the bureaucratic entities that supervise these linkage mechanisms, call conventions, and manage elections (party committees). These party organizations not only campaign (and so absorb a variety of campaign workers and candidate organizations) but reconvene in subsequent election years to launch new campaigns (and so provide the organizational continuity behind the party label between elections). Teams of office seekers attempt to harness these organizations for their own personal ends, and large groups of voters identify with major party labels. However, party business is conducted in a thick institutional network of organizations, rules, and assemblies. Their design has an impact on outcomes independent of teams of politicians and voter alignments.[19]

---

[16] Formisano, "The 'Party Period' Revisited," 94.

[17] Joel Silbey, *The American Political Nation*; Kleppner, *The Third Electoral System*; see also Larry Bartels, "Electoral Continuity and Change, 1868–1996," *Electoral Studies* 17:3 (September 1998), 301–26.

[18] Martin Shefter, "The Emergence of the Political Machine: An Alternative View," in Willis D. Hawley and Michael Lipsky, eds., *Theoretical Perspectives on Urban Politics* (Englewood Cliffs: Prentice-Hall, 1976), 14-44. Scott James, "Patronage Regimes and American Party Development from 'The Age of Jackson' to the Progressive Era," *British Journal of Political Science*, January 2006, 3. Stephen Erie similarly notes that "the full-fledged or mature urban machine did not emerge until the third party system entered an advanced stage in the 1870s and 1880s," but still acknowledges that this development had "roots in the second or Jacksonian party system of the 1820s and 1830s." *Rainbow's End*, 2.

[19] The rules that shape party behavior are "invisible participants" in party decisions, say James Lengle and Byron Shafer, and they "distribute power in one way rather than in others."

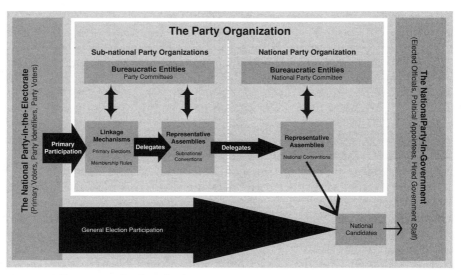

FIGURE 1. Party organizations in the party system.

The party organization is distinct from the party-in-government (elected officers who identify with the party) and the party-in-the-electorate (the members of the electorate who identify with the party).[20] As Figure 1 illustrates, the path through the linkage mechanisms and the representative assemblies progressively filters out the party-in-the-electorate and produces candidates for whom the general electorate votes in the general election. Successful candidates constitute the party-in-government.[21]

Second, it is helpful in examining nineteenth-century parties to think of there being distinct party organizations at the local, state, and national levels (clarified in Figure 1 by the division between subnational and national party

"Primary Rules, Political Power, and Social Change," *The American Political Science Review*, 70:1 (March 1976), 25–40, at 40.

[20] The tripartite distinction is classically articulated in V. O. Key, *Politics, Parties, and Pressure Groups*, 3rd ed. (New York: Thomas Y. Crowell, 1956).

[21] Figure I, and this discussion generally, omits consideration of the variations of subnational conventions (including ward or district conventions, county conventions, state assembly district conventions, and congressional district conventions – to name just a common few), as well as various types of committees (including general committees – often large assemblies that resembled legislatures – executive committees that were selected by general committees, and primary committees, which were usually only empowered for the purposes of presiding over primaries and usually appointed by local executive committees). Elected officials at the local, state, and congressional levels are also left out, although they complete the party-in-government. It omits various political jurisdictions, such as precincts, wards, assembly districts, counties, senatorial districts, judicial districts, and congressional districts that had somewhat distinct party organizations. The complexity that emerges from these additional layers would lengthen the analysis without providing a better explanation than that offered by simplifying them as "local." Further, because these organizations were often not truly distinct but were composed of ex officio officers of the basic local party organizations, the simpler account is more realistic.

organizations). The state and local components of the party organizations were both older than the national organizational component and significantly independent of the national component. The Jacksonians combined existing political organizations into a single national alliance; although they melded them into a national organization, they were careful to limit its power to interfere with the political objectives of local party elites. As Aldrich explains, "to knit together those already in place in local politics, the national party had to yield them autonomy. Each local unit needed the freedom to establish its own definition of benefits in the collective good."[22] The result was an organization designed to empower the preferences of state and local party organizations. Thus, although the various organizational layers were connected by a common organizational framework and party label, that framework provided each unit with considerable freedom, particularly the freedom to define the margins of the party label in ways that were helpful in local campaigns. Thus, the republican orientation of the Jacksonian mode both preserved local influence and served the interests of local elites.

This distinction between national and subnational (state and local) organizations is a reminder that the various organizational levels often exhibited contrary motives. The national organizations focused on winning national elections, for instance, but subnational elites, although they benefited from national victories, rarely subordinated parochial power for national purposes, because "their decisions were influenced by their calculations as to the effects their commitments would have on their own political fortunes."[23] Teams of elites competed for control of the subnational organizations because the party label was important to the electorate and was thus a valuable political tool. In its penetration of popular political culture, Van Buren's model was remarkably successful; most voters identified with one of the major parties (which provided voters with valuable informational cues and a sense of empowerment through a partisan community), so the party label bestowed considerable legitimacy on office-seeking elites. Further, the party organization facilitated relationships with a variety of self-interested party workers who were essential for maximizing turnout. Outside of the parties, few institutions were capable of generating similarly reliable resources. This is not to say that politicians were not interested in principles but that party principles and the practical value of the party label can be conceptually separated. This often created a gap between cultural ideals and institutional reality because elites hijacked the party organization and label for the advancement of their team.

This makes it difficult to identify coherent interests among parties in the nineteenth century, but in all parties, mixed motives and political ambitions cloud common purposes; instability emerges chiefly when the motives that drive their decision-making processes are incongruent with voters' expectations. In this case, as long as voters' political horizons were focused on subnational politics, the privileging of subnational political power was acceptable.

[22] Aldrich, *Why Parties?*, 124.
[23] McCormick, *The Second American Party System*, 331.

However, the new national citizens glaringly exposed the Jacksonian organization's disjunctions.

Party Regularity

As noted earlier, this book defines party organizations as consisting of bureaucratic entities created to manage elections and maintain the continuity of the parties between elections (party committees), the representative decision-making assemblies that select candidates (party conventions and primary election meetings), and the mechanisms that link these entities with the electorate (primary elections and membership rules). In each case, control of the party organization conferred the power to police, what was called, in the lingo of the time, party "regularity." Regularity was recognition of the right to take part in party politics, either as an individual voter or as a state or local organization that claimed affiliation with one of the national parties.[24] Although this term came to carry cultural connotations – voters took pride in identifying themselves as a "party regular," and politicians believed that maintaining regularity conveyed a sense of one's trustworthiness as an ally – should not be taken as the whole of the concept. It also described a specific organizational status defined by rules, processes, and precedents, which shaped the practice of intraparty democracy. Regularity demarcated who was and who was not allowed to participate in party affairs. "Regular nominations," concludes Silbey, "were the centerpiece of party affairs,"[25] and *The Century* reported in 1892 that "the most useful word in the vocabulary of the man who makes a mere business of politics is 'regularity.' "[26]

Clarifying the character of party regularity is helpful for students of nineteenth-century party politics. Given the diversity of subnational party organizations across the country, explaining how dissimilar entities fit into a common organization inevitably glosses over an array of exceptions. Nevertheless, among all state and local party franchises in the late nineteenth century, one common feature applied: maintaining "regular" status formalized their position in the party system. The institutional status of regularity distinguishes between the ubiquitous local party organization and teams of elites who controlled them, as well as the economic interests that they represented.[27] Parties

---

[24] As a sketch of the nature of intraparty relationships, this chapter demonstrates the ways in which the parties were articulated, in Maurice Duverger's terminology. Duverger's concept of organizational articulation, or the manner in which the component parts of party organizations are linked together, describes the degree to which the rules linking organizational units and power relationships are formalized. Articulation "guarantee[s] that each basic element plays its part in the total life of the party," through regulations prescribing intraparty relations in more or less restrictive detail. *Political Parties: Their Organization and Activity in the Modern State*, trans. by Barbara and Robert North (New York: John Wiley & Sons, 1963), 44.

[25] Silbey, *The American Political Nation*, 66.

[26] "Regularity and Independence," *The Century*, 44:1 (May 1892), 156.

[27] Ostrogorski defines a machine as "an aggregation of individuals...bent solely on satisfying their appetites by exploiting the resources of a political party," drawing a distinction

were different in New York City and Atlanta and San Francisco but in each place were represented within the national organization through the procedural framework of party regularity. As Theodore Roosevelt observed in his 1886 study of party politics, "although with wide differences in detail, all these bodies are ordered upon much the same general plan, and one description may be taken, in the rough, as applying to all."[28] The component parts of the party organizations thus shared more than a label; they shared an institutional structure that governed their relationships with one another.

Regularity was not an arbitrary distinction; in fact, it was essential to maintaining the integrity of Jacksonian organizations. Conventions were assemblies of independent associations that claimed allegiance to a larger party label but otherwise might have little in common on which to base their association. The *North American Review*'s description of conventions as "voluntary associations of obscure men" was, in this sense, accurate.[29] Formalizing the nature of membership among dispersed constituencies also allowed comprehensive representation of all relevant political districts. Recognizing the relationships between organizations in the various political jurisdictions ensured organizational continuity by providing a thread of succession from convention to convention – both from place to place and from election year to election year.[30] As a Topeka editor warned,

suppose no authority of this character is conferred upon any body? The result necessarily is that an unorganized mob meets, and declares itself a republican state convention. It may prove, afterwards, that the mob is really a duly elected representative body, and that those assuming to act as delegates have proper credentials. But unless this claim is investigated and passed upon prior to the meeting for temporary organization, who can say whether it is or is not fairly made?[31]

between party organizations and the interests that embody them. The "immediate object" for the machine was the primary election, where "each [boss] strives to assert himself" to "be 'recognized' [as regular] by the higher Organization of the party impassively contemplating the struggle." Machines were groups that exploited the institutional rewards of regularity across multiple elections. *Democracy and the Organization of Political Parties, Vol. II*, 371, 370.

28 Theodore Roosevelt, "Machine Politics in New York City," *The Century* (November 1886), 76. Political scientist Daniel Remsen found that, despite the lack of a common set of written rules providing national uniformity, "usage and custom have however brought a degree of uniformity to all parties," and that "in the absence of rules the traditions and customs of the party are ordinarily followed." Remsen, *Primary Elections*, 37–8. Even where there were minor variations, general consistencies prevailed across the nation. Silbey confirms that "organization was decentralized, but it looked and generally acted the same everywhere," in *The American Political Nation*, 70. McCormick, *The Second American Party System*, 342.

29 Silbey, *The American Political Nation*, 62. Sidney G. Fisher, "Nominating Conventions," *The North American Review*, January 1868, 245.

30 *Proceedings of the Democratic State Convention, Held in Albany, January 21, and February 1, 1861* (Albany: Comstock and Cassidy, Printers, 1861), 39; "The City Republicans," *New York Times*, January 18, 1882, 2.

31 "Action of the State Central Committee," *The* (Topeka, KS) *Commonwealth*, July 13, 1882, 2.

Certifying delegates required identifying those lower-level political entities that were authorized to be represented in the parties' formal proceedings. Emphasizing the need to draw some boundaries between the party and the public, the *Chicago Tribune* insisted that "there is no other way of conducting party politics."[32]

Regularity demarcated those who were and were not allowed entry to the nomination process – only the acts of the regular organization were "recognized as the acts of the party."[33] Under the formalized proceedings of regularity, convention delegates were seated "by virtue of a right" derivative from their organization's regular status; only representatives possessing this right passed from local to state to national conventions. Maintaining regular status required following generally accepted procedures ("party usages and party necessities," as a claimant for regularity described them in 1894) for calling and holding primaries and conventions in the selection of delegates to conventions held at higher levels. As a Boston Democrat explained,

if the [state] convention met in the place where it was called to meet, and was called to order by a member of the State Committee in good standing, and was properly and duly organized by legal delegates, and performed its business in an orderly, parliamentary manner, it must be regarded as the legal convention, and should be recognized by the Democracy of the State and of the nation.[34]

In similar terms, a Nebraskan described regularity as flowing through orderly procedures between conventions:

[a] convention was called by the . . . "regular" State Committee of the Democratic Party. That convention selected a new State Committee in the usual way, which organized and through such organization called the state convention . . . . The State Committee was the legitimate successor of the old committee, over whose jurisdiction there was no question. Hence this convention was regularly called and should be recognized by the convention of the party, and its delegates seated.[35]

Delegates elected by conventions that were called by irregular committees or followed irregular procedures, when challenged by delegates elected by conventions called by the regular party committees, were not supposed to be given a place in party councils. Individuals, factions, and interests that could not prevail within the regular party process were excluded from party affairs.

Regularity did more than exclude nonparticipants; it empowered those groups within those boundaries by declaring them the official local custodians of the party label. As Amy Bridges points out, "party divisions are not simply

[32] "Party Loyalty by Resolution," *Chicago Tribune*, June 5, 1884, 4.
[33] "A Long Step toward Harmony," *New York Times*, September 1, 1894.
[34] "Was It Regular?" *Boston Globe*, September 19, 1878, 2.
[35] Thomas Malory to William Jennings Bryan, June 2, 1896, box 4, William Jennings Bryan Papers, Manuscript Division, Library of Congress.

the epiphenomena of 'natural' divisions." They "work to promote some solidarities and undermine others."[36] Regularity delimited the kinds of political divisions allowed into party life; in particular, Jacksonian mode parties were ordered along the lines of the geographical divisions that also composed the electoral system, obscuring divisions based on ideology, ethnicity, or interest. Popular movements or interests that did not coincide with those geographical divisions were shut out of the process, magnifying the distinction between the local party establishment and the party-in-the-electorate. The Jacksonian party mode facilitated a limited role for popular influence, limiting it to that which could pass through the framework of regularity, in contrast to the ideal depiction of Jacksonian Democracy as a direct chain of command between the national organization and the people.

This preference for geographical organizational units had three underlying props. First, it reinforced the Jacksonian-republican prescription for the primacy of organic local communities as the best security for the common man's political efficacy. Second, it resolved a strategic problem; because the national electoral system was itself demarcated by discrete geographical constituencies, parties needed to maintain organized support across a range of geographical locations. Regularity aided this by providing openings and incentives for elite participation in every electoral unit. Finally, geographical regularity "reduced the chances of intraparty competition for the same office... since, unlike the caucus, every geographic and electoral division of government was directly consulted."[37]

Two effects of regularity in the Jacksonian mode affected national party leaders. First, it made subnational party leaders gatekeepers, separating the national party organization from the national party-in-the-electorate and made the national organization more responsive to the demands of subnational party leaders than to the party-in-the-electorate.[38] Second, because regularity was a procedural and not an ideological designation, it provided no remedy for the problem of local elites who obscured national purpose for local politics. Thus, as Silbey explains, "the great issues of the day were filtered through the prism of local outlooks."[39] Combined, then, these two effects insulated subnational party leaders from popular opinion and limited the effectiveness of national popular leadership of the party-in-the-electorate.

This nonideological gatekeeping role produced pathologies that obscured public opinion. Party leaders worked in a world of procedure, but one in which the details of the procedures mattered less than the plenary control of

---

[36] Amy Bridges, *A City in the Republic: Antebellum New York and the Origins of Machine Politics* (Ithaca: Cornell University Press, 1987), 13, 12.

[37] Chase, "Jacksonian Democracy and the Rise of the Nominating Convention," 89.

[38] Reynolds, *The Demise of the American Convention System*, 102–3; Marcus, *Grand Old Party*, 120.

[39] For the perspective of a period politician on the matter, see William L. Wilson, *The Cabinet Diary of William L. Wilson, 1896–1897*, edited by Festus P. Summers (Chapel Hill: University of North Carolina Press, 1957), 93; Silbey, *The American Political Nation*, 174.

TABLE 1. *Regularity and the Components of Party Organization*

Components of Organization	Opportunities for Control of Regularity
Linkage functions	– Membership lists – Party label as promotional tool
Representative functions	– Calling conventions and primaries (including scheduling and selecting locations) – Composition of electoral ticket
Bureaucratic entities	– Selection of committee members – Allocation of patronage and election funds

the regular apparatus that enforced them. Understanding intraparty conflict as oriented toward organizational control and thus the power to demarcate the boundaries of party regularity clarifies a great deal about nineteenth-century manipulations of party procedures. Regular subnational party organizations controlled the linkage mechanisms in their location and so controlled entry to the network of regularity. State and national parties tended to look the other way when local organizations – the ground forces for their campaigns – manipulated these linkage mechanisms, and subnational organizations took full advantage of their forbearance; as the *New York Times* observed of the rise of Roscoe Conkling's New York State machine, "every petty technical advantage has been seized. The most rigorous enforcement of the forms of party rule has been insisted on, where that has been to the advantage of the machine."[40] Roosevelt is again a valuable witness; exploiting the benefits of regularity, politicians were "able to become perfectly familiar with all its workings, while the average outsider becomes more and more helpless in proportion as the organization is less and less simple."[41]

The three components of party organization (Table 1) demarcated the parameters by which local party organizations, through the status of regularity, controlled entry to the party. First, regularity provided control over party membership lists (which allowed access to nominating primaries), and so provided considerable authority over the principal mechanism by which members of the party-in-the-electorate were effectively linked to the party organization. American parties have never had clear requirements for official memberships, but in the nineteenth century, the right to participate in primaries was not effectively regulated by the state (although some state and local governments enacted registration laws in the 1880s and 1890s). As voluntary associations,

[40] "The Cost of a 'Boss'," *New York Times*, June 17, 1881, 4. Conkling's biographer confirms this judgment: David M. Jordan, *Roscoe Conkling of New York: Voice in the Senate* (Ithaca: Cornell University Press, 1971), see chaps. 7, 8, 15, and 21.

[41] Roosevelt, "Machine Politics," 76. Daniel S. Remsen found that a lack of printed rules facilitated the control of regulars by obscuring the requirements for successful rebellion, but even when rules were written down, committees could routinely "amend, modify, enlarge, repeal, or suspend the whole or any part of the plan and rules." *Primary Elections: A Study of Methods for Improving the Basis of Party Organization* (New York: G. P. Putnam's Sons, 1894), 40.

local party organizations kept variously constituted membership lists that controlled public access to primaries. Even when elites did not arbitrarily eliminate voters from their lists, the necessity of maintaining a list provided barriers to entry, and regular elites found it relatively easy "to keep the ward or precinct list of party voters small and 'select.' " David Remsen's 1894 survey of state and local party practice found the following qualifications for primary election voters in place in various locations across the country:

[participants must] reside within the district, be a voter, have voted the party ticket, have been registered at the last preceding election or show cause for his failure, not be a member of any other [partisan] organization, must attend personally, sign a pledge stating intention to support the candidates of the party and to submit to the legally expressed action of the district or county committee.... [and] must be endorsed by one or more members and passed upon by a committee and in some cases by a vote of the members at the regular meeting subsequent to the one at which the name is proposed.[42]

Philadelphia Republican party rules adopted in 1872 provided that voters could be added on only one day of the year during a four-hour period. Voters were required to "prove to the satisfaction of a majority of the Registering Officers that they are Union Republican voters, and entitled to vote in said Division," and regular party members could challenge individual names. The Board of Registering Officers was appointed by the regular executive committee of each ward, and the executive committee (the president of which also kept the rolls for his ward) served on the board ex officio, making it easy to control the rolls.[43] Different locations had different arrangements, but in all cases, regular party organizations maintained plenary power over the right to participate in internal party procedures. As a San Francisco Democratic state committeeman complained of a similar arrangement to Democratic boss Christopher Buckley in 1884, "if I have the President, Secretary, and keeper of the roll, the way things have been carried on I would not care a twenty-cent piece whether I was in the minority ... or not, so far as the bona fide voters were concerned." Buckley responded: "of course you wouldn't. You've been too long in the business for that."[44]

Second, regularity was a powerful promotional tool for politicians, certifying a candidate's affiliation with the party and thus enabling voters to link candidates' names with their historical commitment to the party regardless of their policy preferences. Regularity was thus "a great advantage, if not absolutely essential to success" in the nineteenth-century party polity.[45] Voters had little time to sort through the claims of various factions to represent the party's

[42] Remsen, *Primary Elections*, 60, 49.
[43] *Rules of the Union Republican Party, Adopted May 24, 1872* (Philadelphia: William White Smith, Publisher, 1872), 6–7.
[44] "Harmony," *San Francisco Examiner*, March 13, 1884, 4; "Reorganization," *San Francisco Examiner*, February 14, 1884, 1.
[45] "Nomination and Election," *New York Times*, October 23, 1881, 8; Chase, "Jacksonian Democracy and the Rise of the Nominating Convention," 89.

"true" position and preferred to allow the party process to resolve these disputes; they relied on regular leaders for voting cues, barring an extraordinarily popular claim by an irregular faction. Regularity also provided a powerful form of community pressure. Voting the "regular ticket" became a measure of one's membership in a partisan community, and willingness to vote for an irregular ticket was a betrayal of that community; as James Kehl observes, "party regularity was interpreted as a specific kind of trustworthiness."[46] For this reason, organizations recognized as regular had "the political *apostolic succession*," as "the *body* of the party . . . will be awed into not only adhesion but activity."[47] The cultural appeal of regularity thus insulated party leaders from popular ire, heightening the disjunction between popular opinion and the votes cast for nominees and delegates in party conventions. There was "an assumption . . . that the voters need not trouble themselves speculating about the nominees."[48] Elites exploited this by choosing candidates according to political considerations rather than popular support for particular candidates or issues. As *The Century* complained, party loyalists "would vote for Satan himself if he got the regular nomination."[49]

Third, local committees called the conventions that both selected local candidates and sent delegates to state conventions. Theoretically, local party organizations were close to the people, and delegates should have therefore been in touch with local opinion. However, when party committees manipulated convention results for their own purposes, as often happened, the link between the people and the parties was broken; party candidates would "in reality be elected, not by the many who voted for him, but by the few who offered him to be voted for."[50] "Under such provisions," noted Remsen, "the created is able to dominate the creator. The servant is greater than the master."[51]

The power to call conventions allowed organizations to control the scheduling and location of the conventions that selected delegates in the nominating process; together with the power to staff conventions and to compose electoral tickets, this enabled them to control the mechanisms that were designed to make party decisions representative of the party-in-the-electorate. Remsen found that in states that had written rules (he assumed that the same applied in states without published rules), "the procedure at all primaries and conventions . . . [was] directed by the [regular party] committee," and as such "the committee is lord of the party."[52] What Ostrogorski described as "a concentration of power and

---

[46] James A. Kehl, *Boss Rule in the Gilded Age: Matt Quay of Pennsylvania* (Pittsburgh: University of Pittsburgh Press, 1981), 81–2.
[47] "New York Politics," *New York Times*, September 7, 1853, 2. Emphasis in original.
[48] Reynolds, *The Demise of the American Convention System*, 29.
[49] "On 'Voting Straight,' " *The Century*, 55:3 (January 1898), 474–5.
[50] Sidney G. Fisher, "Nominating Conventions," *The North American Review*, January 1868, 237.
[51] Remsen, *Primary Elections*, 22.
[52] Remsen, *Primary Elections*, 21–2. The *New York Times* noted that such local primaries were "where the power to nominate is first delegated. Here the voters commission certain of their

a compression of public opinion and of its preoccupations, which increased at each stage of the Organization," began at the primaries, gradually substituting the demands of organizational maintenance for popular opinion.[53]

Local committees used their authority to set primary dates, times, and locations to maximize their ability to control outcomes. Primaries could be scheduled at short notice, or in obscure locations, or with poor advertisement, exploiting the regular organization's power over the delegate selection process by limiting the scope of conflict within it. In Philadelphia in 1872, reformers complained that the Republican executive committee called delegate elections a day before the date of the convention and that "the shortness of time before the election renders thorough ward and precinct organization of the taxpayers impossible."[54] In Chicago, "respectable" citizens grew disillusioned with party democracy when they recognized in 1877 that "a shrewd politician can always manage his own or a friend's success by manipulating the primaries," and primaries held in 1880 were poorly attended because "the polling-places were not made known, and, without exception, were held in unfrequented saloons, where the saloon-keeper, the [election] judges, and a few vagrants met and elected themselves."[55] Regularly called primaries did not require massive turnout for authority to speak for the local party-in-the-electorate, as Topeka Republicans recognized, when, in 1880,

[a] member of the county central committee from the Third ward, stationed himself behind the counter, and after rapping sharply with a weight, announced that nominations for judges were in order, then named five men, three for judges and two for clerks, whom he said were suggested. He called for an affirmative vote and it was given, but no call for the negative was asked. None was demanded because the friends of the opposition had before been told that no concessions would be made, and it was useless to attempt what would surely result in defeat.[56]

Such maneuvers were common not only in cities; surveying 1881 primary elections in New York State, reformer George Walton Green documented turnout-dampening manipulations in smaller towns as well. In Bethlehem, "the notice was posted in the evening for an election to be held on the following day." In New Scotland, "the call was posted on Thursday for a meeting on Saturday to elect delegates to Monday's convention." In Waterloo, "no meeting was held

---

members to act for them in district or state conventions." "Party Representation," June 15, 1880, 4.

53 Ostrogorski, Democracy and the Organization of Political Parties, 115; Bensel, Passion and Preferences, 125.

54 "The Republican Executive Committee," (Philadelphia) *Evening Bulletin*, April 1, 1872, 4; "Political," (Philadelphia) *Evening Bulletin*, January 25, 1872, 8.

55 "Regulating Primary Elections," *Chicago Tribune*, April 4, 1877, 4; "A Complaining Democrat," *Chicago Tribune*, August 15, 1880, 10.

56 "Yesterday's Primary," *The* (Topeka, KS) *Commonwealth*, September 2, 1880, 2. See also "Dishonest Party Government," *Chicago Tribune*, October 9, 1882, 4; "Republican Factions at It," *New York Times*, August 3, 1894, 3.

nor any notices given, yet at the convention two delegates claiming to represent that place were promptly on hand."[57]

The party committees that called conventions to order also influenced the selection of the conventions' leadership. They selected the slate of temporary officers, who were supposed to organize the convention long enough to secure the selection of permanent officers by the convention. (The temporary leadership recognized that conventions were often approached by contesting delegations; temporary officers secured the selection of credentials committees and waited for their work to be completed before calling for the selection of a permanent chairman and officers.) Temporary chairmen presided over the selection of committees on rules, resolutions, and permanent organization, as well as credentials committees. Shaping the composition of these committees could determine the character of the convention. The temporary chairman often simply appointed these working committees (only sometimes following the suggestion of the delegates; more often they reflected agreements worked out among party leaders ahead of time).[58] In some cases temporary chairmen were chosen in advance by the reigning party committee; in Philadelphia, the city executive committee picked the temporary chairmen of all conventions held within its jurisdiction, including county conventions, congressional district conventions, senatorial conventions, state representative conventions, and legislative conventions, allowing it to shape party affairs across the city.[59] Control

---

[57] George Walton Green, "Facts about the Caucus and the Primary," *The North American Review*, September 1883, 259–60.

[58] Evidence that this was a common procedure in nominating conventions at the state and local level is too abundant to list completely, but so sporadic as to render a more rigorous documentation awkward. Among the sources that confirm it are the following: "Worcester," *Boston Globe*, September 17, 1879, 1; "County Convention," *The* (Topeka, KS) *Commonwealth*, August 3, 1882, 4; "Democratic State Convention," *The* (Topeka, KS) *Commonwealth*, June 3, 1880, 4; "Democratic Convention," *The* (Topeka, KS) *Commonwealth*, September 29, 1881, 4; "Congressional Convention, Third District," *The* (Topeka, KS) *Commonwealth*, June 1, 1882, 3; "Democratic," (Philadelphia) *Evening Bulletin*, August 29, 1876, 8; "Nomination Day," (Philadelphia) *Evening Bulletin*, June 24, 1875, 8; *Proceedings and Address, of the Democratic County Convention, Held at Galena, in the County of Jo Daviess, in the State of Illinois, on the 22nd February, 1839* (Galena: *Galena Democrat and Advertiser*, 1839), Library of Congress collection; *Proceedings of the Democratic State Convention, Composed of Delegates from the Several Districts and Parishes of the State of South Carolina, Assembled at Columbia, on the 22d May, 1843*, (Columbia: The "South Carolinian" Office, 1843), Library of Congress collection; *Journal of the Democratic Convention, Held in the City of Montgomery on the 14th and 15th of February, 1848* (Montgomery, AL: M'Cormick & Walshe, Printers, 1848), Library of Congress collection; *Proceedings of the Republican State Convention, Held at Sacramento, June 20, 1860*, Library of Congress collection.

[59] Evidence that this was a common procedure in nominating conventions at the state and local level is too abundant to list completely, but so sporadic as to render a more rigorous documentation awkward. Among the sources that confirm it are the following: "Political," (Philadelphia) *Evening Bulletin*, June 20, 1874, 8; "The Republican Convention," (Philadelphia) *Evening Bulletin*, June 19, 1875, 8; "The Republican Committee," (Philadelphia) *Evening Bulletin*, September 7, 1878, 8; *Proceedings of a Meeting of the State Central Committee of the Union Republican Party of Georgia, Held at Atlanta, Wednesday, November 24, 1869* (Atlanta: New

of credentials committees shaped the membership of the convention; because it was easy "to get up a contest" over the regularity of a ward delegation, it was not unusual for committee members to encourage fraudulent delegations, which could be accepted over duly elected delegations by a compliant convention leadership.[60] Control of the temporary organization also enabled regular organizations to control the committees on resolutions, which created party platforms and could block popular input on platforms.[61]

Fourth, local regular organizations made up ballots, completing the list of representative functions of the party organization. Ballots were informally printed and distributed by the parties, with no state regulation. This mattered in general elections as well because many voters voted the regular ticket without inspecting its contents.[62] However, it also had bearing on convention delegates, whose access to the primary ballot was also controlled by the regular organization. Because convention delegates were the only institutionalized means by which popular input on national candidates was taken, the quality of local party democracy shaped the quality of national party democracy. The primary process was so easily manipulated by the regular organization that "in very many places," wrote a contemporary student of the nominating process, it was "customary for the members of the ward or town committee to make up a

---

Era Job Office, 1869), Library of Congress collection; *New York Republican State Convention, Held at Syracuse, September 18 and 19, 1856*, Library of Congress collection; *Proceedings of the Democratic State Convention, Held at Charlottesville, VA, September 9 and 10, 1840*, Library of Congress collection; Chairman of the (Pennsylvania) State Committee, *Proceedings of the Pennsylvania Democratic State Convention, at Lancaster, Wednesday, March 22, 1876*, (Lancaster: Steinman & Hensel, Printers, 1876).

[60] This practice is documented in "Action of the State Central Committee," *The* (Topeka, KS) *Commonwealth*, July 13, 1882, 2; "County Convention," *The* (Topeka, KS) *Commonwealth*, August 3, 1882, 4; "The State Central Committee," *Boston Globe*, October 17, 1878, 4; "The State Central Committee," *Boston Globe*, October 17, 1878, 4; and "Mr. Chase Insubordinate," *Washington Post*, January 12, 1888, 3. In his *Nominations for Elective Office in the United States* (New York: Longmans, Green, and Co., 1897), Frederick Dallinger observed that the phenomenon was common at local conventions; further, "by its control of the organization of the convention, and consequently of the appointment of the committee on credentials, is able to unseat a sufficient number of [opposing] delegates (filling their places with its own friends) to nominate whomsoever it pleases," 69.

[61] The chairman of an 1889 Chicago city convention refused to take resolutions from the floor and insisted that other lists handed to him were unauthorized and the committee on resolutions "ought to ignore them" ("Selection of Election Judges," *Chicago Tribune*, January 13, 1889, 13). More prosaically, the 1872 Democratic State Convention in Pennsylvania, "for the purpose of facilitating business," provided that all resolutions from the floor would be sent to the committee on resolutions "without debate or reading," despite the open knowledge that "gentlemen from all parts of the State" were present "with their views in writing" (John C. Barr, H. H. Cummin, Herman Kretz, and John O'Connor, *Proceedings of the Democratic State Convention of 1872, Nominating Governor and Auditor General, Judge of the Supreme Court and Congressman at Large, Selecting an Electoral Ticket, and Electing Delegates to National Convention, at Baltimore* [Pittsburgh: Barr & Myers, Printers, 1872], 4.)

[62] See Herbert J. Bass, *"I Am a Democrat": The Political Career of David Bennett Hill* (Syracuse: Syracuse University Press, 1961), 97.

ticket or 'slate,' as it is sometimes called, of candidates and delegates previous to the caucus" without popular input.[63] In Philadelphia, it was reported that delegates to state conventions were "elected without any reference whatever to the chosen candidate."[64] John Reynolds's study of the convention system found even where the party-in-the-electorate selected delegates directly, "it was rarely clear where any prospective delegate stood with respect to candidacies or causes."[65] The convention system's capacity to signal popular will to the national conventions was thereby diminished.

Fifth, primaries selected local committee members, either directly or indirectly (as when committees were appointed by conventions), so control of primaries allowed teams of elites to perpetuate their position across election cycles. It was through primaries that committees' claims to regularity were renewed, but as Ostrogorski observed, "the direct influence of the electors on the composition of the committees expires on the threshold of the committee of first instance," because the committees then gained power over local party affairs.[66] It is little surprise, then, that the *Boston Globe* reported the local primaries as the place where "the politicians work most assiduously"[67] or that a San Francisco party member claimed that local committees were the determinative institutional component in the nominating process: "committee ownership is nine points, in the estimation of the ward politician, in shaping the election of delegates to the various conventions."[68] Local committees were also commonly appointed rather than elected, further limiting popular input.[69]

---

[63] Dallinger, *Nominations for Elective Office in the United States*, 60. This was aggravated by the fact that, in many places outside of urban or highly contested areas, nomination procedures were informal in nature. Alan Ware, *The American Direct Primary: Party Institutionalization and Transformation in the North* (Cambridge: Cambridge University Press, 2002), 63.

[64] "The Fourth District," *Philadelphia Evening Bulletin*, September 24, 1874, 4.

[65] Reynolds, *The Demise of the American Convention System*, 27–9. Local committees often simply appointed delegates to higher-level conventions, although it is less clear that this happened frequently in the selection of delegates to conventions selecting national delegates. For examples, see "Local Politics," *Chicago Tribune*, March 24, 1880, 1; "Republican Meetings," *Chicago Tribune*, October 17, 1875, 9; "Wild Tumult," *Cleveland Press*, July 16, 1887, 3; "Biff! Square in the 'Leader's' Face," *Cleveland Press*, July 12, 1890, 3; "The Fourth District," (Philadelphia) *Evening Bulletin*, September 24, 1874, 4; "Democratic Municipal Convention," *Boston Globe*, November 18, 1873, 5; and "Caucusing," *Boston Globe*, September 21, 1876, 4. That practice is documented in Kleppner, *The Third Electoral System*, 333–4, and Remsen, *Primary Elections*, 42.

[66] Ostrogorski, *Democracy and the Organization of Political Parties*, 36.

[67] "On the Verge of the Campaign," *Boston Globe*, August 18, 1874, 4.

[68] "War of the Factions," *San Francisco Examiner*, March 3, 1892, 4

[69] The Arkansas Democratic State Central Committee was selected by a committee convened at the state convention. "Arkansas Democrats," *Arkansas Gazette*, June 1, 1888, 3. In the Pennsylvania Republican organization, the chairman of the state committee was selected by the gubernatorial candidate and the chairman of the state convention; the state chairman named twelve at-large committeemen (assumed to "be notable for their efficiency in cooperating with the chairman who has chosen them"). Committees at higher levels were often composed ex officio of members of the local committees and statewide, making party organizations an

Sixth, regular status qualified an organization for patronage consideration from higher levels of the party organization. As Steven Erie's intergovernmental theory of party building suggests, the strongest accounts of party development consider parties as a whole – linking the local, state, and national levels of the party to account for the "pivotal role of local alliances with party leaders at the state and federal levels" in securing long-term power.[70] Patronage distribution was a central means by which relations between the national, state, and local levels of party organization were maintained. For regular organizations, "the Executive axe [would] hew off the heads of malcontents, without rest or mercy."[71] Patronage, notes James, was a means of disciplining local workers, and the ability to exploit patronage resources was a central tool with which party politicians responded to local electoral challenges, further securing the careers of regular politicians.[72] Regularity enabled local organizations to maintain the services of party workers, preventing them from carrying intraparty disputes into irregular political activity. Once regularity was established, "the moderate, and especially the *ambitious* ... [would] be *whipped into the traces*, and [would] even support the ticket to escape suspicion." This made patronage "the cement ... used to keep political organizations together," rather than merely a tool to promote the ambitions of individual politicians. Rebellious elites who appealed to the public outside of party bounds were "disciplined by having the patronage, local, state and national, thrown against [them]."[73] Channeling the ambitions of party workers helped the regular organization to control the caucus as it saw fit "and to keep itself in power against the wishes of the party voters of the district."[74] These workers came to "regard offices as rewards of party service, nominations as the special prerogative of partisan workers, elections as tests of the obedience of the rank and file to the commands of their leaders, and government as a means by which the party in power compensates itself for its previous outlays and perpetuates

---

amalgam of ex officio positions staffed largely by a small group of individuals. (See Macy, *Party Organization and Machinery*, 112–19; on ex officio officers, see chaps. 8–14 generally.) In San Francisco in 1892, the forty-five-member Republican county committee added twenty-five new seats, which were given to an irregular organization that had threatened to lead "an independent movement of Republicans." "Martin Kelly Beats Burns," *San Francisco Examiner*, March 22, 1892, 6. In Chicago, the Cook County Republican Central Committee frequently selected new members when less than a quorum of committee members appeared at meetings – in 1875, eight committee members thereby selected eleven new members before proceeding to apportion city convention delegates to the wards. See "Meeting of the Republican Central Committee," *Chicago Tribune*, October 3, 1875, 9; see also "Political," *Chicago Tribune*, October 3, 1875, 9.

70 Steven Erie, *Rainbow's End*, 9.
71 "New York Politics," *New York Times*, September 7, 1853, 2; Harold F. Gosnell, "Thomas C. Platt – Political Manager," *Political Science Quarterly*, September 1923, 462.
72 James, "Patronage Regimes and American Party Development," 39–60.
73 "New York Politics," *New York Times*, September 7, 1853, 2 (emphasis in original); Gosnell, "Thomas C. Platt – Political Manager," 457, 453.
74 Remsen, *Nominations for Elective Office in the United States*, 61.

its own tenure."[75] Again, patronage followed geographic lines, with politicians ensuring that the spoils were spread to ensure an even mobilization effort. This limited presidents in particular from the kind of ideological patronage that would come to mark twentieth-century presidential politics, requiring that appointments be governed by "considerations of a . . . geographical nature," in which "each locality is entitled to have a man of its own."[76]

Regular organizations also exerted "control over the party campaign funds," meaning the power to assess local officeholders and party members, as well as "the full assistance of the State and National Administrations" during elections. The latter arrived in the form of lump cash payments. With little oversight, the self-interested local politician "[can] use his position to get a wad of money, which will be divided between his few friends here and the campaign will have to look after itself."[77] For poll workers and ward heelers, such funds were the reward of party work.

Widespread corruption in the form of vote buying, repeat voting, and miscounting of ballots has long raised questions about the validity of the Jacksonian mode's claim to democratic practice.[78] However, the institutional position of local political parties allowed for elite manipulations that obviated the need for electoral corruption. Glenn Altschuler and Stuart Blumin examined participation in Jacksonian era party affairs and found a number of indications that party organizations tended to be managed by small cliques, leaving many citizens "disengaged from political affairs." Convention delegates routinely failed to attend, breaking the connection between local publics and the party-in-the-electorate, leaving party affairs to what an editor called "party despotism under a show of popular consultation." Spectacular campaign events, on closer examination, suggest "qualification about the depth and extensiveness of popular engagement in campaign rituals," because rallies were often swollen with party hacks.[79] From this perspective, the Jacksonian party mode's localistic bias did more than reinforce an ideological preference for republican politics; it restrained the effective operation of popular opinion to the local level of politics.

The Jacksonian Mode and National Party Politics
Although party regularity shaped politics at all levels, the focus here is on the effects of the Jacksonian mode on the practice of national party politics. From a national perspective, party regularity excluded large portions of the

---

[75] *Boston Advertiser*, quoted in "Cameron, Logan, West, Dorsey," *Springfield* [MA] *Republican*, February 7, 1876, 4.
[76] Milkis, *The President and the Parties*, 54–9; Joseph Benson Foraker to Mark Hanna, July 13, 1887, box 2, Hanna-McCormick Family Papers; Foraker to Hanna, April 27, 1886, box 2, Hanna-McCormick Family Papers, Manuscript Division, Library of Congress, Washington, DC.
[77] Franklin D. Locke to William C. Whitney, August 8, 1892, book 74, William C. Whitney Papers, Manuscript Division, Library of Congress, Washington, DC.
[78] See the charges summarized in Peter H. Argersinger, "New Perspectives on Election Fraud in the Gilded Age," *Political Science Quarterly*, Winter 1985, 669–87.
[79] Altschuler and Blumin, "Limits of Political Engagement in Antebellum America."

party-in-the-electorate, drained national campaigns of common purposes, and substituted the political preferences of local elites for an expression of national popular opinion. The problem was compounded by the Jacksonian mode's campaign operations: the national party organizations relied largely on subnational organizations to conduct national campaigns, and their legendary mobilization prowess was often subverted by the same local interests that undermined the convention process's representative qualities. As popular opinion was filtered by local organizations on its way up to the national convention, national party purposes were filtered by local organizations on their way back down to the people.

This reflected the republican values of the Jacksonian mode. Delegate selection was conducted through a local democratic process, and the preference for preserving local sources of power meant that the party organization was not designed to facilitate a national democratic process that distinguished a national constituency from the aggregation of local constituencies. This prevented the national party from drawing legitimacy from popular opinion and preserved the notion of the local party's authority over a homogeneous community. Further, it appropriated the president's appointing power to shore up local political boundaries and maintain geographically based incentives, even as it weakened a constitutional source of executive power.

National Conventions and Deferential Compromise

National conventions united various state and local organizations to create national nominees and platforms. They functioned more as congresses of distinct and self-interested organizations, however, than as deliberative councils pursuing common substantive goals. They were united by a republican argument for "harmony," because ideological pursuits were discouraged in favor of cooperation among political friends. This, too, originated in the context of the Jacksonian era. The Jacksonians retained the Jeffersonian identification of two parties inherent in human nature, dividing mankind into Whigs and Tories, and hoped to maintain the unity of the former to protect republican government from the latter.[80] Clarifying principles, Jacksonian Democrats believed, only divided republicans, confusing permanent interests with conflicts over transient issues. Conventions were to compromise rather than fight for ideological preferences; delegates were to show flexibility in their advocacy of candidates and platform planks.[81] This justified the delegates in substituting a general notion of representing "the people" for a more exact representation of public opinion.

---

[80] Hofstadter, *The Idea of a Party System*, 27.
[81] On this "search for harmony," see Reynolds, *The Demise of the American Convention System*, chap. 2. Silbey notes that "more than anything else . . . jealousies, indifference, and internal squabbles over candidates had to be prevented. 'Union, harmony, self-denial, concession, everything for the cause, nothing for men,' was how one Democratic congressman put it." *The American Political Nation*, 24.

Critics wondered whether the results reflected public opinion at all. Of the 1879 city primaries, the *Chicago Tribune* complained that "in many of the wards the result did not express the wishes of the Republican voters." It seemed that once "a candidate got his men on the Central Committee, who managed the campaign," they too often "ran it not for the interests of the party, but in the interest of Tom, Dick, and Harry." The (Philadelphia) *Evening Bulletin* complained of an 1872 convention that it "was what is called in the political slang of the day 'a set-up job.' The people had little or nothing to do with it." In 1880, in reporting on the Pennsylvania state convention, which rammed through a delegation pledged to a third nomination for ex–President Grant despite widespread opposition in the state, the newspaper observed that "in view of the really non-representative character of political conventions, impartial judgment will hesitate to accept the result of yesterday's work as settling anything in regard to the condition of the public mind upon the Presidential question." As Reynolds concludes, this was aggravated by the weakness of the link between the delegates and the presidential appointments those delegates supported. Primary voters usually voted for delegates who had not announced a preference for any candidate; in this way, "the hierarchical character of the convention system did little to promote meaningful participation on the part of the citizenry," an observation that "became more true the further one moved up the political ladder."[82] Further, without clearly defined ideological principles as a litmus test for candidates or platforms, voters had few tools to judge the representative qualities of their candidates or platforms. Candidates were praised for being "available," that is, least likely to alienate many local pockets of support, who were thus likely to be most useful for mobilizing voters.

Although there were positions deemed to be "regular," being recognized as a party regular or a regular organization required no profession of political faith other than an intent to vote for the regular party ticket. In Philadelphia, for instance, no Republican could be nominated by a convention without taking a pledge to "abide by the decision of this Convention, and . . . not become a candidate against the regular nominee of the Union Republican party, nor . . . permit my name to be used as such candidate." Evoking the same idea, a resolution proposed in the 1880 Republican National Convention declared that every delegate was "bound in honor to support its nominee, whoever that nominee may be, and no man should hold a seat here who is not ready to so agree." It passed with only three dissenting votes, even though that convention saw a bitter contest between the Stalwart and Half-Breed factions of the party. This fiction of unquestioning party unity provided the designation of "regular" with a sense of unity that did not really exist; minorities who questioned party

---

[82] "Reforming the Primaries," *Chicago Tribune*, September 14, 1879, 3; "Is This Reform," (Philadelphia) *Evening Bulletin*, April 4, 1872, 4; "The Convention" (Philadelphia) *Evening Bulletin*, February 5, 1880, 4; Reynolds, *The Demise of the American Convention System*, 29, 32.

principles, or nominees' attachments to them, were silenced by "powerful pressures against individual action and toward unanimity or, at least, accepting the majority's decision."[83] Critics of the Jacksonian mode argued that the nominating system had become unhinged from the party-in-the-electorate. Thus, *The Nation* opined in 1884 that the "party which votes and the . . . party which acts have become two different things in virtue of a law which seems to govern all organizations. . . . [namely,] the tendency of the leaders and managers, if assured of their tenure of power . . . to drift away from the main body of their constituents."[84]

In no instance was the problem more glaring than in enforcement of the unit rule, a tightly contested component of the convention framework in both parties. Imposed on national convention delegations at state conventions, the rule bound delegates to cast their votes as a unit with other delegates from their state, with the majority of the delegation deciding how the whole would vote. Unit voting was established in the first Democratic convention in 1831 by a rule requiring delegations to cast their votes through their chairmen, which was interpreted to mean that chairmen could cast the state's whole vote according to the preferences of a majority of the delegation. This did not specifically mandate unit voting, but historian Carl Becker argued that "it show[ed] a tendency at the very beginning to leave the decision of all such matters to the state, or the delegations which represent the state." State conventions quickly began to send their delegations with instructions to vote as a unit. Because the Democratic party's convention framework served as a model for Whigs and Republicans, it provided the basis for the rule's use in the Whig party and for attempts to impose it on Republican conventions; as explained in Chapter 6, Republicans only officially abandoned it in 1880 – and then only after an intense fight.[85]

The logic of the unit rule – and of the Jacksonian mode itself – held that national delegates were agents of the state conventions, not direct representatives of the people. This empowered state conventions procedurally, rhetorically, and strategically in shaping the selection process.[86] It also presumed a superiority of state organizations over the rules of the national convention, although it did not deny individuals' right to vote independently; rather, it

[83] "C.C.C.," (Philadelphia) *Evening Bulletin*, July 14, 1874, 8; "The President-Makers," *New York Times*, June 5, 1880, 1; Republican National Committee, *Official Proceedings of the Republican National Conventions, 1868, 1872, 1876, and 1880* (Minneapolis: Charles W. Johnson, Publishers, 1903), 410; Silbey, *The American Political Nation*, 60, 66.

[84] "What Is the Republican Party?" *The Nation*, October 30, 1884, 368. For contemporary complaints along this line, see also "The Work of the Convention," *Weekly Alta California*, May 6, 1876, 2; Sidney G. Fisher, "Nominating Conventions," *The North American Review*, January 1868, 245; Oliver T. Morton, "Presidential Nominations," *The Atlantic Monthly*, April, 1884, 459.

[85] Carl Becker, "The Unit Rule in National Nominating Conventions," *The American Historical Review*, 5:1 (October, 1899), 66, 75–6.

[86] Macy, *Party Organization and Machinery*, 84.

denied the national convention authority to recognize individual votes of delegates against the will of their chairmen. "The authority of the State Convention is held to be exclusive in the matter," argued unit rule defenders, and it "had its origin in the idea that in political matters the State is sovereign and the National Convention has only a delegated authority for general purposes and no power of coercion over the party in any State."[87] The unit rule thus reinforced the republican preference for local autonomy rather than common national purposes.

Through unit voting, state party leaders could silence political minorities and thus "either almost double or eliminate entirely the influence of a faction or a group within a delegation." Binding state delegates "enable[d] the State to exercise a powerful influence in the nomination" by magnifying support for particular aspirants.[88] Hence Pennsylvania's Don Cameron is reported to have said of his delegation, "a majority of one is all that I want."[89] The rule helped quell controversial issues by preventing "discussion which may not otherwise be forced upon the Convention."[90] Because it prevented candidates from combining political minorities across the country into a coherent movement transcending state borders, it forced aspirants to deal with state leaders. This coincided with a republican mistrust of ambition; candidates who played to popular audiences may have boosted their popular support, but there was no way to translate such support into convention votes.

Further, Jacksonian conventions obscured the distinction between state and congressional district delegates, which had an important denationalizing effect. Convention calls in both parties specified that state delegations were to be composed of a combination of at-large delegates, who represented the state as a whole, and congressional district representatives. The distinction was often ignored in practice, again empowering state organizations at the expense of popular opinion. District delegates were frequently selected by state rather than district conventions under the theory that "the State as a whole is to be represented by delegates apportioned in part among the Congressional districts but not representing them directly as separate constituencies." This distanced delegates from the party-in-the-electorate by selecting them from larger and less representative bodies. It also made convention delegations more representative of state organizations than of a broader sampling of the

---

[87] "The Manner of the Nomination," *New York Times*, July 12, 1884, 4.

[88] Paul T. David, Ralph M. Goldman, and Richard C. Bain, *The Politics of National Party Conventions* (New York: Vintage Books, 1964) 164, 204. Howard Reiter concludes that it "not only subsumed individual rights under states' rights but also increased the power of states that exercised the option." *Selecting the President*, 133. See also W. C. McFarland to John Sherman, March 29, 1880, vol. 209, John Sherman Papers, Manuscript Division, Library of Congress.

[89] "From Harrisonburg" (Philadelphia) *Evening Bulletin*, February 5, 1880, 3.

[90] Republican National Committee, *Official Proceedings of the Republican National Conventions, 1868, 1872, 1876, and 1880*, 420. As Reynolds points out, the parties' "obsession with harmony dictated that all potentially disruptive influences be cast aside." Reynolds, *The Demise of the American Convention System*, 60.

party-in-the-electorate.[91] This facilitated favorite son candidates; as one politician remembered, "where the machinery of the party was in the hands of a few men who controlled party affairs, delegations could be taken to the convention in support of any candidate who might have sufficient local [that is, statewide] pride back of him."[92] Thus, even without the unit rule, "the cohesive power of state pride, and the power of a large majority"[93] could hold a delegation together. Favorite son candidates, who were more often stalking horses for the ambitions of state party leaders than genuine popular favorites, rode roughshod over local preferences for nationally popular candidates; once favorite sons bowed out, state delegations remained bound by the unit rule, enabling state party leaders to deliver their entire delegations and maximize political debts.

Jacksonian Mode Campaigning

When national party leaders sought, in the late nineteenth century, to perfect their connection with the electorate and generate national mandates, they confronted the Jacksonian mode's conventional campaign wisdom as well as its delegate-selection procedures. Fitting the Jacksonian mode's localistic republicanism, national committees were composed of representatives of state organizations, and they largely confined their activities to localized fundraising operations. The national organizations relied on subnational regular party organizations to present the parties' case to the voters. Even as the national organizations relied on their local affiliates, however, the Jacksonian mode did not provide the former with any reliable mechanisms to control the conduct of the latter. Jesse Macy noted in 1912 that "the state central committee in each state ... exercises much leeway as to its course in respect to matters purely local" and otherwise "[is] organically independent of the national committee." Silbey's account of the solidification of the Jacksonian party organizations found that the parties' "pyramidal structure did not mean power from the top down to each successive component below."[94] Thus, not only was public opinion filtered on its way up the chain of party hierarchy, national party purpose was filtered on the way back down to the electorate in the form of campaigns.

The absence of national control over campaign appeals gave subnational party leaders leeway to slant national campaign themes to suit local preferences. As a result, national campaigns failed to present a consistent case to voters across the nation and thus failed to provide clear mandates for national policies. Tammany Hall's Richard Croker provided a cogent defense of this old order:

the Democrat of New York and the Democrat of Iowa are agreed on certain fundamental doctrines, and in order to put these in action they forbear to press the acceptance of

---

[91] "The Unit and Two-Thirds Rules," *New York Times*, July 9, 1884, 4.
[92] Dictated Statement of Charles Dick to John B. Morrow, February 10, 1906, p. 6, box 4, Hanna-McCormick Family Papers.
[93] W. C. McFarland to Sherman, March 29, 1880, vol. 209, Sherman Papers.
[94] Macy, *Party Organization and Machinery*, 10, 81–2; Silbey, *The American Political Nation*, 70.

ideas as to which they are at variance. They only vote for the same candidate once in four years; at other elections they choose Governors, Representatives, etc., who are at liberty to entertain widely different views as to the extent to which certain political theories should be made to operate.[95]

Croker's argument was practical as much as principled; aggressive efforts to educate the public detracted from mobilization, risking debilitating factional disputes, and national issues caused divisiveness and weakened the party when unity was most necessary.[96]

Avoiding efforts to lead public opinion beyond parochial concerns, party leaders assumed that "when a political canvass is to be entered upon politicians have to take the condition of the public mind as they find it," and unfamiliar issues risked alienating voters.[97] Looking back at the period from the vantage point of 1905, Frank Chandler, an associate of Mark Hanna's, recalled that "under the old system of party management it was necessary to give one's personal effort toward getting the voters to the polls and to see that elections were fairly conducted and ballots honestly counted."[98]

This organizational norm had three effects on national campaigns. First, they encouraged national party platforms to be generalized to the point of vapidity, in what one editor called "the policy of dodging important issues in the hope of reconciling antagonistic elements."[99] Platforms were written so that they could "be stretched into more shapes than were ever assumed by Proteus," to touch "a common cord," rather than rousing "the asperities of faction."[100] As Douglas Jaenicke explains, parties strove in the construction of platforms "to avoid political choices that might drive disaffected groups from the party."[101] This is not to deny the presence of ideology in party politics, which John Gerring has adeptly documented. Rather, it is to point out that national campaigns did not effectively articulate national partisan principles. Instead, explains Richard Bensel, parties relied on "coded language" that was "intended to gloss over

---

95 Richard Croker, "Tammany Hall and the Democracy," *North American Review*, February 1892, 225–6. A popular expression of this principle was the ancient dictum: "in essentials, unity; in non-essentials, liberty; in all things charity." New York Democrat David Hill, quoted in "A Big Battle of Words," *New York Times*, May 2, 1896, 1.

96 Silbey, *The American Political Nation*, 24, 46.

97 "Associated Reform Work," *New York Times*, December 4, 1888, 4.

98 Dictated Statement of Frank M. Chandler to James B. Morrow, May 13, 1905, Hanna-McCormick Family Papers, Box 4. Richard Jensen argues that during the period, "the candidates and their managers thought in military terms. The election was conceived as a great battle pitting the strength of two opposing armies and the genius of their generals." The task was to get as many men onto the field as possible. *The Winning of the Midwest: Social and Political Conflict, 1888–96* (Chicago: University of Chicago Press, 1971), 164.

99 "Reading Out," *Arkansas Gazette*, March 25, 1884, 4.

100 Untitled article, *Arkansas Gazette*, July 1, 1884, 4.

101 Douglas W. Jaenicke, "The Jacksonian Integration of Parties into the Constitutional System," *Political Science Quarterly*, 1986 (Centennial Edition), 98. See also "The Beauties of Platform Making," *Arkansas Gazette*, June 17, 1882, 2; untitled article, *Centreville* (MD) *Observer*, June 27, 1871, 2; "An Era of Political Quackery," *Chicago Tribune*, September 30, 1886, 4.

differences between factions in the convention and the party at large."[102] In the absence of clearly articulated partisan agendas, national popular mandates for rule were impossible to achieve.

This was complicated by the second effect of Jacksonian mode localism on national campaigns. Recognizing the difficulty of imposing a single platform on a range of diverse localities, the spirit of deferential compromise forgave subnational organizations for obscuring national platforms in campaign appeals, and the national organizations avoided appealing directly to voters. Kleppner explains that "each party's electoral coalition was a loosely structured alliance of subgroups or subcoalitions functionally related to each other for the purpose of winning elections. Since subgroups of the population were asymmetrically distributed across the nation, the exact mixture of each party's social coalition varied from locale to locale." Thus "each party's mobilizers pursued success by showing voters the consonance between the party's character and their own concerns."[103] For this reason the *Chicago Tribune* complained that in local campaigns, "genuine Republicanism was thrust aside and in its place were paraded conspicuously views either flatly hostile to the principles of the party as defined by the National Convention . . . or else questions foreign to the platform of the National Convention."[104] Local Democrats were similarly allowed to take positions they thought would make them the strongest with their immediate constituents, believing that "the undisguised policy of the National Democratic Convention was to leave the matter open to that course."[105] The resulting national campaigns were a crazy quilt of diverse local interests and strategies, further hampering the development of coherent national mandates.

---

[102] John Gerring, *Party Ideologies in America, 1828–1996* (New York: Cambridge University Press, 1998), 114. Richard P. McCormick concludes that the parties "functioned best in securing agreement on candidates, conducting campaigns, mobilizing their partisans in the electorate, and sustaining and rewarding a large corps of organizers. They were less successful in articulating issues," in *The Presidential Game: The Origins of American Politics* (New York: Oxford University Press, 1982), 166.

[103] Kleppner, *The Third Electoral System*, 209. Bensel points out that "party organizations in the individual states regularly chose to ignore or dissent from national party declarations when the latter impaired their competitiveness in local elections." His analysis of state and national party platforms reveals that "differences were adjusted in national conventions in such a way as to gloss over conflicts and highlight consensual positions which promised advantage over the opposition," *Political Economy of American Industrialization*, xviii, 103, 124–32. Benson's case study of New York Democrats in the 1840s found similarly that state platforms deviated from national platforms to "maximize its appeal for the New York electorate, . . . direct attention to long-settled issues, and *thereby reinforce party loyalty*," in *The Concept of Jacksonian Democracy*, 233, emphasis in original. There were limits beyond which the terms of party regularity would not stretch, although "that was a message most politicians were not willing to convey publicly." Silbey, *The American Political Nation*, 116.

[104] "Republican Mistakes in New York," *Chicago Tribune*, November 18, 1887, 4.

[105] "Speaker Carlisle Lectures the House," *Chicago Tribune*, December 7, 1887, 4; see also William Garrott Brown, "A Defense of American Parties," *The Atlantic Monthly* (November 1900), 578.

Finally, it was believed that national candidates with clearly defined views reduced local campaigners' flexibility, and doing so was perceived to be dangerous to party success and individual careers. This reimagined the republican trope that candidates should stand for election rather than campaign openly, long after that façade had any bearing on political reality. This diminished presidential party leadership, because presidents could claim no substantive national leadership over a party that had not depended on them for substance in the campaign.[106] Hence, the *Chicago Tribune* warned that "it is a matter of little practical importance what may be the personal opinion of any of the candidates. . . . It is the duty of the convention to define the position of the party on this question, and the candidate selected will have nothing to do but accept or decline the commission."[107] Supporting this was what Daniel Webster had called "the sagacious, far-seeing doctrine of availability," whereby candidates were considered acceptable not because of the specific positions they championed but because of their generic acceptability to all factions. Ostrogorski defined availability as "not possessing a strongly marked individuality and not having compromised [onself] in the controversies of the day or in the struggles of factions."[108] Although "available" nominees kept the parties harmonious, they obscured popular choices. As the *Springfield* (MA) *Republican* observed, availability "has one meaning in the mouths of the politicians, and another, quite different meaning in the minds of the plain people," meaning that popular support was a secondary concern for the former; "the less record and the fewer enemies he has made, the greater his attractions for your average party-saving American politician."[109] Thus, the practice of Jacksonian mode politics reinforced the republican character of the Jacksonian organization by proscribing independent national leadership.

This electoral arrangement between national and subnational party organizations worked relatively well, ensuring campaigns with a national scope. However, its operation often fell short of the ideal, especially when state and local leaders were "more interested in keeping control of the machines in their states for their own future than in upholding true party principles for

[106] Reynolds, *The Demise of the American Convention System*, chap. 3. Jeffrey K. Tulis, in *The Rhetorical Presidency* (Princeton: Princeton University Press, 1987), argues that candidate reticence was the result of widely shred values about constitutionally appropriate behavior for presidents, but the norm of candidate reticence was at least as much a result of the demands of deferential compromise as of notions of constitutional propriety. See also Melvin Laracey, *Presidents and the People: The Partisan Story of Going Public* (College Station: Texas A&M University Press, 2002).

[107] "Candidates Can't Make Platforms," *Chicago Tribune*, May 29, 1888, 4. See also untitled article, *Arkansas Gazette*, March 18, 1882, 2.

[108] Daniel Webster quoted in Joseph B. Bishop, "Humor and Pathos of Presidential Conventions," *The Century*, 52:2 (June 1896), 306; Ostrogorski, *Democracy and the Organization of Political Parties: Volume II*, 130.

[109] "Available Men," *Springfield* (MA) *Republican*, February 6, 1876, 4. See also Oliver T. Morton, "Presidential Nominations," *The Atlantic Monthly*, April, 1884, 458; "A Brake on the Machine," *The* (Topeka, KS) *Commonwealth*, May 6, 1880, 1.

which they care only as the advocacy of such principles tends to their personal advancement."[110] Many subnational politicians, argues Robert Marcus, "were glad to concede an honor they did not need – that of being the president-maker – for a power in their state that was their political livelihood."[111] Subnational leaders often failed to mount credible national campaigns, preferring to devote more effort and resources to state and local campaigns, which might be more tightly contested or more central to their interests.[112] On occasion they negotiated elaborate trades with their local opposition to swap votes on the national ticket for votes on the local ticket.[113] To make good on threats, they might sit out campaigns or conduct them listlessly. In the Jacksonian mode, national leaders had few tools with which to combat this and no choice but to work with the regular local organizations. Even nationally sponsored speakers were sent out only at the request of the state organizations.[114]

The Hurrah Campaign

Along with decentralization and a preference for compromise rather than discord, the Jacksonian party mode maintained a particular style of campaigning

---

[110] Wilson, *The Cabinet Diary of William L. Wilson*, 118–19.

[111] Marcus, *Grand Old Party*, 74. Alan Ware argues that autonomy was centered at the county level of party organization, which even resisted concentration of power in the state party organizations. *The American Direct Primary*, 86.

[112] A variety of source material supports this, including Wharton Barker to John Sherman, February 5, 1888, box 4, Wharton Barker Papers, Manuscript Division, Library of Congress; "Victory for the Plucking," *New York Times*, June 8, 1892, 1; George F. Parker to Grover Cleveland, August 23, 1892, series 11, box 9, Grover Cleveland Papers, Manuscript Division, Library of Congress; Edwin Bailey to Whitney, September 3, 1892, book 75, Whitney Papers; James Russell Reed, Circular Letter, October 25, 1890, Young Men's Democratic Club of Massachusetts, Massachusetts Historical Society, Boston, MA; Charles E. Benedict to William C. Whitney, August 11, 1892, book 74, Whitney Papers; F. M. Hayes to Grover Cleveland, October 20, 1892, series 11, box 6, Cleveland Papers; Thomas Malory to Bryan, June 14, 1900, Bryan Papers, box 24; "Mr. Brice Coming Back," *New York Times*, September 16, 1888, 5; J. C. Miller to George B. Cortelyou, n.d., box 27, George B. Cortelyou papers, Manuscript Division, Library of Congress.

[113] Research by John F. Reynolds and Richard L. McCormick supports the view that ticket splitting mattered in nineteenth-century elections; "Outlawing 'Treachery': Split Tickets and Ballot Laws in New York and New Jersey, 1880–1910," *Journal of American History*, March 1986, 835–58. See also Ware, *The American Direct Primary*, 36–8, and Marcus, *Grand Old Party*, 146. For a variety of primary source material, see "What Will Tammany Do?" *New York Times*, September 28, 1884, 3; Theodore Roosevelt, "Machine Politics in New York City," *The Century*, November 1886, 80. D. C. Robinson to Whitney, November 8, 1892, book 77,Whitney Papers; R. W. Story to Bryan, November 5, 1890, Bryan Papers, box 2. See also, Frank J. Morgan to Bryan; W. E. Johnson to Bryan, October 16, 1890, box 2, Bryan Papers.

[114] For a clear example of the impotence of the national party to control local affiliates as late as 1896, see "Stop It! Hanna's Command to Quarreling Local Republicans," *Cleveland Press*, August 14, 1896, 1; "Ultimatum: Chairman Hanna Reads the Riot Act," *Cleveland Press*, August 17, 1896, 2.

known in the lingo of the time as a "hurrah campaign" – meaning an emphasis on spectacle and enthusiasm over substantive appeals, all centered on turnout maximization. Research on voting patterns in the nineteenth-century United States suggests three important features of electoral behavior to consider in making sense of this style. First, after the Civil War, neither party commanded a steady majority of voters nationally, resulting in instability in election returns and increasing the salience of bolts and third-party challenges.[115] Second, most voters were "core" voters who voted consistently with one party across multiple elections.[116] Finally, voting was heavily shaped by community loyalties, and "most American political communities... could be counted on to vote in great numbers in regular fashion," despite considerable mobility in society as a whole.[117] All three patterns contributed to the Jacksonian mode's campaign style; given the consistency of most voters and the competitiveness of elections, it made sense for the parties to maximize turnout.

Because the focus of party activity was on bringing party identifiers to the polls, local organizations relied on the kind of entertaining spectacles that have always drawn democratic citizens into the public realm. Aldrich argues that this hoopla was integral to the Jacksonian mode and that it "can easily be seen as an attempt to highlight the social, political, and personal value of being on the right side." Bolstering the social benefits of voting was a key factor that made nineteenth-century parties so successful – it was not merely an epiphenomenon of the limited entertainment choices of the period but a central component of the parties' routine operating procedures.[118]

The communal nature of the spectacle further reinforced the communal commitments so essential to the Jacksonian republican vision. Public spectacle provided republican citizens an opportunity to demonstrate to their community that they were not "shirkers" or "deserters." As the *Philadelphia Evening Bulletin* argued in 1874, it was the partisan's "duty to be present to assist in the demonstration."[119] Much partisan language of the day conveyed this sense

---

[115] Kleppner, *The Third Electoral System*, 34–5; on spread of turnout across competitive and noncompetitive districts, see 23–44. Alan Ware has demonstrated that competitiveness was not evenly spread across the country (only around 32 percent of states were consistently competitive), but Kleppner's analysis reveals that although there was a correlation between competitiveness and turnout, high turnout was nevertheless spread relatively evenly across the country. Ware, *The American Direct Primary*, 164–66. Taken together, Ware and Kleppner's studies suggest an emphasis on mobilization efforts even in areas in which mobilization was not the superior strategy.

[116] Paul Kleppner, *Who Voted? The Dynamics of Electoral Turnout, 1870–1980* (New York: Praeger, 1982), 24; William Claggett, "Turnout and Core Voters in the Nineteenth and Early Twentieth Centuries: A Reconsideration," *Social Science Quarterly* (September 1981), 443–9. Silbey, *The American Political Nation*, conveys a good sense of this argument, 150.

[117] Silbey, *The American Political Nation*, 150–1; Kleppner, *The Third Electoral System*, 367–9.

[118] Aldrich, *Why Parties?* 102. Marcus points out that the parties' "principle method was to stir up 'enthusiasm' to bring their potential voters to the polls, or, less frequently, to demoralize the opposition into staying home." *Grand Old Party*, 12.

[119] Untitled article, (Philadelphia) *Evening Bulletin*, October 10, 1874, 4.

of duty with martial urgency. Thus, in 1878, "indifferent Republicans" were "stirred to activity" by the charge that "if the Republican party hopes to win in the coming election it will have to rally its last man to the standard."[120] In 1881, the *Oregon State Journal* thus invoked the Jacksonian mode's norm of participation in declaring that citizens who did not "give the necessary time to attend its primaries and conventions . . . [were] not fit to hold any office or profit or trust under the American Government."[121] Some period observers were convinced that these public rites did little to elevate or even involve public opinion. "The forces on which the parties seem chiefly to depend," scowled *The Century*, "are physical forces; noise, parade, spectacle, 'demonstrations,' strike the physical senses and do not appeal to the reason." Those joining in these "caparisoned companies" that adorned themselves "with tinsel and trumpery" to go "marching night after night" were attuned to listen to repeated partisan attacks and platitudes but were unlikely to be engaged in serious discussion.[122] Such displays stunned British observer James Bryce, who noted that although "the parade and procession business, the crowds, the torches, the badges, the flags, the shouting, all this pleases the participants by making them believe they are effecting something," their actions contained little substance: "in short, it keeps up the 'boom,' and an American election is held to be, truly or falsely, largely a matter of booming."[123]

Local hurrah campaigns often "had little to do with government or public policy, or even with the choice of officials" but instead were intended to "stimulate the faithful and, if possible, convert the wayward."[124] An 1880 newspaper account of a Republican rally in Topeka emphasized the presence of party marching clubs that "went through some of their evolutions," fireworks, and banners (among which were those emblazoned with the slogans "How are you, democrats?" "Grant to Sherman – 'Push things'," and "Garfield fought under Lincoln's orders," although none were quoted that mentioned the party's substantive positions). Only two speeches were delivered, one that was described as "full of loyalty, and enthusiasm for the old republican party, and defiance to the Solid South in their attempt to override the wishes of a majority of the people of the United States"; of the other, it was said that "the tone of his entire speech was rejoicing over the recent victories and those which will

---

[120] "Skulkers to the Front," (Philadelphia) *Evening Bulletin*, August 20, 1878, 4.

[121] "Civil Service Reform," *Oregon State Journal*, March 19, 1881, 1.

[122] "The Degradation of Politics," *The Century*, January 1885, 460. See also John L. Cleaner to Bryan, October 13, 1894, box 3, Bryan Papers.

[123] James Bryce, *The American Commonwealth, Vol. II* (London: Macmillan, 1890), 203. Observing this spectacle, Bryce (p. 331) warned of the "fatalism of the multitude" inherent in mass democratic society, in which large-scale displays of majority fervor "inspire a sort of awe, a sense of individual impotence, like that which man feels when he contemplates the majestic and eternal forces of the inanimate world. . . . a self-distrust, a despondency, a disposition to fall into line, to acquiesce in the dominant opinion, to submit thought as well as action to the encompassing power of numbers."

[124] McCormick, *The Second American Party System*, 350.

certainly follow."[125] At a San Francisco Republican rally in 1884, "all economic questions were thrust aside. All constitutional problems were laid away.... It opened familiar vistas. The ground it disclosed was enchanted ground. They had often trod it before, and with success," and "although the revenue question is the absorbing topic of discussion in political circles, and the present revenue laws were framed and adopted by a Republican Congress, the caucus had absolutely nothing to say about it."[126] A Democratic speaker at a San Francisco rally in 1888 insisted that "we are scarcely here to discuss the issues of the coming campaign," but to "kindle the fires of patriotism and to recruit our ranks."[127] Even this minimally engaged level of speechmaking was often drowned out by flash, as occurred at Tammany Hall's 1894 Fourth of July celebration, during which the neighborhood political organizations "tried to outdo the others in the point of fireworks and illuminations," and "the confusion caused by the fireworks had become so great that it was thought best to abandon further speechmaking," although a musical concert was held, and one orator "pointed out some of the differences between the Democratic and Republican Parties" in a perfunctory manner.[128] As Altschuler and Blumin conclude, "many elements of the political rally had nothing to do with public issues or specific candidates," because citizens paid more attention to fireworks, theatrics, and music than to substantive debate.[129]

From the hype of the hurrah campaign came its cynical opposite, embodied by those politicians who "'didn't believe in a speechmaking campaign' but pinned their faith to the good old-fashioned 'still hunt,'" in which one party avoided public displays early in the campaign, saving resources for a late date, after which, it was hoped, the opposing party would not have time to mount a countercampaign.[130] Like the hurrah campaign, the still hunt presumed the important work of party politics to be mobilization rather than persuasion. Neither strategy was rooted in explicating national issues to voters. Thus, although the national organizations were assured of local mobilization efforts, there was little expectation that their local partners were effective in contributing to national political mandates.

The republican values embedded in Jacksonian mode campaigns thus presented a significant barrier for national party leaders. Convention procedures

---

[125] "The Maddest, Merriest Night," *The* (Topeka, KS) *Commonwealth*, October 28, 1880, 4.

[126] "The Republican Key Note," *San Francisco Examiner*, February 3, 1884, 4.

[127] "The Democracy," *San Francisco Examiner*, May 4, 1888, 4.

[128] "Speeches, Music, Fireworks," *New York Times*, July 5, 1894, 8.

[129] Altschuler and Blumin, "Limits of Political Engagement in Antebellum America," 872.

[130] George Walton Green, "Victory for the Plucking," *New York Times*, June 8, 1892, 9. John Reynolds points out that Jacksonian mode campaigners avoided early campaigns because of the cost and effort involved in *The Demise of the American Convention System*, 21. Other primary source confirmation of this phenomenon is found in "A Still Hunt," *The* (Topeka, KS) *Commonwealth*, April 3, 1884, 4; Walter H. Beecher to Grover Cleveland, October 2, 1892, series 11, box 3, Cleveland Papers; "Canvass Badly Managed," *New York Times*, October 13, 1888, 5.

obscured platforms and so obscured ideological and policy commitments, local campaigners eroded statements of national party purpose, and campaign spectacle avoided substance – all weakening the national party apparatus's connection with the national party-in-the-electorate. Further, these features of Jacksonian mode campaigns strengthened subnational political leaders by preventing national movements from providing a source of local political rebellion. Establishing a durable connection between the national party organizations and the national party-in-the-electorate and empowering the newly nationalized citizen in partisan life thus required a reworking of these fundamental features of party life.

Patronage and Presidential Politics in the Jacksonian Mode

A pivotal consequence of Jacksonian mode localism was the erosion of presidential power. As the singular nationally elected office and the office around which the party organizations emerged, the presidency was deeply affected by the Jacksonian party mode. Like the constitutional checks on power that pit the three branches against one another, the Jacksonian organizations were "rife with checks on independent action and resistant to claims of personal authority."[131] In no area of politics was this clearer than the Jacksonian party mode's appropriation of presidents' appointing power.

Prevented from direct popular appeals, presidents had few institutional tools with which to persuade members of Congress – other than the veto – without patronage. Despite the fact that, in patronage, presidents had something members of Congress wanted, the strictures of party regularity constrained presidential freedom because the necessity of meting out offices to the geographical bases of the party effectively distributed the spoils automatically. Patronage, then, did more than undermine effective civil service; it was "the constant, classic threat to Presidential leadership."[132] Patronage had become part of the routines of regular party maintenance and so "created a form of political indenture," rather than warrants for presidential party leadership.[133] "Members of Congress," complained the *New York Times*, "[go] to Washington under a mortgage of all the Federal appointments in their districts to men . . . whose sole recommendation is that they can pack nominating conventions." Presidents, in turn, had "no alternative but to submit" to demands for patronage, largely because "the Senate [stood] combined in solid phalanx for the preservation of the common usurpation. . . . which enables these members of both branches of Congress to perpetuate their own official existence."[134]

---

[131] Skowronek, *The Politics Presidents Make*, 199.
[132] Charles A. McCoy, *Polk and the Presidency* (Austin: University of Texas Press, 1960), 194.
[133] Johnson and Libecap, *The Federal Civil Service System and the Problem of Bureaucracy*, 16.
[134] "The Two Steps in Corrupting the Government," *Chicago Tribune*, March 30, 1876, 4. See Carl Russell Fish, *The Civil Service and the Patronage* (Cambridge, MA: Harvard University Press, 1904), 190.

Careful distribution of patronage provided "an appearance of leadership in legislation" but more accurately reflected attempts "by the President to have the greatest possible harmony between himself and Congress." This "led him to admit congressmen to the greatest practical share in the distribution of appointments." Such exchanges were ultimately a net loss for the presidency, providing a façade of presidential power that obscured a limited freedom to distribute patronage according to presidents' political preferences.[135]

The Jacksonian patronage system developed over time but did so along lines laid out at its founding. Dorothy Ganfield Fowler argues that the congressional control of patronage began as early as Taylor's administration (1849–50) "not only because the presidents were weak, but also because the party machinery had become better organized." The post–Civil War Republican party took patronage to new levels, especially in the South, where federal offices provided a lifeline to isolated Republicans. As the spoils system became more robust, presidents became less authoritative in their ability to use appointments for personal political purposes. As a result, Ostrogorski observed, "the managers of the Organization, disguised as members of Congress, forced the executive to make over the whole federal patronage to them."[136]

The more presidents deferred to Congress, the more accustomed members of Congress became to exercising what they increasingly saw as a right rather than a privilege. Granting patronage to party allies became the sin qua non of presidential duties, not a bargaining chip to enhance presidential party leadership.[137] As members of Congress expected more power over appointments, presidents earned less capital by exercising the appointment power. By 1869, noted Senator George Frisbee Hoar, "the Senate claimed almost the entire control of the executive function of appointment to office. . . . What was called 'the courtesy of the Senate' was depended upon to enable a Senator to dictate to the executive all appointments and removals in his territory." Reflecting the shift of the locus of patronage power to Congress, *Scribner's Monthly* reported in 1872 that "it is notorious that if the President interferes with the assumed rights of the congressman in this matter, and makes an appointment independent

[135] Jacob Dolson Cox, "The Hayes Administration," *Atlantic Monthly*, June 1893, 831; "Congressmen and Patronage," *New York Times*, June 24, 1885, 4.
[136] Dorothy Ganfield Fowler, "Congressional Dictation of Local Appointments," *Journal of Politics*, 7:1 (February, 1945), 57. See also Stanley Hirshon, *Farewell to the Bloody Shirt: Northern Republicans and the Southern Negro, 1877–1893* (Bloomington: Indiana University Press, 1962), 35–6. Ostrogorski, *Democracy and the Organization of Political Parties, Vol. II*, 79, 48.
[137] Leonard White suggests that Congress's demands on the appointment power were "designed to transfer control of the public service from the President to the Senate, and thus to strike a vital blow both to executive power and to the capacity of a President to maintain a coordinate position with the legislative branch." *The Republican Era, 1869–1901: A Study in Administrative History* (New York: The MacMillan Company, 1958), 28.

of him, he brings upon himself the enmity of the latter."[138] By the time of Benjamin Harrison's administration, congressional dictation of patronage had progressed to the point, remembered Harrison aide Elijah Halford, that Pennsylvania Senators Matt Quay and Don Cameron presented the president with a list of appointments that they expected him to make in their state. "The President asked to have some information concerning each of the men indicated," recalled Halford, "but the Senator said that was not necessary, because they were guaranteed by the two Senators." (Halford's recollection may have skewed things in favor of his former boss. Quay's biographer recounts that Quay received little patronage from Harrison, even when requests were accompanied by endorsements from other Republican party luminaries.) If Quay and Cameron assumed a prone presidency on patronage matters, others went further. Senator Charles B. Farwell of Indiana proposed "a fantastic scheme" of routinizing patronage allocation that would have essentially removed the president from the process:

the total of the offices to be filled should be divided between the States and the Congressional districts, and then allocated between them equitably, and referred to the Republican members of the several delegations for nominations, the names to be sent to the Senate when the Republican Senators and Representatives had severally indorsed and recommended them.[139]

Members of Congress were thus poised to take advantage of the increasingly expansive task of filling patronage positions. Presidents who simply signed over appointments to members of Congress frittered away a valuable source of discretionary power.

Presidents who sought to build independent support often found local patronage politics debilitating, however. Because patronage was a scarce and particularistic benefit, presidents disappointed a number of recipients for every office they filled, undermining their ability to unify the party. As Quay observed, "everybody cannot be gratified, and for every single appointment a dozen or more who have been disappointed become disgruntled and indifferent."[140]

---

[138] Hoar quoted in Henry Jones Ford, *The Cleveland Era: A Chronicle of the New Order in Politics* (New York: United States Publishers' Association, 1972, originally published 1919), 19; "Civil Service Reform," *Scribner's Monthly*, November, 1872, 115.

[139] Elijah W. Halford, "Harrison in the White House," in *Leslie's Weekly*, May 3, 1919, p. 671, in carton 1, Elijah W. Halford Papers, Manuscript Division, Library of Congress. Quay's biographer suggests that Harrison's refusal to work with Quay, who chaired the Republican National Committee during the election, revealed a poor understanding of the requirements of national politics. Kehl, *Boss Rule in the Gilded Age*, 115–25. Harrison's most thorough biographer places both incidents in the context of the president's commitment to channel recommendations for appointments through the relevant department heads, thus avoiding the appearance of favoritism between factions and to free his own schedule for more pressing matters. Harry J. Sievers, *Benjamin Harrison: Hoosier President* (Indianapolis: The Bobbs-Merrill Company, 1968), 41–3.

[140] Quoted in Kehl, *Boss Rule in the Gilded Age*, 123.

Advising James Garfield in his appointment strategy, William Chandler warned him to clear out old Republican appointees to build a personal base of support for renomination: "if we do not rotate before 1884. . . . the 'outs' will be more numerous, active and powerful than the indolent and pampered 'ins,' and will win at last, if not through us then in spite of us." Yet although forcing rotations of officeholders would infuse the Republican organization with fresh blood devoted to Garfield, they would also generate significant opposition within the subnational organizations: "to leave out A and retain B, C, and D," Chandler advised, "will be an invidious distinction which will irritate A and his friends without much benefiting the administration."[141] Chandler was doing the work of the Half-Breed faction of the Republican party, clearing out members of the Stalwart faction; but that is just the point. Factions viciously contended for the smallest office (Garfield's confidant James G. Blaine fretted over the appointment of a Stalwart as postmaster of Helena, Montana), and with the Executive Mansion staffed with a miniscule clerical staff, presidents could hardly engage in such political details in any coherent fashion.[142] As one editorialist explained, "the position which [the President] is thus made to occupy by the restless and intriguing politicians in both factions is one that can strengthen neither him nor the party of which he is the responsible chief."[143]

Despite the pitfalls of patronage, in the absence of a viable alternative for generating political capital, presidents clung to it so tightly that presidential leadership on civil service reform was difficult, because "an administration which seeks to abolish the spoils system must expect to lose that appearance of leadership in legislation which has been sustained by the farming out of patronage."[144] "If I were [in Congress]," speculated Chandler, "I would vote for civil service regulations which if President, I would not think of attempting to prescribe for myself. Grant and President Hayes have tried that plan without success." Chandler referred to Grant's and Hayes's attempts at civil service reform by executive order, which failed, Chandler said, because "a president cannot make a system of rules to guide him in his appointments. Being only self-imposed he will often disregard them, when he personally wishes to, or is

[141] William E. Chandler to James A. Garfield, November 22, 1880, reel 105, series 4B, James A. Garfield Papers, Manuscript Division, Library of Congress, Washington, DC.

[142] On the Byzantine machinations of competing factions for patronage in the Garfield administration (and Garfield's artless management of competing claims), see Allan Peskin, *Garfield: A Biography* (Kent, OH: Kent State University Press, 1978), chap. 24; Justus D. Doenecke, *The Presidencies of James A. Garfield and Chester A. Arthur*, (Lawrence: The Regents Press of Kansas, 1981), 38–45.

[143] "Too Much Patronage," *New York Times*, May 1, 1882, 4. Alan Ware concludes that patronage had negative effects on presidents' parties as a whole because "the effort expended in winning contributed to a splintering of support for the winning party after an election – too few expectations of preferment could be satisfied, and the inability to satisfy the demand made it more difficult for that party to maintain its position." *The Democratic Party Heads North*, 56.

[144] Jacob Dolson Cox, "The Hayes Administration," *Atlantic Monthly*, June 1893, 831.

overborne by friends."[145] Far from natural constituents of reform, presidents coveted the appointment power as the flawed but singular accoutrement of office that gave the appearance of party leadership. As civil service reformer Albert Bushnell Hart observed, although "every president wishes to have a good, honest, successful, and popular administration. . . . no president is left to himself. He is deflected by the consideration of his political debts, by the effort to make sure a re-election."[146]

One measure of the frustrations of the spoils is how easily presidents were persuaded to surrender another source of presidential power in order to escape them: re-eligibility for office. Harrison's personal secretary recommended "a constitutional amendment extending the President's term and making him ineligible for at least immediate re-election" because "everything a President may do or not do is prejudged and misjudged in the light of a second term."[147] Two presidents eschewed reelection to escape the patronage trap: James K. Polk and Rutherford B. Hayes swore off a second term, insisting that they would enhance presidential independence by avoiding debilitating patronage struggles involved in reelection efforts.

Polk, arguably the first dark horse presidential nominee (Whigs greeted his nomination with jeers of "Who is Polk?"), had no illusions about the limitations of his position. He complained that "in every appointment which the President makes he disappoints half a dozen or more applicants and their friends, who, actuated by selfish and sordid motives, will prefer any other candidate in the next election."[148] Upon taking office, he pledged that he would not seek a second term, believing this would take his administration out of the hands of the patronage seekers who held the executive hostage by threatening to deny him support in the next convention. Polk could then use the appointment power as a tool to advance his agenda. It is possible that Polk vowed a single term to "triangulate" the issue against his Whig opponents, who opposed second terms on principle; however, his personal defense suggests that his purpose was to trump his party allies, not the Whigs.[149] Polk biographer Charles McCoy concludes that Polk "believed that by not being a candidate he enjoyed the rare advantage of being above the partisan strife and could pursue an independent course."[150] The maneuver brought him relative success,[151] but his refusal to truck to patronage demands cost him dearly in Congressional support. He observed that "at least 20 members of the present Congress have been disappointed [in appointments], and in all the cases . . . they have afterward voted

[145] Chandler to Garfield, November 22, 1880, reel 105, series 4B, Garfield papers.
[146] Albert Bushnell Hart, "Do the People Wish Reform?" *The Forum*, March 1890, 49.
[147] Elijah W. Halford, "At the White House with Harrison," in *Leslie's Weekly*, July 12, 1919, p. 64, in carton 1, Halford Papers.
[148] Quoted in McCoy, *Polk and the Presidency*, 203.
[149] By a strange contingency, no Whig president ever survived his first term to test the party's resolve on this principle.
[150] McCoy, *Polk and the Presidency*, 207.
[151] See Skowronek, *The Politics Presidents Make*, chap. 5.

against the measures which I have recommended."[152] Pledging a single term in office freed Polk to focus on the demands of governing, but it was not an effective means of transforming governing power into electoral power.

Hayes's experience displays the perils of this course, and because his presidency was less successful than Polk's, the significance of both men's strategy has not been seen as a response to the Jacksonian mode's constraints. Hayes's pledge was sincere – he quashed draft attempts, insisting that "I would like to have my personal friends keep my name out of that sort of mention." He wrote to newspaper publisher Murat Halstead that talk of breaking the one-term pledge would "weaken me in my efforts to improve and purify things." After a year in office, he attributed what strength he possessed to this pledge, insisting that "my success has been such notwithstanding that I mean to keep on in the course marked out."[153]

Like Polk, Hayes worried that a nonpartisan president or administration would "of course be feebly supported, if at all, in Congress or by the Press,"[154] and like Polk, Hayes expected to use the single-term pledge to restructure relations with Congress. He understood the limitations of the Jacksonian mode and believed that the temptation to seek reelection was a particular barrier to presidential leadership on civil service reform.[155] He argued that civil service reform required presidents "to break the habit of expecting or hoping to be one's own successor in this place," and so his term would be solely dedicated to "the rescue of the appointing power from the Senate and House."[156] Although Hayes desired reform, he was no antipartisan; to the contrary, he believed that civil service reform would strengthen the GOP in the long run.[157]

Hoping to establish merit-based appointments, Hayes appointed reformers to key positions (including the New York Customs House), instructed his postmaster general to consult with special investigating agents in making hires rather than members of Congress, forbade (by executive order) postal employees from serving on party committees or serving as delegates to national conventions, and prohibited (again by executive order) party assessments of postal workers. To Pennsylvania reformer Wayne MacVeagh, he bragged that "this is the first Administration in half a century that has not employed its office holders to promote its own political purposes."[158] Yet as Fowler concludes,

[152] Quoted in McCoy, *Polk and the Presidency,* 200.

[153] R. B. Hayes to Murat Halstead, July 13, 1878, Hayes Papers, roll 17, frame 102.

[154] Rutherford B. Hayes, *Hayes: The Diary of a President, 1875–1881,* ed. by T. Harry Williams (New York: David McKay Company, 1964) 126, 137.

[155] R. B. Hayes to Rev. Dr. Hatfield, January 16, 1877, roll 176, frames 271–2, Rutherford B. Hayes Papers, Manuscript Division, Library of Congress, Washington, DC.

[156] R. B. Hayes to L. Clarke Davis, June 5, 1879, roll 176, frame 676, Hayes Papers; R. B. Hayes to George William Curtis, December 16, 1878, roll 176, frames 271–2, Hayes Papers.

[157] "Senators shall make the office holders, and . . . the office holders shall make the Senators. How many victories can the Republican party gain on such a platform?" worried Hayes privately. Rutherford B. Hayes, *Hayes: The Diary of a President,* 137.

[158] R. B. Hayes to Wayne MacVeagh, October 30, 1879, roll 176, frame 924–5, Hayes Papers.

"President Hayes was very naïve if he really believed that his executive order had changed the management of the party or had freed office holders from political assessments." The Republican Congressional Campaign Committee resumed assessments in defiance of Hayes's order, wording their appeals as requests for "voluntary" gifts and raising $93,000 from officeholders out of a total 1878 budget of only $106,000.[159] There were other signs of congressional intransigence. After his appointments in New York, a delegation of Republican senators warned him that "if the president wanted the support of the republican party in Congress, he must show that he was willing to act with the party."[160] Frustrated at the resistance, Hayes complained that "the party men do not like it, among the Republicans, and Democrats find no interest in heartily supporting an Adm. they did not select."[161] After two years in office, the *New York Times* praised Hayes's motives, arguing that "the President has done something for reform by his comparative independence of Congressional dictation," even while acknowledging that he had "raised, if he has not thrown off, the yoke of subservience to Congress."[162] That judgment was confirmed when, after he left office, most of his reforms were effectively reversed.

The Hayes and Polk experiences are instructive. Presidents chafed at the Jacksonian mode's limitations on their independence and sought creative means of weakening them, even to the extent of eschewing a source of power constitutionally endorsed by the Founders. The presidential office alone did not provide enough strength for their efforts, however. Cut off from the public by the convention system and indentured to their partisan comrades, presidents were at the mercy of Congress and their partisan allies.

These difficulties grew more complicated over time. The civil service expanded, requiring more appointments to be filled and exacerbating the disadvantage to presidential power,[163] but members of Congress still had fewer offices to be concerned with and fewer office seekers to placate. Thus, they had an advantage over the president in efficiently using patronage. Presidents were increasingly forced to rely on the advice of their co-partisans in Congress. As reformer Carl Russell Fish observed in 1904,

the civil service had by the middle of the nineteenth century become so extensive that the careful supervision which the earlier presidents exercised became impossible; and, as appointments continued to be made by personal selection, organization and division of labor became more and more necessary.[164]

---

[159] Dorothy Ganfield Fowler, *The Cabinet Politician: The Postmasters General, 1829–1909* (New York: Columbia University Press, 1943), 167–71.

[160] Quoted in V. L. Shores, *The Hayes-Conkling Controversy, 1877–1879*, Smith College Studies in History, vol. IV, number 4 (Northampton, MA: Department of History of Smith College, 1919), 239.

[161] Hayes, *The Diary of a President*, 126.

[162] "The President's Power for Reform," *New York Times* (January 4, 1878), 4.

[163] Johnson and Libecap, *The Federal Civil Service System and the Problem of Bureaucracy*.

[164] Fish, *The Civil Service and the Patronage*, 173. Johnson and Libecap make a similar argument in *The Federal Civil Service System and the Problem of Bureaucracy*, 18. As Ostrogorski put it,

Rather than opening up new avenues of presidential power, the expanded bureaucracy complicated presidential party leadership. Simultaneously, the expansion of the political universe meant that patronage strategies had to reconcile claims over a greater expanse of territory and population; "with the growth of the population," observed the *New York Times*, "and the very great and complicated interests that have developed in a party large enough to carry a national election the claims for spoils are out of all proportion to the amount to be divided."[165] Even Matthew Quay, who fought bitterly with President Harrison over appointments, believed that, in this environment, "patronage [was] a positive disadvantage to a party and particularly to a politician."[166] Harrison's frigid attitude on patronage drove Quay, the chairman of the Republican National Committee, and James Clarkson to abandon their positions in protest; the post of Republican National Committee Chairman sat empty for months, because every politician prevailed on by Harrison refused to serve.[167] The experience of Harrison and his predecessors affirms Skowronek's observations about the tendency of secular time to "flatten out differences in the potential political prospects for presidents," enhancing the power of the below-average president (strengthening him by connecting him with a ready-made cadre of local supporters) but weakening the above-average president (by making him dependent on parochial allies who resist his "order-shattering" goals). Over time, sources of authority that initially appear helpful to presidential power become traps, tying presidents to the labors necessary to maintain them.[168]

Jacksonian democracy was not the participatory idyll that many of its extollers suggest. Popular opinion filtered unevenly through primaries and conventions, obscuring popular choices. Local organizations campaigned listlessly and selectively for national platforms, forgoing national coherence for local political advantage. Presidential candidates maintained a judicious silence that allowed local campaigners to project desired qualities on them. National party leadership centered in the presidency was stymied by the spoils system.

By the late nineteenth century, this republican party order appeared antiquated. Its tendency to elevate representation of local party establishments over the representation of national interests became problematic as local party establishments multiplied. Its tendency to exclude the losers of conflicts at

---

expanded government operations made it "less possible . . . for the legislative and the executive to act separately or at a distance from each other," complicating the executive's ability to judiciously withhold patronage from all but issues central to his position. *Democracy and the Organization of Political Parties: Volume II*, 131.

[165] "The Spoilsmen's Outlook," *New York Times*, April 3, 1889, 4.

[166] Quoted in Kehl, *Boss Rule in the Gilded Age*, 123.

[167] This follows closely on Jensen's analysis in *The Winning of the Midwest*, 162. Kehl's account of the 1892 nomination and election campaigns is a thorough explication of the problems inherent in Harrison's position. *Boss Rule in the Gilded Age*, chap. 10. On Quay and Clarkson's defections, see Sievers, *Benjamin Harrison*, 203, and chaps. 12–15.

[168] Skowronek, *The Politics Presidents Make*, 31.

each stage of the telescopic delegate-selection process shut the parties off from disaffected populations at a time when such populations could more effectively organize than ever before. The pressure for unity produced a mentality of compromise among political leaders that required members of the party-in-the-electorate either to ratify party leaders' choices or to abandon longstanding party loyalties. This was problematic in an age in which new forms of political controversy raised questions about the usefulness of the parties as a means of ordering national political conflict, because compromise on pressing issues suggested that the parties stood for little more than the advancement of political careers.[169] Further, the norms of campaigning that allowed local campaigners discretion in shaping campaign themes undermined the parties' efforts to generate national mandates for rule and thus their capacity to demonstrate their representative character to a diversifying national society.

Nonetheless, a cadre of new men – the late-nineteenth-century counterpart to Van Buren and the new men of the Jacksonian era – envisioned more ambitious purposes for the national party organizations. They rejected the republican notion of restraining national power and maintaining the salutary influence of local communities. They expressed instead a liberal preference for the free interplay of interests. Party leaders were threatened and inspired by the emergence of this extra-partisan associational universe that increasingly mobilized citizens for national political purposes in ways that would transform the operating assumptions of both major political parties.

[169] Gerring, *Party Ideologies in America*, 196.

2

The Nineteenth-Century Associational Explosion and the Challenge to the Jacksonian Mode

In the late nineteenth century, Americans organized themselves into national civic associations at a frenzied pace, especially Americans who felt excluded from the traditional party organizations. As they constructed new national publics, these groups resisted the Jacksonian mode's republican notion of the fundamental coherence of community identities, defending and demonstrating a politics of national aspirations and self-interested policy pursuits. They aggressively challenged the parties' dominance of the political sphere, claiming to offer a more accurate and nimble representation of national public opinion. Impressed by their success at mobilizing national publics, national party leaders transplanted some of the new national associations' methods to the national party organizations, hoping to transfer some of their legitimacy into the parties as well. These associations taught party leaders the potential of national politics and so contributed to a new idea of party, particularly the notion of a nationalized party-in-the-electorate. For this reason, understanding the national party leaderships' adoption of these new methods requires an understanding of their operation in the universe of national citizens' associations.

In the years following the Civil War, American civic associations thrived on the expansion of national communications and travel networks that had occurred during the war, generating a newly nationalized consciousness among many citizens. As Gerald McFarland observes, "Americans regrouped themselves into organizations appropriate for industrial conditions," as "various occupational groups – farmers, industrial workers, and professional men – heretofore largely unorganized, now formed themselves into national associations."[1] The U.S. political system underwent an associational

[1] Gerald W. McFarland, "The Mugwumps and the Emergence of Modern America," in Gerald W. McFarland, ed., *Moralists or Pragmatists? The Mugwumps, 1884–1900* (New York: Simon & Schuster, 1975), 8, 7. Howard Reiter attributes party nationalization to "the transportation and communications revolutions, greater centralization of government power in Washington and the Presidency, and the ensuing nationalization of American politics in general"; *Selecting*

explosion, much like the "advocacy explosion" that Jeffrey Berry argues took place in the 1960s, 1970s, and 1980s.[2] National voluntary associations had been around from the beginning (in the 1830s, Tocqueville found "a hundred thousand men publicly engaged not to make use of strong liquors" in a national temperance campaign[3]), but with the exception of abolitionists, such associations had not had the associational explosion's impact on party politics.[4] Where government or tradition failed to provide anything other than local solutions, organizations such as the National Association of Manufacturers, the American Bankers Association, the American Federation of Labor, the American Protective Association, the Woman's Christian Temperance Union, the National Congress of Mothers, the Sierra Club, and the American Bar Association stepped in to organize citizens for national coordination and public advocacy.

These new associations and the citizens that they attracted disdained the Jacksonian mode's republican localism. Whereas traditional parties preferred compromise to self-interest, these associations faulted them for poorly representing popular demands. Whereas traditional parties sought to preserve the local party organizations' gatekeeping role, they pointed to their national membership as an alternative form of authority. Finally, whereas traditional parties evaded substantive arguments, the new citizens' associations boasted educational methods designed to enlighten self-interest.

As such, the newly nationalized citizens came to recognize, in Gordon Wood's words, that "the people were not an order organically tied together by their unity of interest but rather an agglomeration of hostile individuals coming together for their mutual benefit to construct a society."[5] The liberalism that Wood finds at the Founding was subverted (but not uprooted) by the republican values that underlay the Jacksonian mode and that spun out their own implications for political behavior. The point is not to suggest that liberalism was not a dominant ideological paradigm in the United States but to recognize that within American political thought, a variety of sometimes conflicting political values have vied for attention. As Samuel Huntington suggests, "if one had to apply one adjective to them, 'liberal' would be it, but even this term does not convey the full richness and complexity of the amalgam."[6] Liberalism

---

the President, 134. Alan Ware argues that "decentralized parties can only transform themselves into more centralized structures over time if the political system becomes less fragmented"; *The American Direct Primary*, 13.

2 Jeffrey M. Berry, *The Interest Group Society* (Boston: Little, Brown, 1984).

3 Alexis de Tocqueville, *Democracy in America*, Harvey Mansfield and Delba Winthrop, eds. (Chicago: University of Chicago Press, 2000), 492.

4 For instance, Bensel argues that labor organization tended to focus on local conflicts with local employers, limiting the impact of the labor–capital division on national politics; *The Political Economy of American Industrialization*, 12–13.

5 Gordon Wood, *The Creation of the American Republic, 1776–1787* (New York: W. W. Norton, 1969), 607.

6 Samuel P. Huntington, *American Politics: The Promise of Disharmony* (Cambridge, MA: Harvard University Press, 1981), 16.

cannot be treated as monolithic or all-encompassing; the presence of "multiple, incongruous authorities operating simultaneously" can be as important as coherent ideologies in shaping political development.[7] In this case, Jacksonian mode republicanism operated uneasily but not impossibly within what was otherwise a liberal regime. The emergence of the new national citizen and newly enlarged national political associations were not responsible for reintroducing liberalism to Americans but for modeling an associational order grounded in liberal values that contrasted with the dominant party mode of operations. They were a "carrier group" for a model of national, liberal organization.[8]

The national scope of the new associations challenged the Jacksonian mode by drawing attention to political conflicts that transcended the parties' traditional geographic boundaries and forcing the parties to respond. For national party leaders, however, the new methods also suggested a means of renewing the parties' connections with the electorate and maintaining the partisan loyalties of the new national citizens. Thus, although the influence of antiparty reformers is often overstated in histories of the late nineteenth century,[9] the new associational models did popularize new preferences in political organization, exploit popular concerns about the parties, and provide correctives to traditional party methods.

The Crisis of the Late Nineteenth Century

The renovation of the parties' organizational values was shaped by massive societal transformations in the mid-nineteenth century that reoriented many voters' political horizons. During and after the Civil War, Moisei Ostrogorski noted, "everything became inflated . . . in public life and in the economic sphere, the citizen began to feel himself more and more a small part of a great whole." The dislocations of the time were existential, he suggested, a response to the generalizing effects of industrialization:

at the bar of his conscience man became responsible not only to his own society in the restricted sense of the word, but to society in general, to his country, to the nation, even to humanity. Thus a readjustment of forces took place in man's social existence between the particular which constituted nearly all his being and the general which was occupied by a small portion of it.

The scope of national life had passed a point at which a change in quantity had produced a change in quality as "the extension of markets again stripped

---

[7] Orren and Skowronek, *The Search for American Political Development*, 108–18. See also Karen Orren, *Belated Feudalism: Labor, the Law, and Liberal Development in the United States* (New York: Cambridge University Press, 1991).

[8] Nancy L. Rosenblum, "Replacing Foundations with Staging: 'Second Story' Concepts and American Political Development," in James W. Ceaser, *Nature and History in American Political Development* (Cambridge, MA: Harvard University Press, 2006), 126–7.

[9] John M. Dobson, *Politics in the Gilded Age: A New Perspective on Reform* (New York: Praeger Publishers, 1972). Mark Wahlgren Summer, *Rum, Romanism, and Rebellion: The Making of a President, 1884* (Chapel Hill: University of North Carolina Press, 2000), xiv.

buyers and sellers of their concrete individuality, and resolved them into the general categories of tradesmen and customers. Railways, by bringing together for half an hour men who saw each other for the first and perhaps last time, reduced them to the general notion of travelers, all placed on an equal footing by a uniform ticket."[10] The old fiction that the states had definitive and unitary interests collapsed as voters increasingly identified themselves with amorphous groups that stretched beyond state boundaries. Many voters – especially in the economically vulnerable regions of the South and West – felt isolated from the partisan mainstream. Voters brought these sentiments into politics and challenged the geographic particularity encouraged by the Jacksonian mode. A broader awareness of national politics exposed the parties' calculating compromises on contentious issues because, as a New York editor insisted, "'all things to all men' does not serve in an age of telegraphs."[11]

As Morton Keller has documented, the post–Civil War American polity was shaped by trends that intensified during wartime. The experience of powerful private associations such as the United States Sanitary Commission and Union Leagues "schooled many of the nation's elite in the possibilities of public power," and generally, "the war's daily lessons in the value of organization ... schooled potent groups in the possibilities of organization, and left them restive under a polity that did not readily satisfy their demands."[12] As this transformed associational universe encountered the communications technologies that had expanded during the war, it was poised to challenge the Jacksonian mode's operating assumptions.

After the war, voters, intellectuals, and the popular press revived the decades-old debate about the propriety of party organization, especially "that tendency to convert party organization from means into ends."[13] There was a growing perception that the parties had failed, as a Populist orator put it, because of a "fatal mental inability in both Democratic and Republican parties to comprehend the new and strange conditions of our modern industrial and social life, an utter inability to cope with the new and vexing problems which have arisen out of the vacillation of this latter day."[14] Many of the new associations and their members questioned whether the personal compromises required of party members were really worthwhile if the parties could no longer meet popular demands. "The importance of cohesion and solidarity in a political

---

[10] Moisei Ostrogorski, *Democracy and the Organization of Political Parties: Volume I: England*, Seymour Martin Lipset, ed. (Chicago: Anchor Books, 1964, originally published in 1903), 72, 73, 32, 31.

[11] "Democratic Incongruities," *New York Tribune*, August 11, 1880, 4.

[12] Keller, *Affairs of State*, 9–12.

[13] "The Democratic View of Democracy," *North American Review*, July 1865, 120.

[14] Quoted in Lawrence Goodwyn, *The Populist Moment: A Short History of the Agrarian Revolt in America* (Oxford: Oxford University Press, 1978), 212. Ignatius Donnelley argued that the Republican Party had "but two issues left – protection and the bloody shirt. Both are sectional issues, neither takes in the continent. When it puts on protection its western extremity is exposed to the cold; ... when it puts on the bloody shirt ... its southern limbs are exposed to the wind," in "The Jubilee at St. Paul," *The* (Red Wing, Minnesota) *Argus*, December 4, 1884, 1.

party is not to be denied," complained the *New York Times*, "but it is more than doubtful whether it is to be secured by disregarding the wishes and smothering the voice of the minority."[15] Charges of corruption are a familiar part of the critique of party organization, but the popular theme of organizational failure ran deeper than mere corruption, as did *The Nation*'s observation that "whenever you have organizations you have to have leaders or managers, and the tendency of the leaders and managers, if assured of their tenure of power... and plentifully supplied with money, is to drift away from the main body of their constituents, to lose sympathy with them and comprehension of them."[16]

The associational explosion rejected the Jacksonian-republican mistrust of self-interest and offered a pluralist vision of a politics that could accommodate a variety of interests. In contrast to the parties' mobilization tactics, the associations used what they called educational methods to appeal to citizens' purposive and self-interested aspirations. They recognized voters to be more interested in private pursuits than in political life and worked to make politics an extension of private life, abandoning republican notions of a broader common duty to community. Presuming that individuals had interests distinct from those of other members of their community, they reached voters directly through the distribution of printed literature to evade the community pressures that reinforced traditional party loyalty. In contrast to the parties' geographic particularity, they were consciously designed to endow citizens with a national perspective on political issues. As McFarland notes, "the national character of these new groups was a prominent trait, the adjective 'American' almost invariably introducing their names, and the values stressed in the groups' literature were those of the modern order: education, specialization, and scientific methods."[17] Due largely to this associational explosion, the *Cleveland Press* could observe by 1892 that the "methods and means of influencing the public mind have likewise undergone such changes that campaigns cannot be carried on as before."[18]

Because their local chapters were separated geographically, the new associations kept members in touch through newsletters, pamphlets, and other forms of printed literature and with national conferences that fostered the circulation of elites. Whereas the parties demobilized at the end of campaigns, the new associations maintained activity throughout the year, keeping individuals tied to the cause and priming them for political action long before primaries or elections were held. The flexibility of party platforms stood in stark contrast to the national associations' earnest appeals to the consciences of their constituencies; as the *New York Times* reported in 1884, party mobilization efforts "[proceed] on a theory of party relations which is narrow, and

---

[15] "The Pennsylvania Plan," *New York Times*, February 6, 1880, 4.
[16] "What is the Republican Party," *The Nation*, October 30, 1884, 368.
[17] McFarland, "The Mugwumps and the Emergence of Modern America," 9.
[18] "At Issue: The Questions Face to Face," *Cleveland Press*, May 14, 1892, 2.

which, though it was once extremely strong, has decidedly lost favor in the last decade."[19]

Because party loyalties influenced citizen perceptions of politics so extensively, these new national associations had to create a new political space in which they could both escape the restraints of party politics and challenge the parties for the loyalties of voters. Despite differences in political purposes, a range of national civic associations adopted a similar set of solutions to this problem. First, describing their contact with voters as "educational" obscured their disruptive potential because it suggested that the information they delivered to voters was merely supplemental and preparatory to traditional partisan political action. Educational efforts also presumed, however, that parties failed to sufficiently equip voters for politics and sought to perfect citizens by clarifying their interests and elevating them above localism and partisanship. This required that the associations break down traditional party loyalties, drawing voters away from the major parties. This was no easy task; "large numbers of voters had to unlearn their identities as partisans and learn to behave as voters with interests beyond party, willing to vote for whichever candidate promised more of what they wanted." This task required, as Elisabeth Clemens points out, "disassembling – at least in part – the politics of party."[20] Hence, Lawrence Goodwyn's assessment of the Populists: they "were engaged in a kind of cultural pioneering" designed to prime voters' minds for a clean break from the hold of the major parties.[21] To do so, they played to the cynicism many Americans had developed about party methods; the new associations' methods were meant to highlight a purer form of political activism than that practiced in the parties. Instead of parades and primaries, the new associations' "educational" opportunities took place in the private home or in the reputable atmosphere of a lecture hall. Instead of patronage, the new associations offered general interest or purposive incentives. Compared with the restrictions of regularity, membership in these groups was extraordinarily open.

Second, they reached out to voters in a communications context that was not dominated by the parties. Private mailings that went straight into citizens' private homes, lecture circuits that posed as schools, and private societies that imitated urban gentlemen's clubs all became forums for reaching voters outside of the traditional partisan community, and all promised substantive discussion of political issues. When the parties avoided divisive issues or compromised to circumvent friction, reform journals complained that "the old parties had ceased to represent any distinct principles, and the old leaders were decidedly unwilling that principles should be made an issue."[22] When they

---

[19] "Party Allegiance," *New York Times*, June 5, 1884, 4.

[20] Elisabeth Clemens, *The People's Lobby: Organizational Innovation and the Rise of Interest Group Politics in the United States, 1890–1925* (Chicago: University of Chicago Press, 1997), 3.

[21] Goodwyn, *The Populist Moment*, 211.

[22] "The Educational Value of the Present Campaign," *The Nation*, August 30, 1888, 163.

evoked sentimental issues to trigger party loyalties, the labor-affiliated *Cleveland Press* proclaimed that "the people will no longer enthuse over 'bloody shirts' or wise declarations about national issues, or stereotypical promises that are never thought of except on election day. They want an issue that means something...and the party which first clearly and honestly presents that issue will have the advantage."[23]

Finally, the new associations directed their members to act as a swing vote to be "always ready to transfer their votes from one party to the other."[24] In this way, they could pressure parties into particular policy initiatives, leading voters out of regular party membership and into an ostensibly nonpartisan political arena. As reformer Charles Francis Adams phrased it in 1880, "every child knows that the boy on the center of the tilting-board can make either end, if the ends are equally weighted, go up or down at pleasure"; independents, he believed, could serve an analogous role in relation to the parties.[25] In some cases, these associations helped bridge the gap between dissatisfaction with the parties and third-party organizations. The People's or Populist party imitated the institutional form of the major parties, although it originated in and maintained the practices of the Farmers' Alliance, which worked more like a national network of political schools than a party. Although they often "fused" with major parties for particular elections, they defended their right to independence, and they organized permanent independent associations to rally voters outside the boundaries of party regularity. Thus, even when the network of reform organizations referred to as Mugwumps claimed affiliation with one of the major parties, they were careful to work explicitly outside the bounds of party regularity, institutionalizing political independence with the aid of legal reforms such as the Australian Ballot (or the secret ballot, which both made bribery more difficult and gave the state a larger role in supervising elections), which were designed to make it easier for citizens to vote their convictions rather than the party line. Interest groups, such as the protectionist American Iron and Steel Association, worked to break down ties of partisanship by reinforcing voters' awareness of self-interest, even as they allied with members of the party-in-government.

In some cases, there was collusion across organizational boundaries. Populists at times worked closely with labor groups, and Mugwumps sometimes shared an opposition to drink with Prohibitionists. In general, such cooperation was not necessary or possible; the two dominant forces – the Populists and the Mugwumps – had too little in common to bring them together in active collaboration. What is striking is how similar their methods were across the geographic and ideological spectrum and how closely the parties imitated their methods, as explained in Chapters 3 and 4. Over the late nineteenth century,

---

[23] "Issues," *Cleveland Press*, July 19, 1887, 2. See also "The American Party," *Cleveland Press*, July 6, 1888, 1.

[24] "Lessons from the Election," *Outlook*, November 19, 1898, 705.

[25] Quoted in Washington Gladden, "To Bolt or Not to Bolt," *Scribner's Monthly*, October 1880, 912. See also "Ballot Reform and Parties," *New York Times*, January 4, 1880, 4.

these methods gained popular esteem, and came to be perceived as the way of the future; understanding them was an indicator of one's modernity. As such, they influenced the assumptions of politicians and the populace much as the later inventions of the radio, television, and the Internet have all been said to "change politics."

Alongside the discussion of new methods was a liberal wariness of the republican values that informed the Jacksonian mode, growing out of a concern that in parties, the individual routinely felt "called upon to surrender something of his own individuality while seeking for the advancement of certain principles through organized effort."[26] Educational methods emphasized the centrality of independent judgment in constructing a fully representative democratic politics, and its advocates criticized party loyalty as obscuring popular judgment. As a contributor to the *Atlantic Monthly* observed, "we are not, as a people, so well able to make a democracy succeed as we were when the government was founded," largely because "education has not been able to deal with the growth of population, and meet the changes of occupation and modes of life."[27]

The new methods thus promised to unleash a new form of democratic judgment. Charles W. Eliot linked this change to the emergence of more efficient methods of public administration, because traditional republican virtues failed to discern the best policies in new policy domains that "belong to the domain of applied science."[28] Mugwumps followed this strain of thought to question the Jacksonian-republican notion that "one man is as good as another, and consequently that all men have an equal right to office" and insisted that experts were better equipped to staff government offices. They suggested that civil service reform, although purifying public administration, was a matter that effected a "restoration of power to the individual" and was a "reenfranchisement of the voter" because it promised to make the government capable of better responding to popular demands and thus offering choices between viable alternatives. Civil service reform was a gateway to further refinements of public policy and was therefore "the fundamental reform of importance – without which the judgment of the country on any other question cannot be arrived at."[29] Reform would open up a new era in politics in which public administration could be expected to respond more effectively to a greater variety of public demands; a government more capable of expanded and scientific administration would require an educated electorate to guide it.

High expectations on this note were not limited to the theoretical scribblings of the East Coast elite. The Nashville *Daily American* complained that "the old leaders of the party are, by habit, training and instincts, tied to old policies." Rather than appeal to "moderate" voters who were likely to look to hold the

---

[26] "On 'Voting Straight,'" *The Century*, January 1898, 474.
[27] Jonathan B. Harrison, "Limited Sovereignty in the United States," *Atlantic Monthly*, February 1879, 185.
[28] Charles W. Eliot, "One Remedy for Municipal Misgovernment," *Forum*, October 1891, 155.
[29] "Republican Institutions and the Spoils System," *The Century*, August 1884, 627–8.

parties to a pragmatic standard, party leaders relied on the "ignorant, preju-diced, bigoted implacables" who toed the party line; "they think it easier to drag and to drive the moderate along than to turn the ignorant and bigoted out of the old groves."[30] Further, argued the _Daily American_, "the politicians reason as if they created the people and directed their movements, whereas society produces all the movements we see on the surface," and "while the movements of which they speak are going on upon one side, they are sub-ject to vast modification by the movements in the other portion of society."[31] This assertion of a public opinion broader than traditional party organizations played an important role in the new civic associations' self-image as mobilizers of a nascent national electorate. In a dynamic society, new interests would con-tinuously disrupt party lines, rendering traditional notions of party harmony obsolete. Advocates of the new educational methods looked to the day when there would be "a re-grouping of voters with almost every new public question of importance" as voters freely shifted between parties based on self-interested calculations.[32]

The new associationalism was grounded in a decidedly liberal understand-ing of voters as primarily and properly private individuals. As Eliot observed, "democratic freedom inevitably tends to produce [a] devotion to [private] affairs."[33] Instead of a virtuous republic of active public servants, the new associations saw their constituency as "men who can deal effectually with their fellows in business, where the objects are well defined and the methods famil-iar" but who "find it at once difficult and disagreeable to work in connection with large numbers of associates in ways that they are unused to"[34] and who were "politically indolent, partly through absorption in business."[35] Theodore Roosevelt noted that urban elites neglected politics because of absorption in private affairs, only to find themselves isolated when they did attend primaries, where they considered it unpleasant to "stand on an equal footing with his groom and day-laborers."[36] The Farmers' Alliance, insisted its president, was similarly "composed of a class of people who stay at their homes and by their firesides unless stern necessity calls them away."[37] The perception of party politics was that of a world in which "a 'regular' political organization is to be 'run' by those who will give most time to its affairs" and that such men often had "no interest whatever in the questions of the day."[38] The new associations promised individuals an opportunity to participate in public affairs with vot-ers who shared their private concerns, free from the restraints of professional

---

[30] "Dilemma of the Republican Leaders," (Nashville, TN) _Daily American_, April 9, 1878, 2.
[31] "Defective Political Deductions," (Nashville, TN) _Daily American_, January 3, 1878, 2.
[32] "Partyism," _Cleveland Press_, June 7, 1892, 2.
[33] Eliot, "One Remedy for Municipal Misgovernment," 167.
[34] "Property and Politics," _New York Times_, October 22, 1899, 20.
[35] Herbert Welsh, "The Degradation of Pennsylvania Politics," _The Forum_, November 1891, 330.
[36] Theodore Roosevelt, "Machine Politics in New York City," _The Century_, November 1886, 76.
[37] L. L. Polk, "The Farmers' Discontent," _North American Review_, July 1891, 11.
[38] "On 'Voting Straight,'" _The Century_, January 1898, 474.

party leaders. Education would be an ally to personal judgment, steeling the individual to vote his interest in the face of immense partisan pressures within the political community.

As the century wound to a close, these voters loomed large in the calculations of party politicians. In Pennsylvania, a feisty bloc of independent voters in the 1880 senatorial contest convinced Republican Stalwart Don Cameron "that it is necessary to the welfare and continued supremacy of our party to defer... to that independent sentiment which found expression... in the late contest."[39] A Virginian who witnessed the Farmers' Alliance growing in prominence in 1892, noted that the Democratic platform was perceived as a "straddle" on the currency issues and warned that "the farming classes must have some relief, they are almost ready for a revolution and let come what may."[40] Mark Hanna was said to fear "that it would be the Republican Party or Socialism in the future," unless the Republican party revitalized its connections with labor groups.[41] National party leaders recognized the necessity of appealing to the voters attracted by the new associations and looked to their methods as a means of renewing their connections with voters.

Late-Nineteenth-Century Associationalism

Widespread dissatisfaction with politicians and party organizations is hardly unusual in American politics. On its face, such rhetoric as that which emerged in the late nineteenth century might appear as just another artifact of Americans' longstanding mistrust of parties,[42] but late-nineteenth-century antipartyism carried a unique associational component. The critique of party localism and the alternative national associationalism appeared with such consistency across the country and the political spectrum that one sees in it the emergence of a new organizational mode. It grew out of lessons learned in a variety of organizational contexts across the country. The new associations watched one another closely, borrowing organizational forms and political styles. As the associational explosion was cultivated, sustained, and spread by a patchwork of clubs, associations, and minor parties, it institutionalized criticism of the Jacksonian mode. Deployed across the nation and among an array of distinct interests, the associational explosion presented a more stable challenge to the parties than any one organization alone could have accomplished. A single group could have been finessed by politicians offering patronage, token candidates, symbolic gestures, or isolation in local contests – all measures that the new associations individually faced. But the coincidence of multiple groups testing the Jacksonian mode from different ideological perspectives prevented the

---

[39] John J. Mitchell to Barker, March 15, 1881, box 1, Barker Papers.
[40] J. O. Thomas to Whitney, July 6, 1892, book 72, Whitney Papers.
[41] Anonymous Statement, n.d., box 4, Hanna-McCormick Family Papers.
[42] Note Ware, *The American Direct Primary*, 5–12. Ware argues that the argument for American antipartyism is overstated and that it is chiefly a rhetoric exploited by "out" groups.

parties from successfully responding with their usual mechanisms for channeling conflict.

Three manifestations of the associational explosion stand out for their organizational innovations and their distinct political contexts. Public interest associations supplemented traditional interest group lobbying by mobilizing broad national publics to demand the parties' attention. The various Mugwump associations that emerged in the Northeast sought to move the parties to adopt reforms by organizing elite opinion to lead the masses out of the parties. For their part, agrarian populists took their earliest shape as educational associations that moved farmers out of traditional party loyalties. Other associations could be considered in this light. Prohibitionists pioneered some of the same tactics throughout the period,[43] as did women's groups and the Grand Army of the Republic, the powerful veterans' organization.[44] Labor groups did as well, but the use of nonelectoral methods, such as cooperatives and strikes, as well as the substratum of labor organizers who looked to a workers' revolution distinguishes them; labor was eventually diverted into a strategy of unionism, which did not reach its peak of influence until the twentieth century.[45] They are omitted in this chapter largely for reasons of concision. The three groups cited in this section are important to the rest of the story for three reasons. First, they specify the newly nationalized publics held up as a motivating factor elsewhere. The leaders of these associations were national elites generating support among a national constituency. Second, they demonstrate the methods that these national elites devised to mobilize their new national publics. Finally, these groups establish the period's critique of the republican elements of the Jacksonian mode and their embrasure of a liberal understanding of political activity.

Interest Associations

Lobbying has always been a part of American politics, but in the late nineteenth century, interest groups began more systematically to mount national publicity campaigns designed to break down their constituencies' party loyalties. Clemens argues that some groups – women, farmers, and workers – formed interest associations in response to their failure to turn traditional electoral politics to their political advantage, expressed hostility to the parties as a result of their rejection from mainstream politics, and rallied their members into new forms of political action.[46] Political isolation was not the only cause of interest group formation or their rebellion against traditional partisanship, however. Even favored interests were organizing differently in the late nineteenth century, and these groups also challenged the Jacksonian mode. Again, as Margaret

[43] Jensen, *The Winning of the Midwest.*
[44] Skocpol, *Protecting Soldiers and Mothers*; Clemens, *The People's Lobby.*
[45] Martin Shefter, "Trade Unions and Political Machines: The Organization and Disorganization of the American Working Class," in Shefter, *Political Parties and the State.*
[46] Clemens, *The People's Lobby.*

Susan Thompson argues, the experience of the war "created new appreciation for the activated potential of federal governance, and . . . the public would insist that potential be used in new and unprecedented ways" that ranged from citizen demands on the U.S. Bureau of Claims and Pensions to demands for social policies to manufacturers' demands for high tariffs. Thus, beginning in the Grant administration, demands on Congress "more closely resembled those of the twentieth century than those of the antebellum era," even as mistrust of politicians led many Americans to direct those demands through extrapartisan interest associations.[47] Interest groups of all stripes claimed that the parties were, in Brian Balogh's words, "less than adept" at representing the interests of their constituents; as such, they "began replacing political parties as the most reliable media for both ascertaining and responding to the views of segments of voters."[48] Such organizations found a popular reception among the newly nationalized citizens.

Tariff politics occupied much of the period's electoral rhetoric and sparked more interest group organization than any other federal policy, drew them closely into the operations of the federal government, and set the stage for an organizational repertoire that inspired imitation across the political spectrum. Although the Republican party developed a thorough defense of the idea of high tariffs as a means of protecting American industry (and was generally willing to add any new industry to the list of those protected), the tariff was also shaped by interest groups formed by protected industries. As Richard Bensel explains, this does not mean that the tariff was originally the result of interest group pressure but that interest group involvement came as Republicans expanded their coalition through side payments in the form of high tariff rates for favored products. (High tariff rates, in return, inflated government revenues, enabling the party to support veterans' pensions and thus the veteran vote.)[49]

National elites' openness to these new associations is demonstrated by Congress's creation of a tariff reform commission in 1882. The assertion of the bill's sponsor, Senator William Wallace Eaton of Connecticut, that the commission would "take the whole subject out of politics and put it where it belongs" bespeaks the period's enthrallment with extra-partisan political repertoires.[50] Members of the commission toured the country interviewing representatives of various industries on the effects of the tariff. Protected interests flocked to the commission. The president, empowered to appoint its members, was besieged with hundreds of recommendations for members; "nearly

---

[47] Thompson, *The "Spider Web,"* 41, 50.
[48] Brian Balogh, "Mirrors of Desires: Interest Groups, Elections, and the Targeted Style in Twentieth-Century America," in Meg Jacobs, William J. Novak, and Julian E. Zelizer, eds., *The Democratic Experiment: New Directions in American Political History* (Princeton: Princeton University Press, 2003), 222–4.
[49] Bensel, *Political Economy of American Industrialization*, 459–60, 462, and the preface generally. See also Skocpol, *Protecting Soldiers and Mothers*.
[50] "Tariff Amendment," *New York Times*, February 6, 1880, 4.

all of them . . . representatives of special interests or industries."[51] Testimony
before the commission was ostensibly delivered by businessmen engaged in protected industries, but these were often the recognized spokesmen of industry
associations. The Chamber of Commerce, the United States Maltsters' Association, the Metropolitan Industrial League, the Independent Labor Party, the
Silk Association, the Pennsylvania Salt Manufacturers' Company, the Gold-
beaters' Union of New York, the editor of the United States *Tobacco Journal*,
the Manufacturing Chemists Association, the Morocco Leather Manufacturers' National Exchange, the Eastern Pig Iron Association, the Wool Growers'
National Association, the Iron and Steel Manufacturers, the Iron Ore Producers, and the Ohio Wool Growers' Association all sent representatives. For a
larger number of producers, the press reported representation by individuals
who spoke for trade associations, as was the case with flax and hemp growers; importers and manufacturers of aniline colors and dye-stuffs; druggists
and quinine manufacturers; manufacturers of neckware, laces, borders, and
trimmings; the flax-spinning industry; dealers in foreign newspapers, maga-
zines, and periodicals; the Louisiana sugar industry; manufacturers of saddlery
hardware; metal sheathing manufacturers; and yellow metal manufacturers,
among others.[52] American industries were well represented by organized interest associations, and they were well prepared for the opportunity; manufacturers, encouraged by trade associations, had besieged Congress with petitions
urging its creation.[53]

Although much of this testimony bolstered the Republican party's case
for protection, interest associations were not always reliable partners for the
parties. Indeed, writes Thompson, the increased role of lobbyists in national
politics grew out of a frustration with the parties' "lack of responsiveness";
when nonpartisan lobbying efforts were found to be more effective, the discov-
ery "put tremendous pressure on established representational mechanisms."[54]
Having been blessed through the Republicans' coalitional demands, it cost protected industries relatively little to organize so as to maintain and expand the

---

[51] "The Tariff Commission," *New York Times*, May 18, 1882, 1; "The Tariff Commission," *New York Times*, June 8, 1882, 4.

[52] Note the following articles, all from the *New York Times*: "The Tariff Commission," June 11, 1882, 12; "The Flax and Hemp Trade," July 20, 1882, 3; "The Tariff Inquiry Begun: First Session of the Commission at Long Branch," July 21, 1882, 5; "The Tariff Commission's Work," July 22, 1882, 5; "The Tariff Commission: Arguments for and Against the Imposition of Duties," July 27, 1882, 2; "Talks about the Tariff: Further Arguments before the Commission," July 28, 1882; "Discussing the Tariff: Linen Manufacturers Asking for More Protection," July 29, 1882, 8; "The Tariff Commission's Work," July 30, 1882, 7; "Talk about the Tariff," August 5, 1882, 5; "Tariff Reform Theories," August 11, 1882, 8; "The Tariff on Tobacco," August 16, 1882, 5; "Discussing the Tariff," August 19, 1882, 3; "The Duty on Chemicals," July 26, 1882, 5; "Tariff Reform Theories," August 11, 1882, 8; "Prospects of Tariff Reform," January 21, 1886, 1; "Iron and Steel Interests," September 13, 1882, 2; "A Cry for Protection," September 2, 1887, 2.

[53] Untitled article, *New York Times*, September 20, 1882, 4.

[54] Thompson, *The "Spider Web,"* 54, 120.

blessing. These organizations found little reason to limit support to one party – especially in an uncertain political environment – and established inroads to the Democratic party. They found that their organized power transcended party politics; after all, reflected the *New York Times*, "representatives are sure to be influenced in a great degree by local feeling, and by that particular form of it which is aroused by definite local interests," a condition that gave organized interests an advantage "whether Democratic or Republican."[55]

In addition to weakening party lines through piecemeal lobbying, interest associations developed methods that aimed to change citizen relationships with the parties. The American Iron and Steel Association (AISA), representing the two products most central to the Republicans' tariff coalition, provides a helpful illustration. Organizationally, AISA embodied trends seen in all areas of the associational explosion that both undermined traditional party lines and were adopted by the parties. Three of these stand out.

First, AISA largely devoted itself to a popular campaign of political literature designed to shape public opinion in favor of protection. AISA's executive director, James Moore Swank, believed that the party press was incapable of representing the interests of the industry "because [newspapers were] managed by men who have not the ability or education to write editorials" or "because in the multiplicity of duties devolving upon the publisher of a County paper, he cannot find time for writing" appropriate editorials. He thus created his own journal to bypass party newspapers and go straight into the home of the voter. AISA aspired to transform popular attitudes and thus bring popular pressure to bear on national politicians. Swank launched a public literary campaign described as "the chief work" of the organization and distributed 300,000 tracts in 1881. By 1884, AISA found the strategy sufficiently successful that it distributed 600,000 more, and, for the climactic election of 1888 (which, as explained in Chapter 5, Grover Cleveland had made a referendum on tariff reform), it distributed more than a million tracts.[56] This material "could go direct to the address of the voter at his post office, and not in such a way as would lead him to believe that someone was endeavoring to influence him."[57] Reached in a private capacity, the voter was approached outside of any communal partisan obligation, and as an individual with distinct interests.

Second, AISA's organized efforts continued on a permanent basis. As a prominent association leader boasted after the 1888 election, although its distribution of literature spiked during critical political battles, "most of the tracts were distributed [in the] winter and spring, when the people had time to read and form conclusions, and before campaign material of any kind had made its

---

[55] "Politics and the Tariff," *New York Times*, February 15, 1882, 4.

[56] Paul Herbert Tedesco, *Patriotism, Protection, and Prosperity: James Moore Swank, the American Iron and Steel Association, and the Tariff, 1873–1913* (New York: Garland, 1985), 149, 124, 122, 131, 167. I draw heavily on Tedesco's thorough account of AISA throughout this section.

[57] Tedesco, *Patriotism, Protection, and Prosperity*, 149.

appearance." The goal was to beat the parties to the people, shaping public opinion long before the party platform was written and long before the local hurrah campaign shaped campaign themes.[58] Having been exposed to AISA's printed material, voters would be less susceptible to communal pressures to adhere to traditional partisan loyalties during the campaign season.

Finally, AISA practiced organizational refinement and replication. It borrowed organizational tools from other organizations (its journal was consciously modeled on one published by the National Association of Wool Manufacturers), and it encouraged the founding of a number of organizational auxiliaries to pursue the cause of protection in various contexts.[59] It supported a federated national network of "Question Clubs" (modeled on the free trade clubs popular at the time), local groups of interested individuals who sent queries about the tariff to prominent politicians and debated their replies in formal meetings. These clubs provided a forum in which "honest arguments would not be restrained by anxiety for party welfare."[60] They struck a nonpartisan pose that belied their political purpose, obscuring any taint of Republican party affiliation and enabling AISA to undermine party regularity without threatening it openly.

Protectionists were not alone in making use of these methods. The tariff commission also attracted tariff reformers, who organized on the belief that "if the revenue reformers hold aloof from the commission, the report, protectionist as it will undoubtedly be, will be sustained by the testimony."[61] Organizations like the Free Trade Club of New York City testified before the commission, complaining that they could not "do better than to arrange for an adequate presentation for the facts and arguments for the other side." The American Tariff Reform League proposed "to start a campaign for furthering the work by lecture and literary bureaus and any other way that may be deemed expedient" and "to secure branch leagues for active work in every township in the various States." Such groups insisted that "the great body of consumers" were "of at least equal weight with the interests of a few hundreds or thousands of protected manufacturers."[62] They encouraged popular "discussions on tariff, taxation and kindred subjects, and the dissemination of literature and information to the workingman," reflecting a strategy similar to AISA's.[63]

---

[58] James Moore Swank quoted in Tedesco, *Patriotism, Protection, and Prosperity*, 149, 168, 124.

[59] Tedesco, *Patriotism, Protection, and Prosperity*, 50–1.

[60] Samuel W. Mendum, "The Question Clubs and the Tariff," *North American Review*, March 1890, 302.

[61] "One-Sided Evidence," *New York Times*, August 23, 1882, 4.

[62] "A Field for the Free Trade Club," *New York Times*, May 30, 1882, 4; "Tariff Reform," *New York Times*, February 8, 1889, 5; "Protection for American Industry," *New York Times*, September 10, 1881, 4.

[63] F. A. Herwig [of the Workingmen's Tariff Reform Association, Philadelphia, PA] to J. Hampton Moore, March 7, 1888, Series 1a, box 1, folder 6, J. Hampton Moore Papers, Pennsylvania Historical Society, Philadelphia, PA.

Businessmen have always played a role in organized politics, but operating outside of and in contrast to party politics, the new associations lent an air of legitimacy to organized business interests. The rise of interest groups in the late nineteenth century, especially those representing business interests, has contributed to a perception that the entrance of businessmen into politics added to the corruption rampant during the period; but this perception obscures the attitudes of the times and the import of the new associational methods. Business associations such as AISA claimed to be purifying politics from the inefficiencies and corruptions of the traditional parties. Even as they brought new infusions of cash into the party system (which the parties appreciated after assessment of federal officeholders was made illegal by the 1883 Pendleton Act), they bypassed traditional party fundraising techniques such as assessments, which were seen as corrupt. Independent businessmen thus increasingly saw themselves as reformers, especially when they asked that their funds be used to introduce the methods of the new associations to partisan campaigning; they were particularly consoled by the idea of funding educational document campaigns such as those relied on by AISA. Thus, Charles Francis Adams spoke the language of the associational explosion when he qualified a promised donation by insisting: "I will not put money in the hands of party organizations to be used for paying poll taxes, or otherwise wasted in what is commonly known as 'legitimate campaign expenses.'" He thus requested that his money be used for printed material rather than the partisan "hurrah" campaign.[64] Such brazen self-confidence on the part of the business community attests to its newfound sense of associational power. More enduringly, the language of these associations illustrates the growing sense that individual participation in politics was no longer limited to partisans but could be channeled through one's private interest in a form of politics untainted by exclusions of traditional party politics.[65] These new associations thus did more than boost the representation of business interests in national politics; they legitimized new methods of citizen organization.

Mugwumps

There was some overlap between these business-oriented national citizens and the Mugwump[66] movement, although the Mugwumps' sense of the purity of

---

[64] Charles Francis Adams to Moorefield Storey, October 30, 1891, Moorefield Storey/C. F. Adams Correspondence, 1882–1915, Moorefield Storey Papers, Massachusetts Historical Society, Boston, MA. See also Adams to Storey, September 22, 1892.

[65] Theodore Roosevelt, "Machine Politics in New York City." Robert D. Marcus argues that the Cleveland administration was so popular among businessmen, as was his "emphasis on 'economic' rather than 'sentimental' questions," that it made political involvement more acceptable to a class of men who had heretofore scorned it. *Grand Old Party*, 3–4, 136.

[66] The term is used broadly here to describe a variety of "independent" groups. There was no official "Mugwump" organization, and the varieties of temperament and ideology in the movement were numerous. See, for instance, Geoffrey T. Blodgett, "The Mind of the Boston Mugwump,"

public service made many of them recoil at the business lobby's pursuit of self-interest. With influence "out of all proportion to Mugwump members,"[67] the Mugwump movement is best described as a progressive reform faction of the Republican party (not to be confused with the Progressives of the early twentieth century) that gained organizational self-awareness in the 1870s and 1880s. They were at the leading edge of national organization of professional associations like the American Bar Association (1878).[68] Their most effective foray into national politics is usually recognized as the 1884 presidential election, during which they bolted the GOP for Grover Cleveland's Democracy, but the precondition of their long-term influence was their long experience with independent, organized political action in the years leading up to the 1880s. The reform wing of the Republican party nominated its own presidential candidate under the Liberal Republican banner in 1872 in opposition to the corruption of Grant's first term. Their poor showing provoked much hand-wringing about the propriety of forming a third party devoted to ending the two-party system, and "the word [reform] in those days carried a sense of futility, a group seeking hopelessly to achieve something alien to the political mores of the community."[69] Through the remainder of the 1870s, their efforts centered outside of the national electoral system.

At the local level, the dissipated national movement grew organizational roots. A number of elite associations, including bar associations and groups such as New York's Council of Political Reform, Union League Club, and the Citizens' Association made significant efforts in urban reform, although in the 1870s, these were largely aimed at specific reform causes and at exposing corruption. Many "were social clubs with quasi-political functions," and much of their business was in planning for elegant dinners and acquiring suitable

The Mississippi Valley Historical Review, March 1962, 614–34; and Gerald W. McFarland, "The New York Mugwumps of 1884: A Profile," *Political Science Quarterly*, March 1963, 40–58. Blodgett dates the phenomenon from the later Grant administration (they only acquired the label "Mugwump" in the 1884 presidential election) to an anti-imperialist "last hurrah" during the McKinley administration. He identifies two distinct stages to the independent movement; the first was concentrated "in the higher councils of the Republican party" and attempted to sway nominations and cabinet appointments toward reformers. The later generation "shared a more activist bent for tactical organization and maneuver" and worked more closely with Democrats. They were more emblematic of the associational explosion in this second stage. Despite differences, there was much that independents across the political spectrum shared, notably the methods outlined in this section. Hence, following Blodgett's lead, I simplify the larger independent movement under the rubric of "Mugwump." Blodgett, "The Mugwump Reputation, 1870 to the Present," *The Journal of American History*, March 1980, 869.

[67] Geoffrey Blodgett, *The Gentle Reformers: Massachusetts Democrats in the Cleveland Era*, (Cambridge, MA: Harvard University Press, 1966), 19.

[68] McFarland, "The Mugwumps and the Emergence of Modern America," 9. Into this category, McFarland places the American Library Association (1878), the Modern Languages Association (1883), and the American Psychological Association (1892); the American Social Science Association (1865) was born of the same spirit. Keller, *Affairs of State*, 122–3.

[69] Mark D. Hirsch, *William C. Whitney: Modern Warwick* (New York: Archon Books, 1969, first published 1948), 53.

headquarters. However, they also featured speakers from politics, academe, and other reform organizations.[70] Such experience was quickly adapted to political organizing. After a decade of organization, the Mugwumps developed a political strategy that vindicated the false start of 1872.

The political career of Boston Mugwump Moorefield Storey embodied in substance and in style the parameters of the associational explosion, in which technological, cultural, and political trends of the day clashed with the Jacksonian mode. Storey's politics in many ways continued the ideological passion of the prewar Republican party of the 1850s, and he spent his life attempting to re-create that sense of purpose through organized politics.[71] He was an experienced organizer with a firm grasp of associational trends in American life. After the Liberal Republicans' failure in 1872, Storey helped found the Commonwealth Club for the purpose of "the purification of politics." In 1876, it reorganized as the Bristow Club, in support of former Navy Secretary Benjamin Bristow, who unsuccessfully sought the Republican nomination. (Bristow, an avowed supporter of civil service reform, had alienated President Grant by investigating the Whiskey Ring and had become, for Liberal Republicans, "the symbol of reform."[72])

In 1877, having failed twice at presidential politics, Storey helped form the Young Men's Republican Committee (YMRC) "to work for Civil Service Reform and honest money and against the payment of the United States bonds with greenbacks." Although it borrowed the name of the Republican party, advised members to attend primaries, and asked that "each [affiliated] committee co-operate as far as possible with its town or city Republican committee," it insisted on independence from the regular Republican organization.[73] To stimulate public discussion of reform, the YMRC published a weekly pamphlet that was distributed to newspaper editors, who were encouraged to reprint the material therein. Although the club worked (and was given credit) for Republican victories in Massachusetts state elections in 1877, its refusal to toe the party line established Storey's "position as an active Independent who stood ready to fight for what he thought were good causes but was not seeking office," rather than a position of party leadership.[74] By September 1878, the club reported 100 affiliates representing 229 towns throughout Massachusetts.[75]

70 McFarland, "The New York Mugwumps of 1884," 49; Blodgett, *The Gentle Reformers*, 29.
71 McFarland, "The Mugwumps and the Emergence of Modern America," 13.
72 E. Bruce Thompson, "The Bristow Presidential Boom of 1876," *The Mississippi Valley Historical Review* (June 1945), 4.
73 Young Men's Republican Committee, flier, March 26, 1878, box 1, Young Men's Republican Committee Records, Massachusetts Historical Society, Boston, Massachusetts (hereafter YMRC Records); Young Men's Republican Committee, flier, May 11, 1878, box 1; Young Men's Republican Committee, "Notebook, 1877–1881," January 17, 1878 and January 21, 1878, YMRC Records.
74 Moorefield Storey, "Autobiography," Storey Papers.
75 Young Men's Republican Committee, "Notebook, 1877–1881," September 15, 1878, March 6, 1880, YMRC Records.

The association defined itself in opposition to the Jacksonian party mode. Whereas the parties waved the bloody shirt, the YMRC proclaimed that "the issues raised by the civil war are for the most part at rest" and focused on financial and civil service reform. The Jacksonian mode treated platforms with cynical irony, whereas the YMRC claimed to be "formed from those who believe in holding the Republican party firmly up to its pledges in the platforms of the last National and State Conventions." Parties in the Jacksonian mode only convened voters during campaign years, but the association aimed to keep "the younger element alive throughout the year to the questions before the country." The Jacksonian mode was grounded in a series of meetings designed to exclude irregular organizations, but the YMRC exhibited openness, suggesting "that in each city and town a small number of young men who favor reform, come together and organize for political operations in their own locality" without questioning their regularity. Further, although the Jacksonian mode preferred to keep political activity within the geographic boundaries of regularity, the association sought to influence voters across the nation, authorizing its executive committee to do what they could "to induce similar movements to be started in other States."[76]

Storey and his Young Republicans struck a markedly unconciliatory note toward national presidential aspirants. In 1880, they declared against the renomination of Grant, as well as the candidacy of James G. Blaine of Maine, whose infamous involvement in a bribery scandal marked him as representative of "everything offensive in the party during its twenty-year reign since the Civil War."[77] Unable to agree on a reform candidate, the association warned that either Grant or Blaine would lose independent votes and agreed to call a special meeting to plot a response if Grant or Blaine were nominated. Relieved but not satisfied by Garfield's nomination and election, they published a "record" of Blaine's career and sent it to the president-elect, then rumored to be considering naming Blaine as his secretary of state.[78]

In 1881, together with civil service reformers Dorman Eaton and George William Curtis, Storey moved further from his party by founding the National Civil Service Reform League (NCSRL), followed by a Massachusetts affiliate of the League. Through the latter, Storey worked for the 1882 election of naturalist Theodore Lyman to Congress as an independent pledged to civil service reform. Storey was credited with a particularly effective pamphlet that "stated the records of ... prominent Republicans, the facts as to the spoils system, and other weak points in the Republican armor." He claimed that "wherever our broadside went, it was read and every where reversed or greatly

---

[76] Young Men's Republican Committee, "Notebook, 1877–1881," September 15, 1878, March 6, 1880, YMRC Records.

[77] Hirsch, *William C. Whitney*, 236. See also Summer, *Rum, Romanism, and Rebellion*, 62–3.

[78] Young Men's Republican Committee, "Notebook, 1877–1881," September 15, 1878; March 6, 1880; May 12, 1880; January 28, 1881, YMRC Records. If Garfield received the missive, he dismissed it, because Blaine was nominated shortly after his inauguration.

reduced the vote for [the incumbent Republican candidate]. While outside the District where it was not circulated, the voters did not understand the cause of the revolution." Visiting Washington after the campaign, Storey found himself "treated with consideration as a new king-maker" by regular party politicians.[79]

Like AISA, Storey was constantly innovating new organizational formats. The Commonwealth and Bristow clubs' narrowness gave way to the YMRC's general appeal to like-minded reformers. The NCSRL functioned as a civil service reform think tank, pursuing research in and advocating for new reform methods. Storey also aimed to unite disparate strands of independent leadership behind a common political strategy. Following the Lyman campaign, he joined with "the men who had been active in the battle" to form yet another nonpartisan association, the Massachusetts Reform Club, in 1882. Unlike the YMRC, the Reform Club was exclusive, claiming only 286 members (and a long waiting list) by 1889.[80] More than any of Storey's endeavors to date, the Reform Club saw itself as part of a national phenomenon, cultivating relationships with thirty-eight reform clubs in Massachusetts, as well as clubs in Philadelphia, Indianapolis, Chicago, Bloomington (Vermont), and the New York Reform Club, which was formed using a copy of the Massachusetts club's constitution.[81] Its honorary members included a who's who of the national reform cause, such as New York's Dorman Eaton, Seth Low, and Carl Schurz, as well as Indiana's William Dudley Foulke, Philadelphia's Wayne McVeagh, and British political scientist James Bryce.[82] It encouraged the spread of independent clubs, as did the YMRC, and engaged in discussion and research on reform methods, like the NCSRL. Its chief function, however, was to prepare a cadre of leaders to serve as the vanguard of a wider independent movement.

By 1884, Storey's reformers were well organized and looking for new opportunities. Emboldened by the success of the Pendleton Act in 1883 (passed with the aid of Lyman in the House of Representatives and written by Storey ally Dorman Eaton), they put the parties on notice that they would support whichever party proved a devotion to reform.[83] When the Republicans nominated Blaine for the presidency, Mugwumps appeared horrified, although Blaine's nomination was a pretext for a strategy the independents had been plotting for years.[84] When Democrats nominated Grover Cleveland, the New

---

[79] Moorefield Storey, "Autobiography," Storey Papers.

[80] Massachusetts Reform Club, "Secretary's Report," December 1889, Massachusetts Reform Club Records, 1890–1901, Massachusetts Historical Society, Boston, MA (hereafter MRC Records).

[81] Storey, "Autobiography;" Massachusetts Reform Club, "Notebook," box 3, MRC Records. See also Blodgett, "The Mind of the Boston Mugwump," 620. Boston Mugwumps were preceded by a Reform Club in Philadelphia, founded in 1872. See Philip S. Benjamin, "Gentlemen Reformers in the Quaker City, 1870–1912," *Political Science Quarterly*, 85: 1 (March 1970), 66.

[82] Massachusetts Reform Club, "Annual Report, 1891," box 3, MRC Records.

[83] Blodgett, *The Gentle Reformers*, 4.

[84] Blodgett, *The Gentle Reformers*, 3.

York governor who had proven his independence by opposing Tammany Hall and advocating civil service reform, the die was cast.

Although the press portrayed the Mugwumps' bolt as a spur-of-the-moment affair, it was not spontaneous. At the Reform Club's monthly meeting, long-discussed plans were finalized, and "the standard of revolt was raised." A public meeting was organized, which created a "Committee of One Hundred" to coordinate national independent activity throughout the campaign. At least forty-two members of the committee were Reform Club members, and Storey and eight other club members were on its fifteen-member executive committee.[85] Nationally, they provided the central nervous system for the Mugwump campaign of 1884, sending its members around the country on speaking tours, contributing to newspapers and journals, and distributing voluminous literature. It sent delegates to prevail upon New York City Mugwumps to launch their own club and to similarly bolt the party.[86] It was during this campaign that the movement, encompassed by several independent organizations, earned the label "Mugwump." Contrary to conventional wisdom, the term did not identify a creature sitting on a fence "with their mugs on one side and their wumps on the other" but was taken from a Native American word for "great man" and applied derisively to Storey's band of young elites, who presumed too much about their relevance to the world of practical politics.[87]

Along with Storey's YMRC, the Young Men's Democratic Club of Massachusetts (YMDCM) provides a good picture of their organized efforts on the ground (more on the YMDCM is found in Chapter 4). Following the 1884 bolt, a number of Mugwumps (including Josiah Quincy, formerly of Storey's Committee of One Hundred and the Massachusetts Reform Club) marked Cleveland's victory by moving permanently into the Democratic party: as Mugwump-*cum*-Democrat George Fred Williams put it, "we wish the Democratic party to take possession of us." The regular state Democratic party was mistrustful of these well-heeled suitors, and, at the state nominating convention of 1887, summarily rejected the Mugwumps' candidates. In response, Massachusetts Mugwumps embarked on a campaign to prove their usefulness to the party and to educate regular Democrats; the club was their flagship.[88]

By 1890, the place of the YMDCM in state politics had been established and prominent club leaders like Quincy gained positions on the

---

[85] Circular, "To the Members of the Committee of One Hundred," no date, carton 1, George Fred Williams Papers, Massachusetts Historical Society, Boston, MA. For membership, see Massachusetts Reform Club, "Annual Report, 1891," box 3, MRC Records. See Dobson, *Politics in the Gilded Age*, 118. The YMRC, by contrast, had only four members on the Committee of One Hundred; Young Men's Republican Committee, "Notebook, 1877–1881," YMRC Records.

[86] Dobson, *Politics in the Gilded Age*, 119.

[87] Summer, *Rum, Romanism, and Rebellion*, 24. See also McFarland, "The Mugwumps and the Emergence of Modern America," 1.

[88] Williams quoted in Gordon S. Wood, "The Massachusetts Mugwumps," *New England Quarterly* (December 1960), 444; see also 446–7.

Massachusetts Democratic State Committee, formalizing their relationship with the regular apparatus. In addition to providing the state committee a list of club members who were willing to give stump speeches and entertaining prominent out-of-state speakers, the club was asked "to take full charge of distributing documents in the coming [state] campaign."[89] By that time, the club had appointed both a document committee responsible for producing, procuring, and distributing campaign literature and a political information committee authorized to collect statistics and general information for writers, stump speakers, and candidates.[90] It had made itself a central ally of the state party apparatus, but it had brought the educational campaign with it. In 1890, a club member, William Russell, received the regular Democratic party organization's nomination for governor and was elected; with the campaign support of the club, Massachusetts sent seven Democrats to Congress in what was identified as a victory for the club's methods.[91]

The defeat of the Cleveland wing of the Democratic party in 1896 left Mugwumps dispirited and isolated. Insisting on the primacy of elite leadership in reform politics, they were "opposed to virtually every protest movement in the 1890s" and did not cooperate with agrarians or labor groups. Their electoral successes centered in Massachusetts and New York, and although legislative achievements in those states provided a model for later reforms elsewhere, the prominence of New York in national politics between 1880 and 1900 amplified their importance in ways that the System of 1896 did not. Mugwumps turned listlessly to the Republican party after Bryan was nominated in 1896, but largely as individuals; the movement lost its cohesive power. Although Mugwumps had justified independence by pointing to similarities between the two major parties, the ascension of Bryan to the head of the Democratic party brought the platforms of the two parties into sharper contrast. The Spanish-American War and the annexation of the Philippines produced one last blast of moral outrage, but it was not enough to return the Mugwump strategy to prominence.[92]

Agrarian Insurgents

At first glance, the agrarian insurgency that dotted the American landscape in the late nineteenth century appears to be part of a different trend altogether from AISA and the Mugwumps. AISA encouraged federal support for industry;

---

[89] Young Men's Democratic Club of Massachusetts, "Minutes, 1891–1894," August 26, 1891, Young Men's Democratic Club of Massachusetts Records (hereafter YMDCM Records).

[90] James Russell Reed, "Annual Report of the Executive Committee of the Young Men's Democratic Club of Massachusetts, December 1, 1890," YMDCM Records.

[91] Blodgett, *The Gentle Reformers*, 98.

[92] McFarland, "The Mugwumps and the Emergence of Modern America," 10; Burnham, "The Changing Shape of the American Political Universe"; Dobson, *Politics in the Gilded Age*, 182–3; Robert L. Beisner, *Twelve against Empire: The Anti-Imperialists, 1898–1900* (New York: McGraw-Hill, 1968).

agrarians raged against collusion with business, and advocated federal assistance to farmers and workers instead. Mugwumps feared increased democratic
influences in society; agrarians celebrated the common man. Mugwumps were
conservative on economic issues (their affection for free trade notwithstanding);
agrarian economic policies challenged the very basis of capitalism.

Yet stripped of their ideological content, the three groups approached politics in a similar fashion, all using the methods that characterize the associational explosion. Agrarians, interest groups, and Mugwumps alike challenged
the parties' hold on voters, breaking down party loyalty and subverting the
Jacksonian party mode's preference for geographic divisions. They rejected the
parties' preference for compromise and pushed for the articulation of clear
national policy objectives. Their organizations provided sustained educational
efforts and national networks in an attempt to distance their members from
partisan politics. They were constant organizers, innovating with new associations as circumstances demanded. Further, they formed their membership into
an electoral hinge that could be swung between the parties at will, maximizing
an otherwise weak electoral presence.

The most thoroughly organized unit of the agrarian insurgency was the
Farmers' Alliance. The Alliance was an umbrella group encompassing a variety
of state and local organizations; like Storey's Mugwumps, it had a long organizational pedigree and drew on organizational duplication and borrowing. It
was inspired by (and drew membership from) the Grange, a farmers' self-help
union that found success in state and national politics in the 1860s and 1870s,
and the National Greenback-Labor party that promoted inflationary monetary
policies in the 1870s and 1880s. In the South, a group of Texas farmers founded
an Alliance by 1875, only to dissolve in a dispute over Greenback party politics
around 1876; it was revived again in 1879 by another group of Texas farmers
who developed "a surprising... density of social organization."[93] An alliance
was also formed in 1880 in Louisiana, complete with a set of secret rituals based
on old Grange procedures and the Texas Alliance constitution. In Arkansas,
the Agricultural Wheel, a farmers' debating society, formed in 1883 and spread
into several states. These Texas and Louisiana Alliances were united in 1887
and, together with the Arkansas Wheel, became the Farmers' and Laborers'
Union of America in 1889. In 1880, a northern Farmers' Alliance was formed
in Illinois that drew on a short-lived farmer's cooperative founded in 1877 by
former Grangers. Although there were ideological and organizational similarities between the two regional groups, cooperation was limited. A major point
of dispute between them was the admission of black farmers; this the Southern
Alliance steadfastly refused, although it cooperated with the Colored Farmers'
Alliance that formed in 1888.[94] They attempted to ally with labor groups such

[93] Sanders, *Roots of Reform*, 117.
[94] John D. Hicks, *The Populist Revolt: A History of the Farmers' Alliance and the People's Party*
(Lincoln: University of Nebraska Press, 1961). On the Northern Alliance, see 97–8; on the
Alliance in the South, see 104–11; on the Colored Farmers' Alliance, see 114–15. The Northern
Alliance had a shallower grassroots base, resisted some of the Southern Alliances more radical
proposals, and opposed secret rituals; *Roots of Reform*, 122.

as the Knights of Labor, but differences between farmers and labor, as well as regional differences, prevented the formation of a durable grand coalition. Thus, the movement, often considered a monolith (in no small part because the northeastern press and the parties considered the threat to be monolithic), was in reality the accumulation of a number of associational experiences that contributed to a common agrarian phenomenon.[95]

The Alliance's various organizational components were formed by farmers who believed themselves to be victims of the concentration of economic power in the hands of eastern corporations. Its early efforts centered around cooperatives designed to enable farmers to escape the impersonal forces of the national economy and focused on disseminating "as widely as possible scientific agricultural information" that would enable farmers to maximize their economic position.[96] However, as evidenced in the earliest days of the Texas Alliance, the question of political involvement was frequently broached and was always controversial. "The farmer's enemy was not an employer, but a *system*," notes Elizabeth Sanders, "a system of credit, supply, transportation, and marketing," and one that tended to lead the Alliance to radical solutions and to look to the expansion of state power.[97] A crisis over political involvement was narrowly avoided after a heady 1886 convention of the Texas Alliance in Cleburne, Texas, in which more radical (and politicized) members succeeded in passing a series of demands for "such legislation as shall secure to our people freedom from the onerous and shameful abuses that the industrial classes are now suffering at the hands of arrogant capitalists and powerful corporations."[98] These went beyond anything either party countenanced, and more practical members cautioned against unnecessarily antagonizing the parties.[99] The radicals thought this all the better, hoping to engineer an enduring break between adherents to the Cleburne platform and the party regulars and to create a third party.

At this moment a wily organizer named Charles Macune emerged, recommending a course of action that closely tracked the methods of the associational explosion. Having been elected at Cleburne to the state Alliance's executive committee, he persuaded both sides to agree to a middle path. Third-party action by a farmers' group in one state in the Solid South was political suicide, but Macune suggested a massive expansion effort, merging with as many sympathetic farmers' organizations as possible – a path that led them to their rendezvous with the Louisiana Alliance and the Arkansas Wheel – believing that a national presence would lessen the isolation that would come from bolting the major parties.[100]

[95] Paul W. Glad, *McKinley, Bryan, and the People* (New York: J. B. Lippincott, 1964), 53–4.

[96] Hicks, *The Populist Revolt*, 129.

[97] Sanders, *Roots of Reform*, 101.

[98] Quoted in Goodwyn, *The Populist Moment*, 47.

[99] Sanders, *Roots of Reform*, 120.

[100] Lawrence Goodwyn, *Democratic Promise: The Populist Moment in America* (New York: Oxford University Press, 1971), 77–84; Sanders, *Roots of Reform*, 120–1.

In the meanwhile, Macune proposed that the Alliance channel its efforts into becoming "a vast pressure group; a huge farmer's organization to impress the government with the gravity of the farmer's plight and national policy," a strategy that would have been familiar to Moorefield Storey and that Macune hoped would forestall a third-party movement. Believing that earlier failures in politics had resulted from "the want of Alliance literature, the means to employ active lecturers to visit and instruct, and encourage the sub-Alliances and institute new ones," Macune insisted that the new effort involved an expanded "educational campaign." In pursuit of that goal, he urged the Alliance to expand a lecture system that it had originated in the early 1880s.[101] In addition to paid national lecturers, who spread Alliance doctrine and founded local branches, each branch (sub-Alliance) had a lecturer whose job was "to suggest subjects for discussion" and to provide members with books and newspapers borrowed from circulating libraries. They formed local study groups to discuss "questions that were agitating the minds of the people" and developed a "'general system of home culture, somewhat on the plan of the Chatauqua [sic],' with organized classes and a supervised course of study."[102] The lecture system was designed to instill farmers with the intellectual tools that would allow them to break the confines of both capitalist economics and party loyalty. As one contemporary account described a local chapter, secret and business meetings were held once a month, but the sub-Alliance "held open meetings on Saturday night and let our lodge drift into a kind of literary or debating society. At these open meetings all were invited. . . . and our programs consisted of readings, recitations, speeches and debates."[103] The educational pretensions of the Mugwumps, with their university degrees and elegant dinner parties, could be dismissed as an artifact of a high-toned society. Nonetheless, similar methods were central to Macune's strategy for reorganizing the Alliance. Farmers needed both to be convinced that traditional party politics did not suit their self-interest and to be educated about cooperative efforts, which in turn required an economic education. As Sanders concludes, "the lifeblood of the [Farmers' Alliance] was its system of collective education."[104]

In 1889, the Alliance founded (and Macune edited) the *National Economist*, the Southern Alliance's official journal. The journal was integrated into the lecture system, forming the basis of lessons delivered by local lecturers and providing local suballiances with discussion topics and exercises to clarify the

---

[101] Michael Schwartz, *Radical Protest and Social Structure: The Southern Farmers' Alliance and Cotton Tenancy, 1880–1900* (Chicago: University of Chicago Press, 1976), 94, 92; on Macune's role, see also Goodwyn, *Democratic Promise*, 85. A brief description of the Exchange is found in Hicks, *The Populist Revolt*, 134–6. On the Alliance's early lecture system, see Sanders, *Roots of Reform*, 118–19.

[102] Hicks, *The Populist Revolt*, 129; see also Schwartz, *Radical Protest and Social Structure*, 106–7; Goodwyn, *The Populist Moment*, 57–8.

[103] Quoted in Schwartz, *Radical Protest and Social Structure*, 110.

[104] Sanders, *Roots of Reform*, 123.

Alliance's economic theories.[105] The *National Economist* existed alongside a network of hundreds of local Alliance-affiliated newspapers. In 1890, they were invited to join a National Reform Press Association, which sought to coordinate the Alliance's message. That year also saw the formation of a National Economist Publishing Company, which poured forth "a torrent of pamphlets, broadsides, and books."[106] The Alliance also had its share of public rallies, picnics, and campfires, and the Southern Alliance was a secret society that occupied much time with the lodge-style rituals that such involved. The lecture system, however, was predicated on educational appeals bolstered by the interlocking pieces of the Alliance's national structure. "Stump oratory," notes Goodwyn, "was hardly the best medium for dissecting an issue as unusual and controversial" as the Alliance's financial policies.[107]

In 1891, referring to the larger organizational effort, Alliance President L. L. Polk boasted that it had "already accomplished much, in that the largest class of our society has been led by it to study political economies and to examine into methods and machinery of government." Notably, like AISA and the Mugwumps, the Alliance fostered a national political perspective. Polk declared that "its influence as a political factor will be plainly evidenced in such national legislation as may be enacted while it exists as an organization." Also, its structure was intended to allow the Alliance to reach voters in a private capacity, speaking directly to interest rather than appealing to civic duty; as Polk explained, the Alliance was "composed of a class of people who stay at their homes and by their firesides unless stern necessity calls them away."[108] Finally, the Alliance's methods were premised on the assumption that new conditions demanded clear policy objectives. As one western Democrat reported, Alliance members rejected the Jacksonian mode's preference for harmony over substantive specificity:

they talk about harmony, agreeing to abide the results of the convention, and all that sort of thing. They don't mean a word of it; but this kind of talk is consistent with the methods which they have been employing to deceive the people for a quarter of a century.... The friends of the people cannot do this, they must be plain and outspoken, or they can have no power with the people.[109]

The parties were thereby put on notice that traditional party politics was insufficient for quenching the prairie fire of the agrarian movement.

It was difficult to convince farmers who had intense loyalties to one of the two major parties to embark on a separate path, and the Alliance initially avoided alienating party loyalists. There were constant efforts to break into electoral politics, however. As early as 1882, dissatisfied farmers in Nebraska formed an Antimonopolist third party and polled well; although the party

[105] Sanders, *Roots of Reform*, 124.
[106] Schwartz, *Radical Protest and Social Structure*, 120.
[107] Goodwyn, *The Populist Moment*, 116–17, 162.
[108] L. L. Polk, "The Farmers' Discontent," *North American Review*, July, 1891, 11.
[109] David Overmeyer to William Jennings Bryan, February 29, 1896, box 3, Bryan papers.

did not endure, the state party organizations in Nebraska later looked to the Nebraska Alliance affiliate to represent farming interests. In 1884, Alliance members running within the major parties won seats in the Minnesota House. In 1886 and 1887, Alliance-affiliated candidates did well in Iowa. In the six territories applying for statehood in 1889, Alliance members initiated farmer-friendly constitutional provisions. The electoral challenges rarely developed into majority control of state governments, but they did demonstrate the power of organized agrarianism. As John D. Hicks concludes, "the farmers seemed to be in an enviable position: Republicans and Democrats were bidding against one another in order to obtain Alliance support."[110] In the South, the domineering strength of the Democratic party and the threat of black power in the face of a divided white majority kept Alliance members within regular ranks.

The movement peaked in the 1890s, during a series of electoral contests that threw normally predictable voting patterns into question. Partisan control of the House changed hands between the parties in 1888, 1890, and 1894; of the Senate in 1892 and 1894; and of the presidency in 1888 and 1892. As Robert Marcus explains, "the politician found himself no longer certain of his electorate. The degree of predictability had abruptly shrunk."[111] Although there were many causes behind the volatility, the Alliance was a large factor in the minds of politicians in both parties. The correspondence of national party leaders between 1890 and 1892 is full of concern over the direction of the agrarian movement. William Whitney, managing Cleveland's 1892 campaign from New York, kept in close touch with southern Democrats who complained that the campaign would "require much hard work" given the third-party challenge.[112] The Alliance's educational work was undermining traditional party allegiances, and party leaders found that "the small men belonging to the order" could not be controlled by traditional appeals to party loyalty.[113] Former Democrats, influenced by the Alliance, were "declaring that the days of usefulness of the Democratic party were at an end."[114] One reported that third-party voters, most of whom had recently been Democrats, were no longer susceptible to the old appeals: "it is hard to get them to read but *one* side," and that side was provided by the Alliance's press association.[115] Another elaborated that "they will not read anything except such papers as they are advised to read and if you tell them anything you see elsewhere they tell you they still [sic] trying to blind the farmer but that day is past."[116] The chairman of the Tennessee State Democratic Executive Committee warned of the "instructions [Alliance

---

[110] Hicks, *The Populist Revolt*, 148–9.
[111] Marcus, *Grand Old Party*, 167.
[112] M. T. Williams to B. H. Burr, June 14, 1892, book 70, Whitney Papers.
[113] R. H. Ricks to Whitney, book 69, Whitney Papers.
[114] A. B. McKinley to Whitney, September 3, 1892, book 75, Whitney Papers.
[115] B. F. Landon to Whitney, May 30, 1892, book 69, Whitney Papers.
[116] D. Siler to Whitney, May 31, 1892, book 69, Whitney Papers.

members] have received for the past 18 months in their secret lodges not to hear the democratic speeches or read democratic newspapers or literature."[117]

The parties struggled to respond. In Nebraska, where the Alliance had gained influence since the abortive Antimonopolist ticket of 1882, William Jennings Bryan was advised to write the editor of an Alliance paper and "give him a little taffy in regard to his influence and the fact that you are in harmony with most of the principles enunciated in the Alliance platform and see what effect it will have."[118] Recognizing the power of the minor party's educational methods, a Mississippi Democrat who claimed "an extensive experience in the Alliance organization" advised that the Democratic party devise an "Educational Plan of Campaign" that mimicked Alliance methods, such as "building educational camp-fires in the strong-holds of the Southern Alliance."[119] A Colorado Democrat insisted that the party needed "a campaign of conviction on economic questions."[120] That such educational methods went beyond the usual party exertions is indicated by a Tennessee Democrat who hoped "by such education to produce still greater results," although he acknowledged that "this thorough organization was unknown to our methods and people down here; the necessity for it never having heretofore existed."[121]

Even with the Southern Alliance following a more conservative course, the 1890 elections showed the extent of agrarian influence. Following the development of a Macune-inspired plan to have the federal government to sponsor a series of warehouses (he called them subtreasuries) in which farmers could deposit crops to wait for favorable prices (and receive government loans using their crops as collateral), the Alliance launched an effort to utilize its massive communications network to support politicians who pledged support for the plan. Southern Democrats such as South Carolina's Ben Tillman imitated the popular language of the Alliance.[122] Western Alliance sympathizers, running either as independents or within the parties, won five congressional seats, a senate seat, and control of the lower house of the state legislature in Kansas. Alliance-affiliated candidates performed well in Nebraska, South Dakota, and Minnesota. Gubernatorial candidates backed by the Alliance won in Georgia, Tennessee, Texas, and South Carolina, as did a number of congressional candidates elsewhere in the South. Eight southern state legislatures were dominated by the People's party, forty-four sympathetic southern congressmen were elected, and three allied southern (Democratic) governors.[123] Once in office,

---

[117] William H. Carroll to Grover Cleveland, October 4. 1892, series 11, box 4, Cleveland Papers.

[118] H.M. Boydston to Bryan, October 16, 1890, box 2, Bryan Papers.

[119] William S. McAllister to Whitney, August 6, 1892, book 74, Whitney Papers. See also J. S. Green to Bryan, November 1, 1890, box 2, Bryan Papers.

[120] A.B. McKinley to Whitney, September 3, 1892, book 75, Whitney Papers.

[121] William H. Carroll to Cleveland, October 4, 1892, series 11, box 4, Cleveland Papers.

[122] J. Rogers Hollingsworth, *The Whirligig of Politics: The Democracy of Cleveland and Bryan* (Chicago: University of Chicago Press, 1963), 8; Sanders, *Roots of Reform*, 127.

[123] Glad, *McKinley, Bryan, and the People*, 53–60. See also Hicks, *The Populist Revolt*, 178–9, 247–8.

many of these regular politicians either downplayed election promises or turned against the Alliance. Tillman, for instance, turned against the Alliance once in power. In Texas, Governor James Hogg ignored Alliance demands, and many of the Alliance's congressional allies abandoned the subtreasury plan.[124]

Heartened by their success and dissatisfied with the response of major party politicians, the resistance to a third-party strategy gave way. In late 1890, the Alliance's convention in Ocala, Florida, moved toward a break with the parties by issuing a series of radical demands and discussing a third party. Although Macune resisted, his National Reform Press Association provided the backbone of the third party effort. In 1891, a collection of Alliancemen, old Grangers, and members of the Knights of Labor founded a provisional national party committee; in December 1891, a group of Alliance congressmen formed a House caucus that nominated Tom Watson of Georgia for speaker of the House; and in Omaha in 1892, a presidential ticket was nominated under the heading of the People's party. Agrarian insurgents launched People's party tickets in state elections across the country, popularizing them along the networks established by the lecture circuit and literature distribution chain. Southerners joined the flow reluctantly, but in those southern states where the Populists gained the most strength, the Democratic party offered platform support for Populist ideas and played to Alliance members, evoking the strong bonds of party loyalty.[125] The People's party candidate also received twenty-two electoral votes from six Western states in 1892.[126]

The transition from pressure group to third party was not a smooth one. The Alliance had created a network of independent state and local sub-Alliances, and each had carved its own path out of its local political context, and thus it was difficult for some to pull out of regular party politics altogether. In some areas, the minority party co-opted agrarian third parties to take advantage of their major party opponents' woes, draining off Alliance elites and voters. In the South, the People's party looked to combine with Republicans, or at least to find "peoples' party candidates who will be voted for by republicans and all others who wish to defeat the democratic party."[127] In the West, Republicans feared combinations between the insurgents and the Democrats.[128]

Fusion with insurgents carried risks for the parties, however, because it obscured the boundaries of party regularity. Even as they broke the bonds of regularity to achieve short-term gains, the parties struggled to maintain a

---

[124] Sanders, *Roots of Reform*, 127–8; Hicks, *The Populist Revolt*, 171–4; Schwartz, *Radical Protest and Social Structure*, 99–100.

[125] Sanders, *Roots of Reform*, 128–31; Hicks, *The Populist Revolt*, 247–8.

[126] These were largely presumed to be naturally Republican-leaning states, including Colorado (four votes), Idaho (three), Nevada (three), and North Dakota (which gave one of its three votes to the People's Party); Kansas (ten) and Oregon (which gave one of its four votes to the People's Party) made up the rest of People's candidate James Weaver's twenty-two-vote count.

[127] D. H. Albright to B. H. Burr, June 16, 1892, book 70, Whitney Papers.

[128] C. H. Grosvernor to Charles Foster, October 6, 1891, box 2, Hanna-McCormick Family Papers.

distinct partisan character, and cooperation with insurgents undermined their efforts. Colorado Democrats reported "having a struggle to preserve our party integrity against the encroachments of men who claim to be yet Democrats, who attend Peoples' Party conventions, openly denounce the Democratic party, and assert that the local adherents of Mr. Cleveland are enemies to their State."[129] Thomas Carter, soon to become the chairman of the Republican National Committee, warned a Montana crowd in 1888 against fusion, insisting on "preserving the identity of the party free from compromising alliances."[130] In Tennessee, the 1890 campaign saw the Democratic party pandering to Alliance voters, attempting to "bend the principles of the democratic party to fit the cranks of the disaffected," which, one Democrat complained, led to the result that "many of the people lost the idea of what democratic principles meant and it has taken the hardest sort of work to get them back in line."[131] As Peter H. Argersinger has documented, Populist[132] fusion with western Democrats led Republican state organizations to adopt a variety of ballot laws to limit the opportunities for fusion and thus avert one of the key strategies of the People's party. With the formalization of ballot laws, it became more complicated for third parties to appear on the ticket under the auspices of one of the two major parties.[133]

Ballot laws were a significant legal barrier, but fusion also undermined the educational strategy that Macune and the Alliance had pursued since the movement emerged nationally. Expecting the eastern wing of the Democratic party to reject the West's rising insurgency, the People's party scheduled its 1896 convention to convene after both major parties held theirs, hoping that the resulting disaffection would send westerners running into the arms of the third party. As explained in Chapter 5, silver forces within the Democratic party adopted the methods of the associational explosion to seize the party for the silver cause and thus seized the mantle of insurgent reform. When Bryan was nominated, the Populists resorted to the pattern they had followed throughout the 1890s, effecting a national "fusion" with the Democrats.[134] Yet although Democrats significantly reconstructed their organization along the lines of the new idea of party, a fundamental premise of the Alliance's organization had been undermining traditional party loyalties. The 1896 détente was disorienting, much as it had been for the Mugwumps who had followed Cleveland into the Democratic party. Alliancemen had endured political ostracism for

---

[129] A.B. McKinley to Whitney, September 3, 1892, book 75, Whitney Papers.

[130] Unpublished draft of biography of Thomas Henry Carter, reel 11, Thomas Henry Carter Papers, Manuscript Division, Library of Congress.

[131] V. Polk to unknown recipient, October 26, 1892, Series 11, box 9, Cleveland Papers.

[132] Like "Mugwump," "Populist" was also both an organizational inaccuracy during most of the People's Party history and originally a derogatory term for the independent movement. See Hicks, *The Populist Revolt*, 238n.

[133] Peter H. Argersinger, "A Place on the Ballot': Fusion Politics and Antifusion Laws," *The American Historical Review* (April 1980), 287–306.

[134] Sanders, *Roots of Reform*, 139.

their willingness to break from regular party ranks, and returning to the fold did not boost their stature. Further, with a candidate sure to attract farmers at the head of the national ticket, the Populists offered the regular Democracy little. Southern Democrats took the opportunity to outmaneuver the third party. Only in Missouri, Arkansas, Louisiana, Kentucky, and North Carolina did the Democratic ticket deign to fuse with the Populists; in Missouri, the Populists ran no candidate for governor and in Arkansas no candidates for Congress – all in the interests of boosting the national Democratic ticket. In the West, where the Alliance had justified a departure from the Republican party with its critique of the two-party system, moving farmers into the Democratic party required tremendous political capital that never saw a significant return once Bryan went down to defeat. As Hicks concludes, "thousands of Populists... had deliberately gone over to the Democrats, and thanks to the welding influence of a heated campaign against a common enemy, they bade fair to stay where they were."[135] Goodwyn concludes similarly that "the Populist rank and file lost the essential emotional ingredient of collective action – faith in their own movement."[136] The fundamental problem, however, was that the 1896 fusion substituted the promise of political power for the educational and pressure group strategy that worked so effectively in the politics of the late nineteenth century. The emergence of the System of 1896, with the eradication of close party competition in most of the North and South, was thus both cause and artifact of the Populists' failure.

William Wilson, serving as Cleveland's postmaster general, looked at how effectively these insurgent groups were tearing his party apart and saw a connection to modern party politics in Europe:

democracy has permanently and perceptibly degraded representative government, resulting also in breaking up great parties into groups, such as are found in all the parliamentary systems on the Continent... and this chiefly by giving rise to a Socialist party.... The Socialists are springing up under the name of Populists and, if the Democratic party dissolves, as is now not improbable, it may be impossible to crystallize its fragments... and, from that dissolution, and the pressure it will take from the Republican party, we too may have Congress[es] made up of groups and not two great opposing parties.[137]

Wilson's analysis shows just how seriously the parties took the Alliance/People's party threat. They believed it would not only cost the major parties victories in the short run but inflict long-term damage on the viability of the two-party system. Antiparty reformers predicted similar outcomes; one Mugwump insisted that "the varieties of temperament are infinite, and instead of dividing mankind into two parties and two only, as the party system requires, divide them into groups without number, or rather run through the whole mass

[135] Hicks, *The Populist Revolt*, 369–70, 378.
[136] Goodwyn, *Democratic Promise*, 590–1.
[137] Wilson, *The Cabinet Diary of William L. Wilson*, 93.

without forming any distinct line of cleavage; the same man being often Liberal on one class of questions and Conservative on another."[138] Unleashing individual judgment grounded in considerations of self-interest would shatter the fundamental unity on which the major parties depended.

The parties responded to the new associational universe in different ways. Antifusion laws targeted Populists, forcing them to confront more directly the deeply entrenched loyalties of voters.[139] Parties embraced many Mugwump reforms because, as Alan Ware and John Reynolds both argue, reformed electoral processes actually served party purposes.[140] The parties did not merely seek to assuage or restrict their new challengers, however. Rather, as explained in the next chapter, for a critical cadre of national party leaders, this challenge provided a lesson in the potential of national organization in the new sociopolitical environment of the late nineteenth century, and they used it to effect a reorientation of party operations. Like the new associations, they saw the task of campaigning as one in which parties spoke to individual interests rather than rallying homogeneous partisan communities. Like the new associations, the parties generated educational campaigns that presented consistent messages across the Union. Thus, they sought to make the parties more responsible to national publics such as those attracted to AISA, the various Mugwump organizations, and the Farmers' Alliance. Doing so required confronting the Jacksonian mode's republican orientation, however; as they struggled with this confrontation, they groped their way toward a new conceptualization of the party-in-the-electorate that did not rely on representation among distinct and homogeneous communities and a newly nationalized party organization capable of reaching citizens directly. In their defense of these new methods, they developed a new idea of party that left Jacksonian republicanism behind and pursued the liberal individualism embedded in the new associational methods.

[138] Goldwin Smith, "The Spoils of Office," *The Forum*, September 1889, 34.
[139] Argersinger, "'A Place on the Ballot': Fusion Politics and Antifusion Laws."
[140] Ware, *The American Direct Primary*; Reynolds, *The Demise of the American Convention System*.

3

Organizational Transformation and the National Parties

In addition to reshaping Americans' involvement in civic associations, the associational explosion provided a model of national citizen politics that was influential for a critical cadre of national party elites who reoriented national political campaigns in the late nineteenth century. The new campaign style they innovated drew explicitly on the "educational campaign" that was honed in the new associations; it was national in scope (and thus did not rely on local party mobilizers), and it appealed to voters' private self-interest (rather than to their membership in a local partisan community). Although transformative, this new campaign style was insufficient by itself; it required the creation of independent national party organizations, and the Jacksonian mode provided the parties with few organizational tools with which to conduct national campaigns. Beginning in the late nineteenth century, however, national party leaders consolidated control over national campaigns in the national party committees, bolstering their capacities to operate independently of the local party franchises. Republican National Committee Chairman James Clarkson explained that the effect was to "revolutionize" politics "just as dry goods business and all other kinds of business have been revolutionized and conducted on entirely new methods."[1]

Four changes toward this end are highlighted here and in the rest of the book. First, the parties implemented a new style of campaigning, one that adapted the "educational campaigns" of the associational explosion to party purposes. National campaigns ceased to rely solely on local efforts to promote national candidates with local arguments and instead distributed national campaign literature directly to voters. Printed material had long been a part of American campaigning, but in the late nineteenth century, national party leaders latched onto it as a means of controlling the content of national elections in new ways. This limited local campaigners' flexibility, standardizing campaign

---

[1] Clarkson to Leigh Hunt, October 1, 1904, box 2, James S. Clarkson papers, Manuscript Division, Library of Congress, Washington, DC.

themes across the country. Second, the national committees were empowered to conduct campaigns independently of subnational organizations by a centralized national committee apparatus and an independent fundraising apparatus. Third, as explained in Chapter 4, a national network of party clubs, modeled on the extra-partisan reform associations founded by Mugwumps like Moorefield Storey, weakened the geographic boundaries of regularity and substituted a direct relationship between the national party and the party-in-the-electorate. Finally, as Chapters 5 and 6 demonstrate, presidents and presidential candidates assumed a larger role in directing these newly nationalized campaigns.

A number of the Jacksonian party mode's defining characteristics remained after these changes were instituted (especially the shell of the convention system). However, the republican values of the traditional parties were significantly challenged. The result was the emergence of the first truly *nationalized* party organizations, as opposed to the merely *national* network of local organizations of the Jacksonian mode. As Howard Reiter explains, the term *national* "implies more than national power only; it involves the equality of persons and the absence of intervening levels of government."[2] Similarly, the concentration of authority in the national party organizations displaced the state and local organizations from their traditional status. The campaign of education eroded the layers of party authority that lay between the electorate and the national party organization, layers that under the Jacksonian mode had been made rivals of concentrated national power. The development of a competent national committee empowered presidential candidates to present their ideas directly to the people, allowing them to appeal to members of the party-in-the-electorate as individuals, rather than as members of distinct state organizations.[3] By directing appeals to voters as individuals, they not only reached them in a private capacity that took them out of their communal setting, they also facilitated appeals to self-interested policy preferences. Further, by creating a national party organization capable of managing campaigns independently of local affiliates, national party leaders displaced the capacity of subnational party organizations to restrain issues and issue entrepreneurs.

Why did subnational party leaders submit to this reversal? As Gary Cox explains with regard to the similar transformation in Great Britain, an increasing complexity in economic and political affairs, a more influential independent press, and a larger electorate pressured members of Parliament to submit to greater party discipline in exchange for a national party apparatus that strengthened the value of the party label in a more complicated political environment.[4] Similarly, in the United States, the transformed political environment of the late nineteenth century, together with the emergence of the associational explosion, produced a crisis of confidence in the traditional

[2] Reiter, *Selecting the President*, 132.
[3] Reynolds, *The Demise of the American Convention System*, 64.
[4] Gary W. Cox, *The Efficient Secret: The Cabinet and the Development of Political Parties in Victorian England* (Cambridge: Cambridge University Press, 1987), especially 51–65.

party establishment. Reconciling national policies through patronage or securing preferential treatment for local interests became more difficult as local
interests multiplied, diversified, and organized. Extra-partisan organizations
began to focus more critically on government services, increasing pressure on
party officials by drawing national publics' attention to government performance. As Alan Ware writes of party professionals' acceptance of primary
reforms, they accepted change for practical reasons that "a style of politics that
worked relatively well in the 1830s was working much less well in the new
circumstances."[5] As local party leaders' capacity to utilize the particularistic
methods of the Jacksonian mode diminished, local politicians became willing
to allow the national party organization to do the hard work of reconciling
competing national policy claims, especially when national politicians seemed
capable of "making use of the growing social impulse in this country."[6] The
new educational style of campaigning was broadly popular. Local party leaders
became enthused at the prospects of a timely adaptation to new and unfamiliar
political pressures.[7]

National Party Leaders and the Associational Explosion

The late nineteenth century was an age of confidence in the possibilities of reform. Too often this impulse has been solely identified with extra-partisan
reform associations such as Storey's Reform Club. The intensification of the
reform impulse between 1880 and 1912 did produce legislation that reformers
believed would weaken the parties, such as the Australian Ballot (or the secret
ballot, intended to prevent electoral corruption), registration laws (intended to
make voter qualification a matter of public record not party privilege), primary
election laws (intended to subject primary elections to legal supervision), and
civil service reform (intended to deprive the parties of the services of officeholders).

Undue focus on these legal reforms misreads the texture of party change in
the late nineteenth century, however, and a great deal of party change during this time took place at the instigation of party leaders. As Ware, as well
as Ronald N. Johnson and Gary D. Libecap, has documented, party politicians, discerning that political reforms could re-legitimate the parties, often
supported legal reforms.[8] Reynolds similarly explains that party leaders were
willing to accept "hustling" candidates because they helped cement the parties' relationship with their constituents.[9] National party leaders went further
than accepting legal reforms; they adopted a number of nationalizing reforms

---

[5] Ware, *The American Direct Primary*, 21.
[6] James Clarkson to Welker Given, August 18, 1894, box 2, Clarkson papers.
[7] McGerr, *The Decline of Popular Politics*, 98–9.
[8] Ware, *The American Direct Primary*; Johnson and Libecap, *The Federal Civil Service System and the Problem of Bureaucracy*.
[9] Reynolds, *The Demise of the American Convention System*.

of the party organizations that transformed the parties' standard operating procedures.

Central to this transformation was a cadre of national party leaders with experience in the new associational universe. William C. Whitney, advisor to Grover Cleveland, was a product of the New York City culture of Mugwump reform clubs; he was a member of the Young Men's Municipal Reform Association, and helped found a Young Men's Democratic Club in 1871.[10] In 1892, he transformed the Democratic National Committee in imitation of the associational explosion's methods. At the 1884 Democratic convention, doubts emerged about Cleveland's ability to win New York State because of his antagonism toward Tammany Hall. Cleveland's personal assistant, E. P. Apgar, suggested that organized reformers could compensate for Tammany's defection, declaring that "there are a hundred thousand men in the State of New York who do not care a snap of their finger whether the Republican party or the Democratic party, as such, shall carry the election.... They are the balance of power. You must have their vote or you cannot win."[11] Enthusing in the hostility Cleveland had earned from Tammany, Wisconsin delegate Edwin S. Bragg declared that independents "love him [Cleveland] most for the enemies he has made," and the phrase became a rallying call for the Democracy in 1884.[12]

Mark Hanna, the architect of William McKinley's 1896 victory, drew on his experiences in Ohio politics, where he saw firsthand how independent politicized associations could either sustain or interfere with party politics. During the 1880 election, he helped found the Business Men's League, which campaigned for Garfield.[13] He worked to keep labor associations friendly with the Republican party (even recommending that labor groups be given patronage) and corresponded with allies who kept watch on the Farmers' Alliance, clearly wary of the group's potential.[14]

In Nebraska, William Jennings Bryan learned the necessity of linking party to independent political associations. During his 1890 campaign for Congress, he benefited when the normally Republican-leaning veterans' group the Grand Army of the Republic voted against his Republican opponent for U.S. Congress because the latter "failed to do the right thing towards the G.A.R.," many of

[10] Hirsch, *William C. Whitney*, 61.

[11] Quoted in Robert McElroy, *Grover Cleveland: The Man and the Statesman* (New York: Harper and Brothers, 1923), 81.

[12] "Work of the Third Day," *New York Times*, July 11, 1884, 1. This phrase translated into Farmers' Alliance rhetoric, which proclaimed that it "loves Dr. [Charles W.] Macune for the enemies he has made." Goodwyn, *The Populist Moment*, 79.

[13] Dictated Statement of Senator Charles Dick to James B. Morrow, February 10, 1906, box 4, Hanna-McCormick Family Papers.

[14] Mark Hanna to Joseph B. Foraker, November 8, 1888, box 2, Hanna-McCormick Family Papers; Mark Hanna to Joseph B. Foraker, January 12, 1887, box 2, Hanna-McCormick Family Papers; John Sherman to Hanna, April 17, 1889, box 2, Hanna-McCormick Family Papers; C. H. Grosvenor to Charles Foster, October 6, 1891, box 2, Hanna-McCormick Family Papers.

whom then supported Bryan.[15] Local Democrats urged Bryan to seek alliance with the Knights of Labor,[16] and he courted an insurgent antiprohibition group that called itself the "Personal Rights League."[17] Confirming Tocqueville's observation that once individuals organize, they always know how to find one another again, one Nebraskan introduced himself to Bryan as a transplant from Brooklyn, "where as a member of the Revenue Reform Club I was greatly interested in arranging debate and carrying on an educational campaign," and asked how his organizing experience could be of use.[18]

The Farmers' Alliance was a more threatening challenge to Bryan's Nebraska Democrats. It assumed "considerable strength" in the state at the time Bryan entered political life, and he learned to treat the Alliance as a potential ally. "Would it not be well," a Nebraska Democrat advised Bryan in 1890, "to 'cast an anchor' and attempt to secure the Alliance nomination. This would practically ensure success." Another urged him to postpone a speaking engagement because it conflicted with an Alliance meeting, "and we are very anxious to have the Alliance folks out when you speak," and local Democrats collaborated with the Alliance to invite Bryan to address a joint meeting of both parties.[19]

Such lessons of the new associational politics were repeated across the nation. Philadelphia Republican Wharton Barker worked closely with non-partisan associations in New York City to counteract Tammany Hall's hold on Irish voters and learned to bring members of business associations into Republican party fundraising.[20] Elihu B. Washburne, a candidate for the Republican nomination in 1880, corresponded with the Honest Money League of the Northwest, which pursued "methods of disseminating correct information through speeches and pamphlets."[21] Presidential hopeful John Sherman was approached by members of a club in Cincinnati that "has for its leading officers business men.... it is designed especially to give particular expression that [Sherman was] the *business man's* candidate."[22] Increasingly, politicians

---

[15] G. I. Bluedorn to William Jennings Bryan, August 18, 1890, box 2, Bryan Papers. See also an almost identical letter in H. M. Boydston to Bryan, August 18, 1890, ibid.

[16] H. M. Boydston to Bryan, September 1, 1890, box 2, Bryan Papers.

[17] E. W. Schinman to Bryan, October 24, 1890, box 2, Bryan Papers.

[18] G. I. Bluedorn to Bryan, August 18, 1890, box 2, Bryan Papers; H. M. Boydston to Bryan, September 1, 1890, box 2, Bryan Papers; E. W. Schinman to Bryan, October 24, 1890, box 2, Bryan Papers; C. Shalkenbach to Bryan, October 22, 1890, box 2, Bryan Papers.

[19] J. W. Barnhart to Bryan, July 22, 1890, box 1, Bryan Papers; W. B. Morrison to Bryan, August 26, 1890, box 2, Bryan Papers; L. A. Dumphrey to Bryan, August 19, 1890, box 1, Bryan Papers; R. W. Story to Bryan, November 5, 1890, box 2, Bryan Papers; R. W. Story to Bryan, November 6, 1890, box 2, Bryan Papers.

[20] Wharton Barker to Benjamin Harrison, October 9, 1888, box 5, Wharton Barker Papers, Manuscript Division, Library of Congress; John Devoy to William Carroll, September 30, 1888, box 5, Barker Papers.

[21] M. L. Scudder, Jr., to Elihu B. Washburne, November 19, 1878, book 97, Elihu B. Washburne Papers, Manuscript Division, Library of Congress, Washington, DC.

[22] Warner Bateman to John Sherman, January 10, 1879, vol. 200, Sherman Papers, emphasis in original.

recognized the value of appealing to the growing class of associations that defined themselves as outside of the regular party organizations.

The campaign of education figures prominently in correspondence between politicians at the time and suggests that many subnational party leaders were just as willing to accept a new role for the national organizations in pursuing the new methods. When a Minnesota Republican surveyed local politics in January 1887, he advised that steps be "taken in advance to properly educate the people" and prescribed a strategy cribbed from the methods of interest associations such as the American Iron and Steel Association, asking that "some arrangement . . . be made to flood the State with protection literature during the calm between now and the National Campaign – that farmers and laborers might read, think, and understand for themselves."[23] Disgusted with a Republican National Committee speaker who held an 1888 audience captive for an hour and a half, "giving them a weak rehash of all the tariff arguments, rabid appeals to the bloody shirt, abuse of Democracy and individual Democrats," a New York Republican asked the committee "not to allow these fellows to speak at all except they promise to avoid the bloody shirt and the state ticket" and speak largely on national issues.[24] In 1890, a Nebraskan articulated a campaign style that was similar to the associational explosion's campaign of education:

my idea of making votes is, that the best plan is to talk to men one at a time and demonstrating to them that it is to their private interest to vote with your party. Of course there must be speech making, torch-light processions etc. etc. to keep up the enthusiasm of the multitude but the quiet work is what changes votes.[25]

In one New York county in 1892, the local party leadership asked the national party to send national material "to give to doubtful voters," adding their financial endorsement of the new methods: "we have some funds on hand and we think this a good way to spend it."[26] When Bryan urged Democrats in 1897 to continue educational efforts for the silver platform, one Democrat confirmed that the party planned on "carrying on an educational campaign of bimetallism during the coming winter . . . every month after the election last fall, up until the hot weather."[27] As national elites moved to adopt the new methods, they were encouraged by their local affiliates.

By the middle of the 1880s, then, the role of these extra-partisan associations in American politics was well established in the minds of those politicians who worked most effectively with them. In addition to cooperating with the new associations, however, they appealed to nationalized citizens by mimicking the associational explosion's methods, reorienting party resources and efforts toward the parties' capacities to a nationalized style of politics. The

[23] Eugene G. Hay to Barker, January 11, 1887, box 2, Barker Papers.
[24] John Devoy to Barker, October 19, 1888, box 5, Barker Papers.
[25] James B. Meikle to Bryan, August 26, 1890, box 2, Bryan Papers.
[26] J.H. Brown to Whitney, June 30, 1892, book 72, Whitney Papers.
[27] M. F. Dunlap to Bryan, November 11, 1897, box 20, Bryan Papers.

concept of an educational campaign soon entered the political lexicon as a shorthand term for a campaign that abandoned the republican values of communal appeals, compromise, localism, and mobilization, emphasizing instead substantive appeals that were national in scope, appealed to voters' interests, and questioned traditional partisan lines. The *New York Times* observed with satisfaction in 1888 that "the political campaign of the present year will be the most salutary through which the country has passed since the great civil war" because of the educational campaign's "popular agitation, arousing the attention and exciting the keen interest of the great mass of the people."[28]

The Campaign of Education

The new associations described their efforts to woo voters as "educational campaigns" and centered their promotional efforts on educating voters through directly distributed, printed political literature. The educational style was contrasted with the Jacksonian mode's conception of party principles as subject to compromise and local interpretation, as local campaigners stretched party platforms to suit public opinion; educational campaigns were designed to change public opinion, and educational campaigners attempted to do this with substantive literature crammed with facts and figures. Although the campaign of education was initially defined in opposition to partisan campaigns, however, national party leaders came to identify two advantages to educational campaigns, as Indiana Republican R. S. Robertson explained in an 1888 *North American Review* essay. First they allowed for a freer interplay of interests within the parties, helping the organizations to better aggregate and represent interests. This empowered the party, because "an organization which invites, collects, and disseminates the best thoughts of the best elements of the party, crystallizes them into declarations of principle, and brings about the most effective methods for instilling these principles into the minds of the people," is more likely to maintain popular appeal than an "organization which, in secret caucus, plots measures to thwart the will of the people." Second, by presenting the decision to vote for the party as an individual judgment rather than a communal imperative, the parties could claim that party victories were collective decisions about distinct policy commitments, empowering the parties to pursue positive policy agendas. Hence, through "the diffusion of the latest information in political affairs, intelligent action upon the information ... the collective judgment of the party attains its maximum strength."[29]

This empowered the national party in ways that the Jacksonians had hoped to avoid. Local partisan communities gave way to "the interests of the people as individual citizens," interests that heretofore had been hidden by party methods that "kept the people back from that practical study which must at last guide their action." Freed from vapid campaign ploys, the people's "sound

---

[28] "A Campaign of Education," *New York Times*, June 10, 1888, 4.
[29] R. S. Robertson, "Permanent Republican Clubs," *The North American Review*, March 1888, 248–9.

common sense can be reached and their convictions stirred," providing a clearer exercise of "that authority over the legislation and the administration of the affairs of the country."[30] Advocates of the campaign of education were quick to emphasize that traditional rallies, conventions, and public meetings were easily manipulable by local party leaders; as Ostrogorski observed, "campaign meetings are attended almost exclusively by the faithful followers of the party; not only the adherents of the opposite party but even the 'doubtful' electors keep away from them."[31] In light of the period's frequent revelations of political corruption, these traditional methods appeared even more disreputable. James Clarkson, a prominent national campaign of education advocate, recalled that "the brass band, the red light, and the mass meeting seemed suddenly to have lost their power."[32] Methods that reached the people directly, in contrast, were highlighted as opening the political process to popular judgment. From a more cynical twenty-first century perspective, it is easy to dismiss such faith in printed materials, which are also easily manipulable. What mattered at the time, however, was the contrast with the lack of substantive discussion in traditional party campaigns. A similar transformation was pushing newspapers into a more objective form of journalism, emphasizing "impartial gathering and reporting of the news" and a "growing independence of editorial opinion from partisan pressures." As one newspaper man reported in 1872, the people "want no ready-made opinions, they demand the *data* for forming independent conclusions."[33] The campaign of education provided material that resembled this journalistic trend (the presentation of factual data in an ostensibly neutral tone was a definitive feature of much of the educational literature produced by the parties), and it also allowed the parties to provide plate material (which could be inserted directly into presses) that matched the tone of the papers in which it appeared, thus compensating for journalists' increasing efforts to maintain a nonpartisan stance. In this format, the parties could convincingly claim to be appealing to voters' independent judgment.

Written material, which could be conveyed directly to voters from the parties' national committees, enabled national party leaders to project campaign themes across the country, cutting out local political middlemen, just as the Mugwump and interest associations relied on printed matter to unite their far-flung constituencies. It was, as Grover Cleveland maintained, "the manner in which access has been gained to the plain people of the land."[34] By 1896, it

---

[30] "A Campaign of Education," *New York Times*, June 10, 1888, 4.

[31] Ostrogorski, *Democracy and Political Parties*, 154.

[32] James S. Clarkson, "Annual Address of James S. Clarkson, President of the National Republican League of the United States, box 4, Clarkson Papers.

[33] Edwin Emery and Henry Ladd Smith, *The Press and America* (New York: Prentice-Hall, 1954), 317; Frank Gilbert quoted in Frank Luther Mott, *American Journalism: A History of Newspapers in the United States through 250 Years, 1690 to 1940* (New York: The Macmillan Company, 1941), 389, emphasis in original.

[34] Grover Cleveland, "Address in Response to the Toast, 'The Campaign of Education,'" Albert Ellery Bergh, ed., *Letters and Addresses of Grover Cleveland* (New York: The Unit Book Publishing Company, 1909), 276–7.

was said that Republican party headquarters "were run like a great publishing house,"[35] and the priorities of the parties had been so reoriented that it could be said that "money is used in political campaigns to convince the doubtful voter (sometimes with torch-light processions and brass bands, but oftenest now with the argument of cold facts)."[36]

The campaign of education thus upset many of the traditional inclinations of the Jacksonian party mode. "The idea that a party is an army bound by rigid rules of command, is repudiated," wrote the (Portland) *Morning Oregonian*. "[T]he true idea has taken its place that party is a voluntary association of men united to promote the common interest upon certain general principles on which they are agreed."[37] As Richard Jensen describes the new style, "the platforms and slogans of the parties became less of an army-style device to encourage morale and more of an intellectual appeal to the needs and wants of the voters... the new emphasis was on the man who might be swayed by intelligent argument."[38]

As Richard Hofstadter argues, the idea that "there is a *twofold* party division that is really natural – that men are, by instinct or impulse, natural Whigs or Tories," was central to the Jacksonians' embrasure of a two- (and only two-) party system on the principle that "controversies were most conductive to the general interest if they were waged between *two* parties, in what could even then already be called the national tradition."[39] Although the sharp division between the advocates of the few and the many was hard to maintain in an age in which both party coalitions contained a diverse sampling of social orders, postwar Americans maintained a notion of the parties as reflecting fundamental and persistent social divisions that were not easily bridged. Partisans insisted that "the reason for party divisions lies deeper than any consideration of the questions of the day. It is a curious study of habits, of temperament, of sympathies, of associations, of subtle and complex conditions of life and mind,"[40] and a party's history revealed these "tendencies" more reliably than platforms.[41] Thus, party loyalty was "a life-long ardor, a grand combination of all the loves, passions, interests, and opinions," notes Joel Silbey. "[T]here was a sense of individual and group commitment to the parties [that was] almost impossible to shake."[42] Parties were "composed of an enormous, drifting mass of individuals

---

[35] Dictated Statement of Hon. C. N. Bliss to J. B. Morrow, October 30, 1905, box 4, Hanna-McCormick Family Papers.

[36] Thompson Brown, quoted in Herbert Adams Gibbons, "Politics – how J. W. entered," in drawer 18, Herbert Adams Gibbons Card Files, John Wanamaker Papers, Pennsylvania Historical Society, Philadelphia, PA.

[37] "Another Look at Politics," (Portland, OR) *Morning Oregonian*, January 17, 1883, 2.

[38] Jensen, *The Winning of the Midwest*, 165.

[39] Hofstadter, *The Idea of a Party System*, 27, 225, emphasis in original. See also Ceaser, *Presidential Selection*, especially 135–8.

[40] "Party Divisions," (Portland) *Morning Oregonian*, February 23, 1883, 2.

[41] "Shall the South Rule?" *Denver Daily Times*, October 27, 1884, 2.

[42] Joel Silbey, *The Partisan Imperative: The Dynamics of American Politics before the Civil War* (New York: Oxford University Press, 1985), 56, 13.

who have had the same common bond of sympathy which one may get at by studying the party's history," and so it was by "broad generalizations that one can truly estimate the political organizations of the day."[43] This was no popularized simplification; as educated an observer as Theodore Roosevelt argued that "a party is a bundle of traditions, a bundle of tendencies," and thus that "there are certain questions on which the parties frequently do not commit themselves."[44]

Late-nineteenth-century party leaders abandoned this notion of parties as representing persistent divisions, arguing instead that "party identification was fluid and ephemeral and that political reorganization was the appropriate response to new conditions."[45] Instead of representing permanent interests, enduring communities, or fundamental divisions, the new national elite envisioned parties that "would be like other societies where members come and go without destroying the main body itself." Much as the Mugwumps and other components of the associational explosion hoped, the result would be to "let the existing bodies take up the new questions as they present themselves, the individuals remain the same and the human desires and plans remain unchanged."[46] The educational campaign presumed a fractious public motivated by conceptions of self-interest and in a constant process of revision; the coherence of interest embodied in the Jacksonian notion of the common man simply did not do justice to the array of interests present in the national society. Instead, a more pluralistic vision of society emerged – an amalgam of interests competing for the parties' attention. Jacksonian mode parties went into campaigns assuming a largely fixed base of support within subnational partisan communities. National party leaders emphasized the capacity of the new methods to appeal to voters "in their especial interests,"[47] transforming their localistic views through exposure to the national party organization. "There has never been a people more susceptible to the power and influence of education than the American people," exclaimed Mark Hanna, echoing the educational campaign's enthusiasm for reconstructing the polity's basic partisan alignments.[48] For Clarkson, the new strategy was similarly premised on the idea that "if all the voters in this country could be made fully to understand the principles, theories, purposes and record of the Republican party, that it would always be able to command the majority of votes in the Nation."[49] Democrats, too, were confident that Republicans could be converted through "the enlightenment of an educational

[43] "J. R. Hawley: An Eminent Republican's Views," *Cleveland Press*, April 2, 1892, 6.
[44] "Voice of a Republican," *New York Times*, May 12, 1887, 5.
[45] Keller, *Affairs of State*, 57.
[46] James P. Foster, "Permanent Republican Clubs," *The North American Review*, March 1888, 242.
[47] Clarkson to Welker Given, August 18, 1894, box 2, Clarkson papers.
[48] Mark Hanna, *Mark Hanna: His Book*, Joe Mitchell Chapple, ed. (Boston: The Chapple Publishing Co., 1904), 30–1.
[49] James S. Clarkson to Welker Given, August 18, 1894, box 2, Clarkson papers.

campaign, one where the issues shall be forced fairly and squarely upon their attention and the fullest information regarding them."[50]

Following the new idea, the *Cleveland Press* insisted that parties had become untethered from their organizational histories: "political parties never stand still. They are constantly moving one direction or another.... Political discussion, like a Storm center, cannot be localized or anchored to any fixed moorings."[51] The educational campaign allowed the parties more flexibility to respond to emergent national issues than did traditional campaigns – which was especially timely, because the invective of bloody shirt rhetoric was largely played out and the parties turned to national economic issues that affected voters' pocketbooks more directly.[52] National party leaders could respond nimbly, free from the restraints of sluggish local party establishments; voters would require substantive campaigns because the issues would never be completely familiar to them given that they would be renewed in each election cycle to keep the parties relevant. As Jerrold Rusk demonstrates, other institutional changes of the period, such as the adoption of the secret ballot and direct primary laws, encouraged voters to react quickly to short-term electoral forces by breaking down the mechanisms that enforced traditional party loyalty.[53] However, it was only the parties' capacity to envision new methods of reaching these voters that kept the parties in command of the American political system. California Republican Morris Estee understood this, linking a party's success to its ability to adapt to changing interests: "men live, die, and are forgotten, but the principles of a great party must be made to fit the interests of a great people."[54]

Cleveland advocated the campaign of education, and in a series of talks in 1890, he outlined his understanding of its implications. The public, he argued, was less easily mobilized by traditional methods and was more willing to reflect on the parties' pledges; in fact, making policies clear became the new imperative of party work. "The labor of [voters'] education in the campaign," he argued, "has consisted in persuading them to hear us; to examine the theories in party organizations and the ends to which they lead; to recall the promises of political leadership and the manner in which such promises have been redeemed." The campaign of education invited voters into a conversation with the parties, "to counsel with us as to the means by which their condition could be improved."[55] This obliged the party to "be prepared to meet all the wants of the people as they arise, and to furnish a remedy for every threatening evil" and to "urge constantly upon our fellow-citizens of this day and generation the sufficiency

[50] Melbert B. Cary to Grover Cleveland, August 19, 1892, series 11, box 3, Cleveland Papers.

[51] "At Issue: The Questions Face to Face," *Cleveland Press*, May 14, 1892, 2.

[52] Hirshon, *Farewell to the Bloody Shirt*; Jensen, *The Winning of the Midwest*, 177.

[53] See Jerrold Rusk, "Comment: The American Electoral Universe: Speculation and Evidence," *American Political Science Review* (September 1974), 1049.

[54] Morris M. Estee to James S. Clarkson, May 20, 1897, box 2, Clarkson Papers.

[55] Cleveland, "Address in Response to the Toast, 'The Campaign of Education,'" in Bergh, *Letters and Addresses of Grover Cleveland*, 277.

of the principles of true Democracy."[56] Echoing the associational explosion, Cleveland rejected the image of voters as ideal republican citizens because "the busy activity of their occupations, and the consequent neglect of political subjects," kept many people away from politics. The campaign of education, for Cleveland, was oriented toward a public that was presumed to be more narrowly focused on individual concerns than on homogeneous community interests.[57]

Enhancing the National Committees

Adopting the campaign of education as a model for national party campaigns required more than printed material. It required a national party apparatus possessing organizational capacities to reach voters directly, bypassing state and local organizations. In the Jacksonian mode, however, national party organizations were essentially nonexistent. As Paul Kleppner explains, "the appearance of a hierarchical or pyramidal organization has always been wholly illusory, for it has never been a hierarchy in which the flow of authority has been from the top downward as in a corporation."[58] Educational campaigns required a fundamental reordering of the national party organizations. National party leaders struggled to shift the organizational balance of power away from the local party franchises to the national party organization, concentrating resources in national campaign management. As Clarkson declared in 1888, the parties were thus "nationalized and made so broad as to cover every state in the Union."[59] This is not to say that the national parties *became* pyramidal, hierarchical organizations but that the assumption of power by the national committees was a watershed moment in the development of a new idea of party that accepted a larger role for party nationalization. The newly independent national committees conducted national elections separately from the subnational local party framework even as they absorbed relatively little direct control over subnational party organizations. Indeed, in the decentralized American political system, it is difficult to see how the local organizations could have been eliminated. They remained considerably free from oversight and in many cases continued traditional campaign styles into the twentieth century. Nonetheless, the legitimacy of independent national campaign apparatuses was secure.

There were two transformative elements of late-nineteenth-century national committee centralization. First, national committees became capable of conducting national campaigns independently of subnational organizations. This involved the creation of distinctly national campaign committees and the maintenance of permanent national committee offices, as well as a distinct

56 Cleveland, "Address in Response to the Toast, 'The Principles of True Democracy,'" in Bergh, *Letters and Addresses of Grover Cleveland*, 282.
57 Cleveland, "Address in Response to the Toast, 'The Campaign of Education,'" 277.
58 Kleppner, *The Third Electoral System*, 208.
59 Quoted in Hirshon, *Farewell to the Bloody Shirt*, 157–8.

national fundraising apparatus that enabled the national committee to act without regard to the financial support of subnational organizations. Second, as explained in the next chapter, the national committees encouraged the formation of a national network of party clubs, modeled on the new national associations of the associational explosion, ancillary to party regularity, and devoted to educational methods of campaigning. National committee independence was more enduring, but the clubs demonstrate the extent to which national party leaders reconceptualized the party-in-the-electorate – providing a body for the new national organizational head.

Jacksonian mode national committees exerted little control over subnational organizations in the conduct of national campaigns. Democrats did not even create a national committee until 1848, when "coming as late as they did, and in a nation still decentralized in focus, the national committees served less to direct or coordinate matters than to do whatever they could to help the state committees throughout the Union."[60] By the time national committees were established, years of practice had taught subnational organizations self-reliance, and the expertise they developed as a result strengthened the republican inclinations of the Jacksonian party mode. National committee members were responsible and responsive to regular state party committees; they spent most of their careers working for their state or local party organizations. In contrast, as Democrat Chauncey Black observed with chagrin, "the National Committee has been, throughout its whole history, an expediency committee. It goes out of business with the conclusion of the Presidential campaigns."[61] Fundraising was also localized; national committee members raised campaign funds in their home states and lobbied for national funds to be sent to their states' campaigns. Clarkson recalled that "the National Committeeman has never been given authority under any Committee for twenty years, to my knowledge, to expend money in his State on his own judgment."[62]

In addition, state delegations to national conventions often chose national committee members before presidential candidates were selected, so national committee selection was not linked to presidential candidate selection; this made for cross-purposes between candidates and committees.[63] In 1884 and 1888, for example, although Grover Cleveland ran as a tariff reformer, the national party chairman was an avowed protectionist who was accused of campaigning unenthusiastically for Cleveland and who later went to work for the protectionist American Iron and Steel Association.[64]

---

[60] Silbey, *The American Political Nation*, 52.
[61] "Work of Democratic Clubs," *New York Times*, February 9, 1894, 4; "The Democratic Societies," *New York Times*, May 27, 1889, 4.
[62] Clarkson to H. G. McMillan, October 5, 1896, box 2, Clarkson Papers.
[63] Ralph Goldman, *The National Party Chairmen and Committees: Factionalism at the Top*, (New York: M.E. Sharpe, 1990), 129.
[64] See Allan Nevins, *Grover Cleveland: A Study in Courage* (New York: Dodd, Mead & Company, 1934), 416; and Hirshon, *Farewell to the Bloody Shirt*, 145.

Lacking national authority and cooperative relationships at the top, the national organizations initially struggled to impose campaigns of education on recalcitrant state organizations. Thus, in 1888, "nothing was done by the so-called Democratic leaders" in Oregon, complained a Democratic editor; the chairman of the state committee had done "less than nothing. After the election we found two waggon [sic] loads of campaign literature addressed to him in the Portland P.O. which he had refused time and again to take away and distribute."[65] This was especially disheartening because the Republican margin of victory in Oregon in 1888 tripled that of 1884, which had been tantalizingly close (only 2,256 votes separated Democrats from Republicans in 1884 – and in 1876 and 1880, the vote had been even closer). A New York State Committee representative grumbled in 1892 that the national organization wanted to start the campaign too early, when "the farmers up the State are busy with their crops. And it's too hot. There will be time enough when the cool weather comes. It would be unusual to begin active work so soon," (this in a state that swung its presidential vote back and forth between the parties every presidential election year between 1876 and 1896.)[66] From Ohio, where the 1892 margin of difference between the two major parties was 577 votes (and where more than 40,000 voted for third parties), one Democrat warned in 1892 that "the impression is very general here amongst Democrats who are supposed to know that it is the purpose of the State Democratic Campaign Committee to make a 'still hunt' of this contest rather than a boldly aggressive fight," a tactic antithetical to the lofty goals of the campaign of education.[67] National committees had no authority over local organizations, no direct relationship with the party-in-the-electorate, and no way to counteract local shirking.[68]

Even where contrary motives did not exist, some subnational organizations were ill-equipped to handle the new campaigns. "The tariff issue is a hard one to fight in the country," reported one commentator from New York State, "where the leaders of the towns and villages are unable to go deeply into a subject that requires special training and a good knowledge of political economy." As a result, "whether from want of knowledge, absence of system, or lack of ability, the interests of the national ticket certainly suffered at the hands of the State Committee in the 'pivotal' State" of New York, in the 1888 election, and "the principal [educational] work in the campaign is being done by patriotic citizens not necessarily affiliated with the party organization."[69] Campaigning by "patriotic" amateurs was an ideal, but national party leaders recognized that to make the educational campaign effective, they would have to formalize the national organizations.

---

[65] G. P. McCall to Whitney, July 7, 1892, book 73, Whitney Papers.
[66] "Politics at the Oriental," *New York Times*, July 25, 1892, 5.
[67] Walter H. Beecher to Cleveland, October 2, 1892, series 11, box 3, Cleveland Papers.
[68] The election returns–based information in this paragraph comes from Walter Dean Burnham, *Presidential Ballots, 1836–1892* (Baltimore: Johns Hopkins Press, 1955), 633, 677.
[69] George Walton Green, "Victory for the Plucking," *New York Times*, June 8, 1892, 9.

As national elites sought to gain control over national campaigns, they began to operate the national committees on a more permanent basis, mainly to prepare for educational campaigns. National party leaders believed that such appeals were best conducted by long-term campaigns that persuaded voters over time, rather than by launching educational efforts in the heat of election season. Educational campaigns started earlier than the Jacksonian norm (which usually saw campaign activity begin in earnest as late as October), "so that even more than the ordinary period for organization will be afforded."[70] One local Democrat explained "in the heat of the fight the best of campaign literature amounts to naught, but in the next two months [July and August of 1892] much can be accomplished with strong, readable matter, put up on an attractive style, with suggestive head lines."[71] Party leaders learned that the new methods required sustained organized efforts; for this reason, they made the work of the national committees permanent. By the 1880s and 1890s, the campaign of education had been extended to cover nearly the entire year before an election. Because voters were more inclined to leisure than to politics, the "time to educate" was "when the minds of men are comparatively at rest or not excited by partisan feeling."[72] Arguing for more permanent work by the national committee, Democratic chairman Calvin Brice credited his party's successes in the off-year elections of 1889 to the long-term effects of the national committee's work during and since the presidential campaign of 1888. "The results of these elections," he explained, "show the effects of what was sneeringly alluded to by some last year as the educational campaign."[73] The next year, Republican chairman Matthew Quay established, for the first time, a permanent party headquarters in Washington, "in order that the party's interests throughout the Nation may not be lost sight of between Presidential elections." Quay's focus on national breadth as well as temporal endurance reflected his recognition of the new demands of campaigning; the campaign of education required persistent work and thus a persistent organizational home; "very little practical good is accomplished by the distribution of political literature during an exciting campaign," Quay observed.[74]

In 1892, Democrats further consolidated national power. The Democratic National Committee authorized its executive committee to maintain permanent operations and to create two specialized committees to coordinate campaign activity. An advisory committee would supervise fundraising; further, a campaign committee would "be the working organization of the campaign, and by division into sub-committees it will attend to the details of the work, such as the distribution of literature, the arrangements for speakers, the securing

[70] Samuel Tilden to Daniel Scott Lamont, September 11, 1871, container 1, Daniel Scott Lamont Papers, Manuscript Division, Library of Congress.
[71] R. B. McCrory to Whitney, June 25, 1892, book 71, Whitney Papers.
[72] A. J. Pethoud to Bryan, November 9, 1894, box 3, Bryan Papers.
[73] "Chairman Brice Is Delighted," *New York Times*, November 7, 1889, 1.
[74] "Coupons for Party Service," *New York Times*, May 8, 1890, 4.

of reports from the several States, and the outlining of plans of battle in the various sections of the country," effectively insulating day-to-day campaign operations from the national committee. It was composed of only nine members – chosen by the national chairman – who were not necessarily members of the national committee, which significantly displaced the Jacksonian mode imperative of incorporating all states; and no recourse to the full range of subnational jurisdictions was necessary. The campaign committee was also "given more authority in the ordering of the campaign than has been the custom," enabling its members to shape national campaign strategy more effectively than ever before. Separating the three functions recognized the growing sense of the party as a coherent national entity.[75]

This institutionalization of the national committees proved enduring. Elmer Dover, who worked for the Republican National Committee in 1896, recalled that "before the campaign of 1896 the National Committee headquarters in Washington were open for four or five months. After the campaign the headquarters were nominally closed but were actually continued for a year with some fifteen or twenty clerks." (Dover may have forgotten Quay's earlier efforts or not known about them, because Dover had not been involved in national politics until 1896.[76]) By 1912, political scientist Jesse Macy found that "the powers of the national committee have in recent years been brought more prominently into public notice than ever before."[77]

The national chairmanship also took on new relevance, even as it gradually fell under the influence of the presidential candidates. A trend toward distinction in the national chairmanship began in the legal wrangling that followed the controversial election of 1876.[78] The candidates were unwilling to make public statements in the tense atmosphere, so the party chairmen, especially Republican Zachariah Chandler, took on a larger public role than before. Chandler was the first Republican chairman with a genuine national reputation before his elevation to the chairmanship, having served as a U.S. senator and as secretary of the interior; by accepting the position, he lent it prominence. Chandler's coordination of state party efforts and public pronouncements following the contested election were so visible as to cause uproar among Democrats and earn praise from Republicans. In the burst of public attention, the chairmanship came "to assume exaggerated proportions."[79]

---

[75] Untitled article [Resolutions in Regard to Democratic Committees], no date [1892], book 72, Whitney Papers; "Already Hard at Work," *New York Times*, July 28, 1892, 8; "Harrity Made Chairman," *New York Times*, July 22, 1892, 1.

[76] Dictated Statement of Mr. Elmer Dover to J. B. Morrow, September 1905, box 4, Hanna-McCormick Family Papers. Dover can be forgiven for his omission of Quay's work; the Pennsylvanian had opposed the nomination of William McKinley. As explained in Chapter 6, Hanna prided himself on running the RNC by "business methods," which he claimed were unknown in the party at that point.

[77] Macy, *Party Organization and Machinery*, 84.

[78] Marcus, *Grand Old Party*, 26.

[79] "Mr. Chandler's Telegrams," *New York Times*, November 17, 1876, 1; "Hayes and Wheeler Elected," *New York Times*, December 14, 1876, 1; "The Secret Investigations," *New York*

Chandler's successor, Senator Don Cameron – another politician of national renown – used his position to promote Grant's renomination in 1880, maneuvering on the eve of the national convention for parliamentary procedures that would secure the enforcement of the unit rule. His overreaching discredited him, first in the public eye – trained by Chandler to watch the chairmanship – and then in his own committee, but the episode drew attention to the strategic position of the national chairmanship. Dispirited by Garfield's nomination, Cameron resigned, and the national committee turned to the candidate for guidance for the first time in its history, setting a precedent for the selection of chairmen who were close to the candidates.[80]

In 1884, Republican chairman Benjamin Franklin Jones continued to enhance the visibility of the position, issuing "An Appeal to the South," urging southern Republicans to drop the bloody shirt (in cooperation with the candidate, James Blaine, who hoped to focus attention on the tariff instead of war issues) and asking for "the sympathy and cooperation of all the citizens of all sections who recognize the supremacy of the great and living questions that rise above all old issues." Jones's term was prescient: asserting control over the use of bloody shirt rhetoric by campaign orators was among the earliest efforts of the national committees to shape the content of campaigns. Under Quay, the Republican National Committee patrolled the speeches of Republican orators, urging them to avoid sectional issues and firing those who refused. By 1888, concludes Stanley Hirshon, "the National Committee controlled the campaign," at least insofar as it enforced the decision to "ignore completely the race issue."[81]

A similar consolidation was underway in the Democratic party. The *New York Times* reported that in the 1892 Democratic campaign plan, with its variegated committees designed to allow the national committee more control over the national campaign, "the Chairmanship of the National Committee is made a position of unusual importance and influence in the conduct of the campaign."[82] Chairman William Harrity's close relationship with Cleveland and his chief strategist William C. Whitney only further enhanced the position in that year. Remarking on the "unusual circumstances" surrounding the first meeting of the Democratic National Committee after the convention nominated Cleveland, a reporter noted that Cleveland himself was present and that Whitney, although not a member of the committee, held a proxy vote and was "one of the leading spirits in the committee meeting." (It is likely that

Times, January 15, 1877, 1; "General Political News," *New York Times*, January 16, 1877, 1; "Management of the Campaign," *New York Times*, January 21, 1877, 2; William Chandler to James Garfield, June 14, 1880, book 49, William Chandler Papers, Manuscript Division, Library of Congress, Washington, DC.

[80] Marcus, *Grand Old Party*, 39. See also Goldman, *The National Party Chairmen and Committees*, 127–31.

[81] Hirshon, *Farewell to the Bloody Shirt*, 163–4, 125. For Hirshon, this is a point of criticism; he suggests that this shift betrayed southern Blacks to southern Democrats.

[82] Untitled article, *New York Times*, July 22, 1892, 4.

Whitney himself wrote the resolutions that restructured the national organization's work in that year and forced the choice of Harrity as chairman.[83]) A close relationship between the national candidate and the national chairman was becoming routine.

On the Republican side, similar evolutions were afoot in 1892. Clarkson, who succeeded Quay as chairman, spent his brief term angling for Blaine's nomination to replace Harrison and was forced out by allies of the president, who argued that "the President ought to have something to say on the question [on the chairmanship], and they are at a loss to understand how he can select the man who was going round the country for weeks before the convention predicting that Harrison could not carry the country."[84] Clarkson stepped down, and, following the Garfield precedent, Harrison sent the national committee a list of five potential chairmen. From this list, the committee selected William Campbell, who named an executive committee composed of Harrison allies and then resigned in a little over a week, precipitating a succession crisis but securing an executive committee friendly to the president. For nearly two weeks, the committee remained leaderless because a number of prominent politicians refused to accept the chairmanship.[85] Finally, Montana's Thomas Carter took the position, although it was clear that he was the president's surrogate, whom the party had determined could run his own campaign. Carter thus declared that "Mr. Harrison intends to superintend his own campaign through personal agents."[86] As Robert Marcus concludes, "the administration had taken the responsibility for naming the chairman away from the national committee."[87]

The fiasco indicated not a decline in the chairman's significance but growing pains in the evolution of an independent national organization. Harrison never lost control of the committee; indeed, at every step it was agreed that it was the president's committee. The *New York Times* editorialized that this was the root of the problem:

if it is understood that the President is to conduct his own campaign and that the Chairman of the National Committee is to act in a ministerial capacity, and as the ministerial agent of the candidate rather than of the committee or the party, it is natural that leading politicians should be reluctant to consider themselves as candidates for that position.[88]

---

[83] "Harrity Made Chairman," *New York Times*, July 22, 1892, 1. This conclusion is borne out by the existence of a handwritten memorandum outlining these changes in Whitney's papers; Untitled item [Resolutions in Regard to Democratic Committees], no date [1892], book 72, Whitney Papers.

[84] "The President's Dilemma," *New York Times*, June 27, 1892, 4.

[85] "Whom Can Harrison Find?" *New York Times*, July 14, 1892, 3; "The Headsman Beheaded," *New York Times*, June 28, 1892, 5; "Campbell Will Not Serve," *New York Times*, July 6, 1892, 1; "Campbell Picks His Nine," *New York Times*, July 8, 1892, 4.

[86] "Carter's Five Advisors," *New York Times*, July 26, 1892, 8; Sievers, *Benjamin Harrison*, 237.

[87] Marcus, *Grand Old Party*, 176–7.

[88] "The Chairmanship Difficulty," *New York Times*, July 16, 1892, 4.

The association of the national chairman with the interests of the national candidate further solidified the national committee's independence. This was particularly critical for Harrison; his troubles with the committee stemmed in part from his quarrels over patronage with Quay and Thomas Platt of New York, both of whom controlled their state organizations (and influenced the choice of their national committee representatives). Harrison had come to share the realization of a number of Republicans that "if there is to be any work done in New York [and Pennsylvania] for Harrison, it must be done by the National Committee" because "the State Committee [would] do nothing for Mr. Harrison."[89]

The increasing profile of national elites whose political status grew out of their service to national candidates marks the evolution of the national committee as an independent entity. John Wanamaker was prominent for his national department store chain, but he earned political fame and position (as postmaster general) from his service to the Republican advisory committee. Whitney, who served as Cleveland's convention manager, became a sort of folk hero among Cleveland supporters. Hanna was acknowledged with a standing ovation at the 1896 national convention, and cartoon satire of him became iconic during the McKinley administration. By 1896, according to Macy, the chairman had "been constantly before the country as a distinct political force."[90] The centralized national party committees served presidential ambitions, a theme that takes on greater focus in Chapters 5 and 6.

Fundraising and National Organization

A key change in national committee capacity was the development of an independent national fundraising apparatus, which gave national committees greater leeway to conduct campaigns. Traditional national committees raised money on a paradigmatically Jacksonian basis: state committeemen were responsible for raising money within their home states. There was a reluctance to share money across state borders, which hampered the parties' ability to speed money to those locations that needed it most in a national campaign; national committees were therefore at the mercy of the generosity of state organizations. When state organizations faced shortfalls, they routinely turned to party leaders in flush states (who could be prevailed upon for personal reasons) rather than to the national committee (which could not require contributions). This did little to coordinate national action; more problematically, it failed to ensure sufficient funds for national campaigns. The problem was compounded in states where the wealthier elements of society were aligned chiefly with one party, as Democrats found in New England and Republicans found in the

---

[89] "Harrison Fears New York," *New York Times*, July 1, 1892, 1.
[90] Macy, *Party Organization and Machinery*, 84–5.

South.[91] More troubling, state organizations often used what national money they did raise to maintain their own organizations, and thus some complained that "whenever money may be distributed by the Committee it will naturally go into the hands of a class of men with which he affiliates and if so, a large portion of it will be lost."[92]

Local fundraising was sufficient for mobilization campaigns, which relied on resources that local voters could readily provide, especially the time to participate in parades and rallies.[93] The campaign of education complicated this arrangement; producing, printing, and distributing campaign literature over longer periods of time raised campaigns costs, which were also more concentrated, rather than dispersed into state-specific efforts. As Johnson and Libecap report, presidential campaign expenses jumped from a mere $300,000 in 1872 to $1,850,000 in 1876, to $4,050,000 in 1892, and $4,025,000 in 1896.[94] Charles Dawes, who kept the books for the Republican National Committee in 1896, reported that fully 29 percent of his budget went to expenses associated with the party's literary department and shipping (a figure that incidentally approximated the budget priorities of the Young Men's Democratic Club in 1888). Only direct payments to state organizations amounted to a higher percentage, with 46 percent of funds going to that source. A mere 7 percent went to campaign speakers, and 13 percent went to "organization," that is, the costs associated with funding Republican clubs and rallies.[95]

The campaign of education's year-round operation also strained state organizations' resources. As Reynolds points out, the reluctance to begin campaigns early contributed to the absence of substance in rushed late fall campaigns.[96] Advocates of the campaign of education realized that if national leaders expected greater substance and long-term campaign efforts, they would have to contribute significantly to their costs. Early campaigns meant tapping regular donors earlier and more often, straining traditional fundraising methods.[97] A common refrain was echoed in 1892 by a Virginia Democratic district committee member who found his state's executive committee reluctant to spend money even in October: "we need some funds *now* – one dollar

[91] B. B. Smalley to Whitney, July 3, 1892, book 72, Whitney Papers. See H. M. Stewart and C. J. Jones to John Sherman, March 20, 1880, vol. 208, John Sherman Papers, Library of Congress; Foraker to Hanna, September 15, 1886, box 2, Joseph Benson Foraker Papers, Manuscript Division, Library of Congress, Washington, DC; Hanna to Foraker, September 25, 1886; and Foraker to Hanna, November 5, 1886.

[92] C. S. Gary to Cleveland, August 18, 1892, series 11, box 3, Cleveland Papers; see James W. Scott to Whitney, August 13, 1892, book 75, Whitney Papers.

[93] Henry D. Strocker, Jr., to Bryan, December 20, 1895, box 3, Bryan Papers.

[94] Johnson and Libecap, *The Federal Civil Service System and the Problem of Bureaucracy*, 23.

[95] Charles Dawes, *A Journal of the McKinley Years*, Bascom N. Timmons, ed. (Chicago: The Lakeside Press, 1950), 106.

[96] Reynolds, *The Demise of the American Convention System*, 21.

[97] Wilson S. Bissell to Lamont, October 23, 1882, carton 81, Lamont Papers.

is worth *more now* than 2 on day of election."⁹⁸ The state committee chair insisted that he had "exhausted every resource within sight" and yet raised only $15,000 by early October.⁹⁹ From an Iowa Republican came the report that fundraising was difficult for the 1896 campaign of education there: "we are doing three or four times as much work as ever before in a campaign ... and of course you can well understand the expense is very heavy" because it was "necessary to open Headquarters and commence our campaign a month earlier than usual." The problem was that "we have had great difficulty in raising the necessary means to carry on our campaign" and that "neither the congressional nor the national committee were prepared to meet the emergencies of the case. They could not furnish us with the literature we needed in time to meet the requirements of the situation."¹⁰⁰ These pleas carried special significance in a tightly contested electoral environment: with the party facing a nationwide threat from the Populists, a meek investment in the novel educational campaign strategy would prove more disastrous than a traditional campaign and would have undermined trust in the national leadership. Enforcement of the Pendleton Act also dried up a major traditional source of campaign funds by prohibiting financial assessments of officeholders, and parties increasingly turned to wealthy donors to make up the shortfall.¹⁰¹ As noted in Chapter 2, the newly politicized associational community identified itself as a purifying force in politics. These new donors preferred making donations when they could be assured that party funds would be spent for educational purposes rather than servicing the traditional local party establishment. They also preferred clear accounting, resented repeated informal appeals from politicians, and demanded transparent finance committees as an assurance that their donations were used "properly." They increasingly pooled their donations in the hands of spokesmen (like Republicans Mark Hanna, Wharton Barker, and John Wanamaker and Democrat William Whitney) who could oversee expenditures and maximize influence.¹⁰² Donors such as Philadelphian John Sellers favored

⁹⁸ George Cassell et al. to Whitney, October 29, 1888, book 55, Whitney Papers, emphasis in original. See also Hugh Preston to Whitney, October 31, 1888. Preston, chairman of the Executive Committee of the Montgomery County Committee, also reported that the State Committee was not giving enough money.

⁹⁹ Basil B. Gordon to Whitney, October 7, 1892, book 76, Whitney Papers.

¹⁰⁰ H. G. M. McMillan to Clarkson, September 5, 1896, box 2, Clarkson Papers.

¹⁰¹ Marcus, *Grand Old Party*, 86–7, 79; Skowronek, *Building a New American State*, 74–8. The congressional campaign committees were more affected than national committees by the Pendleton Act because they relied more heavily on assessment of officeholders, most of whom had been appointed at the request of members of Congress. Weakening the former actually cleared the way for the consolidation of power by the latter. Macy, *Party Organization and Machinery*, 31–2. Marcus, *Grand Old Party*, 25; "Asking for More Money," *New York Times*, August 24, 1884, 7; "Political Assessments," *New York Times*, June 20, 1882, 3; "The Party Assessors," *New York Times*, July 26, 1882, 3.

¹⁰² Ohio Republicans such as William Hahn found that Hanna's standing within the business community helped establish trust among donors and urged that out-of-state donors "should send [donations] through you, because I believed that if we were allowed to use your name

giving only to "authorized Committees appointed for the purpose of collecting Campaign Funds," believing that "the money thus collected, will do more good in the hands of an organized association for its distribution, than through individual effort" and declared their intention to forego such individual efforts.[103] To translate businessmen into party funders required a formalization of party methods – the transformation of party into something more like a business.

The parties responded. In 1884, the Democratic National Committee distributed circulars reassuring financiers that their donations would be "expended with economy and fidelity, and accounted for publicly at the conclusion of the canvass."[104] Hoping to prevent cross-purposes and to ensure that the national committee could control as much of these new resources as possible, Republican Chairman Quay routinized the party's fundraising by keeping a list of "registered contributors" to the national party to prevent multiple appeals. He sent donors certificates to distribute to associates, allowing individuals to become fundraisers and thus tapping donors who might have been reluctant to give directly to the parties.[105]

The real innovator of the 1888 campaign was John Wanamaker. He was the spokesman of a pool of protectionist Pennsylvania businessmen donors who opposed National Chairman Quay locally and who used their fundraising prowess to drive a wedge between Quay and Harrison. Seeking to isolate Wanamaker, Quay offered to make him Pennsylvania's representative on the Republican National Committee. Wanamaker refused to serve in this capacity; instead, arguing that "old methods would not elect Harrison," he recommended the formation of an "Advisory Board to National Committee made up of business men, with a treasurer" that would be "limited in number" (thus not composed of representatives from each state) and given the "power to supervise expenditure as well as [the] raising of money."[106] This advisory committee played into the business community's growing sense of its own role as a reforming element of American politics by promising to bypass local politicians and reach national political leaders directly. Wanamaker insisted on serving as chairman of this committee, from whence he coordinated expenditures and contributions, quelling donors' concerns about how their funds were used by emphasizing his adherence to business methods.[107] Wanamaker's

---

it would be of vast benefit to us." William M. Hahn to Hanna, September 30, 1891, box 2, Hanna-McCormick Family Papers. See also Marshall Jewell to Barker, September 30, 1880, box 1, Barker Papers; Marshall Jewell to Barker, October 3, 1880, box 1, Barker Papers.

[103] John Sellers, Jr. to Barker, August 6, 1888, box 4, Barker Papers.

[104] Manton Marble, "Draft of an Address by the Democratic National Committee to the Democracy of the US," August 1884, book 57, Manton Marble Papers, Manuscript Division, Library of Congress, Washington, DC.

[105] "Coupons for Party Service," *New York Times*, May 8, 1890, 4.

[106] Herbert Adams Gibbons, "Pres. Campaign (1888) – J. W.'s rôle," drawer 18, Herbert Adams Gibbons Card Files, Wanamaker Papers.

[107] Quoted in Herbert Adams Gibbons, "Pres. Campaign (1888) – Wanamaker's methods in raising money," drawer 18, Gibbons Card Files, Wanamaker Papers.

relations with Quay revealed the subversive implications of the new committee; he "was opposed to the old methods of the party managers"[108] and used the advisory committee to bypass subnational leaders and direct national expenditures in ways that he saw fit. In 1892, a Republican advisory committee was set up to bypass New York party leader Thomas Platt, who was opposed to Harrison's reelection and who, as head of the New York Republican State Committee, controlled his state's national committeeman. Harrison approved the selection of the advisory committee personally, and when the committee sent a representative to distribute money to Western states, it was Harrison's personal friend Louis Michener who went.[109]

Whitney, like Wanamaker, declined to serve on the Democratic National Committee in 1892 even though he was popularly acknowledged as the mastermind of Cleveland's unprecedented third nomination and was thought to deserve the chairmanship.[110] Instead, he chaired a newly created advisory committee, which had, with Whitney in mind, been authorized by the Democratic National Convention to be composed of members "from without the membership of the Democratic National Committee" and appointed by the national chairman.[111] The committee would "devote itself to what may be called the 'larger politics' of the campaign," as a member of the national committee described it,[112] although it was "generally understood that the function of the committee is not to be that of giving advice, but of raising money"[113] (the name appears to have been intended to convey the impression that donors not only gave money but guided the conduct of the campaign). Its membership was "formed of business men all over the country," chiefly big donors who could also be counted on to solicit donations from their peers – thus formalizing the pooling of donations that had occurred in previous elections.[114] With Whitney's aid, the Democrats raised "as much or more money than the Republicans" for the first time since the Civil War.[115]

[108] Herbert Adams Gibbons, "Pres. Campaign (1888) – J. W.'s not optimistic," drawer 18, Gibbons Card Files, Wanamaker Papers. See also Kehl, *Boss Rule in the Gilded Age*, 97.
[109] "Carter's Five Advisors," *New York Times*, July 26, 1892, 8; "Michener in Nebraska," *New York Times*, October 14, 1892, 5; Marcus, *Grand Old Party*, 178.
[110] Whitney received a number of letters to this effect, suggesting that, in the words of Boston Mayor Nathan Matthews, "there is a wide spread and, in my judgment, well founded opinion that the value of your name at the head of the committee would, of itself, be a great source of strength to the party in the campaign throughout the nation." Nathan Matthews to Whitney, June 27, 1892, book 71, Whitney Papers.
[111] Untitled item [Resolutions in Regard to Democratic Committees], no date [1892], book 72, Whitney Papers.
[112] "Already Hard at Work," *New York Times*, July 28, 1892, 8.
[113] Untitled article, *New York Times*, August 11, 1892, 4.
[114] Dictated Statement of Hon. C. N. Bliss to J. B. Morrow, October 30, 1905, box 4, Hanna-McCormick Family Papers; "To Capture Mr. Platt," *New York Times*, July 24, 1892, 13; "Five Hours of Conference," *New York Times*, August 13, 1892, 5.
[115] Hirsch, *William C. Whitney*, 238, 209.

As Republicans used their advisory committee to bypass unfriendly subnational politicians, Democrats used it to thwart their own localistic cliques. Tammany Hall, which opposed Cleveland's renomination, had agreed to support the campaign only after Cleveland's allies made a number of concessions, including the selection of Tammany ally Robert B. Roosevelt as National Committee Treasurer.[116] When Boston Mugwump Josiah Quincy, heading the critical Literature Bureau (which printed and distributed campaign literature), complained that Roosevelt refused to fund the bureau's operations, Roosevelt was gradually shut out of the party's most important fundraising efforts; he complained to Whitney: "I suppose that a good deal of the money you get will be distributed directly as has been done without it going through my hands at all" (it had instead been distributed by the advisory committee).[117] Roosevelt was not even allowed to know the names of donors or informed of meetings of the finance committee.[118] Cut off from institutionalized access to the national party, subnational party leaders were correspondingly limited in their ability to control campaign expenditures, either for corrupt or for merely traditional ends.

Beyond their ability to access funds that would not otherwise have been entrusted to the parties, advisory committees helped establish an independent role for the national committees themselves. This was a departure from the Jacksonian mode's restraints on the independence of the national committee. Freed from the oversight of the localistic elements of the party organization, national party leaders were able to pursue campaign strategies independently of subnational party leaders. Although nominally independent of the national committees, the advisory committees were ready at hand when party leaders with a national perspective rose to party leadership.

Hanna, for instance, had a firm grasp of the committee's usefulness. Hanna had learned the value of centralized financial administration during his career in state politics. For John Sherman's 1891 Senate Campaign, Hanna perfected a statewide organization in Ohio designed to provide central direction of funds and keep expenditures efficient and legal, "so as not to engage any officer of the Government." He systematized the distribution of funds by channeling money to competitive districts, ensuring efficiency and weakening opportunities for graft.[119] When Hanna became national chairman, he used the advisory committee to raise record amounts and to control fastidiously the conduct of the campaign, organizing "the business of collecting contributions as carefully as that of distributing reading matter" and demonstrating business methods that appealed to business donors. He appointed "responsible men" to work within their localities to collect national funds. He made assessments

---

[116] Cleveland to Whitney, August 23, 1892, book 75, Whitney Papers.

[117] Robert B. Roosevelt to Whitney, September 25, 1892, book 76, Whitney Papers.

[118] Robert B. Roosevelt to Cleveland, October 22, 1892, series 11, box 10, Cleveland Papers.

[119] John Sherman to Hanna, October 6, 1891, box 2, Hanna-McCormick Family Papers.

on businesses – rather than officeholders – basing his requests on the value of their assets and "always did his best to convert the practice from a matter of political begging on the one side and donating on the other into a matter of systematic assessment according to the means of the individual and institution."[120] "I think that Hanna himself decides how the money shall be expended and divided,"[121] remarked Clarkson with equal measures envy and admiration.

In his pivotal essay on the "System of 1896," Walter Dean Burnham charged that the election of 1896 saw the elevation of business interests in American politics and argued that the subsequent decline of participation protected the capitalist economy from more radical claims on wealth. Although he offered no evidence for this assertion other than the sudden demobilization of the electorate – there was, for instance, no evidence provided of collusion between business interests and the parties – he concluded that "the blunt alternative to party government is the concentration of political power...in the hands of those who already possess concentrated economic power."[122] The evidence Burnham needed might well be construed out of the rise of the advisory committees, but this is a limited reading of the evidence. In the new willingness to appeal directly to the self-interest of businessmen, one discerns a willingness to abandon the republican notion of a common public interest and a turn to a more calculating appreciation of individual interest as a legitimate motive force in party politics. However, this new view tied into a faith that self-interested appeals evoked more considered individual judgment and thus a more effective representation of public opinion than that provided by the traditional party organizations, which is why "businessmen" like Hanna believed they were purifying politics.

These developments also strengthened nationalist forces in the parties generally, and, as suggested by the 1896 Democratic campaign, nationalized parties could be put to use by forces hostile to business as well as those friendly to it. Although Republicans outspent their Democratic rivals in 1896, the Democrats' adoption of the advisory committee model proved critical in funding William Jennings Bryan's campaign. Bryan's nomination turned the party upside down, leaving the candidate with a national committee composed of a number of gold Democrats opposed to the national party's new ideological tilt. The result was, as a Colorado Democrat wrote to Bryan, that "in many of the States where the Democratic sentiment is overwhelmingly for free coinage the committeeman has ideas entirely in conflict with those of his constituency."[123]

[120] Herbert Croly, *Marcus Alonzo Hanna: His Life and Work* (New York: MacMillan Company, 1923), 219, 220.
[121] Clarkson to H. G. McMillan, October 5, 1896, box 2, Clarkson Papers.
[122] Burnham, "The Changing Shape of the American Political Universe," 27. For another perspective, suggesting that the contribution of businessmen to the parties "may be regarded as 'conscience money'," see Macy, *Party Organization and Machinery*, 239.
[123] C. J. Thomas to Bryan, June 1, 1896, box 4, Bryan Papers.

Northeastern Democrats in particular had a difficult time swallowing the Bryan candidacy. In Massachusetts, for instance, where Cleveland Democrats had taken over the party, in many places "the city or town committees are in the hands of men of doubtful loyalty," which "[are] merely clogging our efforts and awaiting the time when the old management will be restored."[124] In such areas, Democrats struggled to maintain abandoned subnational organizations or to seize control from recalcitrant Cleveland Democrats. In these cases, it was the ability of the party's advisory committee to fund campaign activities that enabled it to continue to contest the campaign across the nation.

Democratic National Committee Chairman James Jones appointed advisory committees in both 1896 and 1900. In 1896, the committee was composed of representatives of organizations that were "working together with the Democratic Party in common cause," including Populist party members and Silver Republicans who could tap into those factions' donors – especially silver mine owners in the West. Jones explained that "it is necessary that we should have free consultation and expression of ideas as to what ought to be done and what ought not," but in reality, the committee enabled the Democrats to stoke a variety of sources of campaign funds and to maintain campaigns in "doubtful" states.[125] Without the advisory committee, the national organization would have performed much less admirably than it did. The campaign of education, formulated as a response to the changed political environment, changed the financial realities of campaigning. The increased involvement of businessmen like Hanna, then, should be read less as a hostile attempt by capitalists to take over the parties and more as a confluence of interests. The parties were just as intent on borrowing the social respectability of the business community as the business community was intent on making use of the parties, and the parties' use of "reformed" campaign methods helped convince businessmen that the parties were reliable partners. "It was not Hanna," recalled one Republican who had worked on the 1896 campaign, "but the conditions that existed at the time that caused the enormous expenses."[126]

[124] George Fred Williams to Bryan, November 10, 1897, box 20, Bryan Papers.
[125] "Jones Will Have Advisors," *New York Times*, August 28, 1896, 6; "Jones Selects Advisors," *New York Times*, August 29, 1896, 3; "Jones's Strange Advisors," *New York Times*, August 9, 1900, 6.
[126] Dictated Statement of Hon. C. N. Bliss to J. B. Morrow, October 30, 1905, box 4, Hanna-McCormick Family papers.

4

National Campaign Clubs and the Party-in-the-Electorate

As they adapted the methods of the associational explosion to partisan purposes, national party leaders abandoned many of the Jacksonian mode's republican values; in their place, they developed a distinctly national and liberal vision of a party-in-the-electorate attracted to the parties by direct appeals to self-interest. Their ambitions for a national party membership were most clearly demonstrated by the creation of an ambitious, if short-lived, network of party clubs. These clubs were locally based but sponsored by the national committees, and they created a sphere of national party membership that overcame the restrictive geographic boundaries of party regularity. The club plan gave a body to the national committee head; as national chairman and club plan advocate James Clarkson argued, without the clubs, "the National Committee itself has no more organization than if the party did not exist."[1] The club networks were an accoutrement to the campaign of education; by providing the national organizations with direct access to voters, the club plan enabled them to spread their educational work across a broad swath of society, much as the Farmers' Alliance lecture network allowed that organization to extend its reach in the 1880s. Drawing explicitly on groups such as Moorefield Storey's various reform clubs, this "club plan" intentionally evoked the method and mood of the associational explosion.

The clubs did not last long, but they were a massive undertaking during the 1880s and 1890s, suggesting that any attempt to understand political parties at this transformative moment in their history requires understanding exactly what party leaders thought they were accomplishing with them. The National League of Republican Clubs claimed 1.5 million members in 1892 and 2.25 million members in 1896; the membership resided in more than 18,000 clubs in cities and towns across the country. Democrats soon followed suit; in 1888, the New York Young Men's Democratic Club, together with its counterparts in Brooklyn, Boston, and Milwaukee, called for a similar national league,

---

[1] Clarkson to Welker Given, August 18, 1894, box 2, Clarkson papers.

which resulted in the formation of the National Association of Democratic Clubs. Democratic National Chairman Calvin Brice warned in 1891 that "it is evident that [Republicans] expect decisive results upon their extensive and well-organized system of Republican clubs." He believed that the Republicans' plan could "be met only by an equally extensive and well-organized system of Democratic societies." By 1900, there were reportedly 7,353 Democratic clubs nationwide, comprising 2 million members.[2]

Despite this auspicious beginning, the club plan was a short-lived phenomenon. Nevertheless, it helped national party leaders visualize a new form of connection with a national electorate and trained a generation of voters to engage national party politics directly, outside the rigid channels of party regularity. They legitimated the logic of the educational campaign and provided it with a network of local supporters in the days of its infancy. By demonstrating to party leaders and voters the potential in breaking down the barriers of regularity, they spread the new idea of party throughout the polity and helped establish something that the Jacksonian mode never intended to accomplish: a coherent national party-in-the-electorate, capable of infusing national party organizations with mandates for national policies.

The National Club Network

The club plan grew out of the Mugwump reform movement highlighted in Chapter 2 but was quickly adopted by the regular party organization. In 1887, the Young Men's Republican Club of New York City sent its president, James P. Foster, across the country to promote a national association of Republican clubs. In December, a convention of delegates from local Republican clubs founded the National League of Republican Clubs. Confident that the league represented the triumph of the associational explosion's aspirations to effect national party responsibility, Foster announced that the league "would virtually control the politics of the Republican Party," much as the Young Men's Democratic Club of Massachusetts had come to control Democratic politics in that state.[3]

[2] "Republican National League," *New York Times*, 2; "A League for Work," *San Francisco Examiner*, March 16, 1888, 4. *Appleton's Annual Cyclopedia and Register of Important Events of the Year, 1888* (New York: D. Appleton, 1889), 780, lists 6,500 clubs with 1 million members in 1888. "True Democratic Lines," *New York Times*, March 5, 1888, 8; "Democratic Club Work," *New York Times*, July 2, 1891, 1. (Circular letter from Democratic National Committee, dated July 1, 1891); "Democratic Clubs Meet," *New York Times*, October 4, 1900, 3.

[3] "Blaine's Great League," *New York Times*, December 18, 1887, 1. A national convention of Republican clubs met in Indianapolis in 1880, but it did not result in a permanent national organization. "National Club Convention," *The* (Topeka, KS) *Commonwealth*, September 23, 1880, 1; "Meeting of Republican Clubs," *New York Times*, September 16, 1880, 1. The 1887 convention was composed of representatives from twenty-three states and approximately 1,500 delegates; *Appleton's Annual Cyclopedia and Register of Important Events of the Year, 1888*, 780.

All of the elements of the associational explosion and the campaign of education were present in Foster's scheme. There was the notion of permanent campaign efforts and a focus on substantive discussion over spectacle: "by all is admitted," he enthused in an article written the next year, "the great value of a headquarters open every day and evening, where stated meetings are held and papers read and speeches and discussions had." There was an emphasis on direct appeals to interest, a sense that party lines would became more fluid in the privacy of the voter's reasoning, and a notion of a more enriched participatory experience: "the fact of every voter having a personal and direct interest in the result of every election, and hence his duty to array himself on one side or the other of every great question forming party issues in a great campaign." There was also a preference for national perspectives over localism: "like any order of fraternity or secret society, or the church denominations," Foster reasoned, "there is no good reason why the Republican party should not be organized as a National party on a permanent basis."[4] Believing that an organized manifestation of the reform sentiment swirling about the country could take advantage of the geographic decentralization of the Jacksonian party organizations, Foster hoped to seize the political legitimacy of the party label and attach it to a network of citizens organized along the lines of his own extra-partisan organization.

If Mugwumps like Foster inspired this foray into organizational innovation, their insurgent spirit did not constrain party leaders' co-optation of the club idea. Indeed, Foster's founding of the Republican league was soon eclipsed by the leadership of Iowa Republican James Clarkson, who was elected to the new league's executive committee. Clarkson was no Mugwump; he sarcastically referred to independent reformers as "Pharisees." He was a party politician who proudly declared that "party zeal was an active and practical form of public patriotism," dismissing the Mugwumps as idealistic moralists who did not understand the realities or benefits of practical politics. Indeed, as a longtime supporter of quadrennial presidential favorite James G. Blaine, a candidate who had built a national following that failed to materialize into effective national leadership, Clarkson had struggled to free his nationally popular candidate from the constraints of the Jacksonian mode. In the National League of Republican Clubs, Clarkson saw a tool for empowering national publics. The league was a means of reviving the spirit of the "first Americans" (that is, the Founding generation) who had "found party necessary" and nurtured the "spirit and . . . pride of party" that reinforced the republic during its first century.[5] Clarkson was in a unique position to effect this transformation; he was elected to the Republican National Committee's Executive Committee in 1888; in 1891, he was elected both president of the Republican's club league and chairman of the national committee. In that capacity, he urged that

---

[4] James P. Foster, "Permanent Republican Clubs," *North American Review*, March 1888, 241–2.
[5] James S. Clarkson, "The Politician and the Pharisee," *North American Review*, May 1891, 613, 614. On Clarkson's work for Blaine, see Marcus, *Grand Old Party*, 62–3.

the committee "do itself the justice of perfecting a systematic organization, whereby all voters could be reached and made to understand our principles and intentions," specifically that "the time had come when the club idea should be utilized in [party] politics." The club network was only part of his "thorough subsoiling plans for reaching the people as a mass," which required a medium "through which a campaign of education could be carried on universally."[6]

Clarkson was also not blindly partisan. He understood the criticisms lodged against the parties and warned that "there is a palsy of political parties just now." He identified the parties's authority as rooted in an educative function that was often forgotten: he revered the Founders' establishment of party, noting that "for a hundred years American boys were taught love of country, pride of party, and promotion and protection of liberty through patriotism of party."[7] The campaign of education was therefore not an innovation but a renewal of the parties' founding purposes. As Michael McGerr notes, Clarkson gave the campaign of education "its fullest partisan expression in the late nineteenth century."[8]

Clarkson recognized that the distribution of national literature by the national committees alone was not enough. Years of innovation by the parties with national literary bureaus, formed in the wake of nominating conventions and viewed as simply supplemental to the broader campaign work, had revealed the need for a "new and more universal form of party method and work" than the Jacksonian mode had provided. Observing the success of the associational explosion, he predicted "the change of political discussion from the field, as in Lincoln's day, to the private home where each family began to examine and discuss for itself the policy of the parties to find which party promised the most for the elevation and comfort of that special home."[9] He looked to this education of private interest for public purpose as the best means to resolve the parties' inability to address emergent issues: "it is on the hearthstones of this country," he insisted, "that all great political questions are finally settled."[10]

Clarkson's ambitions were not unique. In the Democratic party, club leaders rejected their heritage by identifying themselves not with Jackson or Jefferson but with the irregular but nationally oriented Democratic Societies that sprang up during George Washington's second administration. As one Democratic club flier explained in 1891,

the Democratic Society was the first organization of the Democratic Party in the Union. It was to their bold assertion of popular rights, their stubborn defense of sound republican

---

[6] Clarkson to Welker Given, August 18, 1894, box 2, Clarkson papers. On Clarkson, see also McGerr, *The Decline of Popular Politics*, 90–5, 179.

[7] Clarkson, "The Politician and the Pharisee," 617, 614, 618.

[8] McGerr, The Decline of Popular Politics, 95.

[9] James S. Clarkson, "Annual Address of James S. Clarkson, President of the National Republican League of the United States, box 4, Clarkson Papers.

[10] Clarkson, "The Politician and the Pharisee," 618.

principles, that we owe the first overthrow of the Federalist Party, the election of Mr. Jefferson, and the blessed era of Democratic rule, almost unbroken, from 1800 to 1860. The truly Democratic club has ever been the engine of liberty endangered.[11]

The reference bypassed a partisan history that might alienate potential converts (if the clubs sprang from a pre-Jacksonian party consciousness, they predated the Democratic party's troubling relationship with secession). It also envisioned the Democratic party's foundation in a popular movement, which attached the club idea to the national electorate. Like the Democratic Societies but unlike the Jacksonian mode establishment (which drew its authority from regularly organized political processes), the new party clubs derived their authority from their status as independent associations of citizens exercising independent judgment.[12]

The clubs' permanent organization further reinforced the distinction between their national constituency and the localistic orientation of the Jacksonian mode. Chauncey Black, president of the National Association of Democratic Clubs, pointed out that the clubs were uniquely "fitted for a continuous educational campaign"[13] and so remained organized after national elections had passed, perpetuating citizen involvement long after the Jacksonian mode dismissed routine voter involvement in party affairs. The Republican league held annual conventions (until the early 1900s, when it began holding conventions every other year), because "one convention each year secures permanency," and clubs were encouraged to "have regular meetings of the club at least once a month," even in noncampaign years.[14] This permanence was consciously contrasted to traditional organizations, which convened in their popular capacity as conventions only during election years. The permanent presence of the clubs would supply "a regulator on this machine of politics," able to "control political sentiment and party action" when party regulars were not engaged in party politics.[15]

Membership qualifications reinforced the clubs' distinctiveness. Enrollment in the regular organization was closed to individuals who did not vote for the party, regardless of their position on the issues of the day, but the party clubs invited membership on the basis of affiliation with national party principles – thus welcoming potential converts. "The only qualification for membership" in the Young Men's Democratic Club of Massachusetts, for instance,

[11] "Democratic Club Work," *New York Times*, July 2, 1891, 1. (Circular letter from Democratic National Committee, dated July 1, 1891.)

[12] Hofstadter, *The Idea of a Party System*, 92–5.

[13] "Work of Democratic Clubs," *New York Times*, February 9, 1894, 4.

[14] *Pocket Manual of the National Republican League* [1898–1900], box 233, folder 3, J. Hampton Moore Papers, Historical Society of Pennsylvania, Philadelphia, PA, 9, 16, 20–21; Addison B. Burk, *Republican Club Book, 1904, Pennsylvania Edition* (Philadelphia, PA: Dunlap Printing Company, 1904), 13. See also "National and State Leagues," *New York Times*, December 17, 1887, 2.

[15] Morris C. Baum, "Permanent Republican Clubs," *The North American Review*, March 1888, 264.

was "adhesion to its declaration of principles."[16] The Republican league only required "that he is a resident and will support the principles of the party"; members weren't even required to be registered voters. It even extended its reach beyond the ranks of legal voters, admitting "young men who have not attained their majority" and women.[17] This openness bespoke the clubs' attempt to persuade voters outside of the bounds of party regularity and also to form an irregular "shadow party" more universal than the regular apparatus, thus representing a broader array of interests. Because membership was not restricted, the clubs provided the party with a better "means of ascertaining the sentiment that prevails among the Democratic masses in different parts of the country" than did the Jacksonian convention system.[18]

Club leaders took care to distinguish their meetings from traditional party politics and avoided hurrah campaign spectacles. They were not used to ratify party nominees or to promote enthusiasm. "Our League organizations should be clearly distinguished from a mass meeting," insisted the Republican organization's handbook, "it is intended to be a school of Republicanism, where the best political literature can be secured, and where the principles of the party are unmistakably taught."[19] Democrat Black noted that the clubs were devoted to "spreading generally a just idea and a better knowledge of what the party is seeking, of how it will affect the interests of every class, and the means by which it can be reached."[20] Clarkson argued that the form of the club meeting would transform the nature of party debate, with the clubs providing "a system for maintaining the strength and evenness of settled opinion as to party principles or public issues," in contrast to the "sudden change or oftentimes artificial decision of a convention or mass meeting."[21] They thus freed individual judgment from the shifting enthusiasms of electoral seasons.

Local clubs were not an innovation of the late nineteenth century. The Jacksonian mode relied on voluntary associational forms, especially campaign clubs organized to arouse popular enthusiasm in hurrah campaigns; they organized just before elections and dissolved just after them. Encouraged by local party organizations, and in most cases simply creations of local organizations, clubs such as the E. P. Lewis Battalion and the Cleveland and Thurman Mounted Brigade, the Jefferson Club, and the Cleveland and Thurman Club of Flushing,

---

[16] Josiah Quincy, "Report of the Executive Committee of the Young Men's Democratic Club of Massachusetts, November 30, 1889, in Young Men's Democratic Club of Massachusetts, "Minutes, 1887–1891," December 16, 1889, YMDCM Records.

[17] *Pocket Manual of the National Republican League* [1898–1900], box 233, folder 3, Moore Papers, 14.

[18] Untitled article, *New York Times*, August 12, 1891, 4; on the concept of a shadow party, see Goodwyn, *The Populist Moment*.

[19] *Pocket Manual of the National Republican League* [1898–1900], box 233, folder 3, Moore Papers, 19.

[20] "Work of Democratic Clubs," *New York Times*, February 9, 1894, 4; "The Democratic Societies," *New York Times*, May 27, 1889, 4.

[21] James S. Clarkson, "Permanent Republican Clubs," *The North American Review*, March 1888, 261.

Long Island,[22] spent much of their campaign efforts marching in parades and organizing rallies. The traditional rallies and parades were a central component of the hurrah campaign, providing opportunities for demonstrations of loyalty to the local partisan community.[23]

National leaders complained that these "irregular and voluntary clubs" were "too frequently managed by individuals for individual purposes, or by factions for factious purposes" and as such had become merely means to mobilize numbers and contest local nominating primaries and conventions.[24] Each convention season provided these clubs with new reasons for frenetic activity but did little to draw voters into national party politics. Many observers blamed the growing distrust of the parties on the use of these Jacksonian clubs by self-promoting cliques to reinforce parochial purposes; as a Minnesota Republican complained in 1888, "the party has . . . been divided into factions, each of which spent its best energies in trying to control nominations." Voters "finally became suspicious, then indifferent, and party lines in great measure disappeared."[25] By contrast, the clubs avoided Jacksonian mode politics to avoid "offending the popular aversion to the 'politicians'" and thus turned the new associations' attraction to partisan ends.[26] The Republican league advised its local affiliates to "avoid the danger . . . of getting too many party Committeemen into the League offices."[27] Club leaders hoped that by maintaining a personnel distinct from the regular office-seeking politicians, there would "be no one left to raise the absurd cry against the 'machine,' which has its effect upon unthinking voters."[28] Standing apart from the politics of regularity, the new clubs would "belong to the party and the party alone" rather than serving the careers of particular individuals.[29]

What did it mean to belong to the party alone? Club leaders were beginning to define the party as a national-party-in-the-electorate, marked by shared beliefs and interests, rather than members of distinct local partisan communities. Through a broader engagement with party principles, "the partisan who has heretofore measured everything by the footrule of local prejudice [would]

---

[22] "The Last of the Campaign," *New York Times*, November 2, 1888, 8.

[23] Aldrich, *Why Parties?*, 102.

[24] Chauncey F. Black, John D. Worman, and J. Marshall Wright, "Pennsylvania Democratic Societies," April 20, 1892, carton 3, folder 6.15, George Fred Williams Papers, Massachusetts Historical Society, Boston, MA.

[25] D. Harry Hammer, "Permanent Republican Clubs," *The North American Review*, March 1888, 254.

[26] Warner Bateman to John Sherman, January 10, 1879, vol. 200, Sherman Papers.

[27] *Pocket Manual of the National Republican League* [1898–1900], 22. In the Arkansas state Republican league, for instance, only fourteen of the league's seventy-five officers also served in one of the state party organization's fifty-two offices; *Pocket Manual of the Arkansas State League of Republican Clubs*, 2–6.

[28] Hammer, "Permanent Republican Clubs," 254.

[29] Black, Worman, and Wright, "Pennsylvania Democratic Societies," April 20, 1892, carton 3, folder 6.15, Williams Papers.

become imbued with broader and national ideas."[30] This comported with the campaign of education's vision of elevating the electorate above its organic local communities.

The National League of Republican Clubs was organized in a pluralistic manner, emphasizing the campaign of education's liberal appeals to distinctive interests. It approached voters "with especial appeals to them in their especial interests or class,"[31] targeting individual interests rather than communal loyalties: "instead of trying to capture men by enthusiasm in the mass, the system is to go to them in detail and to reach them along the lines of effective influence," wrote Clarkson. The clubs approached voters as members of groups who had distinct needs, so that "the different nationalities, the different secret societies, the different church organizations, college organizations, college clubs, university clubs, the various elements of the different nationalities are all considered.... in every way each individual voter who is eligible to Republican conquest is reached directly and personally and by the one who has the most influence with him." Individual clubs specialized in issues that spoke to the unique interests of their members. Clarkson explained that "wherever mechanics are strong I had Clubs made up entirely of mechanics, where foreign elements are strong Clubs made up of the same foreign elements."[32] One period sourcebook on American politics noted that under the club plan "innumerable clubs appeared under diverse names: Irish Republican clubs; Bohemian Republican clubs; Jewish Republican clubs; traveling men's Republican clubs; students' Republican clubs – clubs for every race, occupation or condition."[33] Clarkson even encouraged women's clubs, and by 1900, the National League of Republican Clubs was affiliated with a National Women's Republican League.[34] Similarly, the Young Men's Democratic Club of Massachusetts described itself as "representative in its membership of every element, geographic or other; of which the party is composed."[35] Pluralism, as a conscious prescription for the distinctive representation of interests, had arrived – for the parties if not quite yet for political science. Understanding pluralism as an "attempt to explain and justify a feasible and desirable social order" as well as "a condition of diversity, which prevents any one group or point of view from attaining preeminence," this pluralistic vision of party order

---

[30] John A. Caldwell, "Permanent Republican Clubs," *The North American Review*, March 1888, 262.

[31] Clarkson to Welker Given, August 18, 1894, box 2, Clarkson papers.

[32] Clarkson to Leigh Hunt, October 1, 1904, box 2, Clarkson papers.

[33] Andrew Cunningham McLaughlin and Albert Bushnell Hart, *Cyclopedia of American Government* (New York: D. Appleton and Company, 1914), 711.

[34] "Private from Clarkson," *New York Times*, August 9, 1892, 1; *Pocket Manual of the National Republican League* [1898–1900], box 233, folder 3, Moore Papers, 2, 7.

[35] Josiah Quincy, "Report of the Executive Committee of the Young Men's Democratic Club of Massachusetts, November 30, 1889, in YMDCM, "Minutes, 1887–1891," December 16, 1889, YMDCM Records.

sought to do more than merely appeal to voters in new ways.[36] It reenvisioned the elements composing the social contract of party membership.[37] The clubs saw themselves as facilitating such shifts, and so the Bushwick Democratic Club of Brooklyn reported that its meetings "reach[ed] a class of independent voters who . . . can be influenced to vote for Cleveland *this time*," although they might not later,[38] and the Ridgefield, Connecticut, Cleveland and Stevenson Campaign Club, was formed "to convert many [Republicans]" through "the enlightenment of an educational campaign, one where the issues shall be forced fairly and squarely upon their attention."[39]

The clubs insisted that they allowed the party-in-the-electorate to influence the party more directly than did the national conventions. Pennsylvania Republican league member J. Hampton Moore suggested that the clubs provided a more accurate "means of ascertaining the sentiment that prevails among the Democratic masses in different parts of the country"[40] by providing an outlet for those minority voices dismissed from the Jacksonian convention system. For this reason, Grover Cleveland argued that the clubs demonstrateed the Democratic party's commitment to popular opinion. "Its best service," he wrote, "has been an enforcement and demonstration of the truth that our party is best organized and most powerful when . . . it quickly responds to the sentiments supplied by an enlistment in the people's cause."[41] Voters would come to see, hoped one Kansas Republican club leader, "that they are recognized as members of a great party made up of members like themselves, and that as the individual is so will the party be." The clubs would "show the wavering person that while he differs from the party on some points, he can find no other party from which he does not differ more, and he will again act with the party which most nearly represents him."[42] The appeal to distinct interests reinforced this effort; not only did it provide the parties with direct access to voters' interests, it emphasized the parties' ability to speak to the needs of a diversifying populace. As Brian Balogh explains, "the ability to distinguish between one's constituents in a more selective fashion than Republican or Democrat, Pole or German, southerner or northerner, laid the groundwork for crafting public policies that expanded the scope of government to serve select (and powerful) constituencies."[43]

[36] John Higham, *Send These to Me: Jews and Other Immigrants in Urban America* (New York: Atheneum Press, 1975), 197.

[37] Bensel, *Passion and Preferences*, 126.

[38] Saul S. Whitehouse to William C. Whitney, October 19, 1892, book 77, Whitney Papers. Emphasis added.

[39] Melbert B. Cary to Cleveland, August 19, 1892, series 11, box 3, Cleveland Papers.

[40] Untitled article, *New York Times*, August 12, 1891, 4.

[41] Grover Cleveland to Chauncey Black, printed in *New York Times*, April 23, 1894, 4.

[42] J. G. Slonecker, "Permanent Republican Clubs," *The North American Review*, March 1888, 259.

[43] Brian Balogh, "Mirrors of Desires," 224. See also Brian Balogh, *A Special Form of Associative Action': New Liberalism and the National Integration of Public and Private* (New York: Cambridge University Press, 2008).

In this, leaders in the club movement were influenced by the associational explosion's challenge to traditional party politics and identified the clubs as a response to this challenge. Clarkson's experience in politics brought him into contact with a number of extra-party groups as they engaged the party process. He reached out personally to Prohibitionists, urging them to stay within the party.[44] The Greenback party fused with Democrats in his home state of Iowa (and in doing so reduced the Republicans' 78,000 majority in 1880 to 18,000 in 1884),[45] free trade clubs threatened to negate efforts made by Republicans among the Irish in New York City,[46] the nativist American Protective Association threatened to defeat Republican candidates for Congress,[47] and Clarkson warned that, in Chicago, "there [were] from fifty to seventy thousand votes there, Socialists and others, that slosh around from one party to another."[48] He believed that the clubs would enable the Republican party to "fight the Farmers' Alliance with its own weapons.... by making the clubs rivals of the Alliance as social organizations."[49] Black, similarly believed the work of the clubs to be "necessary to prevent the sudden disorganization of the Democracy, which has so frequently befallen it, South and West, from temporary popular delusion," as expressed in alternative forms of political organization, especially third parties.[50] In this sense, the club plan both mimicked the emerging organizations and undermined their novelty by using the club impulse for partisan ends.

National Organization

Club leaders were cautious not to challenge visibly the traditional lines of party authority. They claimed that their network was, in Republican William Chandler's words, "by no means intended to supplant, but rather to supplement, the regular National State and County organizations by and through which the Republican party has heretofore voiced its sentiments." Chandler explained that "there is little danger that these new clubs will clash with the regular organizations.... all are working for a common purpose and will endeavor to avoid conflict."[51] Republicans insisted that their league would "not in any manner endeavor to influence the action of any National, State, County or Municipal convention," nor "indicate ... any preference for any candidate before any

[44] As is implied in Mrs. A. E. McMurray to Clarkson, August 5, 1885, box 1, Clarkson Papers.
[45] Edward H. Stiles to Clarkson, June 9, 1884, Clarkson Papers; Walter Dean Burnham, *Presidential Ballots, 1836–1892* (Baltimore: Johns Hopkins Press, 1955), 413.
[46] E. R. Kirk to Clarkson, July 23, 1884, box 1, Clarkson Papers.
[47] Thomas H. Carter to Clarkson, November 23, 1894, box 2, Clarkson Papers.
[48] Clarkson to Samuel Fessenden, October 15, 1896, box 2, Clarkson Papers.
[49] "Gen. Clarkson's Plans," *New York Times*, May 1, 1891, 2.
[50] "Work of Democratic Clubs," *New York Times*, February 9, 1894, 4.
[51] William E. Chandler, "Permanent Republican Clubs," *The North American Review*, March 1888, 247.

political convention.[52] In handbooks distributed to local clubs, the national league warned local leaders to "permit no conflicts to arise between your club and other organizations of the Republican party" and reminded them that "your club does not take the place of, but is auxiliary to, the regular committee of the party."[53]

These disavowals did not preclude political action generally, however. The clubs primed voters for political action outside of party regularity, even if they were not directed toward taking over the regular party process. Democrats encouraged club members to "discuss political questions and methods and to arrange for work to be carried on in their immediate localities," so that they were clearly to be actively involved in politics rather than mere observers.[54] Black urged that meetings be used "not only to discuss the issues of the canvass and to make each member familiar with the irresistible arguments in favor of our ticket, BUT TO CONSIDER THE MEANS OF VICTORY."[55] A Democratic club in Mariontown, Pennsylvania, concurred with Black's vision, describing itself as "an organization whose chief aim is to discuss and to develop and maintain an efficiency for permanent Democratic strength."[56] By itself, this sounds like little more than the usual exhortation for party loyalists to work for the cause, but in light of the nationalizing ambitions of the educational campaign, the work of the clubs was hardly neutral to the Jacksonian mode's balance of power.

The club plan fit into a larger vision of nationalizing the party. As chairman of the Republican National Committee, Clarkson expanded the committee's publication of printed campaign material by establishing a literary bureau, sent plate matter to local newspapers, and even recommended founding a publishing company devoted to the purposes of producing campaign literature.[57] From his position at the top of both organizations, he worked to, in his words, "put the entire club organization under the general management of the National Committee and make it one of its working forces," thus giving the national committee a lifeline direct to the local party-in-the-electorate.[58] Simultaneously, he took a leading role in urging the party away from the old sentimental issues of war and reconstruction toward accommodation with the interest-based politics of the associational explosion.[59]

---

52 *Pocket Manual of the National Republican League* [1898–1900], 10. See also *Pocket Manual of the Arkansas State League of Republican Clubs*, June, 1900, box 233, folder 3, Moore Papers.
53 *Pocket Manual of the National Republican League* [1898–1900], 20–1.
54 "Work of Democratic Clubs," *New York Times*, February 9, 1894, 4; "The Democratic Societies," *New York Times*, May 27, 1889, 4.
55 Chauncey F. Black, John D. Worman, J. Marshall Wright, "Pennsylvania Democratic Societies," April 20, 1892, carton 3, folder 6.15, Williams Papers, emphasis in original.
56 W. H. Rankin to Grover Cleveland, August 10, 1892, series 11, box 10, Cleveland Papers.
57 Clarkson to Welker Given, August 18, 1894, box 2, Clarkson papers. On Clarkson, see also McGerr, *The Decline of Popular Politics*, 90–5, 179.
58 "Gen. Clarkson's Plans," *New York Times*, May 1, 1891, 2.
59 Hirshon, *Farewell to the Bloody Shirt*.

Like the traditional parties, the national leagues had a federated structure opening membership to "any permanently organized State or Territorial League"[60] and that "contemplate[d] the connection from the central to the remotest organization." The league was composed of "a series of organizations extending from the State League to the local clubs through the closely connecting District and County Leagues," which supervised local clubs. State leagues were given "full supervision over all the subordinate leagues in its jurisdiction" during national campaigns, and district leagues directed congressional campaigns. Below the district leagues, the Republican league constitution specified that "the County League has full jurisdiction of League work within its territory as do the township or local clubs in theirs," although there was no responsibility given to the local organizations to conduct local campaigns, probably because more than one club could exist in a given locality and the national focus of the clubs, which kept them out of local political conflicts.[61]

The clubs thus fostered the kind of national "life and power and rule" of the sort that the Jacksonian mode explicitly discouraged. Even in the states' rights–oriented Democratic party, the procedures for integrating new clubs into the national association were designed to bring local clubs under the influence of national party leaders, breaking their members away from their traditional localistic boundaries. "As soon as a club has been thoroughly organized for the campaign," noted the secretary of the Democratic association, "we have their secretary send us in a list of members with their addresses, and we send documents direct from this office to the individual addresses."[62] Not respecting the boundaries of the regular organization, the Republican league sought to make "the Republican clubs . . . so numerous and universal as to take in every active Republican voter," crafting a national entity out of what had always been an alliance of state and local organizations.[63] The club plan would be particularly useful in embracing voters previously excluded from party ranks or dissatisfied with their local party leadership, but its aim was to absorb all party identifiers. Clubs were even allowed to overlap several party jurisdictions and the territory of multiple local clubs.[64] For the first time, a truly national party-in-the-electorate was coming into being.

State presidents were empowered (and encouraged) to appoint club officers in districts where no clubs existed,[65] and the league also had a paid staff that

[60] Burk, *Republican Club Book, 1904,* 12.

[61] *Pocket Manual of the National Republican League* [1898–1900], box 233, folder 3, Moore Papers, 13–14.

[62] Lawrence Gardner to Cleveland, August 3, 1892, series 11, box 5, Cleveland Papers.

[63] D. Harry Hammer, "Permanent Republican Clubs," *The North American Review,* March 1888, 254.

[64] Joseph Chelleur to Cleveland, September 29, 1892, series 11, box 3, Cleveland Papers. Chelleur was a traveling salesman who together with some colleagues "formed ourselves into a Democratic Campaign Club for the purpose of distributing campaign documents to those settlers" in frontier settlements.

[65] *Pocket Manual of the National Republican League* [1898–1900], 15.

traveled the country organizing clubs.[66] Relatively loose requirements for the founding of local affiliates encouraged the proliferation of a wide variety of groups.[67] In 1891, the National Association of Democratic Clubs

> prepared a plan under which it is intended to have an aggressive Democratic organization in every voting precinct in the country when the Fall campaign opens. In addition to the Vice President of the National Association in each State, a superintendent and organizer will be appointed for each county, and the work of all will be supervised by the National Association, acting with the co-operation of the National, State, and Congressional Committees.

Extending its reach throughout the nation and down to the local level, its "central body will be in direct touch with the best Democratic workers in every county in every State in the Union, and not a point in the country where effective work can be done for the party can escape detection."[68] This enabled the association to pursue national party goals even when they met subnational recalcitrance, clarifying national purpose in ways that the traditional organizational mode could not: "there are States in which, under certain circumstances, this organization furnishes the only refuge for true Democrats intent upon national work, such as tariff reform, where machines unfriendly to political progress or economic reform have taken possession of the old state organizations, or where populists or other third parties have seized them." Hence, the clubs' efforts were "wholly distinct from the usual campaign work."[69] In Boston, the Young Men's Democratic Club of Massachusetts, one of the founding members of the National Association of Democratic Clubs, maintained its work was "a large and distinct field of its own" and that its members can perform work that could not "in the nature of things be accomplished by the regular party committees."[70] The Republican league was similarly devised to "supply local wants where the national organization... cannot reach in detail," again "where voluntary labor must be relied upon."[71] This was a striking claim for a national committee affiliate to make because it suggested party authority arising outside of the procedures of intraparty democracy, violating the Jacksonian faith in the primacy of localistic party processes.

Thus even without intervening in the convention process, the clubs envisioned a dramatic shift of power away from the regular subnational organizations to the national level of party organization by providing the national party

---

[66] *Pocket Manual of the National Republican League* [1898–1900], 2; Burk, *Republican Club Book, 1904*, 14.

[67] *Pocket Manual of the Arkansas State League of Republican Clubs*, June, 1900, box 233, folder 3, Moore Papers, 12.

[68] "Work for Democratic Clubs," *New York Times*, June 21, 1891, 20.

[69] "Work of Democratic Clubs," *New York Times*, April 23, 1894, 4 (speech to the Executive Committee of the National Association of Democratic Clubs).

[70] Quincy, "Report of the Executive Committee of the Young Men's Democratic Club of Massachusetts, November 30, 1889, in Young Men's Democratic Club, "Minutes, 1887–1891," December 16, 1889, YMDCM Records.

[71] A. M. Clapp, "Permanent Republican Clubs," *The North American Review*, March 1888, 251.

organizations with new means to shape national partisan mandates, as "by permanent organization of clubs there would be a concentration of unlimited political power, and these organizations would mold the opinion of the party in advance of conventions."[72] National elections could be grounded in something deeper than the contingencies of subnational factionalism and thereby generate national policy agendas. Where disagreement existed within the party, the clubs "would form a tribunal whose decrees measurably would determine matters of policy," submitting the conflicts of politicians to the judgment of the party-in-the-electorate. The result would be greater substantive discipline – responsibility, in language that would become popular in the twentieth century – as "leaders of cliques would find that their personal ambitions must yield to the larger interests of the party."[73] Thus, if the clubs did not mark out the institutional pattern of twentieth-century party development, they did help flesh out the idea of party that would come to define the theoretical aspirations of the parties.

A Local Club in Action

As noted in Chapter 2, the Young Men's Democratic Club of Massachusetts (YMDCM) was an early advocate of the nationalization of the club idea. Considering the founding membership's relationship to Moorefield Storey's Young Men's Republican Club and Reform Club of Massachusetts, classifying it here, with the national party clubs, rather than in the consideration of Mugwump groups, is problematic. There are good reasons to do so, however. Chief among these is the fact that the YMDCM explicitly chose to affiliate itself with the Democratic party and thus to embrace a traditional form of partisanship that Mugwumps of Storey's ilk resisted. As explained in this section, the YMDCM became the bulwark of the Democracy's brief rise to power in Massachusetts in the early 1890s. Further, it was a model for clubs across the nation (many later clubs drew on its constitution in their own founding), and its operations provide a lens into the club style of political organizing.

The YMDCM was modeled closely on Storey's Young Men's Republican Club, and although it was designed "to foster and disseminate Democratic principles," it kept itself conspicuously independent of the regular party. Rather than an accoutrement to the party's mobilization efforts, it announced its goal as being "to publicly declare the specific measures to which it desires to see the Democracy pledged in coming elections." Reaching outside the bounds of party regularity, the YMDCM declared that "the only qualification for membership is adhesion to [the club's] declaration of principles" and welcomed the participation of "those who have hitherto been indifferent to political duties, or who have been prevented from performing them" because of exclusion from or

---

[72] Hammer, "Permanent Republican Clubs," 253.
[73] Morris C. Baum, "Permanent Republican Clubs," *The North American Review*, March 1888, 264.

disgust with the procedures of the regular party organization.[74] It appealed to sympathetic voters across the state to organize affiliates.[75] Much as the American Iron and Steel Association (AISA) believed permanent organization would help undermine party loyalty, the YMDCM insisted on a "continuous effort to accomplish the objects of our club."[76]

It also provided a forum for political discussion, as evidenced by the club's statement of political principles, which was under constant revision as members debated old and recognized new issues.[77] Their meetings were spent discussing policy and forming working committees on federal and state legislation, on civil service, on prohibitory legislation, and on the abolition of the poll tax. The club formed committees to report on particular areas of legislation, to expand club membership, and to schedule lectures on political issues of the day. Club records indicate that at various times, the lecture committee scheduled presentations and discussions on the Bland Silver Bill, eliminating import duties on iron ore and coal, funding the Civil Service Commission, reforming pension laws, the tariff's effects on New England, the income tax, currency issues, the initiative and referendum, registration of land titles, labor troubles, immigration laws, postal reform, and more.[78] In purpose, then, it neatly paralleled the Farmers' Alliance's lecture system and the AISA's question clubs.

As Storey's organizations had done, the club promoted national contacts, coordinating with Young Men's Democratic Clubs in New York to plan the first national convention of Democratic clubs, and it met frequently with its New York counterparts.[79] Following Storey's (and AISA's) insight as to the power of printed literature, it specialized in the distribution of literature that focused on substantive discussion of issues of national policy.[80] It formed the Committee on Campaign Literature and spent more than 30 percent of its $10,000 annual budget on literature production and distribution (the rest being spent on headquarters expenses, clerical help, expenses related to those rallies they did hold, expenses for attending the National Convention of Democratic Clubs, and direct subsidies of local affiliates across the state). Its membership dwarfed that of Storey's Reform Club at just over two thousand, and had affiliates in more than 250 cities and towns in Massachusetts.[81] Because it admitted

---

[74] YMDCM, "Constitution, By-Laws, and Declaration of Principles," March 1891, Box 3, YMDCM Records.

[75] Quincy, "Report of the Executive Committee of the Young Men's Democratic Club of Massachusetts," November 30, 1889, YMDCM Records.

[76] YMDCM, "Minutes, 1887–1891," December 17, 1888, YMDCM Records.

[77] See printed declarations of principle for March 1888, February 1889, March 1891, 1893, 1894, and 1898, in YMDCM Records.

[78] See generally, YMDCM, "Minutes, 1891–1894," YMDCM Records.

[79] YMDCM, "Minutes, 1887–1891," February 20, 1888, April 9, 1888, and July 12, 1888, YMDCM Records.

[80] Henry W. Swift, circular letter, October 1, 1890, YMDCM Records.

[81] YMDCM, "Constitution and By-Laws of the Young Men's Democratic Club of Massachusetts," March, 1892, YMDCM Records.

members from a wide array of occupations, it was not an elite organization like some Mugwump organizations.[82]

The club was a veritable publishing and distribution house of campaign literature. In 1888 alone, it reported distributing 1,508,500 copies (a number that approximated that distributed by AISA in the same year, as noted in Chapter 2) of twenty-five documents on weighty topics (including "What the Mills Bill Means for the Laboring People," "What High Tariffs Did for Ireland," "A Woolen Manufacturer on Free Wool," "Twenty Reasons Why a High Tariff Does Not Make High Wages," "Iron Making in New England," and "The Mills Bill"). Document distribution was systemized and coordinated with local club members and club organizations, so that "only such documents were sent out as were, in the opinion of the receivers, suited to the locality, and every town but two received documents at one time or another." Ever mindful of national purposes, the club sent 219,400 documents out of state in that year.[83] Its proficiency in distributing campaign literature was noted by the regular state Democratic committee and it was asked "to take full charge of distributing documents in the coming [state] campaign."[84] Although all local clubs could not be expected to replicate the Massachusetts club's publishing prowess, the centrality of pamphlet distribution to the club's sense of purpose was common across the club network, and the YMDCM saw itself as playing a special role in the national club plan by providing its fellow clubs with material for distribution.

The club did take part in campaign activity but was careful to avoid the routine activities of the regular organizations. Early in its history, the club concluded that "it was not deemed advisable... to attend to the work of the assessment or registration of voters throughout the State," – work closely associated with the regular organization. It focused instead on educational campaigning and resisted the temptation to become absorbed in regular politics.

[82] In circular letters announcing applicants for admission between 1890 and 1891, the following occupations (among others) were listed: accountant, architect, armorer, baker, banker, bank teller, bill collector, brewer, builder, carpenter, cashier, chemist, civil engineer, clerk, clock maker, clothier, commercial traveler, conductor, contractor, dentist, deputy sheriff, druggist, dry goods salesman, editor, electrician, engraver, expressman, farmer, florist, foreman, grain dealer, grocer, hardware salesman, hotel clerk, hotel proprietor, innkeeper, insurance salesman, jeweler, journalist, lawyer (Louis Brandeis was a member in this category), lithographer, lumberman, merchant, metalworker, milk contractor, mill agent, miller, minister, musician, paint dealer, painter, photographer, physician, plumber, porter, postmaster, printer, professor, salesman, shoe cutter, shoe dealer, stenographer, stevedore, student, tailor, teacher, tobacco dealer, undertaker, watchmaker, wholesale fruit seller, and wool-sorter. See YMDCM, circular letters of September 24, 1890; October 8, 1890; October 21, 1890; October 28, 1890; November 12, 1890; December 11, 1890; July 18, 1891; September 3, 1891; September 23, 1891; September 30, 1891; October 3, 1891; October 14, 1891; October 29, 1891; and November 11, 1891, box 3, YMDCM Records.

[83] "Report of the Treasurer of the Young Men's Democratic Club of Massachusetts, November 1888," YMDCM Records; YMDCM, "Minutes, 1887–1891," December 17, 1888, YMDCM Records.

[84] YMDCM, "Minutes, 1891–1894," August 26, 1891, YMDCM Records.

The club even refused to rent space in its club headquarters to the regular party to maintain a firm distinction between itself and the regular organization.[85]

Like the national party clubs, the YMDCM flourished between 1888 and 1900 but faded thereafter. One explanation of the clubs' failure is that the tumultuous election of 1896 threw a number of old political alliances into question, much as the Farmer's Alliance was decimated by the turn to the Democracy in the same year. Bryan's nomination proved disastrous because the clubs' elite membership balked at the party's new silver plank. The club called for a rump convention of Gold Democrats, declaring that it refused "to follow the Chicago platform of July 8, 1896, or to support the nomination of Messrs. Bryan and Sewall."[86] The next year, a committee was appointed to gauge support for "forming Democratic-National Clubs" (that is, Gold Democratic clubs), and it met mixed results. In 1899, they declared against "imperialism" and trusts – indicating continued mistrust of the Republican party – but there was significant soul searching. There was talk of disbanding; "we had better keep quiet," urged one member, and others agreed that there was no point in campaigning if they were not certain they would support the party's nominee.[87] After Bryan's renomination, a weak resolution was passed that "without endorsing the [Republicans'] Kansas City platform, opposes McKinleyism, and believes that the success of the Democratic candidates is preferable to a continuance of the present Republican party."[88] When in 1902 the club's campaign committee sent a circular letter to former party leaders, only half replied, and only half of those expressed interest in working for the Democratic party.[89] With the Mugwump leadership gone, Boston's Irish Democrats attempted to revive the club, but the Irish working class was not as enamored with the club plan as their WASPish predecessors had been.[90]

The clubs carved out a space in politics for voters who disdained the rough-and-tumble of local politics, a space that continued to animate amateur politicians throughout the twentieth century, although they were never again the center of a coherent effort by the national parties to reach a national electorate.[91] Thus, even as the club plan exposes the nationalizing tendencies implicit in the new idea of party, it is also a reminder that nationalization is not uncomplicatedly invited by the American constitutional order. A number of factors explain the failure of the club plan to achieve lasting institutionalization within the two-party system. First, contingent political factors surrounding the 1896

---

[85] YMDCM, "Minutes, 1887–1891," July 12, 1888 and October 17, 1888, YMDCM Records.

[86] YMDCM "Minutes, 1895–1903," July 27, 1896, YMDCM Records.

[87] YMDCM, "Minutes, 1895–1903," April 22, 1897, March 23, 1899 and July 18, 1900, YMDCM Records.

[88] YMDCM, "Minutes, 1895–1903," September 10, 1900, YMDCM Records.

[89] YMDCM, "Minutes, 1895–1903," May 28, 1902, YMDCM Records.

[90] Daniel F. Buckley to Prescott F. Hall, October 5, 1903, YMDCM Records.

[91] James Q. Wilson, *The Amateur Democrat: Club Politics in Three Cities* (Chicago: University of Chicago Press, 1966).

election undermined the clubs' appeal to their targeted membership. Urban–rural divisions became more apparent, and party competition decreased as one of the two major parties came to dominate politics in many electoral districts. For many voters, shifting between the Republican and Democratic parties was more difficult after divisions between them became more apparent following Bryan's nomination. The YMDCM, for instance, declined as its elite membership flocked back to the Republican party; most members did so without fanfare, reluctant to announce their move by joining similar Republican clubs.

Second, subnational party organizations resurged at the turn of the century, undermining the clubs' usefulness. The late nineteenth century's relatively closely contested political environment gave way to a period of reduced political conflict in many areas. The consolidation of machine control over major northern cities enhanced the value of traditional local organizations to the national parties, leading to a golden age of machine politics. The new idea of party transformed the parties' campaign style but did not remove the organizational vestiges of the Jacksonian mode; hence, the localistic structure of the parties remained firmly in place. The relevance of traditional local organizations had not dissipated, however, if only because the national party clubs had never been grafted onto the traditional power structure. As Alan Ware notes, there were a number of twentieth-century developments that transformed the relevance of state and local politics. The declining registration of new immigrants and the passage of antiparty reforms that actually helped machines consolidate control of local politics led to the consolidation of urban political machines after the 1890s, making "the following 30 years or so...the heyday of the urban machine." This benefited different parties in different cities, but it generally enabled one party to regularly dominate the other. In this environment, playing for those voters who sat in the middle was less rational than allowing the dominant machine to mobilize the requisite voters.[92] In this environment, the clubs served less of a purpose for the national parties. For the club membership, the consolidation of machine politics meant a loss of the respect it had garnered from the regular party establishment, thus undermining its ability to dictate the terms of its participation in politics.

Further, the new form of presidential politics highlighted in Chapters 5 and 6 caused an erosion of the clubs' political status. The centralization of the national party organizations provided presidential candidates with new opportunities to shape national party politics through their own direct line of communication to voters. This was further complicated by the fact that both the Republican and the Democratic club networks fell victim to the manipulations of individuals seeking to boost the aspirations of particular politicians, despite their intention to avoid factional fights. Clarkson's longtime association with the Blaine wing

---

[92] Erie, *Rainbow's End*; Jessica Trounstine, "Dominant Regimes and the Demise of Urban Democracy," *Journal of Politics* (November 2006), 879–93; Ware, *The Democratic Party Heads North*, 96.

of the Republican party and later with presidential aspirant William B. Allison, coupled with his past disloyalty to Harrison, made Clarkson and his league suspect in the McKinley camp.[93] Under Hanna's leadership, the National League of Republican Clubs, which had not been "under control of the committee as much as desired," was "swallowed up" by the national committee, enabling Hanna to control its campaign content, much as he consolidated control over the Republican Congressional Campaign Committee.[94] As noted in Chapter 6, the McKinley campaign made use of the club idea chiefly by forming McKinley clubs whose loyalty was to the candidate, not the party. Such clubs were not likely to continue for long stretches, to maintain voter interest between elections, or to retain members as new candidates were nominated.

The National Association of Democratic Clubs came under the influence of William Randolph Hearst, who was elected its president in 1900. The association became "the publisher's personal property," and he used it to boom his name for the 1904 presidential nomination. In the meantime, Hearst (following his election to Congress in 1902, and his campaigns for mayor of New York City and governor of New York) came to be known as an unreliable partisan ally. He was left "a one-man party" that both of the major parties distrusted. Disappointed by the 1904 convention, Hearst feebly supported the candidacy of Alton B. Parker.[95] Democrats continued to make use of the nationalized committee apparatus, but the National Association of Democratic Clubs was no longer trusted as an impartial entity.

The systemic cross-pressures of U.S. politics thus tore the institutional viability of the clubs apart. Local party clubs continued to meet and organize, but they never again played such a significant role in the national party organizations. Two conclusions that have been drawn about the clubs by historians are particularly unwarrantable, however. First, Robert Marcus concludes that the club phenomenon was insignificant, considered by professional politicians to be a "Sunday School political organization" that was never taken seriously.[96] In

---

[93] See, Dictated Statement of Senator Charles Dick to James B. Morrow, February 10, 1906, box 4, Hanna-McCormick Family Papers, Manuscript Division, Library of Congress. Clarkson privately complained that Hanna refused his offer of help during the 1896 campaign and that his influence in the party was "nil." Clarkson to Samuel Fessenden, October 15, 1896, box 2, Clarkson Papers; Clarkson to H. G. McMillan, October 5, 1896, box 2, Clarkson Papers.

[94] "Now in the Background," *New York Times*, September 26, 1896, 1. McGerr notes that the Republican's league never again managed to gain the support of prominent Republican politicians. McGerr, *The Decline of Popular Politics*, 180.

[95] John K. Winkler, *W. R. Hearst: An American Phenomenon* (New York: Simon & Schuster, 1928), 170–94. Under Hearst's leadership, a 1902 election night celebration at New York's Madison Square sponsored by the National Association of Democratic Clubs ended in tragedy when a fireworks display exploded in the crowd, killing twelve and injuring eighty. Subsequent investigations found both the city (which suspended a pyrotechnics ban for the event) and the association responsible. "To Fix the Blame for Madison Square Tragedy," *New York Times*, November 6, 1902, 1; "27-Year-Old Suit Nets City $30,000," *New York Times*, September 19, 1936, 19.

[96] Marcus, *Grand Old Party*, 137.

the end, politicians did abandon the club networks but only after sinking considerable resources into them in a period of particularly tense political conflict. Presidential candidates afterward – from McKinley to Hearst to (as described in the Conclusion) 1920 presidential aspirant Leonard Wood – mounted their own national networks of clubs specifically oriented to their candidacies, all designed to bypass local organizations and create direct links with voters. What seems more accurate is that national politicians became more aware than ever of the use of irregular amateur political associations as they came to rely more effectively on national publics as they had previously relied on the regular subnational party establishment. However, just as the regular party organizations were susceptible to factional politics, so, too, were the club networks.

Michael McGerr similarly attributes the decline of the club plan to the emergence of "advertised politics," a bastardization of the educational campaign that substituted pithy slogans and candidate personality for the substantive minutiae of the campaign of education. "There was not much need for educational clubs," McGerr concludes, "in the world of advertised politics."[97] This mistakes the method of the club plan for its institutional import. The clubs *were* designed to thicken political debate, but national politicians also promoted them because they helped strengthen the national party organization. Both incentives were present, and both continued to influence politics into the twentieth century. Although the "advertised" methods that McGerr describes did move political discourse to a more simplified version of the campaign of education, it is too simplistic to suggest that a single new campaign style claimed an empire over the conduct of national politics going into the twentieth century.

Most important, the clubs shaped the notion of a national party-in-the-electorate with a direct relationship with the national party organizations. They created a valid notion of party identification that transcended traditional geographic notions of regularity, focused on commitments to party proposals rather than on local partisan communities, presumed self-interest to be an acceptable form of appealing to voters, and insisted that the national party organizations were strengthened by formalized input from the people. They served as vehicles for the "carrier groups" of the new national idea of party, and in their – albeit limited – relations with the local party establishment, they helped legitimate and promote this new idea. As explained in the following chapters, this idea found a more enduring form in the relationship between the presidency and the people.

97 McGerr, *The Decline of Popular Politics*, 180–1.

5

Grover Cleveland and the Emergence of Presidential Party Leadership

As part of its broader effort to limit national political forces, the Jacksonian mode constrained the presidency's independence. The late-nineteenth-century idea of party, however, complemented presidential power and inspired a series of transformative presidential administrations. Grover Cleveland's attempts to force his party to take up tariff reform led to his unprecedented three popular vote victories. William McKinley's portentous reconstruction of the Republican coalition in 1896 was grounded in a crafty convention strategy that took advantage of the previous decades' convention reforms to force his nomination on resistant subnational party organizations. Even the diminutive Benjamin Harrison's oft-derided "front porch campaign" of 1888 was a daring demonstration of presidential candidates' ability to define the terms of their campaigns. Far from a period of presidential forbearance, the years between 1880 and 1900 saw a resurgence of presidential power that changed popular expectations of the presidency.[1] These efforts at carving out political space for national party leadership sped the breakup of the Jacksonian party mode and released presidents from forty-plus years of republican restraints on presidential power.

The Jacksonian nominating convention, paralleling not only the electoral college but also the political geography of the legislative branch, was a distinctive Jacksonian contribution to the American presidency. It canceled out the Founders' decision to make the president responsible to a political constituency distinct from that of the national legislature. The Founders intentionally distinguished the geographic basis of the electoral college from that of the House (electors represented entire states), leaving open the possibility of a significant distinction from the Senate. (Although the Senate was selected

---

[1] Sean Dennis Cashman argues, to the contrary, that presidents at the time "thought of themselves as administrators rather than as party leaders. What authority they did have was based on political influence rather than popular appeal." *America in the Gilded Age: From the Death of Lincoln to the Rise of Theodore Roosevelt* (New York: New York University Press, 1993), 244.

by state legislatures, the states were constitutionally allowed to select electors by popular vote – and soon all did.) The Founders clarified this distinction by prohibiting members of Congress from serving as electors. The convention system essentially undid this by providing the same organizational elites who were influential in selecting members of the legislature with a central role in selecting presidents. Thus, although the constituencies of the president, the Congress, and even state and local politicians were constitutionally distinct, the convention system blended them together. The Jacksonian idea of party celebrated this as a material improvement over the Founders' undemocratic system; Republican Oliver Morton observed in 1877 that "the practice has contradicted the theory for the last sixty years in every particular" and insisted that "this departure from the original theory is the very best feature in the electoral system . . . and is the only guaranty against the corruption of the elector."[2]

Were conventions the truly democratic institution that the laudators of Jacksonian democracy often make them out to be, scholars could suggest, along with Morton, that the Jacksonian party organization had opened the federal establishment to more popular influences. Yet whereas the Founders sought to protect the choice of the president from the influence of "any preestablished body" to gain "the sense of the people" from a group of "men chosen by the people for the special purpose, and at the particular conjuncture,"[3] the parties ensured that presidents would be chosen by a cohesive body of elites possessing distinct organizational interests. "Structurally and institutionally," after all, "party organizations were, more often than not, dominated by the professional leaders who set up and ran the apparatus."[4] It was not unusual for members of Congress to serve in prominent roles in local, state, and national nominating conventions, undermining the Constitution's prohibition of a role for legislators in the presidential selection process. One cannot press the point too far, because the result was hardly a lockstep party-in-government, but instead of presidents constitutionally elevated by means of a constituency distinct from traditional local elites (acting as a national check on local impulses), presidents were elevated only through the influence of subnational elites (and thus reinforced local impulses).

Ensuring local influence was essential for providing that sense of unity that was, according to John Reynolds, "the rationale behind much that was done under the rubrics of the convention system."[5] Nominations made for one office were balanced later by nominations for others. Constituencies left disappointed in one convention were placated in the next. Nominees were selected for their tendency to maintain existing coalitions. Further, campaigns were conducted by local party organizations. National nominees usually avoided

---

[2] Oliver P. Morton, "The American Constitution," *North American Review*, May 1877, 342.
[3] "Federalist 68," Hamilton, Madison, and Jay, *The Federalist*, 435.
[4] Silbey, *The American Political Nation*, 64.
[5] Reynolds, *The Demise of the American Convention System*, 34.

personal campaigning for fear of reducing these local campaigners' flexibility, and so campaigns rarely produced effective mandates.[6]

The disruption of these organizational restraints on the presidency can best be explained by the emergence of competent national party organizations, and the emergence of a new idea of nationalized parties, in the late nineteenth century. Part of this transformed presidency centered on the new form of nationalized, substantive, and interest-oriented campaign appeals; presidential aspirants found new opportunities in this environment to identify themselves with particular policy positions as a means of vying for national party leadership. When such candidates were nominated, their parties appeared to make a commitment to the positions they had taken in their quest for the nomination. National elections came to be seen as contests over presidents' agendas rather than pitched mobilization battles grounded in the efforts of local party organizations. In this way, elections came to be identified as mandates for the candidates' specific positions instead of moral victories for their parties' general principles. Notably, the success of this form of presidential leadership did not originate in the legitimization of presidential rhetoric, as Jeffrey Tulis argues, or in the development of presidential administrative power, as Sidney Milkis argues, but in the availability of a newly nationalized party apparatus that enabled presidents to control more effectively the terms of national campaigns.[7] With the newly nationalized committee apparatus, presidents could "challenge jurisdictional monopolies, changing the boundaries of institutional authority" by taking advantage of the parties' national pretensions.[8] Subnational party organizations accepted this because presidents greatly simplified their task of presenting increasingly complicated national issues to their local audiences, sharpening the focus of the electorate on particular policies and highlighting the party's fitness to address emerging issues.[9]

The patterns of presidential electoral politics took a dramatic turn at this point, as presidents became increasingly capable of asserting party leadership. Between Jackson and Cleveland (1828–1884), only Abraham Lincoln, a wartime president, and Ulysses S. Grant, a popular general closely tied to congressional Republicans, were reelected (see Table 2). Reelection was clearly outside the norm of the Jacksonian party mode. Over the next 56 years (1888–1944), by contrast, presidents were reelected eight times.

A more telling sign of the increasing importance of presidential candidates to party success is the fact that between 1828 and 1884, only four sitting presidents

---

[6] Gil Troy, *See How They Ran: The Changing Role of the Presidential Candidate* (Cambridge, MA: Harvard University Press, 1996).

[7] Jeffrey Tulis, *The Rhetorical Presidency* (Princeton, NJ: Princeton University Press, 1987); Milkis, *The President and the Parties*.

[8] Adam D. Sheingate, "Political Entrepreneurship, Institutional Change, and American Political Development," *Studies in American Political Development* (Fall 2003), 186.

[9] Gary W. Cox notes a similar phenomenon in the establishment of cabinet government in Britain; *The Efficient Secret: The Cabinet and the Development of Political Parties in Victorian England*, (Cambridge: Cambridge University Press, 1987).

TABLE 2. *Presidential reelections, 1789–2004*

1789–1824	1828–1884	1888–1944	1948–2004
Washington	Jackson	Cleveland*	Truman
Jefferson	Lincoln	McKinley	Eisenhower
Madison	Grant	T. Roosevelt	Johnson
Monroe		Wilson	Nixon
		Coolidge	Reagan
		F. Roosevelt	Clinton
		F. Roosevelt	G. W. Bush
		F. Roosevelt	

* non-continuous reelection of 1892

received their party's renomination, although between 1888 and 1944, sitting presidents received this honor eleven times (see Table 3). The trend began with Cleveland, who was renominated twice, once after he had been defeated in the previous election (for a total of three nominations, hence his unique claim to be the only president to have served nonconsecutive terms). Accounts of the rise of the modern presidency must take this into consideration, for only when presidents became valuable enough to their parties to be renominated did they emerge as authoritative leaders of national politics; in the nationalized post-Jacksonian organizational mode, presidential leadership was valuable, because it provided a rallying point for the national organization. When, for instance, renominations in the 1828–1884 and 1888–1944 periods are compared with the 1948–2004 period, the kinship of the post-Jacksonian mode presidency to the "modern" presidency becomes more apparent.

The pattern suggests a strong tendency toward presidential party leadership throughout American history that subsided during the years in which the

TABLE 3. *Presidential Renominations, 1789–2004*

1789–1824	1828–1884	1888–1944	1948–2004
Washington*	Jackson*	Cleveland*#	Truman*
Adams	Van Buren	Harrison	Eisenhower*
Jefferson*	Lincoln*	McKinley*	Johnson*
Madison*	Grant*	T. Roosevelt*	Nixon*
Monroe*		Taft	Ford
J. Q. Adams		Wilson*	Carter
		Coolidge*	Reagan*
		Hoover	G. H. W. Bush
		F. Roosevelt*	Clinton*
		F. Roosevelt*	G. W. Bush*
		F. Roosevelt*	

*indicates successful reelection
#not a sitting president when renominated in 1892

Jacksonian party organization was in place and reemerged when it was weakened in the late nineteenth century. Between 1789 and 1824, and again between 1888 and 2004, presidents managed to develop enough political capital to be renominated (and often reelected) relatively frequently. Between 1828 and 1884, however, only exceptional presidents were reelected because presidential renomination was the exception. This suggests the Jacksonian party mode's strong gravitational pull on presidential authority and its erosion in the late nineteenth century. There is thus good reason to think that at least part of the distinction political scientists draw between the "modern" presidency and a "premodern" presidency is an epiphenomenon of the rise and decline of the Jacksonian party organization, not the emergence of new political phenomena in the twentieth century or even the force of recurring patterns of politics in time. The result can be thought of as "modern" presidential leadership, but it also revived a potential role for the presidency that was envisioned at the Founding, after a forty-year-plus interregnum in which the Jacksonian mode restrained that potential.

The confluence of party development and presidential ambition points to the three persistent ingredients of presidential power highlighted by Daniel Carpenter and Keith Whittington. First, presidents have independent bases of authority rooted in the Constitution, bolstered by the separation of presidential powers from congressional encroachment. Second, the president's status as "the sole authority in American politics whose electoral constituency is the entire nation" bolsters presidents' claims to party leadership because of the unique ability of presidents "to form cross-national, diverse coalitions" that "cut across the existing structure of congressional interests to build new coalitions on their own terms." Third, presidents have the power to set agendas. Here, Carpenter and Whittington argue that the agenda-setting power is a relatively recent innovation, although James Sterling Young argues that the absence of an alternative "adequate political process for producing consensus upon which to govern" implied that "the only position in the Washington community which might have supplied that leadership was the Presidency," a persuasive argument that suggests a longer pedigree for agenda setting as a pervasive calling for presidential power.[10]

The Jacksonian mode undermined each of these sources of power, even though it did not constitutionally alter them. In turn, the Jacksonian mode was challenged as presidents learned to exploit powers inherent to the executive office more effectively in conjunction with the late nineteenth century reform of the party organizations. The strengthening of independent national party organizations, the increasing role presidents played in their election campaigns, and the decreased role of subnational party organizations in national nominating conventions (especially in the Republican party) all worked to enhance the

[10] Keith E. Whittington and Daniel P. Carpenter, "Executive Power in American Institutional Development," *Perspectives on Politics* (September 2003), 498–501. Young, *The Washington Community*, 250, 251.

presidency's intrinsic opportunities to set partisan agendas and thus to portray alternative sources of leadership in the party system as "the more blinkered and parochial concerns of legislators."[11] Only when presidents coupled the source of their political power with the potential inherent in their constitutional position was the full weight of presidential authority thrown behind their "deep-seated impulse to *re*order things . . . [to] alter system boundaries and recast political possibilities."[12]

The two main strains of the modern presidency argument obscure this. The "rhetorical presidency" strain posits the chief executive's growing capacity to "go public" to forge closer relationships between presidents and mass publics, overwhelming the constitutional system's checks and balances and granting the president a newly dominant position in American politics. The rhetorical presidency argument is limited by its tendency to exclude nonrhetorical forms of presidential leadership from consideration and to emphasize the kind of communications technology that facilitates the projection of presidential rhetoric.[13] As Melvin Laracey's study of presidential communication points out, a scholarly bias toward modern rhetoric obscures the fact that "presidents might have used other ways to communicate with the public at other times in our history."[14] An exclusive focus on rhetorical presidential communication – especially a tendency to emphasize the effects of twentieth-century communications technology – actually obscures the effect of other technological advances (such as the railroad, telegraph, and cheaper forms of printing) on the presidency. A focus on rhetoric also obscures certain types of presidential communication, for instance, bypassing all presidential state of the union addresses (then called annual messages), in particular Grover Cleveland's dramatic 1887 annual message, which shaped the message of the Democratic party for years to come and established his then-unprecedented dominance of the party (between Thomas Jefferson and Woodrow Wilson, no annual message was delivered by a president in person). Indeed, Tulis's account of the rhetorical presidency moves abruptly from a consideration of Andrew Johnson's ill-fated 1866 speechmaking tour (which resulted in his impeachment) to Theodore Roosevelt, who successfully used public rhetoric as a means to rally support for presidential policies, missing Cleveland's innovative exertion of party leadership altogether.

Cleveland was no Roosevelt, but leaving out his example obscures the broader process of political learning. For instance, in Tulis's account, a social taboo against presidential leadership "*required*, the proscription of most of the rhetorical practices that have now come to signify leadership."[15] Although

---

[11] Whittington and Carpenter, "Executive Power in American Institutional Development," 499.
[12] Skowronek, The Politics Presidents Make, 4.
[13] Tulis, *The Rhetorical Presidency*; Kernell, *Going Public*.
[14] Laracey, *Presidents and the People*, 8.
[15] Tulis, *The Rhetorical Presidency*, 27, emphasis in original; see also 59. Troy's useful history of presidential campaigns makes a similar argument, arguing that nineteenth-century publics recoiled out of principle from presidential campaigners who campaigned too publicly; *See How They Ran.*

this taboo did shape candidate behavior, it is incorrect to posit it as a monolithic constraint on behavior. Instead, presidents were constantly probing the boundaries of acceptable presidential leadership. The trappings of the modern campaign of full-blown speechmaking tours would wait until Bryan's losing effort in 1896, but short tours by James A. Garfield in 1880 and James G. Blaine in 1884, as well as the "front porch campaigns" of Benjamin Harrison in 1888 and William McKinley in 1896 accomplished the same thing. That the Republican party led the way in this is not accidental. As explained in Chapter 6, reforms of their convention process in the 1880s paved the way for more aggressive nomination campaigns by presidential aspirants and thus brought campaign rhetoric into the forefront of campaign strategy. Presidents also accomplished similar objectives with different tools. In 1884, 1888, and 1892, Democrats were represented by a candidate who disliked speechmaking (Cleveland excelled at producing effective written messages) but was wildly effective at placing himself as the popular head of the party-in-the-electorate. By 1896, with the accumulation of experiences and increasing legitimacy of the new idea of party, presidential rhetoric had become much less controversial. In fact, as explained in Chapter 6, the popularity of the new campaign style put pressure on presidential candidates to engage in more popular rhetoric.

The "administrative presidency" strain of the modern presidency argument posits the growth of national administrative capacities and executive branch exploitation of these new powers as the central difference between modernity and premodernity. In this interpretation, modern presidents are more capable of controlling political outcomes through administrative management than through congressional bargaining or party leadership, luring presidents into the appearance of popular leadership at the expense of genuine reconstructive possibilities. However, these exercises of administrative power hardly contribute to expanded presidential power without the capacity of presidents to explain themselves using the broader tools of national political leadership. For instance, Terry M. Moe argues that presidents have come to be held responsible for administrative performance because "the president is the only politician with a national constituency," which has in turn led to presidents increasingly seeking to expand political control over the federal bureaucracy. The president's singular national constituency does not describe the presidency's administrative character, however, but its political character. So long as the Jacksonian mode restrained presidents' ability to appeal directly to their national constituency, the president's administrative power was not simply focused on "efficiency or effectiveness or coordination per se" but on putting that power to use in ways that were appealing to a different reelection constituency, influenced by subnational political leaders.[16]

---

[16] Terry M. Moe, "The Politicized Presidency," in John E. Chubb and Paul E. Peterson, eds., *The New Direction in American Politics*, (Washington, DC: The Brookings Institution, 1985), 239.

These different strains of the category concept of the modern presidency propel different candidates for the title of "first modern president" into the spotlight. Proponents of the rhetorical presidency strand look to either Theodore Roosevelt or Woodrow Wilson as the originator of modern presidential leadership; proponents of the administrative presidency strand look to Franklin Roosevelt's reconstruction of the executive branch during the New Deal (although Louis Gould provocatively suggests William McKinley as a candidate, largely for his mastery of the task of administering the nascent executive branch).[17] The successful assertion of presidential leadership during the late nineteenth century suggests that the office contained inherent leadership qualities that have become more prominent since the twentieth century but that remained undeveloped during much of the nineteenth. This argument has been more thoroughly articulated by David Nichols, who points out that the presidency enshrined in the 1787 Constitution is itself the root source of the modern presidency. Nichols argues that the American Founders sought to reconcile the tension between democracy and executive power in part by limiting the presidency's dependence on Congress and subnational bodies and empowering it with a vibrant connection to the people; "it was the American invention of the democratic executive [in 1787] that took the decisive step in uniting executive power and popular government."[18] Indeed, this was Woodrow Wilson's analysis, as he noted of the election of Grover Cleveland, that "in him we got a president . . . by immediate choice from out of the body of the people, as the Constitution has all along appeared to expect."[19]

To suggest that the end of the Jacksonian mode was simply a wholesale return to Founding intent is also misguided, however, because the passage through the Jacksonian mode left distinctive markings on the presidency. In foreclosing the caucus model of party organization that selected all of the pre-Jacksonian presidents besides Washington and John Q. Adams, the Jacksonian organization drew the presidency away from the closer relationship with Congress that had the potential to develop out of the caucus – which also shut off a potential source of strength for the office.

---

[17] Proponents of Roosevelt's role include Gerald Gamm and Renee Smith, "Presidents, Parties, and the Public: Evolving Patterns of Interaction, 1877–1929," in Richard Ellis, ed., *Speaking to the People: The Rhetorical Presidency in Historical Perspective*, (Amherst: University of Massachusetts Press, 1998); Tulis suggests that Wilson was the first modern rhetorical president in *The Rhetorical Presidency*, as does Ryan L. Teten in "Evolution of the Modern Rhetorical Presidency: Presidential Presentation and Development of the State of the Union Address," *Presidential Studies Quarterly*, (June 2003); and Ceaser, *Presidential Selection*. Gould, *The Modern American Presidency*.

[18] Nichols, *The Myth of the Modern Presidency*, 26–7, 166. See also Harvey Mansfield, *Taming the Prince: The Ambivalence of Modern Executive Power* (Baltimore: Johns Hopkins University Press, 1993). Daniel Galvin and Colleen Shogan similarly argue that "many of the characteristics of the presidency that are claimed to be distinctively modern are, in fact, transhistorical," in "Presidential Politicization and Centralization across the Modern-Traditional Divide," *Polity* (April 2004), 477.

[19] Woodrow Wilson, "Mr. Cleveland as President," *Atlantic Monthly* (March 1897), 289.

Did it have to be thus? Americans' Revolutionary era preference for strong legislatures over strong executives was constitutionally revised by the Founding, but the ideology of strong legislatures still maintained a strong cultural hold and considerable state-level institutionalization. In most states, legislative caucuses rather than popular conventions selected nominees, suggesting that political practice continued to uphold what the 1787 Constitution was supposed to discourage. Given these strong cultural, intellectual, and institutional indicators, the possibility of a continuance and strengthening of the caucus system even after the failures of 1824 and 1828 is not beyond the realm of reasoned inference. Had this occurred, a subsequent intensification of party discipline and programmatic party politics along the lines of British parliamentary development was not outside the realm of the possible.[20] Political science has not given the extinction of caucus-based party government the attention it deserves, instead drawing a rather uncomplicated link between the expansion of suffrage and an increasingly popular presidency. Yet the rise of universal white manhood suffrage alone is not enough to point to an inevitable shift of party leadership to the presidency, even if "the president was the sole authentic spokesman for and representative of national majorities."[21] The expansion of suffrage in Britain, for instance, contributed to the consolidation of parliamentary control over the executive functions of government through the creation of the cabinet system.[22] Perhaps in such a counterfactual scenario it would be the legislative leader Henry Clay, not Martin Van Buren, who came to be hailed as the father of the American party system.

The Jacksonian mode also provided an institutional basis for a democratized presidency – indeed, given the limitations on American media, communication, and transportation systems, it was possibly the *only* means of democratizing the presidency at the time. Compared with the caucus-dominated party system that existed before, conventions marked a revolution in popular participation. Again, it did not have to be thus. Both the electoral college and the mechanism of sending deadlocked presidential elections to the House offered institutional models for a less-democratic presidency. Without the Jacksonian convention system – or without a judiciously constructed one that could similarly integrate diverse states and regions – alternative outcomes might have resulted in

---

[20] The decline of the caucus was no isolated phenomenon. The period saw dramatic declines in suffrage restrictions (most often falsely attributed to the rise of Jacksonian democracy); indeed, while legislatures were "suffering [the] loss [of the caucus], they were also experiencing general curtailment of their elective functions, as evidenced by the trend toward the popular choice of electors, governors, and other state officials." Richard P. McCormick, "Political Development and the Second Party System," in William Nesbit Chambers and Walter Dean Burnham, eds., *The American Party Systems: Stages of Development* (New York: Oxford University Press, 1975), 105. My argument for a caucus-based counterfactual draws heavily on McCormick's argument.

[21] Robert A. Dahl, "On Removing Certain Impediments to Democracy in the United States," *Political Science Quarterly* (Spring 1977), 6.

[22] Cox, *The Efficient Secret*.

more frequent recurrence of this kind of mechanism. An injudiciously balanced convention framework, coupled with the ever-present threat of sectionalism, might have provoked factional secession from the major parties, as it did in 1860 when the Democratic party was fragmented into sectional blocs, or led to alternative localist paths to the nomination, as occurred in 1824 and 1828 when state legislatures nominated prominent candidates in the absence of a strong consensus behind the congressional caucus nominee. It is not beyond the realm of possibility that this outcome, repeated over time, could have produced a tendency toward coalition presidencies (perhaps among regional legislative blocs) grounded in political horse-trading in the electoral college and the House of Representatives, rather than recourse to the people through majoritarian parties. Although it is tempting to assume that political elites would have devised some popular remedy, there is again no reason to be confident that political leaders would have inevitably turned to popular solutions. Just as likely, members of Congress would have preferred to let presidential selection recur to the House frequently, strengthening Congress's hold on the executive branch and the political agenda.[23]

The choice of the Jacksonian organizational mode thus more muscularly shaped the contours of American political development than is accounted for when one views the convention system as a natural outgrowth of the expansion of suffrage in the early republic; as such, it should be considered as a contributor to the character of the modern presidency. During its forty-year-plus period of dominance, it reinforced the propriety of extra-legislative presidential selection, even though it simultaneously limited the independent action of presidents by holding them captive to congressional patronage demands. It also reinforced a powerful logic – if not a reality – of presidential responsibility to the national public, an important step in a regime still uncomfortable with notions of direct democracy.

There is thus reason to consider the birth of the "modern presidency" to be a story about the removal of the Jacksonian mode's restraints on persistent sources of presidential authority, rather than the creation of completely novel sources of power. By this reasoning, the modern presidency is not really all that modern after all but an example of the remarkably conservative (a term meant with a descriptive rather than an ideological connotation) nature of American political development. Although "disruption of the status quo ante is basic to the politics presidents make" and presidents are constantly "scrambling for fresh sources of political influence to sustain their leadership projects,"[24] the course of the development of presidential power in the United States has been relatively stable. The careers of the late-nineteenth-century presidents (and

---

[23] These are precisely the outcomes that Van Buren and his copartisans hoped to prevent. Ceaser, *Presidential Selection*, 131–49.

[24] Skowronek, *The Politics Presidents Make*, 4; Scott C. James, "The Evolution of the Presidency: Between the Promise and the Fear," in Joel D. Aberbach and Mark A. Peterson, eds., *The Executive Branch* (New York: Oxford University Press, 2005), 4.

of the most important failed presidential candidate, Bryan) demonstrate just how the tradition of "modern" presidential leadership is intertwined with the abandonment of the Jacksonian mode.

Grover Cleveland, William Jennings Bryan, and the Emergence of Presidential Party Leadership

Rarely do successive presidential candidates of the same party conjure up such divergent historical images as do Grover Cleveland and William Jennings Bryan. Cleveland is routinely portrayed as dowdy, conventional, and conservative; Bryan is billed as electrifying, innovative, and radical. Bryan's performance in the 1896 campaign marks him as a prophet of the personality-driven presidential politics of the twentieth century. Cleveland's status as the only president to serve nonconsecutive terms in office strikes modern sentiments as smacking of the unprincipled, organization-dominated politics of the nineteenth century. Indeed, the differences between the two men feed the perception of a stark difference between modern and premodern presidential leadership.

The politics of the period invites such contrasts. Cleveland was viewed as the Democratic party's savior in 1884, 1888, and 1892, a principled reformer of tremendous personal popularity within his party. He was a symbol of what would come to be called "progressive" reform, speaking of the necessity of civil service and tariff reforms. By 1893, however, Cleveland's image had changed. In the midst of a dramatic depression, Cleveland appeared ineffective, steadfastly resisting popular demands for inflationary monetary policies, conspiring with Wall Street to save the gold standard, and sending in U.S. troops to shut down the 1894 Pullman strike. By the time of the 1896 election, there was little left to distinguish the Cleveland Democrats from McKinley Republicans on the single issue that defined the party split: the battle over whether to maintain the gold standard or to inflate currency by basing it partly on silver. The 1896 Democratic party platform, written by silverites, was a nearly point-by-point refutation of the Cleveland years; attacks on the Republican party were practically an afterthought.[25]

There were, however, considerable continuities between the political careers of Cleveland and Bryan, and these are part and parcel of the quiet unleashing of presidential authority due to the erosion of the Jacksonian party mode. Despite the fierce antagonisms that existed between both men and their followings, they practiced a very similar form of politics. Both recognized the value of the associational explosion, drawing on extra-partisan organizations to undermine the boundaries of party regularity and build independent political authority for themselves. Both turned the educational campaign and nationalized parties into partisan authority. Further, both broke out of the traditional

---

[25] Louis W. Koenig, *Bryan: A Political Biography of William Jennings Bryan* (New York: G. P. Putnam's Sons, 1971), 188–9; Bensel, *Passion and Preferences*, 94–6.

Jacksonian party mode, and both did so for the purpose of reorienting the principles of the Democratic party and thus renewing its popular appeal. Between them, Cleveland and Bryan dominated thirty years of Democratic party politics (between 1884 and 1908, they were nominated three times each, with only the nomination of Alton B. Parker in 1904 breaking the succession). They also provided an important bridge between the party transformations of the late-nineteenth-century and twentieth-century presidential politics; there is a clear line of influence from Cleveland to Bryan to the "modern presidencies" of Democrats Wilson and Franklin Roosevelt. Indeed, differences between the former and latter pairs can, in many ways, be chalked up to timing; Wilson and Roosevelt came to power after years of work by Cleveland and Bryan in eroding the Jacksonian mode.

Cleveland's Early Executive Experiences

Grover Cleveland was not, as many assume of nineteenth-century presidents, a favorite son, a dark horse, or a figurehead for behind-the-scenes power holders; nor is Lewis Gould's derision of "the law-office approach of Grover Cleveland" accurate.[26] Rather he was an experienced and thoughtful career executive who had spent his political career working out ways to transform executive power into popular political power. He made expert use of the political trends of the late nineteenth century and understood how those trends shaped party strategy. Although he assumed the presidency with a more traditional executive pose than he had as mayor and governor – insisting that he would be a "constitutional president" – by the end of his first term, he returned to the vigorous executive party leadership he had practiced in lower executive offices.

Before 1882, Cleveland's political career was decidedly local and conspicuously executive, including stints as sheriff of Erie County in 1870 and mayor of Buffalo in 1881.[27] He was supported locally in his mayoral campaign by the kind of reform-minded businessmen who were building extra-partisan reform organizations in the late nineteenth century, and his success as a reformer won him prominence among men of that sort statewide. In 1882, he was elected to the New York governorship, and during his single term in that post, he won national renown as an opponent of Tammany Hall. Two years later, he was nominated for the presidency, supported by reformers who were said to "love him most for the enemies he has made."[28] His rise was meteoric, fueled at every step of the way by the reformist element then beginning to make itself felt in politics. For this reason, Robert Kelly insists that "the most important fact about Cleveland may have been the way in which he was so summarily plucked

---

[26] Gould, *The Modern American Presidency*, xiv.

[27] As sheriff he personally presided over executions, making him the only president who could claim to have been an "executive" in the fullest sense of the word.

[28] "Work of the Third Day," *New York Times*, July 11, 1884, 1.

from obscurity and hurried to the White House," by the trend of antimachine reformism.[29]

Although he was by no means a populist, Cleveland combined a Jacksonian notion of the executive as the people's tribune with the late-nineteenth-century ambitions of the campaign of education. This combination of early- and late-nineteenth-century usages of party leadership proved a potent one[30] and contributed to his sense of "an almost mystical bond between himself and the nation at large."[31] If Cleveland's personality encouraged such notions, it is clear that few such men had had their predilections ratified by the party system since Jackson himself. That it did so in 1884 both flowed from and accelerated the new national citizens' ambitions for American politics.

Although Cleveland was the object of the Mugwump bolt to the Democrats in 1884, Cleveland was no Mugwump. Rather, he saw himself as bringing order to the confusion of nineteenth-century party politics without shattering the otherwise useful bonds of party loyalty (much as James Clarkson had done in his work with the National League of Republican Clubs); Cleveland was insistent on making his accomplishments party accomplishments. Accepting his party's nomination for governor, he observed that "the platform of principles adopted by the convention meets with my hearty approval" and vowed to "impress them upon my administration." In his presidential nomination acceptance letter two years later, he insisted that "when the wisdom of the political party . . . has outlined its policy and declared its principles, it seems to be that nothing in the character of the office [of president] or the necessities of the case requires more, from the candidate . . . than the suggestion of certain well-known truths, so absolutely vital to the safety and welfare of the nation that they cannot be too often recalled or too seriously enforced." When renominated in 1888, he intoned: "the political party to which I owe allegiance both honors and commands me. It places in my hand the proud standard and bids me bear it high at the front in a battle which it wages bravely."[32]

Cleveland had, from the beginning of his career, a sense that the party-in-the-electorate empowered the partisan executive vis-à-vis his party, as well as a sense that an alliance with the people against party elites expanded independent executive power. At a Democratic rally during his gubernatorial campaign he declared that he would "show to party managers that the elective franchise is not held by the people to perpetuate them in power and place, and that the people are not mere puppets to dance when they pipe, without regard to the

---

29 Robert Kelly, *The Transatlantic Persuasion: The Liberal-Democratic Mind in the Age of Gladstone* (New York: Alfred A. Knopf, 1969), 322.
30 "Grover Cleveland," *Buffalo Sunday News*, July 26, 1882, carton 107, Lamont Papers.
31 Kelly, *The Transatlantic Persuasion*, 322.
32 Grover Cleveland, "Letter Accepting Nomination for Governor," 3; "Letter Accepting Nomination for President," 10; "Speech to the Committee on Notification," 13, all in George F. Parker, ed., *The Writings and Speeches of Grover Cleveland* (New York: Cassell Publishing Company, 1892).

methods which made the music."[33] Thus, he advised that "the party which leads in an honest effort to return to better and purer methods will receive the confidence of our citizens and secure their support," suggesting that reform was not a means of weakening party but of perfecting its function as a popular mouthpiece.[34] This was not merely the overexcitement of a novice politician; in 1890, he similarly warned Tammany that the people would "revolt against the dominance of any political party which, intrusted with power, sordidly seeks only its continuance."[35] Cleveland's public posture of the party outsider, battling for the good of the people, was one twentieth-century presidents turned into an art form.

Then, as now, the public response often obscured the fine distinction between popular leadership and party leadership. "Mr. Cleveland dwells on the welfare of the people, not of a party,"[36] enthused the *Buffalo Express* during his campaign for governor. His gubernatorial letter of acceptance was declared "a platform of itself, and one upon which all good citizens, of whatever party, can stand."[37] This stance appealed to independents, insurgents, and Republicans, belying traditional notions of regularity as the safeguard of party unity. "There could be no better evidence of the extraordinary obliteration of party issues that has come upon the country," wrote the *Utica Herald* with some wariness, "than the fact that a democratic candidate for governor of New York state announces no principles to which any republican can take exception."[38]

Cleveland also understood how to use the new associations to undermine traditional party lines and build momentum for his leadership. Rallying such groups prepared a ready-made constituency to support his popular appeals. During his gubernatorial campaign, he and his managers encouraged independent Republicans to bolt to the Democratic candidate by founding and funding independent Republican clubs that directed them into the Cleveland camp.[39] He encouraged interest-based associations to organize for political action, urging them to bring their private interests into the public realm.[40] To an assemblage of farmers in 1883, he dismissed the notion that "politics is a disgraceful game, and should be left untouched by those having private concerns and business which engages their attention," insisting instead that "this

---

33 "The Buffalo Democracy," *Lockport* (NY) *Union*, n.d., carton 107, Lamont Papers.

34 Cleveland, "Letter Accepting Nomination for Governor," "Address as President, at Washington (March 4, 1885), Parker, *Writings and Speeches*, 6, 32.

35 Grover Cleveland to Abraham B. Tappan, June 30, 1890, Bergh, ed., *Letters and Addresses of Grover Cleveland*, 228.

36 "A Marked Contrast," *Buffalo Express*, October 10, 1882, carton 107, Lamont Papers.

37 "The Ring of True Metal," *Syracuse Courier*, n.d., carton 107, Lamont Papers; "Cleveland's Letter," *Rochester Union*, October 10, 1882, carton 107, Lamont Papers.

38 "It Will Meet with Hearty Approval," *Utica Herald*, n.d., carton 107, Lamont Papers.

39 W. S. Bissell to Daniel S. Lamont, October 13, 1882, container 1, Lamont Papers.

40 When Cleveland's assistant George Parker edited a collection of his papers in 1892, he featured five chapters of addresses to farmers' organizations, business associations, religious and charitable organizations, professional bodies, and political clubs, indicating the importance Cleveland attached to such appeals. See Parker, *Writings and Speeches*.

neglect serves to give over the most important interests to those who care but little for their protection." To a Farmers' Alliance lodge in Ohio, he derided the "indifference" shown by farmers to the tariff and urged that they "insist that this cost shall not be increased for the purpose of collecting revenue." To an annual meeting of the Pennsylvania Grange, he praised the methods of the associational explosion, and the "discussion, and the comparison of views which necessarily are the accompaniment of such a meeting."[41] He spoke similarly to business associations, urging "the business men of this country [to] cultivate political thought" and to "cease to eschew participation in political action." He reminded a merchant's association in Milwaukee that "their duty is not entirely done when they have exercised their suffrage and indicated their choice of the incumbent" and recommended advocacy for business interests. To the New York Chamber of Commerce, he expressed hope that through extra-partisan associations "there may be impressed upon the administration of our government a business character and tendency free from the diversion of passion."[42]

Cleveland's actions suggested an understanding of the new idea of party. He resisted the deferential compromise insisted upon by traditional party politicians and drew attention to the popular and associational sources of party renewal that he cultivated.[43] When assessing Democratic victories, he parsed the distinction between "the triumph of Democratic principles" and the fact that their "success was made possible by the co-operation of many who are not to be considered as irrevocably and under all circumstances members of our party." He riled party regulars when he noted that independent Republicans "trusted us and allied themselves with us in the late struggle because they saw that those with whom they had acted politically were heedless of the interests of the country and untrue to the people."[44] He embraced the campaign of education, explaining that "it was deemed important to appeal to the reason and judgment of the American people, to the end that the Democratic party should be reinforced as well as that the activity and zeal of those already in our ranks should be stimulated." This was, Cleveland argued, "the manner in which access has been gained to the plain people of the land, and the submission to their reason and judgment of the objects and purposes for which the campaign was undertaken." Just as the extra-partisan associations recognized, Cleveland argued that the dominance of the regular party organization was not due to "the ignorance of the people which had led them to submit to the evils

41 Cleveland, "At the Oswegatchie Fair," 135–6; "To a Steubenville (O.) Lodge of the Farmers' Alliance," 142; "To the Annual Grange Picnic of Pennsylvania," 141, all in Parker, *Writings and Speeches.*
42 Cleveland, "At the Commercial Exchange, Philadelphia," 144; "Before the Milwaukee Merchants' Association," 146; "To the New York Chamber of Commerce," 147, all in Parker, *Writings and Speeches.*
43 See Nevins, *Grover Cleveland,* 495, on Cleveland's hostility to Tammany in particular.
44 Cleveland to the Young Men's Democratic Association of Canton, Ohio, November 25, 1890, in *Letters and Addresses of Grover Cleveland,* 270–1.

of bad government" but that popular dislocation from the party organizations "was partly owing to the busy activity of their occupations, and the consequent neglect of political subjects, and partly to the rigidity of their party ties and their unquestioning confidence in party leadership."[45]

Cleveland's Executive Messages

Cleveland further had a thorough sense of how to marry the campaign of education to executive power. In particular, Cleveland used executive messages to grab public attention and assert the executive's ability to articulate party commitments, thus marrying the campaign of education to executive leadership.[46] Examples chart the progression of his career. His 1883 gubernatorial veto of a public transit bill became a legendary testament to his political wherewithal. A Tammany-sponsored bill proposed to lower fares on New York City street railways from ten to five cents and received tremendous popular support as a service to working men; Cleveland called it a breach of contract between the state (which had granted the railway builders a franchise on the basis of a ten-cent fare) and the railways (which had invested their capital with the ten-cent fare in mind), and thus an abuse of legislative power. Despite clear opposition, Cleveland sent a strongly worded veto to the state legislature, intoning that "the State should not only be strictly just, but scrupulously fair, and in its relations to the citizens every legal and moral consideration should be recognized,"[47] then waited for the political backlash.

To his surprise, the press and the public responded in resounding affirmation of his veto. In the state legislature, Theodore Roosevelt, a formerly "conspicuous" advocate of the bill, admitted that the governor's message had changed his mind, and voted to sustain Cleveland's veto. The response etched in Cleveland's mind (and Roosevelt's as well[48]) the ability of an executive officer to lead his party through popular appeals. In a phrase repeated throughout Cleveland's career, the *Albany Evening Journal* claimed that Cleveland had become "bigger and better than his party."[49] When Tammany legislators retaliated by refusing to confirm some of his appointments, he fumed to an aide, "give me a sheet of paper.... I'll tell the people what a set of D – d rascals they have upstairs." He then composed a scathing message to the state senate, decried its refusal to confirm his appointees, and released it to the press.[50] The public declarations of the executive, he learned, focused the people in dramatic ways.

His first effort at national party leadership occurred after his first presidential election in 1884, but before his 1885 inauguration, with a public letter on

---

[45] Cleveland, "Address to the Toast, 'The Campaign of Education,'" Parker, *Writings and Speeches*, 276–7.

[46] Bruce Miroff, "The Presidential Spectacle," in Michael Nelson, ed., *The Presidency and the Political System*, 8th edition (Washington, DC: Congressional Quarterly Press, 2005).

[47] Quoted in Nevins, *Grover Cleveland*, 116.

[48] The event is recounted in Theodore Roosevelt, *Theodore Roosevelt: An Autobiography* (New York: The Macmillan Company, 1913), chap. 3.

[49] Quoted in Nevins, *Grover Cleveland*, 117–19.

[50] Ibid., 122.

civil service reform. Cleveland had come to office on a wave of Mugwump support, but the election of 1884 had not been an educational campaign. The Mugwumps, in fact, contributed to the personality politics so prevalent in the campaign by promoting new information on James Blaine's scandalous dealings with an Arkansas railroad line and investigating rumors of Cleveland's bachelor days in Buffalo.[51] The few stirrings of a new form of presidential campaign had appeared in Blaine's decision to launch a limited speaking tour of the country ("I know no reason why I should not face the American people," he declared[52]). However, this soon turned into a debacle that reinforced the wisdom behind the Jacksonian norm against candidate speechmaking. On a New York stop shortly before election day, Blaine was preceded by the Reverend Samuel Burchard, who decried Democrats as the party of "Rum, Romanism, and Rebellion." The resultant uproar among Catholic voters has long been considered a contributing factor in Blaine's defeat.[53] Cleveland, keeping with traditional expectations of presidential candidates, did not campaign.

An opportunity to break his silence came from one of the new national associations that Cleveland courted so assiduously, Moorefield Storey's National Civil Service Reform League. In a letter to the president-elect, the league expressed its "anxiety lest the party change in the National Executive" roll back the effects of the Pendleton Act by setting off a spate of partisan removals and appointments. They urged the president-elect to take care "in the exercise of the great power with which the American people have intrusted you."[54] The association wanted Cleveland's assurances that his reputation as a reformer would follow him to Washington.

George William Curtis, the letter's author, had reason to know what to expect in response. He had written Cleveland a similar letter during the campaign and received a friendly reply in which Cleveland promised to protect not only those officers protected by the letter of the Pendleton Act but that "the same considerations should apply" to "other officials of a non-political character, to whose retention in place, during the time for which they are appointed."[55] The president, in other words, possessed the discretion to push the spirit of reform past the letter of the law. Now elected, Cleveland publicly

[51] Horace Samuel Merrill, *Bourbon Leader: Grover Cleveland and the Democratic Party* (Boston: Little, Brown and Company, 1957), 61–2.

[52] Quoted in Troy, *See How They Ran*, 93.

[53] Hirsch, *William C. Whitney*, 241, points out that Democrats hired a stenographer to follow Blaine. The audience, Blaine included, missed the remark, but the stenographer rushed the alliterative slogan into print. Troy, *See How They Ran*, 93, follows Democratic National Committee member Arthur Pue Gorman's claim that he caught the remark and directed an "underling" to jot it down. The suggestion in both accounts of a stenographer ready-at-hand suggests Democrats had invested in breaking Blaine's candidacy on the speechmaking tour.

[54] George William Curtis to Cleveland, December 20, 1884, reprinted in "Civil Service Reform," *New York Times*, December 30, 1884, 4.

[55] Cleveland to George W. Curtis, October 24, 1884, in Allan Nevins, ed., *Letters and Addresses of Grover Cleveland* (New York: Houghton Mifflin, 1933), 46.

reiterated his position to Curtis. For authority to do so he acknowledged the statute but only as evidence "that a practical reform in the civil service is demanded," emphasizing instead "the further fact that a sentiment is generally prevalent among patriotic people calling for the fair and honest enforcement of the law."[56] Many subnational Democratic organizations had not made civil service reform a central component of their campaign, but calling on his reputation as a reformer Cleveland was essentially claiming a popular mandate for reform, one that came from the people rather than his party's campaign management.

Cleveland could have pointed to Democrats' role in passing the Pendleton Act or to the practical necessity of proving the party's capacity to enforce the law, but instead he rooted his decision in a personal commitment to the party's standard. "I regard myself pledged to this," he maintained, "because my conception of true Democratic faith and public duty requires that this and all other statutes should be with good faith and without evasion enforced." This claim to have a determinative "conception" of the "true Democratic faith" marked him as distinct from his party's establishment or the convention that had produced the platform. The implication here – that there was a "true" party faith, and that he, as president, was duty bound to enforce that "in good faith" – linked executive prerogative to party leadership. He, not the party elite (who, as most politicians acknowledged, hoped for a weak execution of the law), would be the final judge of the platform's meaning, and he located this authority in his nomination by the party. The party, after all, had chosen him with full knowledge of his reputation as a reformer, and in selecting him, he would have it known, it had not restrained him but restrained itself. Thus, he could declare that "in many utterances made prior to my election as President, approved by the party to which I belong and which I have no disposition to disclaim, I have in effect promised the people that this should be done."[57] Party leaders might kick, but they had used their singular national meeting to declare for his candidacy, and this committed the party as well as its standard bearer. This was, it should be noted, a complete reversal of the notion of presidential "availability" that had limited presidential authority under the Jacksonian mode. The old notion held that the presidential nominee was "available" – capable of representing the widest range of party factions possible – rather than a substantive leader. Cleveland implied the opposite: a party that selected a candidate with a well-known position on an issue came to pledge itself to that issue and so grafted his views onto its official "aura."[58] As the Seattle *Post-Intelligencer* would put it, he was claiming that "he constitutes

56   Cleveland to George W. Curtis, December 25, 1884, reprinted in "Civil Service Reform," *New York Times*, December 30, 1884, 4.

57   Cleveland to Curtis, December 25, 1884, reprinted in "Civil Service Reform," *New York Times*, December 30, 1884, 4.

58   Benson, *The Concept of Jacksonian Democracy*, 216.

party opinion, party caucuses, party conventions, party platforms, nay, even the party itself, all within the circumference of one capacious waistband!"[59]

Driving the point home, Cleveland addressed members of his party who might second-guess that decision. "If I were addressing none but party friends," Cleveland intoned, not completely hypothetically, as he knew the letter would be published (he had not included any such passage in his earlier private exchange with Curtis), "I should deem it entirely proper to remind them that though the coming Administration is to be Democratic, a due regard for the people's interest does not permit faithful party work to be always rewarded by appointment to office." Yet he offered a word of hope to his party friends; referring to Republican officeholders, Cleveland observed that "many now holding such positions have forfeited all just claim to retention, because they have used their places for party purposes in disregard to their duty to the people," and thus "proved themselves offensive partisans."[60] Patronage-seekers believed this was an excuse for housecleaning – after all, so many Republican officeholders had engaged in partisan activity that this qualification was likely to prove fruitful. As removals for this cause proceeded apace, some Mugwumps complained of Cleveland's parsing of words.[61]

At the moment, however, Cleveland's message was an electric charge. Newspapers acknowledged that "the response of Mr. Cleveland is addressed, through the league, to their wide constituency, and it bears out the confident hope which the friends of reform among his supporters have entertained" and declared that "it is one of the most noteworthy political documents of this generation."[62] From Washington came reports that "Gov. Cleveland's letter upon the civil service has been read to-day with more interest than anything else in the newspapers, and in the departments it has been the talk of all employes [sic], great and small." Dorman Eaton, the godfather of civil service reform, affirmed that "it is a platform on the subject to which it relates. The views of the letter are those common to all true statesmen of both parties. These views are those most rapidly growing in the hearts of the people."[63]

Cleveland did not limit himself to proclamations on civil service reform; he consistently instructed his co-partisans on the matter. Testing Cleveland's mettle, Tammany Hall sent him an invitation to its 1885 July Fourth celebration, including an admonition that "the Administration should so discharge all its functions as to merit not only the approbation of the people but at the same time insure a harmonious party united in Jeffersonian Democracy." This was a reminder of the Jacksonian mode practice of "harmonizing" the party through patronage, including factions that, like Tammany, had not supported the

[59] "The Clevelander's Creed," [Seattle] *Post-Intelligencer*, July 8, 1890, 9.
[60] Cleveland to Curtis, December 25, 1884, reprinted in "Civil Service Reform," *New York Times*, December 30, 1884, 4.
[61] Merrill, *Bourbon Leader*, 96–7.
[62] "Mr. Cleveland and the Civil Service," *New York Times*, December 30, 1884, 4.
[63] "Cleveland and Reform," *New York Times*, December 31, 1884, 1.

nominee. Cleveland persisted in the language of his civil service reform letter but couched it in partisan terms. "My conception of the true purposes and the mission of my party," he replied in his public response to Tammany (again touting the primacy of his "conception" of his party's position), "convinces me that if the present Administration merits the intelligent approval of the people, this result of itself certainly should 'insure a harmonious party united in Jeffersonian Democracy.'"[64] He repeated a similar theme in a letter rebuffing a politician's request for patronage: "I understand that the party which succeeded to the Administration in the last election is a progressive Democracy; and it should be really and truly in full accord with the wishes of the people, and willing to base its hopes of a continuance in power upon popular approbation," rather than on deferential compromise.[65]

The popular reception given to Cleveland's public missives gave credence to his faith in the ability of executive leadership to transcend the Jacksonian mode's limits. In a nationalized, media-saturated polity, the president had new opportunities to define partisan objectives; it was observed of his first annual address, for instance, that

Mr. Cleveland's message has been talked of everywhere to-day, and in such a way as to make it plain that even those Senators and Representatives who ask for more time before expressing their opinions have grasped its points and concluded that it is not a merely formal report to them, to be sneered at or kept out of the way.[66]

Tariff reform advocate J. S. Moore noted that "the general favorable reception by a whole people, irrespective of party politics, of the President's message...simply foreshadows the desire of the nation that due heed should be given by Congress to those important recommendations which the President...so clearly urge[s]."[67] Through these messages, Cleveland charted a new path for the presidency.

The 1887 Tariff Message

Although his early messages were well received, it was his annual message of 1887 that secured Cleveland's dominance of the Democratic party. Presidential annual addresses were then, as one correspondent wrote of Hayes's 1879 effort, "more a rehash of events than an expression of ideas, more like the work of a clerk than the production of a thinker."[68] In this context, Cleveland's message was a dramatic departure. The message was devoted solely to tariff reform, omitting even the appeal to God that traditionally began such addresses.

---

64 Cleveland to P. Henry Surgo [Grand Sachem of Tammany Hall], July 1, 1885, in Nevins, *Letters and Addresses of Grover Cleveland*, 66.

65 Cleveland to "A Western Politician" [never mailed], August 25, 1885, in Nevins, *The Letters and Addresses of Grover Cleveland*, 72.

66 "The President's Opinions," *New York Times*, December 10, 1885, 5.

67 J.S. Moore, "Letter to the Editor," *New York Times*, December 17, 1885, 9.

68 "Hayes' Message," *Napa County* (California) *Reporter*, December 5, 1879, 2.

The 1884 Democratic platform demanded "a tariff for revenue only" and recommended lowering tariff rates so as to fund only necessary government operations. Any amount above this, they believed, protected favored American industries, raised consumer costs, and created a surplus of government receipts. The platform did not restrain all party members effectively, however. The doctrine of "deferential compromise" allowed congressional Democrats to advocate protection of industries in their districts, thus preventing any action on reform. In fact, between 1876 and 1881, the Democratic speaker of the House, Samuel Randall, had led a self-conscious bloc of protectionist Democrats who openly defied the party's platform. Cleveland deplored his party's intractability on this signature issue. Lamenting his position, he complained that

I have been here five months now, and have met many people who had no friendship for me, and were intent on selfishly grabbing all they could get, without any regard to the country, the party, or to me. . . . I don't want these friends go; but I am tired of this beating about the bush and all this talk about "second-handed invitation" and "holes in a plank" and that sort of thing.[69]

The issue was so contentious among congressional Democrats that they could not even hold a binding caucus, and when the Democratic-controlled House introduced the 1886 Morrison Tariff Bill, thirty-four Democrats betrayed their platform.[70]

Cleveland initially showed little initiative on the issue. Unlike civil service reform, Cleveland was not closely identified with tariff reform and hesitated to focus on an issue that would divide his party without a clear popular mandate. Beyond routine mentions in his annual addresses, he avoided tariff legislation.[71] Tariff reform had qualities that recommended it to Cleveland's attention, however. First, it was a source of periodic monetary crises that threatened economic stability. The tariff created a government surplus – certain to grow larger with Cleveland's insistence on government frugality – and when tariff revenues ran high enough, it caused monetary contractions, freezing currency in government. Republicans relieved this surplus through veterans' pensions and infrastructure projects, spreading the protective system's appeal beyond the manufacturers who benefited directly from it; Cleveland and the Democrats opposed such expenditures as an expansion of federal government power, and his vetoes of private pension bills spun off from this opposition.[72]

Second, Cleveland believed that the Democrats needed to demonstrate their governing capacities – his was the first Democratic presidency since the

---

[69] Cleveland to Charles Goodyear, August 6, 1885, in Nevins, ed., *The Letters of Grover Cleveland*, 71.

[70] Nevins, *Grover Cleveland*, 269, 280, 287; Bensel, *The Political Economy of American Industrialization*, 476.

[71] Nevins, *Grover Cleveland*, 269–70.

[72] Bensel, *Yankee Leviathan*, chap. 4. On Cleveland's position on government frugality, see Robert Higgs, *Crisis and Leviathan: Critical Episodes in the Growth of American Government* (New York: Oxford University Press, 1987), 83–4.

war – and that the tariff would do this by lowering costs and staving off contraction. Failing to meet the demand would be a disaster for his presidency and his party: "if the first Democratic administration," he wrote, "had failed, thro' deference to 'policy,' to bravely meet the responsibility of leading that attack, the party should never be trusted again."[73] Cleveland thus had incentives to establish the Democratic party as uniquely capable of resolving this persistent economic problem.

Third, tariff reform promised to expand the Democratic coalition by appealing to the growing agrarian insurgency, especially in the West. These states tended to vote Republican, but voting trends during the period revealed a divergence of partisan support between national- and state-level candidates, which suggested to Cleveland the opportunity to generate Democratic votes for the presidency in states where local Democrats were rare – in this way, Cleveland was taking advantage of the presidency's unique ability to construct cross-national coalitions that transcended Congress's parochial divisions, thus making himself indispensable to his party.[74] Although he maintained a deflationary stance on the currency, for which western and southern agrarians distrusted him, Cleveland mitigated the unpopularity of this stance with policies aimed at appeasing westerners, such as support for legislation taxing the sale of oleomargarine (although he thought it violated the spirit of private enterprise), the formation of the Department of Agriculture, and siding with homesteaders over railroads in the Miller's Farm dispute. Tariff reform appealed to agrarian communities because protection raised the cost of consumer products that farmers depended on, and in the summer of 1887, opposition to the tariff was sweeping through the resolutions committees of Democratic state conventions. Like many Democratic leaders, Cleveland "pictured the political revolution which would sweep over the Western States if the Democratic party had the boldness to wage a war in favor of a reduction of the tariff." Further, opening the West would relieve some of the party's dependence on New York State (which forced Democrats to appeal to Tammany-dominated New York City), which caused Cleveland significant problems in both 1888 and 1892.[75]

The tariff also threatened to divide the Republican party's northeastern base from its western political colony. Farming states in the West and South received little benefit from protection (although Republicans included wool and wool products on the tariff lists to draw in western support) but suffered disproportionately from high consumer costs and currency contractions.[76] Tariff reform also had support in nonmanufacturing sectors on the East Coast and was popular among Mugwumps, so the political environment encouraged confidence.

[73] Cleveland to William Endicott, May 10, 1891, quoted in Fowler, *The Cabinet Politician*, 198.

[74] Ware, *The Democratic Party Heads North*, 55; Whittington and Carpenter, "Executive Power in American Institutional Development," 501.

[75] Nevins, *Grover Cleveland*, 359–62, 370; "Secretary Whitney as a Sagacious Politician," clipping enclosed in Edward A. Oldham to William C. Whitney, November 23, 1888, book 56, Whitney Papers; Hirsch, *William C. Whitney*, 402; Ware, *The Democratic Party Heads North*, 15, 65.

[76] Bensel, *Yankee Leviathan*, 265–7.

In 1886, the silver contingent in Congress, representing states such as Iowa, Nebraska, Indiana, and Minnesota, indicated that they would be willing to see legislation on monetizing silver take a back seat to tariff reform, as long as Democrats passed legislation advocating an international agreement on monetizing silver. When the 1886 Congressional elections saw significant agitation from the American Free Trade League and significant support for tariff reform in both New England and the Northwest, Cleveland interpreted the election as an opportunity to create a grand tariff reform coalition.[77] In this, Cleveland has been misunderstood by historians who attribute his tariff reform stance to Mugwump influence. In the context of the late nineteenth century, viewing Cleveland's stance as an appeal to the insurgency without accepting its monetary policies makes more sense than the image of an easterner blithely ignoring the gathering insurgent storm.[78] The strategy presaged Bryan's obverse attempt to unite the West and South in 1896 by committing the Democratic party to silver and because it promised to secure the electoral vote of silver-averse New York, Cleveland's was more strategically sound. By forcing his party into action on an issue of national scope, the president could reshape the political map.

Cleveland's purpose was to establish his reputation as a party leader rather than a windmill-tilting reformer: the address was "intended as a guide to the President's party in the approaching election."[79] Although his earlier messages had defended executive independence, none had so boldly goaded his party on an issue so central to its platform. As such, Cleveland began his initiative by working with party leaders to fashion a reform bill that suited the platform's requirements. He met in September 1887 – two months before the message's appearance – with his Treasury secretary, the Democratic speaker of the House, and the Democratic chairman of the Ways and Means Committee, to begin constructing a tariff bill that would provide a working plan for Congress. They launched a campaign of education for party leaders, shaping elite opinion in advance; Cleveland's consultations with party leaders were covered in the press and "sent a thrill of expectation throughout the party" even before the address.[80]

In the message, Cleveland applied the lessons he learned about executive leadership to the tariff problem. In an 1889 interview, he explained that "all of my speeches and messages . . . naturally led up to that of 1887."[81] He related his thinking to reformer Richard Watson Gilder before the message was issued: "I hated to relinquish the idea that would be likely to do good in the direction of tariff reduction. At last it occurred to me that there is nothing in the

---

[77] Nevins, *Grover Cleveland*, 291, 289–96.
[78] See, for instance, Matthew Josephson, *The Politicos, 1865–1896* (New York: Harcourt, Brace, 1938).
[79] Macy, *Party Organization and Machinery*, 50–1.
[80] Nevins, *Grover Cleveland*, 371–4.
[81] "Faithful to His Trust," *New York Times*, February 23, 1889, 1.

Constitution which required that the annual message should, as is usual, go over the entire public business." The departure from tradition – devoting the entire annual message to a single, substantive policy issue – would grab popular attention, inviting public comment and giving the party-in-the-electorate reason to read the message in the privacy of their homes – it was the campaign of education applied to presidential leadership. "He was so assured of the righteousness and reasonableness of the position assumed," observed Gilder, "that he felt that if the public could only understand the actual situation, there would be an influence upon Congress which would effect the necessary reforms."[82]

Given a hint of the message before it was released, William Whitney, Cleveland's Navy secretary and campaign strategist, wavered because he was as yet unsure "whether it was judicious to urge the policy on the eve of a Presidential election." His reluctance, as with other members of the cabinet, was not grounded in resistance to presidential leadership, but expediency. A campaign of education required "time enough at command of the party to combat prejudice, to overthrow false charges and to educate the minds of the working people up to an understanding of their own interests," and Whitney doubted there was time to educate the people before the election.[83] Other Cleveland allies voiced similar concerns. Former Ohio governor George Hoadly wrote to Cleveland warning that the people needed time to absorb the import of reform, otherwise they might "be swept off their intellectual bearings for a period long enough to endanger the results of the next Presidential election."[84]

Unlike his civil service letter, the 1887 message did not explain a course of executive action; instead he asserted that part of the problem was the *absence* of a "clear and undoubted executive power of relief." This justified his unusual interference in congressional affairs, and it required a broader party initiative. Cleveland evoked a reform popular at the time – giving presidents authority to negotiate rates directly with foreign nations. As Richard Bensel points out, this was a more "economically coherent and efficacious trade policy" than the "interest-group driven construction of the tariff in Congress." It allowed presidents to lend national coherence to a decentralized process and centered a fundamental party-building task of managing the party's larger coalition-building problems in the executive branch.[85] It was also a version of his claim that parties got the presidencies they asked for; if Congress gave Cleveland power to negotiate trade agreements, they would clearly get Grover Cleveland's trade policies. On the other hand, the people would know who to blame in the

---

[82] Richard Watson Gilder, *Grover Cleveland: A Record of Friendship* (New York: The Century Company, 1910), 8, 11–12. See also Ellis Paxson Oberholtzer, *A History of the United States Since the Civil War*, Vol. 5 (New York: The Macmillan Company, 1931), 476.

[83] "Secretary Whitney as a Sagacious Politician," clipping enclosed in Edward A. Oldham to William C. Whitney, November 23, 1888, book 56, Whitney Papers.

[84] Hoadly to Cleveland, November 25, 1887, quoted in C. Joseph Bernardo, *The Presidential Election of 1888*, unpublished dissertation, Georgetown University Graduate School, Washington, D.C., August, 1949, 41.

[85] Bensel, *The Political Economy of American Industrialization*, 519.

event of a failure of tariff reform; "if disaster results from the continued inaction of Congress," he warned, "the responsibility must rest where it belongs," making presidents more responsible for national campaigns.[86]

The message included a critique of partisan discourse that revealed the influence of the educational campaign. Tariff reform, Cleveland warned, "should be approached in a spirit higher than partisanship and considered in the light of that regard for patriotic duty which should characterize the action of those intrusted [sic] with the weal of a confiding people." Here, the language and style of the educational campaign demonstrated its fundamental (and persistent) attraction for the presidency, and reached its fullest nationalizing impact; it enabled Cleveland to stand above the partisan fray and speak to the nation. The problem with partisan passion, Cleveland insisted, was that it substituted the rhetoric of harmony for analysis; "our progress toward a wise conclusion will not be improved by dwelling upon the theories of protection and free trade. This savors too much of bandying epithets." Hence, in the most quoted line of the address, he declared "it is a condition which confronts us – not a theory." Theories were an appropriate realm for Jacksonian-mode partisan conflict, inviting broad disputes over irreconcilable principles; a condition presupposed certain objective facts that required calm study and so was particularly suited for an educational campaign. The line was partly an effort to forestall Republican criticism that Democrats were enamored with British free trade theories, but it also rejected the pluff of vapid party principles and challenged Republicans to present their own economic analysis rather than sentimental claims and hyperbolic charges. Both parties, after all, had advocated some kind of tariff reform in their platforms and so "the obligation to declared party policy and principle is not wanting to urge prompt and effective action."[87] The question was which party could best explicate and defend its economic policies before the public.

Cleveland couched the tariff's relation to the economic system in terms calculated to appeal to agrarian insurgents and inflationists and as such presaged the Democrats' turn, under Bryan, to class-based economic appeals as a means of expanding their coalition. The document in purpose and tone resembled Bryan's "Cross of Gold" speech that enthused Democrats less than ten years later for purposes opposed by Cleveland. Insisting that consumer interests be considered equally with manufacturing interests, Cleveland anticipated Bryan's demand that the business of the farmer be treated with the same respect as the business of the businessman. For instance, cautious tariff reformers advocated reducing tariffs on luxury items, which would reduce surpluses without endangering manufacturers. Cleveland batted this down, insisting that a tax on luxury items "presents no features of hardship"; reform would not be undertaken merely to clear government books, but should relieve the suffering of "the farmer and the agriculturalist who manufacture nothing, but who pay the

---

[86] "The President's Message," *New York Times*, December 7, 1887, 9.
[87] "The President's Message," *New York Times*, December 7, 1887, 9.

increased price which the tariff imposes."[88] The similarities are not coinciden-tal; Bryan was enthused by Cleveland's speech. At the 1888 Nebraska state convention, he insisted that the state party "let the campaign be based... on Cleveland's tariff message of December, 1887." When Cleveland lost, Bryan wrote him that "we would rather fall with you fighting on and for a princi-pal [sic] than to succeed with the party representing nothing but an organized appetite" and invited him to move to Nebraska and seek public office there.[89]

The public response to the message was phenomenal. Newspapers reported that "he has forced upon his party the issue as to which [the] party is... so divided that unless the minority yield it can defeat the will of the majority" and that "it places Mr. Cleveland far above any of the leaders to whom the repub-lican party has of late lent a hearing, and above most of the leaders of his own party." It gave "to the democratic party what it has long lacked – an issue and a leader."[90] The message undermined the politics of deferential compromise, as evasion of tariff reform – as popularized by the president – became politically inexpedient. George William Curtis praised Cleveland's educational purpose, observing that the president "undoubtedly intended that the message should be just what it has been called – an elementary treatise. It furnishes every man who is busy with his daily work both arguments and answers upon the general question it discusses" and exclaimed that the address made Cleveland "virtu-ally the undisputed Democratic candidate for next year and the virtual dictator of the Democratic policy."[91] The *New York Times* declared the opening of a campaign of education:

never before, at least not within the recollection of the present generation of voters, has the question of a sound tariff policy been brought to a direct issue before the people, and consequently the country has never had the education upon the principles and working of such a policy that can only come from a popular agitation, arousing the attention and exciting the keen interest of the great mass of the people.... This subject needs to be treated broadly and thoroughly with reference to its effect upon the interests of the people as individual citizens.[92]

Popular pressure for a tariff reform bill grew in response to the speech. Pennsyl-vania's Samuel Randall saw his state convention endorse Cleveland's position despite his opposition. Philadelphia's Samuel J. Randall Association changed its name to the Eleventh Ward Democratic Club, endorsed tariff reform, and denounced Randall for betraying his party's platform.[93] Democratic state con-ventions in at least thirty states endorsed tariff reform, many praising Cleveland

88 "The President's Message," *New York Times*, December 7, 1887, 9; Nevins, *Grover Cleveland*, 378.
89 Koenig, *Bryan*, 60, 63; see also Paolo E. Coletta, *William Jennings Bryan: Political Evangelist, 1860–1908* (Lincoln: University of Nebraska Press, 1964), 37.
90 "Comments of the Press," *Ashland* (Wisconsin) *Daily News*, December 7, 1887, 1.
91 "The President's Problem," *New York Times*, December 10, 1887, 5.
92 "A Campaign of Education," *New York Times*, June 10, 1888, 4.
93 "His Art Is True to Poll," *New York Times*, May 27, 1886, 5.

by name.[94] The overwhelming response proved the extent to which presidential leadership could pressure the subnational party establishment.

Cleveland's challenge was now to show that presidential party leadership could produce legislative achievements. Here, the result was less striking. Congressional Democrats' work in the months leading up to the address produced the Mills Bill of 1888 (named for Ways and Means chairman Roger Q. Mills), and Cleveland threw the weight of presidential patronage behind it.[95] In the House, Democratic members rushed to the floor to deliver speeches proclaiming their allegiance to Cleveland-style reform. When it came to a vote, only four House Democrats defected (Randall abstained), a significant improvement over Democratic performance on the Morrison Bill.[96] Nonetheless, the bill died as a result of an inability to compromise with the Republican-led Senate, which drove up tariff rates that the House had lowered. Yet the defeat did not diminish Cleveland's value to the party. Tariff historian F. W. Taussig concluded that the message "committed his party, till then but half-hearted, to an unreserved declaration in favor of free raw materials and lower duties on manufactures." Bensel similarly concludes that "the net effect of Cleveland's attack on the tariff was to discipline Democratic opposition to protection," a modest goal to be sure but a striking departure from the Jacksonian mode's low expectations of presidential party leadership.[97]

Stephen Skowronek concludes that Cleveland failed to exploit the "reconstructive possibilities" for coalition-building that the political situation presented him; "instead of moving the Democratic party onto new and broader ground, he effectively scuttled it as a national political alternative and left in his wake a resurgence of Republican hegemony."[98] This obscures Cleveland's strategic gambit and favors a perspective on Cleveland that looks back from the hindsight of Bryan's popular success in 1896. In 1887, Cleveland had good reason to hope that farmers and western states would stand with him on tariff reform and that his stance would secure a new, presidentially secured national coalition. He recognized, though, that financial centers (such as the pivotal swing state of New York) resisted the inflationary measures favored by agrarian insurgents. They believed "Cleveland to be the only rock that could withstand the rising tide of agrarian revolt," and because they were the first to abandon the party after Bryan's nomination, there is reason to agree with Cleveland that binding them to the West was a critical coalitional objective.[99] Emphasizing the tariff, then, *was* a major reconstructive possibility.

[94] "The Convention and the Tariff," *New York Times*, June 2, 1888, 4; "Revenue Reform Urged," *New York Times*, June 2, 1888, 3.

[95] Bernardo, *The Presidential Election of 1888*, 94.

[96] Bensel, *The Political Economy of American Industrialization*, 476.

[97] F. W. Taussig, "The Tariff Act of 1894," *Political Science Quarterly* (December 1894), 585; Bensel, *The Political Economy of American Industrialization*, 470. See also Moisei Ostrogorski, *Democracy and the Organization of Political Parties: Volume II*, 106.

[98] Skowronek, *The Politics Presidents Make*, 48.

[99] Hirsch, *William C. Whitney*, 378.

Cleveland's Renomination

The tariff message simplified the task of renominating Cleveland. Rejecting him meant rejecting his message, which only more forcefully advocated a policy to which the party was already committed and would require either an about-face on the tariff or a difficult effort to explain how another nominee better represented the party's stance. Cleveland had only refined his party's tariff plank, but his interpretation was authoritative. As Curtis put it, "do the politicians imagine that they can retain Mr. Cleveland and enjoy the benefit of his prestige and still discard the policy which gives him his strength, and on which his prestige rests? To refuse to nominate the President would be to reject the general position which he has taken on this subject."[100] Addressing the National Democratic Committee, the national chairman insisted that "it was plain, at the end of the third year of the official term of President Cleveland, that his renomination was desired by the great majority of the members of the entire National Democratic Party."[101] Cleveland's actions demonstrated that the presidential capacity to define party objectives was a valuable partisan tool.

The message also forced Republicans onto the Democrats' chosen ground of battle. From self-imposed exile in Europe, James Blaine (who had long advocated focusing the Republican party's message on economic issues) wrote a public letter attacking Cleveland and laying out his arguments for protection. Most observers correctly identified the move as Blaine throwing his hat in the ring, but it was notable that in doing so, he had been reduced to a meeker imitation of Cleveland's own "letter" to Congress.[102] The 1888 election became a referendum on Cleveland's tariff policy; the personalistic elements of the 1884 campaign were not widely repeated as the nation turned instead to discussions of the intricacies of tariff politics. *The Nation* praised the campaign, noting that "a specific measure of legislation has been proposed in order to cure a particular evil," which "necessarily brings up for discussion the general scope and policy of government."[103] Cleveland's articulation of a clear tariff policy fit perfectly with the campaign of education. His strategy was not simply accidental nor the creation of a sycophantic Mugwump press; he promoted the new campaign style as an indication of his novel approach to party leadership. Shortly after his second nomination, he spelled out the nature of the campaign of education to the president of the National Association of Democratic Clubs. "The plain people of the land...must be reached," he asserted, "we do not proceed upon the theory that they are to be led by others who may or may not be in sympathy with their interests." With such language, Cleveland positioned

---

100 "In Danger of Making a Mistake," *New York Times*, September 22, 1887, 4; "Cleveland Their Sole Hope," *New York Times*, April 23, 1887, 4.

101 William H. Barnum and Calvin S. Brice, "Address of the National Democratic Committee," September 22, 1888, series 1, reel 12, Benjamin Harrison Papers, Manuscript Division, Library of Congress, Washington, DC.

102 David Saville Muzzey, *James G. Blaine: A Political Idol of Other Days* (New York: Dodd, Mead, & Company, 1934), 367.

103 "The Educational Value of the Present Campaign," *The Nation*, August 30, 1888, 163.

his party to take advantage of what John Gerring describes as "the clear implication...that Americans were *not* all the same," which lay "at the heart of
Populist drama." This ideological shift within the Democratic party is too-often
identified with Bryan's 1896 campaign and so simply folded into accounts of
party factionalism. Cleveland's showcasing of similar appeals in 1888 suggests
the new liberal view of party as a root source of changing partisan language.
Thus, "we have undertaken to teach the voters," Cleveland insisted,

> as free, independent citizens, intelligent enough to see their rights, interested enough to
> insist upon being treated justly, and patriotic enough to desire their country's welfare.

> Thus this campaign is one of information and organization.

> Every citizen should be regarded as a thoughtful, responsible voter, and he should
> be furnished the means of examining the issues involved in the pending canvass for
> himself.[104]

The appeals of the campaign would be aimed at individual judgment, avoiding
the blind cant of partisan loyalty. This educational campaign also met the
approval of those extra-partisan associations that had pioneered it. At the
Young Men's Democratic Club of Massachusetts, Josiah Quincy intoned that
the coming campaign was unique:

> it is to be a contest which, more than any other in this or the preceding generation,
> is to be decided according as the people shall find in the one party or the other the
> general principles of government best adapted to secure the progress and prosperity of
> the American Republic.... Thus the conditions of this contest necessitate a return to
> the discussion of the political principles which underlie party policies and measures.[105]

Cleveland's scorn for traditional partisan methods was perhaps premature.
An independent admirer of Cleveland's policies conceded that "he has been
unable to win the loyalty of many of the leaders of his party as he won the loyalty of the party[-in-the-electorate] itself."[106] Cleveland was frustrated by the
daily necessities of party leadership, and his imperious treatment of Randall and
other Democratic dissenters alienated individuals who might have supported
him out of the kind of unswerving loyalty to party that he derided. His failure in
1888 rested to some degree on his failure to win the electoral votes of New York
State, which stemmed from his refusal to placate New York Governor David
B. Hill, who reputedly engineered a deal whereby Republican voters supported
Hill in exchange for Democratic support for Harrison.[107] What is remarkable
is that Cleveland's defeat failed to set back the nationalizing transformations
going on within the parties. As explained in Chapter 3, the centralization of

---

[104] Cleveland to Chauncey F. Black, September 14, 1888, in Nevins, *The Letters of Grover
Cleveland*, 189. Gerring, *Party Ideologies in America*, 196.
[105] August 11, 1888, Minutes, 1887–1892, YMDCM Records.
[106] "An Independent," "Mr. Cleveland's – Failure?" *Forum*, April, 1894, 131.
[107] Harry J. Sievers, *Benjamin Harrison: Hoosier Statesman* (New York: University Publishers,
1959), 394.

power in the national committees took off during the elections of 1888 and 1892, spawning the creation of national advisory committees to free them from state and local recalcitrance, as well as a streamlined and candidate-directed national committee structure. After the election, Cleveland remained both a leader within the Democratic party and a model for later presidents and candidates. He had forced his renomination on a party establishment that believed he had provided a candidacy that was more valuable to the party label than was deferential compromise. If they misjudged his electoral usefulness, they should be forgiven, because he won the popular vote by almost a hundred thousand votes.[108]

Cleveland's Third Nomination

Cleveland's reputation was embellished after he left office. The passage of the McKinley Tariff in 1890, followed by a precipitous rise in the cost of consumer goods, seemed to validate not only Cleveland's proposal but the emotional thrust of his analysis, ushering in a period of nostalgia for the ex-president. When Democrats won a congressional majority in 1890, many claimed that their position on tariff reform – popularized largely by Cleveland – had contributed most to the victory. The *New York Times* claimed that "when, in December, 1887, Mr. Cleveland sent his now famous tariff-reform message to Congress, he outlined with great clearness the ground on which the great fight of this year has been fought and the victory won."[109] The Business Men's Democratic Association echoed this assessment, observing that "the celebrated Tariff Reform message which he sent to Congress, – although defeating him for reelection because the country did not appreciate its import, – was the means of giving us the present house of Representatives by an overwhelming majority."[110] A Pennsylvania Democratic club declared that "to that celebrated tariff message of '87 we attribute the victories of '90 and '91, and without arrogance claim that these are but fore-runners to a more splendid triumph in 1892."[111] Political observers saw significance not only in the congressional victories but in their source. Of the seventy-six seats that the Democrats gained in 1890, 83 percent came from the sixteen states in which third parties won more votes than the margin of victory between the two parties in either 1888, 1892, or both (indicating significant insurgent pressure), including Illinois, Indiana, Iowa, Michigan, Minnesota, Montana, Nebraska, Ohio, and Wisconsin in the critical West and Midwest.[112] Although he lost reelection, the results of 1890 appeared to confirm Cleveland's strategic drive to appeal to precisely those states where his party most needed converts. Clearly, contemporaries felt

---

[108] Burnham, *Presidential Ballots*, 247.

[109] "Mr. Cleveland's Policy," *New York Times*, November 8, 1890, 4.

[110] Forrest H. Parker to Whitney, June 18, 1892, book 70, Whitney Papers.

[111] W. H. Rankin to Cleveland, August 10, 1892, series 11, box 10, Cleveland Papers.

[112] Jerrold Rusk, *A Statistical History of the American Electorate* (Washington, DC: Congressional Quarterly Press, 2001).

Cleveland's assertive presidential leadership to be a boon rather than a threat to the party's fortunes.

Cleveland took advantage of his renewed popularity to maintain his position in the Democratic party. In a December 1890 speech at New York's Reform Club, Cleveland encouraged the connection between his message and the 1890 elections. He referred to the 1890 congressional campaign as a campaign of education; returning to the theme of cooling partisan passions, he argued that the campaign taught Democrats "that we, as a party, had... been tempted by the success our opponents had gained solely by temporary shifts and by appeals to prejudice and selfish interests, into paths which avoided too much the honest insistence upon definite and clearly defined principle and fundamental Democratic doctrine." As politicians followed his argument for tariff reform, the true Democratic party emerged from the electorate, as "traitors were silenced, camp-followers fell away or joined the scurvy band of floaters, while the sturdy Democratic host confidently pressed on, bearing aloft the banner of tariff reform." Cleveland insisted that party principle, traditionally understood, was outdated; in its place was a commitment to meeting the shifting interests of the people. The party thus "should be prepared to meet all the wants of the people as they arise."[113] Cleveland's view of party, guided by national publics and shifting according to changing issues, tracked closely to the new idea of party.

In 1891, responding to an invitation to another Reform Club dinner, Cleveland wrote a letter denouncing the monetization of silver and released it to the newspapers.[114] The letter indicated Cleveland's interest in guiding the affairs of his party, and Cleveland again "began to loom up as the most available candidate in the party" among voters and party leaders.[115] Cleveland's supporters grew ebullient; "the object is not only the nomination of Mr. Cleveland, desirable as that is," wrote one, "but the ascendancy in the party councils of what has come to be known as Clevelandism."[116] As in 1888, Democrats fretted over the consequences of not renominating him. "He has given the Democracy its policy, and set up its issues," wrote one Democrat, "if he is set aside, the very fact is an acknowledgement of weakness."[117] Another wrote that the party "was lifted up by Mr. Cleveland, put on ideal ground, infused with sentiment, transfixed by that arrow of truth which is the canon law of unselfishness, that he who loses his life shall find it" and insisted, "I fear the consequences if we disappoint the popular expectation."[118] As a Boston Mugwump put the party's

[113] "Address in Response to the Toast, 'The Campaign of Education,' Delivered at the Reform Club Dinner, New York, December 23, 1890," in Bergh, *Letters and Addresses of Grover Cleveland*, 273, 282, 285.
[114] "Free Coinage Denounced," *New York Times*, February 12, 1891, 9.
[115] Hirsch, *William C. Whitney*, 379.
[116] S. E. Morss to Whitney, June 13, 1892, book 70, Whitney Papers.
[117] L. L. Price to Whitney, June 20, 1892, book 70, Whitney Papers.
[118] John P. Irish to Manton Marble, March 1, 1892, container 1, Lamont Papers.

conundrum, "the moment Cleveland is set aside the first question is, why was it done? No satisfactory answer can be given."[119]

Cleveland supporters echoed his argument that the selection of the nominee committed the party to that nominee's policies; his nomination would "be accepted as the platform," even "above the resolutions of the Chicago Convention."[120] A member of the Michigan State Democratic Committee wrote to Cleveland begging for one of his public letters to supplement the platform: "our campaign is one of Education.... a letter from you would arouse the Michigan Democracy to the highest pitch of enthusiasm."[121] Abandoning the Jacksonian norm of candidate reticence, Democrats wanted to hear from Cleveland. Whitney advised that Cleveland's drawbacks, including a growing unpopularity in southern states, could be countered by judicious public appeals rather than appeals to party loyalty: "in the South the impression of you got by the people is that you do not appreciate their suffering and poverty.... I think having this in view you might write on the tariff and on silver in a mood sympathetic to them and make a great change in the South."[122] The uproar for direct statements from Cleveland suggests the need to revise the prevailing understanding of the nature of nineteenth century restraints on presidential rhetoric. Although the norm had its origins in eighteenth-century notions of the respectable behavior of public men, it had, by the middle of the nineteenth century, grown into a matter of prudence rather than of propriety.[123] By the late nineteenth century, the benefits of presidential leadership had so overcome prudential concerns that even disasters such as Winfield S. Hancock's 1880 proclamation that "the tariff is a local issue" and Blaine's speaking tour could not prop them up. Successful presidential candidates – James Garfield and Benjamin Harrison – spoke during their campaigns, and Cleveland became a political powerhouse precisely *because* of his willingness to identify himself outside of party principles. Rather than evolving notions of propriety, the rise of presidential rhetoric stems from the increasingly secure place that presidents and presidential candidates built for themselves in the party system. Both voters and party leaders looked to the candidates to articulate party doctrine, a role that was facilitated by the newly nationalized party apparatus.

As the convention loomed, Cleveland's opponents, especially his old enemies in the New York State organization, worked all the angles of the Jacksonian mode to defeat him but were checked by the new methods. New York Democratic leaders called a "snap" state convention in February, violating the tradition of spring conventions; in February, winter conditions hampered travel

[119] R. L. Bridgman to George Fred Williams, February 25, 1892, carton 3, folder 5.18, Williams Papers.

[120] A. E. Burr to Whitney, July 11, 1892, book 73, Whitney Papers.

[121] Thomas F. Carroll to Cleveland, August 9, 1892, series 11, box 3, Cleveland Papers.

[122] Whitney to Cleveland, August 30, 1892, book 75, Whitney Papers.

[123] As evidenced by "Campaign Dangers," *Atlanta Constitution*, August 21, 1892, enclosed in Charles Estes to Whitney, August 22, 1892, book 75, Whitney Papers, perusing the history of presidential candidates causing controversy by imprudent comments and letters.

from upstate districts where Cleveland was strong. They publicized it poorly, instructed its national delegates to vote for the nomination of Tammany ally David B. Hill, and bound them by the unit rule. His favorite son candidacy had little hope for success but was intended chiefly to block Cleveland.[124] Questioning the authority of the regularly (if outrageously) called state convention, Cleveland supporters followed a course of action popularized by the reform clubs in 1884: they held a public meeting, which selected their own slate of delegates to the Democratic National Convention that had no chance of being recognized by the credentials committee but that demonstrated Cleveland's popular support. These "Anti-snapper" delegates followed the regular delegation to the convention, where they served as an observing force and lobbied unsuccessfully to have the convention's rules committee abolish the unit rule (which would free New York delegates and thus open up support for Cleveland).[125]

Cleveland's campaign furthered the decade-long development in the relationship between presidential candidates and national party chairmen. Whitney managed his prenomination campaign, corresponding with Democratic leaders across the country and meeting with allies before the convention assembled.[126] Cleveland was actively involved in preparations for the convention, including the writing of the platform, insisting to Whitney that "the platform on the money question *must* be right if I am to be in any way related to it."[127] Upset with the wording of the tariff plank (Whitney had not deemed it worth a fight, Cleveland's position being so well known), he dismissed the platform altogether: "I think I must stand by the message of 1887 and if I make up my mind to that I shall come pretty near saying so."[128]

Support for Cleveland's nomination was so overwhelming and so rooted in his personal popularity that his nomination was identified as a personal victory, and party leaders were willing to give control of the campaign to Cleveland and his allies. Through his national planning and engineering of the Anti-snapper displays in New York, Whitney was seen as having imposed the outcome on the convention, rather than having negotiated a compromise with subnational leaders. As a result, Whitney was not forced aside as party elites seized on their share of campaign management – the typical fate of such managers – but was hailed as a conquering hero second only to Cleveland. The party establishment had long viewed the national committee as an agent of the party, not the candidate; this was not the case in 1892, when party leaders conceded that the committee reflected Cleveland's dominance of his party. One correspondent

---

[124] Charles Tracy to Whitney, June 9, 1892; Charles Montford to Whitney, June 18, 1892; John B. Castleman to E. J. McDermott, June 16, 1892, book 70, Whitney Papers; Nevins, *Grover Cleveland*, 483–4.

[125] Nevins, *Grover Cleveland*, 486. On the lobbying effort, see Thomas F. Bamy to Whitney, June 22, 1892, book 70, Whitney Papers.

[126] Hirsch, *William C. Whitney*, 391.

[127] Cleveland to Whitney, June 10, 1892, book 70, Whitney Papers.

[128] Cleveland to Whitney, July 9, 1892, book 73, Whitney Papers.

wrote to Whitney, complaining of "the leading members of the committee who have conducted previous campaigns" and warned that "there is an impression in the country that these gentlemen were unfriendly to Mr. Cleveland. If one of them should take charge of the campaign, it would be unfortunate because of this impression."[129] The Democratic Mayor of Boston suggested that a Cleveland-dominated national committee, controlled by Whitney, "would, of itself, be a source of great strength to the party in the campaign through-out the nation."[130] Whitney responded to such concerns with the reforms of the national committee outlined in Chapter 3, giving the Democratic national organization unprecedented centralization.

Democrats took advantage of Cleveland's celebrity. Presidential candidates were traditionally formally notified of their nomination in dour ceremonies at their homes, where they received a committee of convention delegates and read a perfunctory statement of acknowledgment. Whitney and Cleveland planned instead a massive public notification ceremony at Madison Square Garden. The *New York Times* (which called the event "unprecedented") estimated that fifteen thousand attended, with thousands turned away at the door.[131] The event played on the impression that Cleveland was called upon by the people, not the party elite. Governor Hill skipped the event in an attempt to embar-rass Cleveland, but the popular response to Cleveland exposed the clay feet of the traditional party's position vis-à-vis candidates of Cleveland's popular stature.[132] Given his popularity, Cleveland had less use for subnational leaders either to present the platform to local voters or to generate local enthusiasm.

Cleveland's Garden speech focused on the harmful effects of the McKinley Tariff. Repeating the tone of the 1887 address, he appealed to farmers and workingmen, the "plain people of the land" who were "burdened as consumers with a tariff system that unjustly and relentlessly demands from them." He made it clear that he was the candidate of a party, insisting that "for the principles and purposes to which my party is pledged, and for the enforcement and supremacy of which all who have any right to claim Democratic fellowship must constantly and persistently labor."[133] In 1884, he made a reasonable claim that his well-known position on civil service reform made his election a mandate for reform; in case the 1887 tariff message did not correspondingly establish the centrality of the tariff, his Madison Square Garden address removed all confusion. He was not merely running as a president who rose above partisan labels, but as a president who claimed distinct authority to define partisan purposes.

He returned to the point in his second inaugural address. Citing the "man-date of my countrymen," he extended the directive of the people to his

---

[129] W. C. Goudy to Whitney, July 7, 1892, book 73, Whitney Papers.
[130] Nathan Matthews, Jr., to Whitney, June 27, 1892, book 71, Whitney Papers.
[131] "Called by a Great Party," *New York Times*, July 21, 1892, 1.
[132] Troy, *See How They Ran*, 98–9.
[133] "Called by a Great Party," *New York Times*, July 21, 1892, 1.

party-in-government: "the verdict of our voters which condemned the injustice of maintaining protection for protection's sake enjoins upon the people's servants the duty of exposing and destroying the brood of kindred evils which are the unwholesome progeny of paternalism." As he had in 1887, he disparaged partisan rhetoric, invoking the higher calling that came from victory in an educational campaign: "in our efforts to adjust differences of opinion we should be free from intolerance or passion, and our judgments should be unmoved by alluring phrases and unvexed by selfish interests." Building on the theme, he highlighted the insufficiencies of party compromise to resolve economic issues, noting that "when we tear aside the delusions and misconceptions which have blinded our countrymen to their condition under vicious tariff laws, we but show them how far they have been led away from the paths of contentment and prosperity." He explained continued commitment among Republican voters to protection as an indication of "the extent to which judgment may be influenced by familiarity with perversions of the taxing power."[134]

The election gave Democrats control of both houses of Congress as well as the presidency and solidified gains in the 1890 congressional election. He emphasized the election of 1892 as a party victory in which "the people of the United States have decreed that on this day the control of their government in its legislative and executive branches shall be given to a political party pledged in the most positive terms to the accomplishment of tariff reform." Nevertheless, he left no doubt that he was the source of party leadership. "Anxiety for the redemption of the pledges which my party has made and solicitude for the complete justification of the trust the people have reposed in us," he warned, "constrain me to remind those with whom I am to cooperate that we can succeed in doing the work which has been especially set before us only by the most sincere, harmonious, and disinterested effort."[135] The claim of a mandate is particularly striking given that his reelection in 1892 was hardly overwhelming. He polled a mere 46 percent of the vote, compared with 48.9 percent in 1884, and the 47.8 percent cast for Benjamin Harrison in 1888. In Cleveland's mind, the mandate came from the nature of the campaign rather than from the extent of his vote.

The election returns signaled problems for Democrats. Rather than fight for the votes of western states in which the People's party threatened more Republican than Democratic electoral votes, Whitney engineered a massive deception that spoke volumes about the strategic preoccupations of national party leaders in the late nineteenth century. Recognizing that they had little chance of beating the Populists with a candidate who had fiercely defended the gold standard, many western Democratic organizations promoted People's party electors, hoping to draw off enough electoral votes from nominally Republican

---

[134] Grover Cleveland, "Second Inaugural Address," *Inaugural Addresses of the Presidents of the United States from George Washington, 1789, to George Bush, 1989* (Washington, DC: United States Government Printing Office, 1989), 187, 189, 188, 191.

[135] Cleveland, "Second Inaugural Address," 191.

states to have the election thrown into the House of Representatives, where a Democratic majority would elect Cleveland. Whitney authorized national committee members to work out the details in their own states, sometimes to the chagrin of the regular local Democratic organizations.[136] Correspondents indicated that local party leaders in Nevada,[137] California,[138] Nebraska[139] (where Bryan approved of the plan[140]), Kansas,[141] Iowa, South Dakota,[142] and Wyoming,[143] among others, gave votes to People's party electors. James Weaver, the People's party candidate, knew and approved of the plan, claiming himself to prefer Cleveland over Harrison.[144] The Populist gain of twenty-two electoral votes must be read in this light.

It is difficult to discount the impact of this strategy in light of the western insurgency that booted Cleveland Democrats from the party in 1896. Cleveland and Whitney had won a pyrrhic victory, taking advantage of the complications of western expansion without fully resolving them. One Colorado Democrat caught sight of the problem early, warning Whitney that "there has been a large secession of Democratic politicians from the local party, declaring that the days of usefulness of the Democratic party are at an end," and complaining that "we are having a struggle to preserve our party integrity against the encroachments of men who claim to be yet Democrats, yet who attend People's Party conventions, [and] openly denounce the Democratic party."[145] Exploiting the western insurgency was a shrewd short-term maneuver, but it did not promise the long-term dominance of Clevelandism.

Cleveland's leadership position quickly unraveled. He returned to office hoping to continue his fight for tariff reform, but the economic crisis of 1893 intruded. Governed by the 1890 Sherman Silver Purchase Act, the Treasury was required to purchase silver bullion, resulting in an outflow of gold from Treasury vaults that, during the economic depression of '93, threatened to weaken the government's ability to maintain the gold standard. The gold standard primarily benefitted industrial and financial interests dependent on maintaining integration of U.S. and European markets, but it limited the flow of currency into the less developed regions of the South and West. The political consequences of the monetary crisis thus pitted the development-oriented Northeast against agrarian interests in the rest of the country – precisely the interests that Cleveland hoped to attract with the issue of tariff reform.[146] Publicly and

---

[136] A. B. McKinley to Whitney, September 3, 1892, book 75, Whitney Papers.
[137] H. R. Campbell to Whitney, July 6, 1892, book 72, Whitney Papers.
[138] S. W. Fordyce to Whitney, July 6, 1892, book 72, Whitney Papers.
[139] James E. Boyd to Whitney, July 11, 1892, book 73, Whitney Papers.
[140] Bryan to Whitney, August 4, 1892, book 74, Whitney Papers.
[141] G. W. Glick to Whitney, July 12, 1892, book 73, Whitney Papers.
[142] James E. Boyd to Whitney, July 11, 1892, book 73, Whitney Papers.
[143] A. L. New to Cleveland, September 24, 1892, series 11, box 3, Cleveland Papers.
[144] S. W. Fordyce to Whitney, July 13, 1892, book 73, Whitney Papers.
[145] A. B. McKinley to Whitney, September 3, 1892, book 75, Whitney Papers.
[146] Bensel, *The Political Economy of American Industrialization*, 355–6.

personally committed to the gold standard, Cleveland called a special session of Congress and asked for a repeal of the Sherman Act. Revealing to reporters his intention to do so, the president spoke in a manner that had come to be characteristic. Referring to his well-established position on the currency issue, he noted that "there has been no mystery or secrecy in regard to my intention in this matter," then added that "our people should be informed authoritatively that the time is at hand when their Representatives in Congress will be called upon to deal with [the] financial condition." He took the opportunity to urge the people "to take up the subject for themselves and arrive at their own conclusions."[147] Cleveland pressured his divided party to repeal the act, "wielding every political club and blandishing every favor that his position as president and party leader provided him." He succeeded, but undermined his tenuous southern and western support in the process.[148]

The stage was thus set unfavorably for Cleveland's tariff reform initiative, begun in the regular session of Congress that convened in December 1893. The explosion of populism in the South and West obscured the issue, however; despite agrarian insurgents' opposition to protection, it was not as salient as it had been in 1888. The repeal of the Sherman Act left western Democrats less enthusiastic in their support of Cleveland than they might have been had the tariff been taken up first. Still, in the Democratic-controlled House, the Wilson Bill passed with only eighteen Democratic defections. Its fate in the Senate (where Democrats were more closely matched by Republicans) was rougher. A list of 408 amendments protecting or raising tariff rates for state producers was added to the House Bill by the Finance Committee. In conference, where tariff negotiations were finalized, House Democrats loyal to Cleveland stood their ground. At this moment, William Wilson, the House Democratic Chairman of the Ways and Means Committee who authored the original bill, released a personal letter from Cleveland. The letter was the clearest statement yet of Cleveland's notion of party responsibility; it was also clearly Cleveland at his most partisan – he used some form of the word "Democrat" thirty times, and "party" ten times in eleven paragraphs – insisting that tariff reform "is so interwoven with Democratic pledges and Democratic success that our abandonment of the cause of the principles upon which it rests means party perfidy and party dishonor." The effect was devastating for Wilson and the president. Democrats denounced Cleveland, complaining that his claims of treachery belied the hard work they had put into reaching a difficult compromise. The result was a timid bill that barely reduced rates and left the principle of protection in place (it also included an income tax, soon struck down by the Supreme Court). With tariff reform muzzled and the depression weighing on the American people, Cleveland's political capital was spent.[149]

---

[147] "An Extra Session Certain," *New York Times*, June 6, 1893, 1.
[148] Sanders, *Roots of Reform*, 135; Bensel, *The Political Economy of American Industrialization*, 412.
[149] Nevins, *Letters of Grover Cleveland*, 354–7, quote from 355. Accounts of the struggle over the bill can be found in Nevins, *Grover Cleveland*, chap. 31; Bensel, *The Political Economy*

Cleveland's attempts to seize the initiative were frustrated by events. The panic of 1893 set in motion the worst depression in American history up to that time, resulting in the failure of a quarter of U.S. railroads, as well as fifteen thousand businesses, leaving as many as 4 million unemployed. As the stock marked plunged, banks called in loans that could not be repaid, resulting in an especially high rate of bank failures in the South and West.[150] When Cleveland and his Treasury secretary made a private deal selling newly issued government bonds to a conglomerate represented by J. P. Morgan, the result was a momentary influx of gold into treasury vaults (preventing the government from resorting to the redemption of government debts in silver), but the outrage was palpable. Cleveland made a tour through the South to explain himself, but he never conquered the rising belief that he was in league with Wall Street. Tariff reform was further complicated by the fact that, during the depression, prices fell dramatically, making further reductions due to the lifting of tariff support problematic. Not only did Democratic discipline on the tariff fall apart, but the popular mind turned to the more quotidian concerns of surviving the economic downturn. When, in 1894, the government responded with force to Coxey's Army and the Pullman strike, Cleveland's appeal to the "plain people of the land" was undermined.[151]

Cleveland attempted one final effort to assert popular party leadership. The Populist revolt was building steam in the South and West, and Gold Democrats in Illinois, nervous of the popularity of Governor John Altgeld's support for an inflationary currency policy, invited Cleveland to a conference convened in Chicago to demonstrate popular support for the gold standard. Cleveland declined the invitation, but in his letter of declination, he sought to rally the Democratic party-in-the-electorate to his side. In terms that had come to define his view of the campaign of education, he expressed hope that "the event will mark the beginning of an aggressive effort to disseminate among the people safe and prudent financial ideas." He insisted that "it is a time for the American people to reason together" and that the farmer must be reminded "that he must buy as well as sell." He implored the "common people of the land" to see that "in our relation to this question we are all in business." The reference to the efforts of the silver movement to educate its constituency (which he referred to as "the illusions of a debased currency") is hard to miss, as is the parallel to Bryan's "Cross of Gold" rhetoric scarcely a year later.[152] The letter appeared in newspapers across the country, providing a rallying point for gold Democrats, even as it further alienated silver Democrats. Editorials proclaimed that it was "just what was needed" in the fight against silver and "calculated to declare

---

of *American Industrialization*, 478–81; F. W. Taussig, "The Tariff Act of 1894," 585–8 and F. W. Taussig, "The New United States Tariff," *The Economic Journal*, (December 1894), 573–5.

[150] Cashman, *America in the Gilded Age*, 271.

[151] Nevins, *Grover Cleveland*, 662–3, 679–81, 581–3; Sanders, *Roots of Reform*, 135.

[152] "For Aggressive Work," *New York Times*, April 15, 1895, 1; Harvey Wish, "John Peter Altgeld and the Background of the Campaign of 1896," *The Mississippi Valley Historical Review*, March 1938, 503–18.

and define the issue which the people must now meet, and to give the right impulse to the educational work in progress on the subject."[153]

Silver leaders were infuriated by the letter. Altgeld observed that "it is the first instance in the history of the Republic in which a President of the United States, after using all the powers of the Government, has, in addition, condescended to write for the newspapers, in order to serve his masters." Missouri Congressman Richard P. Bland joined in the silver chorus, remarking that "Mr. Cleveland. . . . has forced upon the country a state of affairs that is intolerable to the masses of our people."[154] Hence, when silver forces gained ascendancy in the Democratic party, they ingloriously rejected Cleveland as the spokesman of privilege.

Cleveland's second-term failures revealed the fundamental weaknesses of the leadership role he had staked out for himself. As the singular national position in both his party and the constitutional system, he had tremendous power to take the initiative on matters of national policy. His party was in the process of flying apart at the seams, however, and a coalitional objective that seemed plausible in 1887 was much more tenuous by 1893. In that environment, the presidential initiative only provided agrarian insurgents with a bigger target. The gold standard and the tariff had become symbiotic, two sides of a common insurgent coin. By emphasizing one side and disputing the other, he exposed himself to the attacks of his opponents, helped elevate silver leaders like William Jennings Bryan and Altgeld in party affairs, and deepened the rift in party ranks.[155] As Woodrow Wilson concluded in 1897, Cleveland "forced the fight which drove the silver men to their final struggle for a party." There was a touch of tragic failure to his ambiguous point that "there was only a danger that if the leaders of the party in Congress continued to follow him merely when they were obliged, he would himself presently be all the Democratic party that was left in the country."[156]

William Jennings Bryan and the Election of 1896

In one of the most revealing ironies of the period's politics, William Whitney, who had maximized the power of nationalized politics to triumph over the forces of subnational parochialism in 1892, united with David Hill (whose defense of the gold standard brought him into the Cleveland camp) in 1896 to rely on all the obstructionist potential of the Jacksonian mode to block a massive national popular movement. Southern and western silverites claimed enough delegates to control the convention, and Whitney's only hope was for division among silver Democrats – who divided their support between

---

[153] "His Letter Most Timely," *New York Times*, April 16, 1895, 1; "Just What Was Needed," *New York Times*, April 16, 1895, 2.

[154] "Gov. Altgeld Raves," *New York Times*, April 16, 1895, 2.

[155] Wish, "Altgeld and the Background of the Campaign of 1896."

[156] Woodrow Wilson, "Mr. Cleveland as President" (1897), in Woodrow Wilson, *Selected Literary and Political Papers and Addresses*, v. 1, (New York: Grosset and Dunlap, 1925), 91, 100, 91.

several pro-silver aspirants – and he aimed to stall the nomination, force a compromise, and save the gold standard. Anticipating such a move, silver Democrats toyed with the notion of abandoning the two-thirds rule, which would lower the threshold of victory and allow one of the silver aspirants to seize the prize quickly – thus was the Jacksonian mode ever-challenged – but never quite destroyed – by the impulses of late-nineteenth-century politics.[157] When it came time to name a temporary chairman, the silver men demonstrated their strength by overturning precedent and refusing the national committee's choice.[158] Whitney's obstructionism was to no avail; the silver forces, undecided as they were on a candidate, were nevertheless resolute in beating the Cleveland wing of the party. The chickens that Cleveland had dispersed for so many years had finally come home to roost.

Bryan's "Cross of Gold" speech helped to resolve the silver forces' confusion and directed the silverites' passion toward himself. Bryan's was more than a personal victory, however; the convention's endorsement of silver was embedded in a larger organizational victory that he had helped engineer, not a momentary display of passion. As explained in Chapter 2, the agrarian insurgency was a well-organized movement, embodied in both educational associations like the Farmers' Alliance and political groups like the People's party. The Democratic party's embrasure of silver in 1896 was shaped by an organized movement distinct from the agrarian movement's organizational base in the Farmers' Alliance and the People's party, although it imitated their methods to gain popularity among a national constituency. Many Alliance leaders, by contrast, felt that the silver movement was too narrowly focused on the panacea of silver coinage, which they believed was too shallow to remedy the structural inequalities of American capitalism. They accused politicians like Bryan of creating a "shadow movement" for free silver that had none of the depth of the Alliance's radical critique and only drew their constituency back into the partisan mainstream.[159] Indeed, politicians found the growing popularity of soft money as a form of relief for debt-crushed farmers and its relatively legitimate position within both parties a convenient means of earning favor among Alliance voters.[160] The depression and Cleveland's frantic efforts to maintain the gold standard brought the issue of silver coinage to the nation's

[157] "The Silver Programme," *New York Times*, July 3, 1896, 2.

[158] Richard Franklin Bensel's account of the 1896 Democratic convention is authoritative, and his account of the rejection of Hill as temporary chairman occupies much of chap. 3 of *Passion and Preferences*; Glad, *McKinley, Bryan, and the People*, 133.

[159] On other politicians taking up the currency issue, see Wish, "John Peter Altgeld and the Background of the Campaign of 1896," 506. On the conflict between Western and Eastern Democrats, see Bensel, *The Political Economy of American Industrialization*, 236–7; and Bensel, *Passion and Preferences*, 12–19; also James A. Barnes, "The Gold-Standard Democrats and the Party Conflict," *The Mississippi Valley Historical Review*, December 1930, 422–50. On the "shadow movement" argument, see Goodwyn, *The Populist Moment*, chap. 8 generally.

[160] Sanders, *Roots of Reform*, 110–15.

attention and highlighted the detachment of the party's eastern wing from its western and southern wings. The silver issue thus played into a bold effort by "colonial" Democrats to take control of a party that had been dominated for many years by the eastern "core"; playing for agrarian votes by building off of an element of the Alliance agenda was a means to take advantage of the westerners' natural resources.

Insurgent politicians seized state parties by influencing public and elite opinion through a network of extra-partisan associations that mimicked the Alliance's educational methods. The American Bimetallic League, founded by silver mine owners in 1889, perfected a national organization in 1892, took on a wider public membership during the depression of 1893, and organized massive public meetings across the country throughout the next three years. Under its auspices, pro-silver politicians from both parties, including Bryan, Richard Bland, Henry Teller, and James Jones, met to devise strategy for the upcoming election and coordinated with sympathetic associations such as the National Bimetallic Union (formed at an 1895 conference of silver leaders) and the National Silver Committee (formed at yet another 1895 conference) to form a central educational agency called the American Bimetallic Union. Silver conventions met under its auspices in Salt Lake City, Memphis, and Springfield (Illinois), rallying the faithful and building networks among men who would return home to elect national convention delegates. Using the tools of the campaign of education, silver organizations held public lectures, distributed educational material, and hired a corps of speakers – including Bryan – to tour the country. In 1895, a group of Democratic Senators, mistrustful of their national committee's dominance by the Cleveland wing of the party, organized the Bimetallic Democratic National Committee for the purpose of "controlling the action of the National Democratic Convention of 1896, upon this vitally important question." They appointed a committee member from each state, creating an irregular shadow organization, its members concentrating on organizing silver forces, founding silver clubs in their home states, monitoring the national committee, and coordinating preconvention strategy.[161]

Given Bryan's role in rallying the silver movement before his nomination, the national speaking tour on which he embarked as a candidate was no surprise and should be viewed as the culmination of two decades of party transformation, rather than the uniquely emotional context of the 1896 campaign. Before he was nominated, Bryan was in popular demand as a speaker from silver clubs around the country.[162] Along the way, he organized silver clubs, which

---

[161] Bimetallic Democratic National Committee quoted in William Jennings Bryan, *The First Battle: A Story of the Campaign of 1896* (Chicago: W. B. Conkey Company, 1896), 162; William A. Dunning, "Record of Political Events," *Political Science Quarterly* (December 1895), 740, covers a number of the groups and the conventions. A good account of the working of pro-silver groups can be found in Bryan's account in *The First Battle*, chap. 6. See also Glad, *McKinley, Bryan, and the People*, chap. 6; Goodwyn, *The Populist Moment*, 217; Hollingsworth, *The Whirligig of Politics*, 37.

[162] See correspondence in box 3, Bryan Papers.

were to come to his aid in 1896.[163] Bryan's prenomination activities made him a significant figure within the silver movement, even though he was less well known as a party leader in the regular Democratic organization. He entered the convention with little direct support for the presidency, but his long work for the cause generated his credentials among silver delegates.[164]

Bryan's "Cross of Gold" speech secured his nomination by enthusing the delegates for the silver cause, but it was also a full-throated demonstration of Bryan's mastery of the new idea of party; thus, its genius ran deeper than its emotional content. "Changing conditions make new issues," he insisted, urging his fellow partisans to respond to the popular outcry for silver and ignore past partisan commitments; "the principles upon which Democracy rests are as everlasting as the hills, but that they must be applied to new conditions as they arise." Claiming that judgment on the issue had been "rendered by the plain people of this country" (Cleveland's phrase), he maintained that traditional party ties had lost their meaning as "the warmest ties of love, acquaintance and association have been disregarded." This sentiment reflected the deep and sectional hostilities of the campaign but also the previous two decades' erosion of traditional party lines. Traditional party leaders (like Cleveland) had "been cast aside when they have refused to give expression to the sentiments of those whom they would lead."[165]

Although silver Democrats were undecided as to which candidate should lead them in their crusade against the East, Bensel concludes that in the uproar following Bryan's speech, "somewhere in the mass demonstration that was convulsing the convention hall, the transfer of sentiment from silver as a policy to Bryan as a presidential candidate took place." Bryan became the individual capable of resolving the anxieties of the silver Democrats and unleashing their passion into confident political action, partly because he demonstrated mastery of the new style of politics. Silver Democrats were typically men of less education and polish than their eastern brethren; the presence of Whitney, with his image as an effective political operator, was a calculated effort to awe the westerners into submission, to suggest that their "break with party traditions that underscored the radicalism of the silver faction" was politically amateurish. Further, the threat that gold Democrats with their money, their base in the populous Northeast, and their proven skill at winning national campaigns would bolt the party undermined the silver Democrats' faith in their ability to win the general election. Silverites needed someone to provide a coherent intellectual justification for their dramatic policy departure – not to defend the policy per se but to defend pushing the policy in the face of party disharmony; as Bensel puts it, they "needed someone to tell them – and the gold men – why they must enshrine silver at the heart of the platform."[166] Bryan used his

---

[163] E. G. Epler to Bryan, May 27, 1895, box 3, Bryan Papers.
[164] Bensel, *Passion and Preferences*, 238, 270–6; Hollingsworth, *The Whirligig of Politics*, 61.
[165] Speech reprinted in Bryan, *The First Battle*, 203, 199.
[166] Bensel, *Passion and Preferences*, 236, 107, 223–4.

mastery of the new idea of party to convince hesitant silverites to abandon the Jacksonian mode's republican values.

Bryan's long experience building an associational base for the silver movement accustomed him to the frame of mind of his audience, to their fears and aspirations. He had field-tested appeals and honed passages of his speech among the "plain people of the land," and by the time he reached Chicago, his appeal was pitch-perfect. He began the speech by referring to the associational tools with which the silver cause had gained prominence in the party, referring to a March 4, 1895, letter that grew out of a National Bimetallic Union conference, in which "a few Democrats . . . issued an address to the Democrats of the nation asserting that the money question was the paramount issue of the hour," and to a Memphis convention held under the National Bimetallic Union's auspices.[167] Bryan was clearly indicating the silver movement's affiliation with the new idea of party and the methods of the associational explosion. The evocation of "trendy" new methods that had taken hold of popular understandings of how campaigns should be conducted made their radicalism seem more like relevance. The reason Bryan was echoing Cleveland was to convince his audience that he knew how campaigns could be won.

Bryan's confidence in the associational explosion model was reinforced by his campaign. As Geoffrey Blodgett explains, "the campaign of 1896 left the Democratic party in a broken heap. In few states were Democrats able to preserve intact the subtle machinery of precedent and accommodation which had allowed them to live together under a common label. . . . the campaign precipitated rending discord among local Democrats."[168] Where this occurred, Bryan and his allies avoided the regular party apparatus and followed the lessons they had learned from the silver insurgents: they reached out to the extra-partisan associations, making use of the extra-partisan silver clubs that Bryan had courted in the months leading up to his nomination. Democratic National Committee Chairman James Jones brought Populists and Silver Republicans into his advisory committee, taking the advice of William Joel Stone, Missouri's representative to the committee, that "it would be wise to associate with you . . . some prominent Silver Republicans and some prominent Populists." He further recognized that "it is important that we should as far as possible organize commercial, industrial and political societies in our behalf."[169] The *Washington Post* reported that "the political machinery that served the party in previous campaigns was almost entirely disregarded, and new and enthusiastic men placed in charge of Mr. Bryan's campaign."[170] Without such organized support the Democratic campaign of 1896 would have hardly been the spectacular effort that it was.

[167] Bryan, *The First Battle*, see p. 155.
[168] Blodgett, *The Gentle Reformers*, 205.
[169] William Joel Stone to James K. Jones, July 31, 1896, box 4, Bryan Papers.
[170] Quoted in Jensen, *The Winning of the Midwest*, 273.

Bryan also compensated for the loss of local Democratic organizational support by taking his case directly to the people. His speaking tour suggested just how far the presidency had come from its reticent years, and his relative success (Bryan won a million more votes than Cleveland had in 1892) meant that his efforts could still be considered something of a victory.[171] Compared with Cleveland's staid public letters, Bryan's nationwide expeditions appear to be from a different time. Yet although it was a striking moment in political history, Bryan's remarkable popular campaign for the presidency grew directly out of the previous decade's politics.

Bryan's efforts over the course of the four years following his defeat displayed just how central presidential candidates had become to their parties, and how thoroughly party leaders had accepted the campaign of education. Between 1897 and 1900, Bryan struggled to solidify his party's commitment to bimetallism. He challenged Tammany (and other recalcitrant local organizations that had opposed his nomination) to take up his principled commitment to silver, abandoning deferential compromise to press the acceptance of an idea on which they differed. In doing so Bryan adhered to Cleveland's vision of national party leadership, suggesting that a national party could change rather than merely reflect public opinion and thus create a popular mandate that elevated local prejudices. Writing to one Tammany lieutenant, he insisted that "the democracy of the nation does have a right to expect the democrats of New York to stand by the platform or announce their hostility" and thus step out of the way to allow New York Democrats loyal to the platform to take over the local party apparatus. The party's role was educational, and he laid this task of informing the public at Tammany's feet: "bimetallism will be as strong in New York when it is fully understood as it now is in the West and South, and the sooner the democracy of New York begins the defense of the Chicago platform the sooner will the work of education be completed." Bryan would not defer to local organizations. Refusing to follow the Jacksonian norm that national party leaders did not speak on locally unpopular national issues when visiting local party leaders, Bryan accepted an invitation to visit Tammany in 1898 but added that "it must be with the understanding that I shall not be restricted as to subjects discussed."[172] If Tammany refused to fall into line, Bryan threatened to create an alternative Democratic organization in New York City, declare for the silver platform, and contest the Tammany delegation's credentials at the national convention in 1900.[173]

Bryan's effort to force his party into line was prodigious for a defeated presidential candidate, and he struggled to keep even his allies on track. Cleveland Democrats were isolated within the party. Chauncey Black, president of the National Association of Democratic Clubs, tired of Bryan's attempts to shape

[171] See Hollingsworth, *The Whirligig of Politics*, 108.
[172] Bryan to Willis J. Abbott, March 16, 1898, Box 20, Bryan Papers.
[173] "Bryan Seeks Assistance," *New York Times*, April 18, 1899, p. 2.

even state party politics, resigned to allow Bryan to make "a complete reorganization" of the clubs (he would throw the presidency to Hearst). [174] Bryan and his allies forced off Whitney's old confidant Harrity, who was not reelected as national chairman but nevertheless served on as a national committee member from Pennsylvania. [175] Even Altgeld chafed at Bryan's efforts to keep Democrats on the silver message and reminded Bryan that "the expression of an individual opinion by one member of a party does not commit a great party to any policy." Altgeld resisted Bryan's fervent belief that education could sway urban workers to the silver cause. "While in Nebraska and in perhaps most of the agricultural [sic] states, the silver question is the one that principally interests the people," he warned, "there are in Chicago and in fact all of the great cities, and even in the country in some of the Eastern states, large bodies of men whom we cannot interest in silver at all." They believed that "through the Democratic party they can achieve reforms relating to municipal corruption, etc.," and because "we both need and want the assistance of these people," they would have to be compromised with to maintain the alliance. [176] Altgeld's argument reminded Bryan that even ideological parties must effect some compromise to win, but it also reveals the latter's grand ambitions for educational appeals to remake the party-in-the-electorate. There were, of course, Democrats willing to allow him to shape the party's image. A prominent Democrat who had served on platform committees in 1888, 1892, and 1896 (and thus who had a good sense of the traditional demands of deferential compromise) enthused to Bryan that "my idea was that as you are to be the candidate it is no more than right that the platform on which you are to stand should not only conform to your views but should embody (as far as might be) your chosen form of expression." [177] This was Cleveland's view of presidential party leadership pressed into the service of Bryan's political objectives.

Even as he worked to keep his party on track, Bryan integrated dissident members of the Republican and Populist parties into the Democracy. He struggled to keep Silver Republicans in the fold through patronage, explaining that "if the democrats expect harmonious cooperation from the silver republicans they must be prepared to show some liberality in distributing the offices" and warning that failing to do so "would probably make cooperation impossible and result in our having no offices to divide." [178] Local leaders resisted this violation of the traditional principles of party regularity. In North Carolina,

---

[174] Chauncey Black to Bryan, April 2, 1898, box 20, Bryan Papers; Black to Bryan, December 4, 1899, box 23, Bryan Papers.

[175] Joseph Hawley to Bryan, May 4, 1898, box 20, Bryan Papers. On the effort to oust Harrity, see also James Kerr to Bryan, May 13, 1898; Urey Woodson to Bryan, May 2, 1898; J. G. Shanklin to Bryan, May 3, 1898; W. H. Thompson to Bryan, May 3, 1898, box 20, Bryan Papers.

[176] John P. Altgeld to Bryan, September 20, 1897, box 20, Bryan Papers.

[177] C. H. Jones to Bryan, June 20, 1900, box 24, Bryan Papers.

[178] Bryan to James K. Jones, February 21, 1898, box 20, Bryan Papers.

for example, Democrats defied Bryan's insistence on fusion with Populists to elect a former People's party member, complaining that he aimed "to make the silver issue predominant and before everything else" to the exclusion of traditional party concerns about local issues. Bryan's extraordinary path to power from the associational fringes of the Democracy taught him to disregard the principle of deferential compromise to a degree that would have been unheard of a decade before. As an outraged North Carolinian complained, "surely you do not understand the situation in this State, politically, or you would, I feel assured, be the last man to desire such an action."[179]

Thanks to his aggressive leadership, Bryan's control over his party continued long after 1896, resulting in three presidential nominations. Few presidential candidates – especially failed ones – have had such a longstanding and deep-reaching influence on their party. To be sure, Bryan's success in dominating his party did not turn it into a strictly ideological entity or into a personalistic one. However, his efforts to bring in the silver movement and to dictate party policy shaped the way Americans viewed the national party organizations. The old view of the national parties as grounded in deferential compromise and restrained by local organizations was challenged by a view that recognized the primacy of the national candidate as central to the party's message.

Bryan owed much of his success to Cleveland. Apart from his organized base of support, what hope he had in the 1896 campaign rested in his capacity to persuade crowds to vote for him – a tactical move that would have appeared much more radical in the days before Cleveland became a political celebrity. That the Great Commoner was self-consciously following in Cleveland's footsteps was made apparent when he chose to give his speech accepting the 1896 nomination at Madison Square Garden, from whence Cleveland had rallied the faithful in 1892. Bryan's inheritance of the national committee's fundraising apparatus, which Cleveland had helped develop, enabled the insurgent campaigner to maintain a national campaign even as state organizations defected. As Robert Marcus explains, the 1896 election was "the first clear test of the ability of an amorphous national party system to absorb massive changes in political demands without structural alterations,"[180] but this was only possible because the party had become flexible and independent under Cleveland. If Bryan raised less money than McKinley, part of the reason was that the platform and his campaign drove away support from the business community that Cleveland's careful balancing of his coalitional forces had avoided in 1888, not because the GOP's fundraising apparatus was more organized. In bringing the extra-partisan silver associations into party politics, Bryan was following a strategy legitimated by Cleveland's "naturalization" of the Mugwumps in

---

[179] Solomon Gallert to Bryan, April 11, 1898, box 20, Bryan Papers.
[180] Marcus, *Grand Old Party*, 20.

1884.[181] Further, Democrats conducted a paradigmatic educational campaign in 1896, supplementing Bryan's efforts with documents and lectures.[182]

Cleveland's position on the tariff had paved the way for Bryan's quixotic crusade for silver. It had introduced the Democratic party to the kind of interest-based economic appeals that Bryan would expand. By substituting for a more conciliatory stance on the currency, the tariff fight had occupied Cleveland's strategic map for so long that it allowed silver sentiment to simmer until the 1890s. The associational flurry that surrounded the silver movement's activities during the second Cleveland administration provided the backbone and strategic muscle to the insurgent movement. Without this isolated constituency, Bryan's career could not have risen to the nomination when it did.

Bryan's candidacy, however, undid the political work Cleveland and his national colleagues had done over twelve years. As Bensel explains, the electoral necessity of winning pro-gold, pro-tariff reform New York City had given the Democracy a personality split between East and West, president and Congress; it had maintained its viability largely because of Cleveland's coalition-building skills.[183] The split, however, came at the worst possible time for the Democrats, in terms of the stage of party development in which it occurred. In the Jacksonian mode, parties did not allow candidate-centered campaigns but provided a low-cost campaign apparatus. Under the new idea, popular candidacies alone were not enough – they had to represent a viable coalition between constituencies capable of funding national campaigns and popular constituencies open to the candidate's ideas. Cleveland had built such a coalition by maintaining the gold standard and humanizing tariff reform. McKinley would, in 1896, achieve a similar victory by defending the gold standard and humanizing protectionism into a winnable issue among the northeastern working class. Bryan's insurgent candidacy weakened his ties to the traditional Democratic financial base but he was unable to achieve victory by stoking a new constituency alone.

[181] Ostrogorski, *Democracy and the Organization of Political Parties*, Vol. II, 233.
[182] Jensen, *The Winning of the Midwest*, 273.
[183] Bensel, *The Political Economy of American Industrialization*, 366.

6

Party Transformation in the Republican Party

Party transformation in the Republican party took a different course from that pursued by nineteenth-century Democrats, although it was shaped by the same emergent idea of party. Two differences between the parties stand out. First, Republican party change centered on alterations to convention rules, which opened up new strategic practices for Republican presidential aspirants. In particular, Republican candidates proved more innovative with novel forms of presidential rhetoric than did Democrats in the 1880. Second, with a greater range of "available" presidential aspirants, the Republican party saw a greater variety of approaches to presidential party leadership.

Republican convention reforms reflected the broader party system's repudiation of Jacksonian-mode republicanism. Instead of restraining presidential ambition by forcing presidential aspirants to work with subnational political leaders, the Republicans' revised convention process encouraged presidential contenders to appeal directly to the party-in-the-electorate by expanding the clout of nationally dispersed constituencies and weakening the ability of state organizations to control their national delegations. The reformed process provided opportunities for presidential contenders to broadcast their positions, and thus to build up popular constituencies. This serviced the campaign of education by providing the parties with an educator-in-chief who could take on the difficult work of articulating party commitments in a complex political environment. Convention reforms, in this sense, paved the way for the presidential direct primary in the early 1900s. The impetus behind both reforms was quite similar – both allowed voters to bypass subnational party leaders, accessing national conventions more directly.

Republican presidential candidates responded with a variety of innovations, making for uneven patterns of development. Democrats were more limited in their leadership options – southerners did not make for good presidential candidates, and in an age in which presidential candidates were chosen in part for their ability to carry their home states, the relative lack of Democratic success at the state level in the most prominent non-southern states limited the range of candidates on whom the party could draw.[1] Cleveland's nominations stemmed from the fact that he was from New York – a large northern state where Democrats were competitive – as much as from his credentials; after the war, all Democratic nominees until Bryan were from New York (with the exception of Hancock, who, although from Pennsylvania, was stationed in New York at the time of his nomination). During the critical phase of innovation in presidential party leadership, Republicans drew on a wider range of candidates – each of whom worked to distinguish distinctive leadership credentials – and there were more Republican presidents during this time – four to the Democrats' one. The result was a greater variety of campaign strategies and styles among Republican presidential candidates, each of whom interacted differently with the new idea of party. Further, as Melvin Laracey notes, Republicans had inherited from their Whig predecessors a more modest set of expectations for presidential leadership than Democrats had, and each Republican president responded differently to this tradition.[2] Despite these differences, late-nineteenth-century Republican presidents, in keeping with the new mode of presidential party leadership, undermined whiggish notions of presidential power. Efforts to connect the national parties with the national electorate thus united both parties on the principle of the president as partisan-in-chief, standardizing expectations of presidential leadership and removing disagreements over the scope of legitimate presidential leadership from partisan conflict.

   Convention reforms were a reaction to a bold evocation of the full implications of the Jacksonian mode in the interests of a third Republican nomination for Ulysses S. Grant. James Garfield rode this wave of reform to the White House, only to be assassinated; he was replaced by a Stalwart successor, and the election of Cleveland. Garfield ally Benjamin Harrison seized the nomination by exploiting the new convention environment; once in office, however, he refused to assert party leadership, and he was also replaced by Cleveland. William McKinley explained himself quite differently from his Republican predecessors, and, like Cleveland, linked his innovations in campaign styles to executive power. Thus, the period 1880–96 was marked by a series of tenuous Republican experiments with presidential party leadership, each terminated by Cleveland's elections. This unevenness has done much to obscure the broader trends at work and at the time prevented the consolidation of an unambiguous presidential claim to party leadership. McKinley's election, however, ushered in a period of unparalleled Republican hegemony, which helped secure his model of

[1] Alan Ware reports that between 1877 and 1889, the median percentage of northern state legislative seats held by Democrats was between 29.7 percent and 40.8 percent, and between 25 percent and 16 percent between 1897 and 1909. Between 1879 and 1891, Democratic governors in northern states served a median of 3 years, and 27.2 percent of the time, northern states appointed U.S. senators. *The Democratic Party Heads North*, 105–6.
[2] Laracey, *Presidents and the People*, 117.

presidential party leadership (meanwhile, William Jennings Bryan's continued leadership of the Democratic party maintained the influence of Cleveland's model within that party).

Convention Reform

Between 1880 and 1888, the Republican party made two changes in its convention rules that altered presidential aspirant strategies. In 1880, Republicans abandoned the unit rule, which (as explained in Chapter 1) significantly empowered state party leaders and obscured popular favorites for the presidency (the unit rule was not abandoned by the Democratic party until the twentieth century). Second, beginning in 1880 and continuing in 1884 and 1888, the party solidified the requirement that national convention delegates be selected in congressional districts, rather than at state conventions. The goal – and the effect – of the reforms was to weaken the role of state party leaders in conventions by devolving delegate selection to congressional district conventions that were perceived to be closer to the people, and more representative of the party-in-the-electorate's diversity of views. District representation meant that Republicans placed the power of delegate selection in the hands of (at the time) 325 congressional district organizations, as opposed to the 38 states that composed the Union, making dispersed but national bases of candidate support more effective than before. Earlier presidential aspirants might have achieved significant gains from a small number of state party organizations; after 1880, aspirants needed to build a more dispersed range of support, which also enabled them to make use of scattered support across the nation.

This change is graphically represented in Figure 2. Contrasted with Figure 1 from Chapter 1 (also reprinted here), the Republicans' formalization of their convention system into separate state and congressional district tracks changed very little in the directionality and character of the flow of the party-in-the-electorate's participation in the party organization. It did uncover a new constituency of district delegates that had been muted by the Jacksonian party mode, expanding the sources of input into the national party organization.

As explained in Chapter 1, in the Jacksonian mode "the party organization of each State [was] regarded as independent, and at liberty to carry out the object of the call of the National Committee by methods of its own devising." Delegates were apportioned by congressional districts but were not conceived of as "representing them directly as separate constituencies," even though the states as a whole were technically represented by at-large state delegates.[3] This comported with established practice in other areas of the political system. For instance, most states had chosen presidential electors by statewide winner-take-all elections rather than by separate congressional district elections since the

---

3 "The Unit and Two-Thirds Rule," *New York Times*, July 9, 1884, 4.

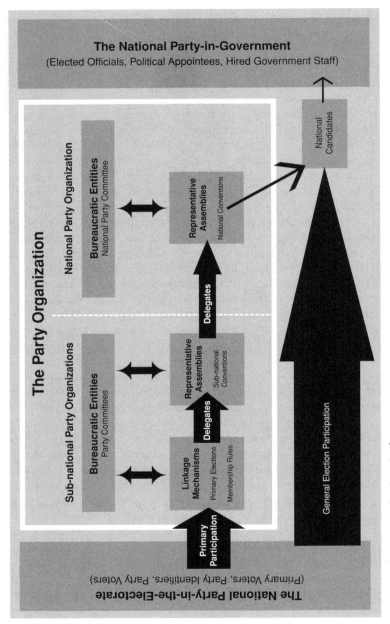

The National Party-in-Government
(Elected Officials, Political Appointees, Hired Government Staff)

The Party Organization

National Party Organization

Bureaucratic Entities
National Party Committee

Representative Assemblies
National Conventions

Sub-national Party Organizations

Bureaucratic Entities
Party Committees

Representative Assemblies
Sub-national Conventions

Linkage Mechanisms
Primary Elections
Membership Rules

Delegates

Delegates

National Candidates

Primary Participation

The National Party-in-the-Electorate
(Primary Voters, Party Identifiers, Party Voters)

General Election Participation

FIGURE I. Party organizations in the party system.

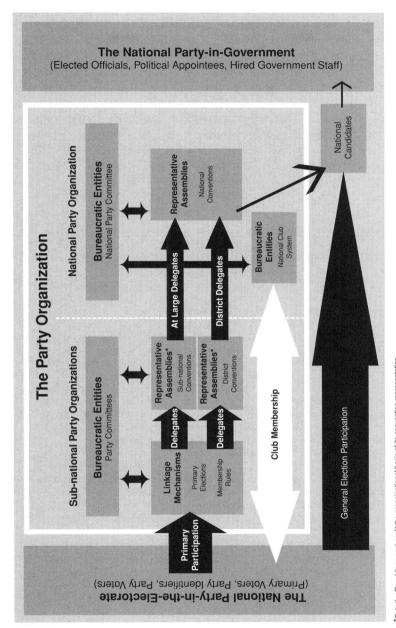

FIGURE 2. Party organizations in the late nineteenth century party system.

*Only the Republican party split the organizational basis of its convention representation

earliest days of the republic, because states realized that their influence on presidential elections was bolstered by a winner-take-all electoral vote allocation.[4] Affirming this logic, the Jacksonian idea of party asserted that "in political matters the State is sovereign and the National Convention has only a delegated authority for general purposes and no power of coercion over the party in any State."[5] Hence "each State has been left to choose its delegates to the National Convention in its own way," and "every State Convention was at liberty to adopt its own method of selecting both the delegates at large from the State and the delegates from the Congressional districts."[6] State organizations could consolidate all district conventions into state conventions, which could divide into separate congressional district meetings after electing state at-large delegates, have representatives of congressional districts vote for their delegates on the same floor, or simply ignore the distinction between district and at-large delegates.[7] This empowered state organizations in shaping the loyalties of national convention delegates. The practice was so common that

---

[4] See Garry Wills, *"Negro President": Thomas Jefferson and the Slave Power* (Boston: Houghton Mifflin, 2003), 68–9.

[5] "The Unit and Two-Thirds Rule," *New York Times*, July 9, 1884, 4.

[6] "States in the National Convention," *New York Times*, May 29, 1880, 4.

[7] *Appleton's Annual Cyclopaedia* contains reports (usually composed by journalists briefly summarizing political events in their states) on state nominating conventions in almost every state in every presidential election. They reveal four things: first, in a few states (such as in the case of Kansas Republicans and Democrats in 1872, Minnesota Democrats in 1872, Connecticut Republicans in 1876, Iowa and Louisiana Democrats in 1880, New Hampshire Democrats and Republicans in 1880, New York State Republicans and Democrats in 1884), the practice of choosing district delegates by use of separate district conventions meeting at the site of the state conventions was clearly and uncontroversially documented. Second, in *some* states, the authors imply that district delegates were chosen directly by state conventions, as in the case of the Florida Republican Convention in 1876, when it is reported simply that "eight delegates were chosen to the National Republican Convention" (p. 295); or in the New York Democratic Convention in that year, when it reported that "four delegates at large, and two from each congressional district, were chosen to represent the party of the State in the St. Louis convention" (p. 601). Third, in *most* cases, district delegates were reported as having been chosen by state conventions without clearly explaining whether they were merely ratifying earlier district conventions, selecting district delegates by on-site district conventions, or unilaterally selecting district delegates on the authority of the state convention alone. In these last cases, however, it is clear that the language of the reports confirms the authority of the state conventions in the matter authorizing district delegates; state conventions were almost uniformly described as having chosen national convention delegates without drawing a distinction between district and at large delegates. In no instance until 1884 (in the account of the New York Republican state convention) is it specified that separate district conventions could be held locally rather than on the site of the state convention, and then it is documented as something of a novel event, occasioning some comment. It should also be noted that New York Republicans retained the option of choosing district delegates at separate on-site district conventions, although no districts choose to do so; New York Democrats continued to choose their district delegates on the site of the state convention. *Appleton's Annual Cyclopaedia* (New York: D. Appleton and Company, 1873); *Appleton's Annual Cyclopaedia* (New York: D. Appleton and Company, 1877); *Appleton's Annual Cyclopaedia* (New York: D. Appleton and Company, 1881); *Appleton's Annual Cyclopaedia* (New York: D. Appleton and Company, 1885).

a Republican editor in Philadelphia even explained the persistence of district elections as a misunderstanding of the nature of party authority:

the action of the district is in reality only a nomination, though in practice it has grown to be looked upon as an election.... there would be no moral wrong in exercising the right in fact, which the convention has heretofore exercised only in appearance.[8]

Republicans' more nationalist political stance did make the position of state organizations in that party's structure more tenuous than in the Democratic party, where the practice of combining district conventions originated. In Republican conventions, as reported in 1880, "the votes of the State delegations have never been considered as units in a National Republican Convention,"[9] and Republicans had, from their first convention call in 1856, specified a distinction between at large and district delegates."[10] Political ideology alone, however, was not enough to effect change. As was the case in the Democratic party, neither the wording nor the spirit of the call for delegates representing congressional districts was strictly enforced before 1880. State-level representation and the unit rule were so compatible with political practice in both parties that efforts had to be made by Republicans to delegitimate them.

The momentum for Republican reform began in 1880 among party elites challenging efforts to nominate Grant for a third term. Grant's supporters claimed that he could energize the Union veteran vote and embolden southern Republicans, staving off Democratic gains made since 1874. Other motives animated the group: during his time in office, Grant had displayed an understanding of the party apparatus that complied with their own. Grant had reportedly "enthroned a directory of Senators and congressmen," providing them with unprecedented control over patronage.[11] As the *Atlantic Monthly* explained,

Grant represents a system which they regard as orthodox. Since he went out of office there has been a mixed *régime* of old ideas and new, very confusing and, as they think, very foolish, and they want to get back to the old plan of senators and representatives in Congress distributing the patronage in their respective States and districts, so that a man will once more know how to go to work to get an office.[12]

Grant's reelection, speculated the *New York Times*, was "calculated to strengthen the power of individual leaders, and to increase the influence of the State in determining the nomination."[13]

---

[8] "The Outlook at Utica," *Philadelphia Evening Bulletin*, February 24, 1880, 1.

[9] "Confusing the Questions," *New York Times*, June 1, 1880, 4.

[10] Victor Rosewater, "Republican Convention Reapportionment," *Political Science Quarterly* (December 1913), 611.

[11] Marcus, *Grand Old Party*, 24. On Grant's relations with his boomers, see Kehl, *Boss Rule in the Gilded Age*, 60; on his granting power to congressional Republicans, see Laracey, *Presidents and the People*, 121.

[12] "Republican Candidates for the Presidency," *The Atlantic Monthly* (April 1880), 552.

[13] "The Pennsylvania Plan," *New York Times*, February 6, 1880, 4.

Anticipating the convention, Grant toured the country, building excitement for the Republican icon. Friendly newspaper editors played into the boom, speculating frenetically about his political intentions. This display of his broad national reputation belied the provincial scheming of his boomers; as Grant careened across the nation, in Illinois, New York, and Pennsylvania, John Logan, Roscoe Conkling, and Simon Cameron, respectively, packed state conventions with their supporters and controlled the selection of district delegates. (Together the three states alone provided 170 votes, or about 45 percent of the votes needed to secure the nomination.) This was not unusual; one defender of the action estimated that half of the 1880 Republican delegates had been elected in this fashion, and the Republican credentials committee of that year heard contests from Alabama, Illinois, Kansas, Louisiana, and West Virginia on precisely this issue (not all of which were the result of pro-Grant manipulations). In the Alabama case, for example, when a duly elected district delegate refused the state convention's instructions to vote for Grant, he was replaced, and the state organization argued "that he was not elected by his district but only nominated, and that except through the action of the state convention ratifying his nomination, he had no authority whatsoever."[14]

The plan was premised on the national convention upholding the unit rule, and when this failed to occur, their delegations fragmented, throwing scattered support to other candidates. Although it was enforced throughout the period in the Democratic party, Republican conventions had never declared that the unit rule was officially tolerated, although Republican state conventions between 1856 and 1880 routinely sent delegations to national conventions instructed to vote as a unit.[15] With the unit rule, the boomers did not have to control every delegate, because a simple majority could cast the entire state's vote – including the votes of Grant opponents – as a unit for the hero of Appomattox. Following this display of state organizational might, "preferences and differences of opinion having been freely expressed and submitted to a recognized arbitrament, [Grant opponents] would have no loyal course but to accept the decision" or risk exile from party regularity. The vote of the minority within the party would be effectively silenced.[16] The outcome depended on the national convention's authoritative interpretation of the convention call, which would determine the size of the aspirants' votes. Grant supporters were particularly concerned about James Blaine, whose popularity was spread relatively evenly across the nation; allowing districts to select delegates without the guidance of state leaders would break up the convention power of their states and empower aspirants who could muster partial support in many states rather than total

[14] "In the Hubbub," *Atlanta Constitution*, June 5, 1880, 1.
[15] "A Defect in Party Organization," *New York Times*, May 17, 1880, 4.
[16] "The Pennsylvania Plan," *New York Times*, February 6, 1880, 4. See also, "Pennsylvania for Grant," *New York Times*, February 3, 1880, 1; "Grant in Pennsylvania," *New York Times*, February 4, 1880, 1; "Pennsylvania for Grant," *New York Times*, February 5, 1880, 1; "Grant Triumphs at Utica," *New York Times*, February 26, 1880, 1.

support in just a few. As noted in Chapter 1, Republicans borrowed their organizational structure from the Democrats. Neither party, however, had granted full recognition to the unit rule or to the practice of allowing state conventions to appoint district delegates. In both parties, the practices were allowed rather than specified; that Republicans picked up what were, for Democrats, informal practices confirms the power of the Jacksonian mode in shaping political practice.

The Grant boomers hoped to count the solid vote of delegations from Illinois, New York, and Pennsylvania, Arkansas, Alabama, Texas, and Louisiana, among others, secured largely through the overpowering position of state party leaders. In these states, Grant sympathizers drew on all the benefits of party regularity. In New York, Conkling forced instructions for Grant before district delegates were even selected, and, on a motion introduced by Chester Arthur, the state convention was empowered to turn out district delegates who refused to be bound by the instructions. Blaine men were outraged and protested that Arthur and Conkling "apparently, draw their views from their affiliations with the Democratic Party." Although this was substantially the same scheme attempted in Alabama, the New York Blaine supporters did not challenge the instructions in their state convention (and so did not present a challenge in the credentials committee) but announced months later, as the publicity around Grant's tour subsided, that they intended to disobey their convention's instructions.[17] Just before the convention convened, twenty-three Pennsylvania delegates declared that they, too, would disobey their state's instructions to vote as a unit.[18] In the Illinois convention, delegate selection produced a bitter dispute between Grant supporters (who controlled the convention by a majority of only about seventy-nine out of a total of six hundred) and Blaine supporters. Drawing on precedent, Grant supporters claimed "that State conventions had the right to supervise the selection of the Presidential delegates." Blaine men insisted that the districts – some of which had been strongly for Blaine – should be allowed to select their own delegates. In the end, the convention's chairman was empowered to appoint a committee that independently named the district delegates, and the state convention instructed all national delegates to vote for Grant as a unit.[19]

Grant boomers conspired to secure the rule by taking advantage of ambiguity in party procedures. As chairman of the national committee, Cameron would announce the committee's choice for the convention's temporary chairman, who would then be voted on by the convention itself. In the balloting, Cameron would recognize the unit rule, securing the selection of a Grant man as temporary chairman. That temporary chairman would then recognize the

[17] David M. Jordan, *Roscoe Conkling of New York: Voice in the Senate* (Ithaca, NY: Cornell University Press, 1971), 324–7. See also, "The Selection of Delegates," *New York Times*, February 26, 1880, 2; "Grant Triumphs at Utica," *New York Times*, February 26, 1880, 1.

[18] "Chicago's Travail," *Atlanta Constitution*, June 3, 1880, 1.

[19] "Illinois in Grant Ranks," *New York Times*, May 21, 1880, 1.

rule in the balloting for permanent chairman, who would recognize it in the balloting for the nomination; the pressure to remain regular would keep disappointed delegates from bolting the convention. Unfortunately for Cameron, Grant opponents on the national committee heard of the scheme and succeeded in passing a resolution in the committee's preconvention meeting that recognized the right of individual delegates to vote against the unit rule, preventing the selection of a Grant man as temporary chairman.[20]

Grant's boomers controlled the votes of the three most populous states, giving them the largest single bloc of votes in the convention. In the credentials, platform, and rules committees, however, each state was represented by only one delegate, and in these committees agents of the anti-Grant candidates united to kill the unit rule and establish the right of district representation. The rules committee (chaired by James Garfield) did not prohibit the unit rule but declared the positive right "of each delegate . . . freely to cast and to have counted his individual vote therein according to his own sentiments, and, if he so decide, against any unit rule or other instructions passed by a state convention." This did not prevent state conventions from imposing the unit rule or delegates from obeying it, but it empowered individual delegates to appeal to the convention if their vote was cast against their wishes – effectively scuttling its usefulness.[21] When the rules report was presented, Grant supporters moved to bypass its adoption and immediately begin balloting for the presidential nomination, but the convention insisted on voting on the rules – and approved them overwhelmingly. The Republican party had officially ruled that state organizations could not control the votes of their delegates beyond the doors of the national convention. In subsequent years, they reaffirmed the decision whenever they voted to adopt the rules of the previous convention.[22]

Credentials challenges also went badly for Grant because a general sentiment in favor of district representation prevailed in the credentials committee. Contests over the Illinois delegation provoked a fight over the issue. Echoing the Democrats' state-based view of the national party organization, the Illinois delegation insisted on "the right of the state convention . . . to determine the methods by which the delegates to a national convention shall be elected." Logan's supporters also defended their action on the basis of expediency, articulating a clear statement of the Jacksonian mode's reliance on state organizations and its insistence on harmonizing conflicting positions:

the denial of such a right and proceeding from this quarter would work results, as we believe, utterly disastrous to the harmonious action of the party throughout the Union. The various states in the Union will not tolerate it, and will not accept the doctrine

---

[20] Carl Becker, "The Unit Rule in National Nominating Conventions," *The American Historical Review* (October 1899), 78–9.

[21] This was especially true as "prominent candidates gained ownership over the delegates," a process that occurred at the state level as well as the national level, as Reynolds documents more closely in *The Demise of the American Convention System*, 79.

[22] Becker, "The Unit Rule in National Nominating Conventions," 78–9.

that the national convention, made up of all the states, shall dictate the methods of proceeding to the convention of any state.... The methods of Massachusetts may, perhaps, be much wiser and better than the methods of Illinois, but Illinois insists on the right of selecting its own methods, and while it will gladly accept suggestions from Massachusetts or Maine, or any other state, denies the right of Massachusetts or Maine, or any other state, to manage its state conventions.[23]

The majority report of the credentials committee articulated the parties' nationalist aspirations, however. It also spoke on behalf of party efficiency but claimed that party fortunes would best be served by a process that reflected the will of the national party-in-the-electorate:

the purpose to be secured in nominating a president is the selection of a candidate the most likely to be accepted by the people, and the nearer we get to the popular feeling, in the manner of selecting delegates, the wiser and safer will be our nominations.... The delegates thus selected by a state convention will not fairly represent the masses of the Republicans of the state, but frequently will misrepresent them. Nominations made by conventions of such delegates will not be so likely to be ratified at the polls.[24]

Here, then, was as clear a statement of the new idea of party's aspirations as any; better representation of diverse citizen interests at the national level would help the party win elections. The convention sided with the majority report and unseated eighteen of the Illinois delegation, replacing them with district delegates opposed to Grant.[25]

The results were decisive. In the eight states closely associated with the Grant boom (Alabama, Arkansas, Illinois, Louisiana, Mississippi, New York, Pennsylvania, and Texas would have given him 250 votes[26]), the rules changes cost Grant 90 votes. Only 30 were lost in credentials contests; 49 votes were then lost by the failure of the unit rule, as Grant delegations split their votes, giving 59 to Blaine and scattering 31 among John Sherman and Elihu B. Washburne – not enough to secure their victory but enough to stall the nomination long enough to allow a dark horse to emerge. On the first ballot, with 379 votes necessary to win, Grant received 304 – the votes he lost from the enforcement of the new rules would have secured his victory.[27] Unable to dominate the convention on the first ballot and thus to demonstrate the party's confidence in a third term, Grant hovered just below a majority until Garfield was nominated on the thirty-sixth ballot.

The backlash set in motion an effort to solidify a more open delegate selection process. Desirous that the spirit of the 1880 rules and credentials committee reports be perpetuated, a friendly floor amendment to the rules committee's resolutions instructed that in the 1884 convention call, "nothing in such rules

---

[23] Rosewater, "Republican Convention Reapportionment," 617.
[24] Rosewater, "Republican Convention Reapportionment," 616–17.
[25] "Roscoe Grows Pale," *Atlanta Constitution*, June 5, 1880, 1.
[26] See Becker, "The Unit Rule in National Nominating Conventions," 77.
[27] "The Tight Squeeze," *Atlanta Constitution*, June 8, 1880, 1.

or method shall be so construed as to prevent the several congressional districts in the United States from selecting their own delegates to the national convention,"[28] redefining convention authority by asserting that "to the representatives of Congressional districts, and to them alone, belonged the right to select delegates to the National Convention, and that the State Convention was absolutely without power to intervene."[29] Reformers argued that the new rule affirmed the party's nationalist orientation, effecting a conscious break from the Democrats' organizational mode. "For purposes of nominating candidates for a Presidential canvass," one editorialist remarked days after the convention, "the Republican Party is a national organization and not a congeries of State organizations." Assuming this to be "the theory" of the Republican party, "the delegates in a National Convention should represent the voting constituencies from which they are sent, with as little interposition of machinery between the voters and the constituted body as possible."[30] If it was not a wholesale reform of the party's nominating procedures, it was an assertion of the party's intent to open participation to the national party-in-the-electorate.

The 1880 rulings put party politicians on alert. As instructed, the Republican National Committee's 1884 convention call highlighted the congressional district requirement. National Committee Chairman Dwight Sabin presented the reform in "a hope that the voice of the people will, beyond recent precedent, be felt in moulding the work you are summoned to perform." He argued that it revived the party's connection to the party-in-the-electorate. A convention governed by the new rules would "win the unhesitating and undeviating support of every lover of those principles, by which the party has heretofore triumphed and yet will triumph" and secure the long-term loyalty of voters.[31]

Still, the 1884 call did not go far enough for some. Although it emphasized the importance of district representation and gave district convention officers the power to accredit district delegates, it also provided that "the Republicans of the various Congressional districts shall have the option of electing their delegates at separate popular delegate conventions.... or by subdivisions of the State conventions into district conventions."[32] The possibility of having district delegates chosen at state conventions – albeit in separate congressional district meetings – presented a problem; geographic separation mattered in the nineteenth century, because meeting at the site of state conventions imposed an extra degree of separation between the delegates and the district party-in-the-electorate. With all of the state's local representatives in one place, even divided into separate district conventions, state leaders could more easily influence

---

[28] Rosewater, "Republican Convention Reapportionment," 618; "The Dark Horses," *Atlanta Constitution*, June 6, 1880, 1.

[29] "Pennsylvania for Grant," *New York Times*, February 5, 1880, 1.

[30] "State and National Conventions," *New York Times*, June 10, 1880, 4.

[31] Republican National Committee, *Proceedings of the Republican National Conventions, 1884–1888* (Minneapolis, MN: Charles W. Johnson, Publisher, 1903), 4, 5.

[32] "The Work of the Committee," *New York Times*, January 18, 1883, 2.

district leaders, ensuring the selection of delegates loyal to the state organization. Thus Pennsylvania Republican Senator John I. Mitchell saw state conventions as a way "to prevent the people acting for themselves in their respective districts, if possible, with a view to controlling the selection of delegates at the State Convention" and warned that "to prevent their [the people's] expressing their real views and desires sums up all that is infamous in political bossism." Through state conventions, party leaders could "steal a march upon the people of the State."[33] As the *New York Times* predicted, it was "comparatively easy, where there [was] a well-organized and powerful machine, to secure a more or less complete concurrence of action by means of consultation and 'pressure.'" On-site district conventions gave state leaders an opportunity to "secure the results of the 'unit rule,' or at least evade the purpose of its abrogation," despite the 1880 declaration against it.[34] The *Springfield* [MA] *Republican* noted to the contrary that state conventions "save trouble and time, and perhaps subject the selection no more to the manipulation of the mere wire-pullers and caucus jobbers of the party."[35] Still, such exceptions made the rule all the more significant; in states where travel costs were at a premium, distant delegates were at greater risk of manipulation by state party leaders. In California, for example, state convention delegates often found travel difficult and could easily be induced to issue proxy votes to those party members planning to attend; because state party leaders tended to be in most frequent contact with far-flung delegates, it was not unusual for state leaders thereby to control a large number of proxies.[36]

The spirit of the new method inspired reformers' aspirations. Enthralled by the decentralizing implications of direct district representation, David McClure, a California delegate to the 1884 Republican National Convention, proposed that the 1888 convention call stipulate that "wherever a majority of the counties or subdivisions containing not less than one-half of the population of the district shall regularly unite in the call and conduct of the Convention, the action thereof shall be valid," which would empower a small number of local residents to select their own national delegates, regardless of the state convention's action and in subversion of the principle of party regularity. The national convention, "the source of all Republican power," could thus elevate itself above the units that composed it by reconstituting the base of its own

---

33 John J. Mitchell to Wharton Barker, February 1, 1884, box 2, Barker Papers.
34 "Choosing District Delegates," *New York Times*, January 26, 1884, 4.
35 "Massachusetts and Cincinnati," *Springfield* (MA) *Republican*, February 14, 1876, 4.
36 The 1860 California Republican convention was disrupted by a debate over the "large number of proxies from remote counties" held by a few elites who thereby possessed "entire control of the Convention and the general management of the Republican party in this State." The Secretary of the State Central Committee held a number of proxies because he was "of course in communication with the several counties of the State." Critics complained that this practice was common in the Democratic party in the state and that it had undermined the credibility of that party. See *Proceedings of the Republican State Convention, Held at Sacramento, June 20, 1860*, Library of Congress Collection, 3–4.

power.[37] McClure's proposal failed, but a more moderate proposal by Galusha Grow of Pennsylvania was adopted, directing the national committee to create new methods for district delegate selection, providing "that such methods or rules shall include and secure to the several Congressional districts in the United States the right to elect their own delegates." Grow's rule stipulated that each Congressional district in the United States would "elect its delegates to the National Convention in the same way as the nomination for a member of Congress is made in said district."[38] Grow's amendment enshrined the option of geographically distinct district conventions into a requirement, ensuring that only delegates selected in separate district conventions would be granted regularity. The *New York Times* praised the clarification; selected through district conventions, national delegations were "in no way dependent upon the opinion or the favor of State Committees, and those bodies should at least not stand in the way of its exercise." State committees had come to be mistrusted "due to [their] action in past times or to the action of others similarly constituted," but "districts which follow this method will have the consciousness of knowing that no extraneous influences, such as a large body of State Committeemen or the large membership of the State Convention itself, will have been brought to bear in the operation." The change to district representation meant that the delegates thus elected came "more directly from the people."[39]

State party leaders responded to the Grow amendment with care. John Sherman understood that the intention of reformed call was to break the power of the state organizations; he wrote to fellow Ohioan Joseph Foraker that "the argument used in favor of selecting them in the way Congressmen are chosen, was that thereby the whole matter would be more certainly relegated to the respective districts, and more completely removed from whatever might be the dominating influence in the State."[40] Sherman recommended that to protect Ohio's delegation from credentials challenges, the congressional committees in each district should issue the call for district conventions.[41] In giving more power to substate party leaders, direct district representation thus required reorganization on the ground, as previously neglected district organizations now had new attractions for ambitious politicians.[42] Mitchell, who was "especially anxious that prompt measures be taken to secure popular election of delegates by the Districts," was relieved to find that the people were "alive to the importance of this work" and organizing effectively.[43]

[37] Republican National Committee, *Proceedings*, 40, 24.

[38] Republican National Committee, *Proceedings*, 70–71.

[39] "District Conventions," *New York Times*, February 9, 1884, 4; "Selection of Delegates," *New York Times*, February 1, 1884, 1.

[40] John Sherman to Joseph Foraker, June 11, 1888, box 2, "Correspondence with Senator Sherman," Foraker papers.

[41] Sherman to Foraker, March 8, 10, and 14, 1888, box 2, "Correspondence with Senator Sherman," Foraker papers; see also Foraker to Sherman, March 20, 1888, *ibid.*

[42] "Choosing District Delegates," *New York Times*, January 26, 1884, 4.

[43] Mitchell to Barker, February 13, 1884, box 2, Barker Papers.

In practice, the 1888 convention interpreted the rule in the radical spirit of the McClure proposal, solidifying the legitimacy of geographically distinct congressional district conventions. Eight of Virginia's congressional districts sent contesting delegations to the convention, providing a convenient test case of the new rules. As part of a wider challenge to the dominance of William Mahone, a white Republican who excluded black Republicans from party affairs, insurgent Republicans organized their own convention in which district delegations selected national delegates in separate district meetings – a clear violation of the new convention call, albeit in the spirit of decentralizing party power. In the national credentials committee, they charged the state organization with violating the spirit of the 1888 convention call by exerting undue influence over the selection of district delegations and appealed to the national convention on the basis that their convention had been an attempt to dethrone a corrupt state party boss, even though it broke the letter of the rule.[44] Seven of the insurgent delegates lost their credentials challenge because they had not been selected within the geographic territories they represented; only the insurgent delegation from the district in which the insurgent state convention had been held was accepted, a strict interpretation indeed. "Where...a demand has been made and insisted upon by any considerable number of Republican voters for the right of local self-government," noted the credentials committee, "and conventions have been held within the district and delegates have been duly chosen, the committee feels constrained to recognize such delegates as chosen in accordance with the letter and spirit of the National call." Thus, the committee emphasized the district party-in-the-electorate's right to govern its affairs without the interference of the state committee and virtually adopted the McClure position that had been rejected four years earlier.[45] Although Mahone's victory recognized the power of a statewide faction that had exerted corrupt measures to influence congressional district conventions, it struck at the heart of the power of the states within the Jacksonian convention framework and came at the price of submitting the state parties to more decisive control by the national convention.

Decentralization of the delegate-selection process strengthened the nationalizing tendencies of the Republican organization. The power of large states was broken, making it harder for candidates without a national profile to secure sufficient delegates through agreements with state party leaders. The size of large states – an advantage under the unit rule – become an invitation to fragmentation under the new rules because favorite son candidates who could not hold their delegation together were revealed to be weak. Indicating just how big an impact this change had, in Republican conventions between 1856 and 1876, the three largest states that the Grant boomers depended on in 1880 (New York, Pennsylvania, and Indiana) voted as a unit on the first ballot approximately 61 percent of the time and cast votes for more than two

---

[44] Republican National Committee, *Proceedings*, 30.
[45] Republican National Committee, *Proceedings*, 65.

candidates only once; between 1880 and 1896, they only voted as a unit 36 percent of the time, and nearly 47 percent of the time cast votes for more than two candidates. In Democratic conventions where the unit rule held and district conventions failed to take hold, these states cast a solid vote 78 percent of the time between 1856 and 1876 and 82 percent of the time between 1880 and 1896.

Weakening the power of subnational leaders changed the strategic environment of Republican party politics by changing how national nominating coalitions were built. Rather than appealing to state party leaders directly, presidential aspirants could appeal to the party-in-the-electorate in congressional districts and build a coalition of support that could not be easily silenced at state conventions. This strategy made popular input into presidential aspirants' campaign appeals more decisive; to win the nomination, they needed to pay more attention to popular opinion and less than before to alliances with state and local party leaders. The dramatic shift away from the tradition that forced presidential candidates to remain silent during campaigns during this time grew out of the new potency of popular campaigns in national party politics. Republicans thus effectively adopted Cleveland's revision of the notion of availability, and candidates claimed that their nomination implied their party's endorsement of their party leadership

Because it was easier for the party-in-the-electorate to influence delegate selection (there were fewer layers of conventions between them and national delegates) and harder for state leaders to dominate (there were more distinct conventions to control), the rules change also transformed preconvention campaigning. John Reynolds's account of the decline of the convention system at this time pivots on the emergence of "hustling candidates," mainly executive nominees seeking to gain ownership over convention delegates by mounting popular campaigns designed to "convert the delegate selection process into a personal plebiscite." Reynolds argues that personalized candidacies did not emerge from direct primaries (a charge common in the decline of party literature) but instead created a political context in which direct primaries were encouraged by a campaign style that made primaries seem reasonable.[46] At the national level, hustling candidates were encouraged by the shift within the Republican party to the district delegate-selection process and the abrogation of the unit rule because the new convention environment encouraged presidential aspirants to engage in preconvention campaign activities designed to develop personal popular followings. Hustling candidates also complemented the campaign of education; because they sought to develop popular support rather than intraorganizational alliances, hustling candidates sought to articulate formulations of party policy that distinguished them from their competitors, inviting more detailed discussion of the issues and providing the campaign of education with material for distribution, encouraging candidates to develop constituencies that could be put to use in educational campaigns.

---

[46] Reynolds, *The Demise of the American Convention System*, 74, 9.

The Garfield Campaign

After Grant's boomers failed to force the 1880 convention to adhere to Jacksonian mode precedents, a stalemate ensued, with supporters of Blaine and Sherman locked in a death grip on the remaining delegates. (With 377 votes between them on the first ballot – the remainder scattered among three minor aspirants – together they controlled the nomination, but each refused to surrender it to the other.) On the thirty-fourth ballot, Garfield, who had helped his own cause by playing a conspicuous role in the proceedings as chairman of the rules committee, was introduced as a compromise candidate; he was elected on the thirty-sixth ballot. Garfield's nomination was the result of a convention deadlock, but his emergence as a dark-horse nominee does not represent the dominance of traditional convention politics. Instead, the Republican convention nominated the man who had, through his presentation of the rules committee report, become personally identified with reform. Garfield's campaign further perpetuated this identification because he took important steps to assert party leadership.

The context of Garfield's assertion of power was a conflict within the Republican party over electoral strategy for the 1880 election. The settlement of the disputed election of 1876 was recognized in some Republican circles as a failure of the party's longstanding ambition to build up a southern Republican party. Hayes had won in 1876 with 185 votes, the barest of majorities out of 369. Yet if the 19 southern electoral votes that snatched victory from defeat could no longer be counted on in the Republican column, the votes of Connecticut, Indiana, and New York – which were closely competitive between the parties – together with the expanding vote of the West through population growth and the addition of new states might provide the start of a new electoral college base.[47] It also meant fighting on different substantive grounds. Although racial violence continued in the South, northern publics were growing tired of Republican appeals that centered on "bloody shirt" rhetoric. "It is clear," observed James Clarkson, "that there is no longer a majority in the North to respond to the nobler issues on which the Republican party has so long stood."[48] Here was surely the dark underbelly of the educational campaign; for many northern elites, Reconstruction gave way to compromise with Jim Crow in exchange for a focus on economic issues.[49]

Garfield believed winning Indiana in particular to be central to a broader strategy for continued victory, knowing that it cast its vote in an early October election and served as a bellwether of the electorate's mood. He wrote his running mate Chester Arthur that victory in November "will be made certainly possible or seriously imperiled by our management of Indiana during the next

---

[47] Burnham, "The Changing Shape of the American Political Universe."
[48] Quoted in Hirshon, *Farewell to the Bloody Shirt*, 157.
[49] Hirshon, *Farewell to the Bloody Shirt*, 29–30; Vincent P. De Santis, *Republicans Face the Southern Question: The New Departure Years, 1877–1897* (Baltimore: Johns Hopkins University Press, 1959), 197–219.

fortnight."[50] Yet a number of Republican National Committee members – including Conkling ally and finance committee chairman Levi P. Morton – placed their hopes in winning back New York's thirty-five electoral votes as the safest strategy and poured money into that state.[51] This set up a conflict between the candidate and the subnational party leadership over the basic strategy for the campaign. This conflict exposed a deeper struggle for party control. Winning through the Midwest placed Garfield at the triumphant head of a ticket that had fought its way through contested territory; winning through New York solidified Conkling's position.[52] If Republicans lost Indiana, Conkling's wisdom would elevate him in party councils and create a sense of Garfield's obligation to Conkling.

With this in mind, Garfield dispatched Stephen W. Dorsey, the secretary of the Republican National Committee, to conduct the Indiana campaign personally. Dorsey's role was curious; a Stalwart, he was forced on the committee as a concession to Logan, who wanted the assurance of a Stalwart presence on the committee. Garfield, however, channeled Dorsey's energies into a direction that served his own purposes. Garfield's biographer suggests that "ambition spurred Dorsey to make the most of the opportunity," and he turned out to be a reliable agent for Garfield.[53] Belying the perception of the Jacksonian mode as a supremely effective party apparatus, Dorsey found the Indiana party's apparatus to be a "paper organization," leaving much of the mobilizing work of the campaign undone. Dorsey built up an entirely independent organization of full-time party workers, all paid by the national committee, and all answerable to Dorsey.[54]

The Garfield campaign in Indiana was not predominantly what would come to be called an "educational campaign." Much of Dorsey's organization was devoted to gathering intelligence on the Democrats and heading off fraud at the polls. In creating an independent organization designed to work independently of the subnational organizations, however, Dorsey moved toward an independent presidential campaign. "This organization being entirely outside the ordinary organization of the State" (and thus violating traditional notions of regularity), he wrote to Garfield's personal secretary, "it seems to me that if we carry it out to the end there can be not reasonable doubt of our success."[55] Left to their own, the state organizations could hardly be trusted – even such a creature of subnational politics as Dorsey understood that. The real problem was building an organization that could successfully contest the election in a way that was faithful to the national party, regardless of the state and local party organizations' enthusiasm.

---

[50] Theodore Clarke Smith, *The Life and Letters of James Abram Garfield, Volume II* (New Haven, CT: Yale University Press, 1925), 1024.

[51] Smith, *The Life and Letters of James Abram Garfield*, 1024.

[52] Ware, *The Democratic Party Heads North*, 49.

[53] Peskin, *Garfield*, 487.

[54] S. W. Dorsey to D. Swain, September 1, 1880, reel 105, series 4B, Garfield papers.

[55] S. W. Dorsey to D. Swain, September 1, 1880, reel 105, series 4B, Garfield papers.

Garfield also reached out to dissident groups and extra-partisan associations in his steering of the Indiana campaign. He encouraged an alliance with the Greenback party, although Indiana Democrats steadfastly refused. He secured the cooperation of the Disciples of Christ, a revivalist network of lay pastors to which Garfield belonged, to distribute campaign material throughout the state and beyond. Garfield also cultivated independent donors like Wharton Barker, a Philadelphia businessman who aspired to play kingmaker and to gain access to the presidency for his protectionist views. He raised money among his colleagues in the Philadelphia business community and sent it directly to Garfield allies in the Midwest (earning a rebuke from National Chairman Jewell, who pleaded that all campaign donations go through the national committee).[56] Garfield's supervision of events in Indiana was not popularly trumpeted, but his careful management was a departure from a party mode that valued subnational control of national campaigns and rigid, geographic lines of regularity.[57] As a result, when Republicans claimed victory in Indiana, it was a personal victory for Garfield, as well as for his party.[58] Election returns revealed that Indiana had gone from a 6,500 Democratic majority in 1876 to a 6,600 Republican majority in 1880. The shift away from southern resources cost the Republicans nineteen of the electoral votes they had received in 1876, but victory in Indiana brought the GOP fifteen electoral votes.[59] Moreover, in seizing control of the campaign despite the resistance of prominent state party leaders like Conkling, Garfield proved that presidential candidates could win without depending on state leaders – a lesson that was not lost on Harrison eight years later.

The campaign was hardly an educational campaign. Garfield avoided policy leadership, claiming that addressing issues beyond the party's platform "would be a violation of the trust they have imposed in me,"[60] and as a dark-horse candidate who had emerged only as a compromise between three popular candidates, he had little legitimacy to do so. In this sense, he and his opponent, Winfield Scott Hancock, were the kind of candidates that the Jacksonian mode encouraged (Hancock was reportedly told "that there was nothing for him to do but to attend to his duties, just as though he had not been nominated"[61]). Garfield's unprecedented leadership, however, demonstrates that a process of political learning among national party leaders was well under way.

Garfield's tentative front porch campaign is further evidence of this. Although Harrison expanded it in 1888, Garfield's use of the technique of

---

[56] Peskin, *Garfield*, 454, 498; Marshall Jewell to Barker, October 3, 1880, box 1, Barker Papers.
[57] Garfield wrote to Whitelaw Reid that "it is hardly possible for anyone to have a fuller knowledge of the forces now at work in Indiana than I. The most minute and comprehensive reports are brought to me daily of the operations there." Smith, *The Life and Letters of James Abram Garfield*, 1025.
[58] Peskin, *Garfield*, 503–12.
[59] Burnham, *Presidential Ballots*, 390–1.
[60] Smith, *The Life and Letters of James Abram Garfield*, 993–4, 1022.
[61] "Campaign Dangers," *Atlanta Constitution*, August 21, 1892.

speaking publicly to large crowds who visited his home was the first substantial effort to campaign in this way. It originated as Garfield was besieged by visitors to his Mentor, Ohio, home, whom he greeted with short, but not politically neutral, speeches.[62] Garfield was also not confined to his home and began a trend of candidate speaking tours. In August, Dorsey urged Garfield to make a trip to New York City to make peace with Conkling. The mission was potentially embarrassing for Garfield, but he turned it into a triumphal procession. He spoke to large crowds throughout New York State, leading James Blaine to remark that "never before in the history of partisan contests in this country, had a successful presidential candidate spoken freely on passing events and current issues."[63] Most of Garfield's speeches were perfunctory, but Harrison, whom Garfield introduced to the crowds and who launched more partisan attacks on Hancock and the Democrats, accompanied him.[64] In New York, Garfield spoke to a crowd of 10,000 in front of the Republican National Committee headquarters.[65] Garfield's popular appeals were an attempt to put the best possible face on the shameful necessities behind his trip, but he also sought to mitigate the effects of Conkling's defection by invading his home turf; just as the "hustling candidates" limited the independence of convention delegates, they undermined the flexibility of subnational party leaders by generating independent constituencies that other politicians ignored at their peril.

Garfield's speeches were popularly received. In imitation, Blaine embarked on a campaign tour in 1884, a move that was marred by his defeat in that year; thus, the legitimation of popular appeals by candidates occurred in fits and starts. Even as Garfield's speechmaking and front porch campaign faced little criticism, his opponent, Hancock, gave an interview to a newspaper in which he declared, somewhat incomprehensibly, that "the tariff is a local issue."[66] Whatever the merits of Hancock's meaning, the phrase became a punch line and cast doubt on the wisdom of presidential candidates publicly campaigning. Scholars such as Gil Troy and Jeffrey Tulis[67] have seen the failure of such campaigns as evidence of a bias against presidential speechmaking, but the reality is that presidential candidates were constantly grasping opportunities to expose themselves; as they did, they furthered a process of political learning, and longstanding norms against presidential speechmaking gave way to emerging norms about presidential candidates' roles. The front porch tactic became a model for later Republican presidents, as did the whistle-stop train tour. When popular statements backfired, they made subsequent candidates more

[62] Peskin, *Garfield*, 499.
[63] Smith, *The Life and Letters of James Abram Garfield*, 1039; Kenneth D. Ackerman, *Dark Horse: The Surprise Election and Political Murder of President James A. Garfield* (New York: Carroll & Graf, 2003), 168–9.
[64] See, for instance, "General Garfield Welcomed," *New York Times*, August 5, 1880, 1.
[65] "The Candidates Honored," *New York Times*, August 7, 1880, 1.
[66] Troy, *See How They Ran*, 87–9.
[67] Troy, *See How They Ran*; Tulis, *The Rhetorical Presidency*.

cautious but did not prevent them from exploring the boundaries of legitimate politicking.

Garfield and Arthur in Office

As explained in Chapter 1, dark horses Hayes and Polk had made extraordinary efforts to turn the restraints of the Jacksonian mode on their head by pledging only a single term in office. If the dark horse Garfield believed that his extended duties as a candidate paved the way for a similarly extraordinary attempt at party leadership through the president's public position, he had little opportunity to make it. His actions during his four months in office before he was shot suggested an old-fashioned determination to bring his fractious party together by placating the Stalwart and Half-Breed factions with patronage; they also betrayed either a startling naiveté or a tendency to be dominated by Blaine (who served as Garfield's secretary of state and a close advisor). Arthur, whose leadership position was much weaker, succeeded Garfield in office; nevertheless, he attempted to make the most of it by relying on traditional methods of patronage allocation. Neither had the opportunity to make the most of the new convention process.

For Garfield, the perils of this traditional approach became apparent almost immediately, for he quickly became embroiled in conflict with Conkling over patronage that demonstrates just how difficult it was for presidents to build political capital with patronage. Hayes's attempts at civil service reform outraged Conkling; the effort to reelect Grant was a reaction to a trend toward reform, and after Garfield's election Conkling resumed the conflict he had begun with Hayes. The nature of the clash, pitting two presidents against a senator of their own party, reveals the intraparty nature of the struggle that produced the nineteenth-century transformation of the parties. Pushing his drive for reform, Hayes had removed Chester A. Arthur, then collector of the New York Customs House, and Alonzo B. Cornell, the naval officer of the Port of New York, for failing to institute civil service reform and appointed reformers in their place. Unable to recognize the political value of civil service reform (he called reform, not patriotism, "the last refuge of a scoundrel"[68]), Conkling thought he saw in the appointment of reformers an attempt by Hayes to undermine his control of New York politics. On a more principled level, his long-term defense of senatorial courtesy and the lengths to which he was willing to put it suggested that Conkling believed that he and not the president might "be allowed to exercise the executive functions of appointment and removal in the State of New York."[69] The Customs House employed hundreds of workers, who could be put to effective use during campaigns and thus had

---

[68] Alfred R. Conkling, *The Life and Letters of Roscoe Conkling: Orator, Statesman, and Advocate* (New York: Charles L. Webster, 1889), 541.
[69] Shores, *The Hayes-Conkling Controversy*, 245, 263.

"a controlling influence in the machine politics of New York, and . . . a controlling influence in Congress, gained and held by appointment favors to senators and members."[70] Conkling fought the removals by engineering the defeat of Hayes's nominees until compromise candidates were arranged. Believing that the ascension of Garfield was merely the replacement of one reformer with another, he had refused to campaign for Garfield until he "had assured him and his followers that he would . . . 'consult' with them regarding New York appointments" (the purpose of the August trip to New York City) before he and his state allies were "willing to lift a finger in the campaign."[71] Following the meeting, Conkling campaigned listlessly for his party's nominee.

Although Garfield quibbled with the extent of just what agreement had been reached in New York, he had few options. Conkling's behavior during the campaign had not demonstrated good faith. Liberal Republicans, so-called independents, and civil service reformers, in contrast, had supported Garfield's nomination and election and had campaigned vigorously for him. If he recognized the former and rejected the latter, he risked an impasse in Congress; if he rewarded Conkling, he risked spoiling whatever political capital he had among independents. Choosing to recognize his campaign constituency, he appointed a reformer as collector of the port, removing Hayes's compromise candidate. However, he also let it be known that he believed Hayes had gone too far in "theoretically holding that Congressmen should not be consulted" and argued that "the Executive . . . should seek and receive the information and assistance of those whose knowledge of the communities in which the duties are to be performed best qualifies them to aid in making the wisest choice."[72] In his limited conception of his role, reaching this understanding meant reconciling the Stalwarts and the Half-Breeds through a judicious use of patronage. Repudiating Hayes's stance on assessments of officeholders, he approved the practice, even as he promised to encourage reform and to "concentrate the weight of public opinion on Congress."[73] Questioning how he could do this while maintaining his strategy of appeasement led his biographer to remark that "so long as the selection of federal appointees in the states was left to be settled by the advice of Congressmen, the essential feature of the spoils system would remain untouched."[74]

The New York appointments came up almost immediately after Garfield took office. When Conkling stalled Garfield's nomination for Collector, Garfield withdrew all of his New York nominations, including those of which Conkling approved, forcing a stand on the issue of whether senatorial courtesy would uphold the prerogative of a single Senator to dictate presidential

[70] Walter Allen, "Two Years of President Hayes," *Atlantic Monthly* (August, 1879), 196.
[71] Smith, *The Life and Letters of James Abram Garfield*, 1103. See also Thomas Collier Platt, *The Autobiography of Thomas Collier Platt* (New York: B. W. Dodge, 1910), 130.
[72] Smith, *The Life and Letters of James Abram Garfield*, 1109–10, 1006, 1003.
[73] Fowler, *The Cabinet Politician*, 172–9.
[74] Smith, *The Life and Letters of James Abram Garfield*, 1007.

nominations. Enraged, Conkling and his fellow New York senator, Thomas C. Platt, showed their disdain for presidential authority by resigning their seats, expecting the New York legislature to reappoint them, embarrass Garfield, and reassert the role of senatorial courtesy. The implications for presidential leadership were significant; if New York reappointed the senators, congressional dictation of appointments would be reinforced. The implications for presidential *party* leadership were also significant, however – perhaps more so, if only because it had a more tenuous hold on conventional opinion than did congressional control over administration. If a president could not reward his own electoral constituency without the blessing of individual senators, then presidents were subservient to the subnational leaders of the party in their reelection efforts. Conkling and Platt's broad political support indicated the strength of the tradition of the congressional wing of the party's influence over presidential patronage; sixty out of eighty-one Republicans in the New York Assembly made a formal objection to the president; a committee of Republican senators visited Garfield to urge the withdrawal of the appointment; and Vice President Arthur, New York Governor Alonzo Cornell, and Garfield's own postmaster general sent formal protests to the president. Garfield's move for independence through patronage was thus controversial enough to generate substantial opposition within his own party. Yet by resigning, Conkling and Platt went too far: the Republican caucus failed to support the New Yorkers, and two days after their resignation, Garfield's New York nominations were confirmed – senatorial courtesy apparently all but forgotten. Garfield was shot before the New York legislature could choose their replacements, but by that time, it was apparent that the Conkling machine in New York State would not be able to overcome the opprobrium that the affair had caused.[75]

Garfield's struggle with the New York senators was bold but exposed the weaknesses of the president's role as party leader in the Jacksonian party mode. As the *New York Times* jeered, "the President's mistake consists in supposing that any conceivable distribution of the spoils would satisfy both factions, and further in failing to see that if the great body of the party – not the office-seekers only – is to be united, it must be by some policy of more importance than the one to which he is just now giving such painful prominence."[76] Whether or not Garfield could have successfully negotiated the struggle between the two local factions designing for control of New York (and the dozens of local factional quarrels elsewhere), struggles over constitutional prerogatives often capture popular attention but rarely inspire popular admiration. The more

---

[75] Accounts of the event are readily available, and vary little; see White, *The Republican Era*, chap. 2; H. Wayne Morgan, *From Hayes to McKinley: National Party Politics, 1877–1896* (Syracuse: Syracuse University Press, 1969), chaps. 1 and 3; Matthew P. Breen, *Thirty Years of New York Politics* (New York: John Polhemus Printing Company, 1899), chap. 51. For a particularly one-sided interpretation, see Platt's *The Autobiography of Thomas Collier Platt*, chap. 7.

[76] "The President and the Party," *New York Times*, May 7, 1881, 4.

presidents struggled to best the Jacksonian mode by playing by its rules, the more distracted they became from governing tasks that played to the executive's strengths. Whether Garfield could or would have been able to achieve the kind of transformative administration that Hayes envisioned cannot be known, but given the distraction of his fight with Conkling during his few months in office, it is unlikely that he would have done so with the tools he was using.

If Garfield came to office on inauspicious terms, Arthur's were impossible. Nominated as a sop to a defeated faction of the party, discouraged from taking the position by the head of that faction, and elevated by an assassin who celebrated his ascension, Arthur had little legitimacy for party leadership. As a party leader, however, Arthur's time in office displayed an awareness of the changed strategic environment of his time. Having observed its ineffectiveness in the 1876 and 1880 elections, Republicans turned against the ideal of building a southern Republican party on the basis of expanded voting rights for black southerners. Yet whereas Garfield had turned almost exclusively northward, Arthur placed his hopes in reorienting the Republicans' southern strategy toward appealing to third-party and independent groups in the South (usually composed of disillusioned white Democrats).[77] Arthur allied with these independents, even to the point of tolerating financial doctrines considered heretical to northern Republicans, in hopes of building a reliable southern base within the party.[78] He supported an independent silverite in Mississippi; independent movements in North Carolina and Georgia; fusion with Greenbackers in South Carolina, North Carolina, Texas, Arkansas, and Alabama; and Mahone's independent movement in Virginia.[79] Although Arthur's scheme was little more than a continuation of the old Republican southern strategy by new means, it did recognize the growing power of third-party movements, and as such reflected a not-implausible move by the president to reshape the conditions of his party coalition.

The strategy did not work for Arthur, nor did it enhance presidential leadership. Southern Republicans resented his interference in their affairs. The Republican Executive Committee in Jackson, Mississippi, requested that Arthur stop sending officeholders to promote his interests: "most of them know little of our affairs: some of them never did know anything about us.... they only use Mississippi as a place to hold office from."[80] Newspapers, outraged that "scores of southern office holders have been sent for, and provided with arguments for use in the South," reported indignantly on Arthur's patronage strategy,[81] and the *New York Times* observed in 1884 that Arthur's agents

---

[77] See Hirshon, *Farewell to the Bloody Shirt*, 99–107.

[78] Vincent P. De Santis, "President Arthur and the Independent Movements in the South in 1882," *The Journal of Southern History* (August 1953), 346–63; Hirshon, *Farewell to the Bloody Shirt*, 105–6.

[79] Doenecke, *The Presidencies of James A. Garfield and Chester A. Arthur*, 116–21.

[80] Republican Executive Committee, Jackson Mississippi, to Chester A. Arthur, 188[?], Arthur papers, reel 3.

[81] "The Presidency," (Portland, OR) *Morning Oregonian*, February 12, 1884, 1.

actually bred more resentment than support: "when [Republicans] read in their newspaper that an Arthur Postmaster or Internal Revenue Collector has 'fixed' the primaries in their county and bids fair to control the district convention they indignantly denounce such proceedings as shameful."[82] Arthur got reelection support from southern independents, but when state elections proved Republican fusion with independents and Greenbackers in the South to be an electoral dead-end, Arthur's strategy was dismissed. In the convention, Arthur's weakness as a popular candidate became apparent. On the first ballot in 1884, Arthur received a paltry 34 percent of the convention's vote, nearly 60 percent of which was from southern delegates, whereas Blaine drew 75 percent of his support from traditionally Republican states in the Northeast and West. Although the fact that he retained a quarter of the convention's delegations largely through his southern strategy testified to the strategic vision of his course, Arthur's lack of appeal to the Republican party-in-the-electorate prevented him from mounting the kind of campaign that would lead later presidents to dominance of their party.

Benjamin Harrison's Campaign and Administration

Harrison was the first Republican presidential candidate to take advantage of the transformed convention environment, but he did not link the new warrants for presidential independence implicit in the nominating process to assertive party leadership once in office. He demonstrated that the assertion of presidential party leadership was a dual track that presented distinct barriers both in the campaign for office and in the office itself. He advanced the process of political learning begun by Garfield, but, perhaps to contrast himself with his predecessor, he shunned the kind of presidential leadership that Cleveland had modeled.

District conventions formed the basis of Harrison's campaign, and they fit neatly with his broader effort to control the national party apparatus and thereby bypass local party leaders, as highlighted in Chapter 3. Seizing on the nationalizing implications of the new delegate selection rules, in what state leaders interpreted as a foray into "enemy territory," Harrison made an 1888 preconvention speaking tour through New York and Pennsylvania, building support within congressional districts. At the convention, it was reported that the result of the Harrison "invasion" was that "the Pennsylvania delegation is hard to handle, and there have been stories circulating all the morning that the Harrison people have succeeded in making a strong impression there, and it is openly boasted that Quay cannot hold his men." Conversely, when New York's Thomas Platt attempted to launch a "favorite son" candidacy for Chauncey Depew, it was seen as "a blunder, destroying the only chance New York had of uniting on a candidate who could succeed, and thus exercise a controlling

---

[82] "The Anti-Arthur Republicans," *New York Times*, April 3, 1884, 4.

influence."[83] According to the *Atlanta Constitution*'s convention correspondent, men like Quay and Platt proceeded on the premise that "the longer we hold out the other candidates against each other, the stronger becomes their unwillingness to yield among themselves," paving the way for the eventual nomination of a compromise candidate. Harrison opponents, however, were unable to hide scattered support for Harrison within their ranks, and the strategy fizzled. An anti-Harrison caucus was called but was unable to unite on a single candidate of national stature, and so it could not compete with the support Harrison built among the now-independent congressional districts. When Harrison received the nomination, the *Constitution* editorialized that Harrison's opponents failed because they "played on the delegates in the old style, and the instruments they used were duplicity and defeat."[84] Harrison did not win because of the delegates he stole from Quay and Platt, but by neutralizing their ability to control their state delegations, he staved off a threat; the decentralization of delegate power opened the door for Harrison's popular campaign at the expense of traditional Jacksonian mode.

Harrison's campaign is often derided as an example of the "front porch campaign," and the technique is too often attributed to the timidity with which nineteenth-century presidents approached campaigning.[85] In reality, Harrison spoke from his front porch because he had undertaken personal control of the campaign in Indiana (which, between 1874 and 1896, alternated its electoral votes between Democrats and Republicans in each election, giving Cleveland a 6,500 vote plurality over Blaine in 1884), much as Garfield had done in 1880 – and Harrison's front porch was, not coincidentally, in Indiana. The campaign proved groundbreaking: in the last six weeks of the campaign, he made speeches (possibly as many as ninety, to three hundred thousand listeners) from his front porch.[86] As in 1880, the candidate and the national committee disagreed about the amount of resources that were dedicated to Indiana; Whitelaw Reid reported that the committee intended to leave Indiana "absolutely to its own resources" and worked to channel private donations directly to Harrison's people in the state.[87] Harrison also desired to be identified as the savior of the state for the Republicans, avoiding indebtedness to Quay, who chaired

---

[83] Morgan, *From Hayes to McKinley*, 402; "No Choice Yet," *Atlanta Constitution*, June 23, 1888, 1; "The First Test," *Atlanta Constitution*, June 21, 1888, 1; "Harrison and Morton," *New York Times*, June 26, 1888, 1.

[84] "Blaine: That Is the Way It Looks at Chicago," *Atlanta Constitution*, June 24, 1888, 1; "The Republican Nominee," *Atlanta Constitution*, June 26, 1888, 4.

[85] Troy, *See How They Ran*, 82–107.

[86] Sievers, *Benjamin Harrison: Hoosier Statesman*, 390; Charles W. Calhoun, *Minority Victory: Gilded Age Politics and the Front Porch Campaign of 1888* (Lawrence: University of Kansas Press, 2008), 133.

[87] Whitelaw Reid to Benjamin Harrison, October 6, 1888, series 1, reel 12, Benjamin Harrison Papers, Manuscript Division, Library of Congress; on the close election in Indiana, see Sievers, *Benjamin Harrison: Hoosier Statesman*, 402; on Harrison's control and efforts to attract resources into that state, see ibid., 403–4.

the Republican National Committee.[88] As had been the case with Garfield in 1880, Harrison's victory in Indiana demonstrated his direct role in the electoral college victory and thus established his credentials.

Judging from the response to Harrison's campaign, the rhetorical presidency – or at least the rhetorical presidential candidacy – had arrived by 1888. Caught up in the spirit of the time, Harrison found it difficult to resist growing expectations of presidential leadership. Requests for Harrison to speak poured in from across the country, perhaps emboldened by Blaine or by Harrison's own speaking role in Garfield's 1880 tour. James Clarkson encouraged Harrison to speak at a tristate rally with politicians from Iowa, Missouri, and Illinois.[89] Other Republicans invited him east, suggesting that "you can do yourself more good in the doubtful states of N.Y., N.J., Conn. and N.H., than all the efforts of any protective tariff organizations or Republican committees can accomplish."[90] From the South came the appeal that "if you could make one or two specific speeches in the South, I am satisfied we could gain many electoral votes there."[91] Such requests were not merely the pleas of intemperate hangers-on but reflected a general shift legitimating presidential party leadership among party leaders, who increasingly believed presidential candidates' speeches were valuable to party fortunes. The president of the Iowa Press Association opined that "a presidential candidate or a president belongs to the whole country and in some way that relationship should be properly manifested." Taking on the role of chief campaigner signified the candidate's aspirations to truly national leadership and thus spoke to his qualifications for the job:

the party and the country are a little restive under the policy of presidents and presidential candidates who are not statesmen but statemen . . . national republicanism owes it to itself to have General Harrison, who is so competent to do it, take on this large national relation as a candidate.[92]

In this context, Harrison's front porch campaign was viewed as neither shocking nor timid. The managing editor of the *Chicago Tribune*, writing to Harrison's private secretary after the election, declared that it was "a great victory indeed, and much of it is due to Gen. Harrison's most admirable reception speeches."[93] If Harrison had been chastened by Blaine's ill-fated 1884 tour, or by a general prohibition against presidential candidate rhetoric, he was also emboldened by his experience and his party colleagues.

Yet although Harrison's campaign was bolder than generally recognized, the distinction between Harrison and Cleveland was apparent from the moment

---

[88] Jensen suggests this in *The Winning of the Midwest*, 12.
[89] James S. Clarkson to Harrison, July 21, 1888, series 1, reel 10, Harrison Papers.
[90] A. C. Carton to Harrison, July 9, 1888, series 1, reel 9, Harrison Papers. Note that the plea also strongly suggests close cooperation between the GOP and national tariff associations.
[91] A. E. Bateman to Harrison, July 17, 1888, series 1, reel 9, Harrison Papers.
[92] A. C. Carton to Harrison, July 9, 1888, series 1, reel 9, Harrison Papers.
[93] W. K. Sullivan to Elijah W. Halford, November 10, 1888, box 1, Halford Papers.

of Harrison's nomination. Harrison's imitation of a classic Whig president appears as more of a conscious maneuver to contrast himself with his opponent than any remaining distinction between the parties on the matter of presidential leadership. Harrison's 1888 campaign, despite his weak presidency, continued a larger trend leading Republicans away from their Whig heritage. Rhetorically positioning himself within traditional Jacksonian organizational notions about the locus of party leadership, Harrison rejected the party leadership that Cleveland pursued and explained his conception of his role in the party and the campaign quite differently from the way Cleveland had explained his. In his letter accepting the nomination, he rejected Cleveland's analysis of the tariff as a practical matter of policy and argued that the election was "not a contest between schedules, but between wide-apart principles," thus speaking the language of the Jacksonian mode by insisting on an inherent divide between members of the two parties. Dismissing calls for a more detailed examination of the tariff, he huffed, "we do not offer a fixed schedule, but a principle." Pushing further, he rejected the notion of an educational campaign by questioning Democrats' honesty and insisting that Republicans not accept Cleveland's arguments at face value: "the legend upon the banner may not be 'free trade;' it may be the more obscure motto 'tariff reform,' but neither the banner nor the inscription is conclusive, or, indeed, very important." If one's opponents could not be trusted to tell the truth, one could not be educated by them. Far from embracing executive party leadership, Harrison pointed to "the methods suggested by our convention" as sufficient for resolving the problem of excess tariff revenues, and he criticized the fact that the Democratic agenda was articulated through "executive acts and messages, and by definite propositions in legislation." His analysis – insisting on the primacy of the convention, mocking Cleveland's messages, and insisting on a fight of general principles rather than policy details – shows that he understood what he was fighting against and how intently he explained himself differently.[94]

Harrison's letter heightened the contrast between his written adherence to Jacksonian mode norms and his actions in his preconvention and front porch campaigns, which demonstrated the capacity of presidential candidates to grab national attention. Yet although Harrison's campaign speeches could have been construed as a bold move to seize control of the campaign, the content of those speeches hardly evidenced bold policy leadership. Critics complained that Harrison had the ability "to speak in public from ten to twenty minutes nearly every day for two or three months without saying something." His letter of acceptance had touched on the tariff in the broadly painted partisan lines of protection versus reform.[95] Thus, although Harrison showcased the potential inherent in presidential candidate performance – and undermined any remaining taboo against presidential rhetoric – he did not use his speeches

---

94 Benjamin Harrison, "Acceptance of First Nomination, 1888," *Public Papers and Addresses of Benjamin Harrison* (Washington, DC: U.S. Government Printing Office, 1893), 2.
95 "Diverse Deliverances of Tippecanoe," *New York Times*, September 20, 1888, 4.

to lay the groundwork for claims of a popular mandate. National Chairman Quay reportedly found the speeches so noncontroversial that he enthused that if the candidate "would continue making those wonderful speeches to the end of the campaign. . . . we could safely close these headquarters and he would elect himself." In keeping with his own understanding of the campaign of education, Quay had the better of Harrison's speeches printed for national distribution.[96]

So although the "front porch" campaign was an innovation, in light of the changes that the parties had undergone since 1880, Harrison appears to have seen it as a campaign tactic alone. This made his homebound campaign seem more reactionary than it was; "there is no apparent reason," observed an editorial, "why the precedent set in [Blaine's] case," meaning his 1884 speaking tour, "should not be followed by Mr. Harrison." As if to emphasize further his timidity, Harrison invited Sherman and Blaine to Indiana for a speaking tour. Blaine continued on throughout the Midwest, "going up and down the land with a zeal and persistency worthy of the restless being to whose attention Job's career was called"[97] – ostensibly campaigning for Harrison but simultaneously reaffirming his own popularity.

Harrison's campaign reveals why the widespread nature of late-nineteenth-century party change was so essential to its success. Had it been isolated in the presidency alone, or in either of the two parties alone, Blaine's failure in 1884 and Cleveland's in 1888 might have deepened the taboo against presidential party leadership. Instead, individuals from both parties, representing different factions and different partisan roles, all contributed to a common result. Garfield's leadership in 1880, Blaine's tour in 1884, Cleveland's messages in 1885–7, and Harrison's front porch campaign in 1888 all legitimated trends that had been drubbed into the consciousness of American politicians by the nationalizing effects of the associational explosion. Dispersed across the political system, it was difficult for any particular failure, or even a weak manifestation of the trend, to discredit the larger trend. That Harrison's performance in 1888 could be viewed with complaisance by someone like Quay, and that Harrison's reactionary intentions were shoehorned into such innovative methods, indicates just how much had changed.

In office, Harrison maintained his election-year stance as an anti-Cleveland. He did not announce clear policy objectives, allowing the major initiatives of the day – such as the McKinley Tariff, the Sherman Silver Purchase Act, and the Lodge Force Bill – to flow out of legislative leadership. This allowed congressional Republicans to bolster their authority to speak for the party.

---

[96] Louis T. Michener, "Harrison's Speeches in 1888," Louis T. Michener papers, Manuscript Division, Library of Congress, Washington, DC; Sievers, *Benjamin Harrison: Hoosier Statesman*, 378; Kehl, *Boss Rule in the Gilded Age*, 100; on the struggle between Harrison and Quay, see Marcus, *Grand Old Party*, 138–45; Homer E. Socolofsky and Allan B. Spetter, *The Presidency of Benjamin Harrison* (Lawrence: University Press of Kansas, 1987), 11.

[97] "Where Is Mr. Harrison?" *New York Times*, October 31, 1888, 4; Sievers, *Benjamin Harrison: Hoosier Statesman*, 403–5.

Rhetoric, then, was not revolutionary in and of itself and was noticeably less revolutionary when used in ways that comported with traditional expectations of presidential leadership. Harrison's inaugural address consciously outlined these traditional expectations. He virtually ceded supremacy in civil service appointments to Congress and defended congressional dictation of patronage as a matter of expediency, acknowledging that "the civil list is so large that a personal knowledge of any large number of the applicants is impossible. The president must rely upon the representations of others." While this was an accurate description of the problems presidents faced with patronage, Harrison was signaling a traditional relationship between presidents and Congress. He also indicated his determination to defer policy matters to his colleagues in Congress. He noted that the financial situation of the country demanded solutions but added that "it [would] be the duty of Congress wisely to forecast and estimate these extraordinary demands." His insistence that "it is the duty of the executive to administer and enforce in the methods and by the instrumentalities pointed out and provided by the Constitution all the laws enacted by Congress" was a remarkably Whiggish claim that further distinguished him from Cleveland.[98]

Sidney Milkis and Michael Nelson describe the Harrison administration as a "retreat in the recent struggle to revive the status of the presidency" and suggest that the weakness of Harrison's leadership "spawned efforts to reorganize the House and Senate to perform their duties more efficiently … by the end of the nineteenth century [Congress] was a complex and well-disciplined institution that was organized to govern."[99] Republican Speaker of the House Thomas B. Reed took advantage of the leadership vacuum and began to rule his chamber with an iron fist, imposing discipline on the body by limiting filibusters, denying Democrats the ability to block quorums, and imposing penalties on representatives who failed to attend sessions. Senate Republicans followed similar procedures, and together the two houses brought "a previously unknown degree of party and procedural unity" to the legislative branch.[100] The result was a flurry of legislation with which Harrison had little to do, and most of it was identified with, and aided the prestige of, competitors with Harrison for national attention.[101] Of course, a variety of factors enabled Reed to seize this opportunity, including a general Republican openness to expanded party power in the House, but Harrison's eschewal of a leadership role contributed to the general sense that Republicans suffered from a leadership deficit at the national level (especially in the wake of Cleveland's demonstration of

98 Benjamin Harrison, "Inaugural Address," *The Inaugural Addresses of the Presidents*, John Gabriel Hunt, ed. (New York: Gramercy Books, 1995), 259, 265.
99 Michael Nelson and Sidney Milkis, *The American Presidency: Origins and Development, 1776–1990* (Washington, DC: Congressional Quarterly Press, 1990), 179.
100 Nelson and Milkis, *The American Presidency*, 180.
101 Socolofsky and Spetter, *The Presidency of Benjamin Harrison*, 81.

the potential of the office).[102] This phenomenon suggests that the development of party in the late nineteenth century did not inevitably lead toward presidential ascendancy. Indeed, it questions the too-frequent tendency among political scientists to assume that "the president's place in the government *had to* become more central if the nation was to have coherent leadership." The trend toward an enhanced, "modern" presidency was not irreversible. That Congress saw a resurgence of power in the vacuum of Harrison's leadership indicated that "new warrants for leadership" abounded in the period but that they remained underutilized until acted upon by willing party leaders.[103] It also demonstrates the depth of the transformation behind the new idea of party. Harrison's administration seemed so reactionary because expectations of acceptable national party leadership had shifted.

The McKinley Campaign

The candidacy and presidency of William McKinley demonstrate just how far this had happened in the Republican party by 1896. The lone Harrison administration and the first McKinley administration were separated by a mere four years, but McKinley's integration of the lessons of the campaign of education and Cleveland's example made for a remarkably different exercise of presidential party leadership. At the very least, McKinley explained himself quite differently than Harrison did. His candidacy carefully laid the groundwork for his presidency, which was marked by prodigious assertions of party leadership.

Another businessman-in-politics, Mark Hanna, masterminded McKinley's campaign. Hanna's biographer, Herbert Croly, noted that Hanna got into politics in the 1870s when his ownership of a street railway company in Cleveland, Ohio, brought him into conflict with the "petty local politicians whose votes usually had to be secured by some kind of influence."[104] Hanna's involvement locally brought him into contact with nationally prominent state politicians like Garfield, Sherman, and McKinley. He supported Sherman's failed campaigns for the Republican nomination and was frustrated when Sherman failed to cultivate popular leadership. In McKinley he saw a popular leader who was capable of building a national constituency that could prove a more reliable basis for a presidential campaign.[105] A major Republican donor, he abhorred the inefficiencies of the Jacksonian mode's fundraising apparatus, and, like Wharton Barker and John Wanamaker, tried to impose order on the

---

[102] Eric Schickler, *Disjointed Pluralism: Institutional Innovation and the Development of the U.S. Congress* (Princeton, NJ: Princeton University Press, 2001), 33.

[103] Gould, *The Modern American Presidency*, xii (emphasis added); Skowronek, *The Politics Presidents Make*, 48.

[104] Croly, *Marcus Alonzo Hanna*, 81, xii.

[105] See, for instance, Bernardo, *The Presidential Election of 1880*, 161–2.

erratic fundraising mechanisms of the traditional Jacksonian organizations.[106] He also saw firsthand how independent political associations could either sustain or interfere with party politics. During the 1880 election, he helped found a Business Men's League that organized across Ohio in support of Garfield.[107] In 1888, he was outraged when elements of the regular party ignored extra-partisan labor groups,[108] and he kept a close eye on the Farmers' Alliance in Ohio, clearly wary of the group's potential.[109]

The lessons of the transformed campaign style were evident from Hanna's earliest efforts to boost McKinley's presidential aspirations. This exposed far deeper fault lines in the GOP than the characterization of McKinley as the candidate of monolithic business interests within the party suggests. In addition to the widespread impression that Democratic gains in 1890 were a reaction to the McKinley Tariff, McKinley lost reelection to Congress in that year. His election to the governorship of Ohio in 1891 revived his career, but in 1893, McKinley was forced into bankruptcy when a friend defaulted on loans that he had endorsed; a group of businessmen donated the funds to retire his debts, which raised eyebrows about the governor's obligations to his financial saviors. By 1894, when the Wilson-Gorman tariff bill passed the House, the failure of McKinley-style protection appeared imminent. Rather than backing away from the tariff, between 1892 and 1896 Hanna and McKinley worked assiduously to "fix protection in the minds of the mass of the Republicans as the cure-all for the economic disturbances." It was a campaign of education at the preconvention stage, designed to create first an impression of the tariff as a cure for the depression, and second "the impression of an irresistible demand for [McKinley's] nomination from Republicans of all classes, sections, and shades of opinion."

Most important, their strategy was grounded in bypassing the traditional subnational party elite. In short, the more popular McKinley was among the party-in-the-electorate (and the more widely broadcast was this impression), the less capable party leaders would be to maneuver an alternate candidate into prominence without public disaffection. In 1892, McKinley undertook a national speaking tour on behalf of Harrison and the Republican ticket, during which "he spoke as far west as Minnesota and Iowa and visited Maine, Massachusetts, Pennsylvania, Indiana and Illinois." By 1894, McKinley's "plain, commonsense talk, easily understood by anyone" was in heavy demand by

---

[106] Hanna to Joseph Foraker, November 27, 1887, box 2, Hanna-McCormick Family Papers; Hanna to Foraker, April 22, 1887, box 2, Hanna-McCormick Family Papers; John Sherman to Hanna, October 6, 1891, box 2, Hanna-McCormick Family Papers.

[107] Dictated Statement of Senator Charles Dick to James B. Morrow, February 10, 1906, box 4, Hanna-McCormick Family Papers.

[108] Mark Hanna to Joseph B. Foraker, November 8, 1888; Hanna to Joseph B. Foraker, January 12, 1887; John Sherman to Hanna, April 17, 1889, box 2, Hanna-McCormick Family Papers.

[109] C. H. Grosvenor to Charles Foster, October 6, 1891, box 2, Hanna-McCormick Family Papers.

party leaders looking for helpful stump speakers in congressional campaigns[110]; Richard Jensen estimates that in 1894, he spoke to 2 million people in a tour of 300 cities in which he gave 371 speeches.[111] McKinley also made contacts with party leaders on the ground in the congressional districts that selected national convention delegates, and beginning in 1892, Hanna and his Ohio allies "conducted a systematic correspondence with men from every State and Territory in the Union and established connections."[112] Shortly after he was reelected governor in 1893, the pro-McKinley *Cleveland Leader* began connecting McKinley's name to the presidency, and McKinleyism was touted as promising a return to business prosperity through protection; by 1894, Hanna was personally distributing copies of the *Cleveland Leader* nationwide. In the midst of this preconvention campaign, the depression of 1893 discredited the Democratic administration, and Republicans regained control of the House and Senate in 1894, contributing to a larger sense of Democratic failure and portending – to the public mind – good things for Republican fortunes in 1896.[113] What once seemed like the candidate's biggest drawbacks had become positive allurements.[114]

Hanna's campaign was not all educational. Between 1894 and 1896, Hanna rented a summer home in Georgia, where he entertained southern Republicans, sewing up their support for McKinley. Despite the reputation of southern Republican delegates as susceptible to corruption, Hanna worked to avoid the appearance of bribery or promises of patronage; Hanna biographer Croly noted that "by making McKinley's personality familiar to Southern Republicans and popular among them, they created a species of public opinion in the South, favorable to his candidacy," that did not require outright corruption. Although this cannot be proven, the real import of Hanna's southern strategy was to block McKinley's opponents from buying southern support. As Thomas Platt recalled, "he had the South practically solid before some of us awakened."[115]

Where state leaders like Quay and Platt voiced their doubts about McKinley's candidacy, his supporters coined the slogan of "The People against the Bosses," playing on popular distrust of the regular organization and promoting McKinley's image as a candidate forcing his popular nomination on a

[110] Margaret Leech, *In the Days of McKinley* (New York: Harper and Brothers, 1959), 60, 72, 61; dictated statement of Senator Charles Dick to Morrow, February 10, 1906, box 4, Hanna-McCormick Family Papers.

[111] Jensen, *The Winning of the Midwest*, 286.

[112] Dictated statement of Senator Charles Dick to Morrow, February 10, 1906, box 4, Hanna-McCormick Family Papers.

[113] Jensen, *The Winning of the Midwest*, 226–7; Silbey, *The American Political Nation*, 234–5.

[114] Clarence A. Stern, *Resurgent Republicanism: The Handiwork of Hanna* (Ann Arbor: Edwards Brothers, 1963), 13; Leech, *In the Days of McKinley*, 61.

[115] Croly, *Marcus Alonzo Hanna*, 176. Stanley K. Jones, *The Presidential Election of 1896*, (Madison: University of Wisconsin Press, 1964), 112, 129, 132; Platt, *The Autobiography of Thomas Collier Platt*, 331.

reluctant party establishment.[116] McKinley representatives attended labor conventions (a practice that Hanna continued during the general election), booming McKinley's name and his argument that the tariff helped working men and again evidencing Hanna's belief in the necessity of courting national extrapartisan associations.[117] Hanna organized McKinley-for-president clubs across the nation to ensure control of local efforts and used the clubs to play on the Harrison strategy of "invading" hostile territory.[118] He sent Charles Dawes into Illinois to organize support for McKinley, outraging Shelby Cullom, Illinois senator and presidential aspirant. Drawing on the experience of the associational explosion, Dawes helped found the Business Men's McKinley Club of Cook County, which sent letters to the chairmen of party committees and to every Republican officeholder in the state, asking who they supported for the presidency and stating their preference for McKinley, thus signifying a groundswell of popular support for the Ohioan. They also provided ground troops for an offensive in local conventions to ensure the selection of pro-McKinley delegates to the national convention.[119] Dawes's organizing efforts appeared particularly fruitful during a January 1896 meeting of the Illinois Republican State Committee, at which McKinley's name was cheered louder than Cullom's, while the Senator fumed onstage.[120] Cullom's later intransigence convinced Dawes that "no alliance can be made with the regular party organization [in Illinois]. It is now McKinley and the people against the 'county' machine and its state branches."[121]

In Pennsylvania, Hanna avoided Quay's attention by working with local groups such as the Philadelphia Young Men's Republican Club and the Workingmen's Protective Tariff League. He encouraged public rallies to "give an opportunity for public demonstration of this strong, popular McKinley desire" and advised organizers to "in a few remarks state that [McKinley's] organization recognized the desire of the public to express itself, *as political managers evidently were not recognizing the public pulse.*"[122] Elsewhere, Hanna's strategy was the same, and in addition to drumming up popular support for

[116] Morgan, *From Hayes to McKinley*, 488.
[117] James S. Clarkson to "Mr. Barnes," July 15, 1903, box 3, Hanna-McCormick Family Papers.
[118] Dictated statement of Senator Charles Dick to Morrow, February 10, 1906, box 4, Hanna-McCormick Family Papers; Leech, *In the Days of McKinley*, 72.
[119] "Open War: The McKinleyites Come Out of the Thicket," *Cleveland Press*, March 19, 1896, 3; "M'Kinley Club," *Cleveland Press*, April 1, 1896, 5.
[120] Dawes, *A Journal of the McKinley Years*, 66.
[121] Dawes, *A Journal of the McKinley Years*, 65–6.
[122] Theodore Justice to J. Hampton Moore, March 25, 1896, series 1a, box 3, folder 10, Moore Papers, emphasis in original. On the Workingmen's Protective Tariff League, see Moore to Charles Grosvenor, April 4, 1896, series 1a, box 3, folder 11, Moore Papers. On Hanna's involvement, see Hanna to Moore, April 6, 1896, April 16, 1896, and April 17, 1896, series 1a, box 3, folder 11, Moore Papers. The response in that city was the formation of three McKinley political clubs, in addition to the support of the existing Young Men's Republican Club. Moore to Hanna, May 18, 1896, series 1a, box 3, folder 12, Moore Papers.

McKinley, he created an organized base with which the campaign communicated directly after the convention. Before the reform of the delegate selection process, such tactics in states such as Illinois and Pennsylvania would have been ill advised because they could have been reliably crushed by state bosses at state conventions and would have antagonized potential convention partners. Cullom's hostility was aroused at "McKinley's 'invasion' of Illinois which he considers his own particular and personal property." Without their traditional control over their states' national convention delegations, however, it was particularly difficult to stop McKinley's broad, decentralized constituency.[123]

McKinley's opponents found that traditional methods of securing delegates to the national convention were undermined by the national scope of Hanna's preconvention campaign. Surveying the scene in early 1895, a Quay ally wrote dejectedly that "their 'missionary work' has extended over a larger area of the country than I had supposed."[124] Illinois Republican John Tanner believed that McKinley's national publicity hardened local politicians' impression of the Ohioan's popularity; "the *Times-Herald*," he despaired, "is pounding away for McKinley all the time, while the *Tribune* is printing Presidential preferences from the Editors all over the country, which shows McKinley largely in the lead, which is helping the McKinley cause to a great extent in our State."[125] This perception of McKinley's unstoppable candidacy went a long way toward securing his position as the front-runner by suggesting a popular uprising in favor of McKinley.[126]

Subnational party leaders turned to manipulation of the nomination process, but this displayed their weakness. As Charles Dick recalled, a "combine" of state leaders, including Quay, Platt, Cullom, and Clarkson, worked feverishly to block McKinley from within state politics: "from every State and district where it was possible upon any pretext to do so contesting delegations were sent to the convention by the combine." State leaders trotted out a series of favorite son candidates, hoping to scatter delegate votes and prevent an early nomination for McKinley, providing them the power to dictate the nomination, or at least to extract concessions from the nominee: "Reed was New England's candidate; Quay was Pennsylvania's; Cullom was supported in Illinois, Manderson in Nebraska, Morton in New York, Allison in Iowa and Davis in Minnesota." Relying on the newly decentralized nominating system, Hanna insisted that "we shall get a delegate wherever we can,'" and this strategy "broke up the solid delegations for the favorite sons."[127] As H. Wayne Morgan argues, "the

[123] Dawes, *A Journal of the McKinley Years*, 65–6.
[124] R. A. Alger to Matthew Stanley Quay, May 8, 1895, box 3, folder 5, Matthew Stanley Quay papers, Manuscript Division, Library of Congress, Washington, DC.
[125] John R. Tanner to James S. Clarkson, February 21, 1896, box 2, Clarkson papers; Tanner to Clarkson, February 17, 1896, box 2, Clarkson papers.
[126] Croly, *Marcus Alonzo Hanna*, 139.
[127] Dictated statement of Senator Charles Dick to Morrow, February 10, 1906, box 4, Hanna-McCormick Family Papers. Whether Croly's enthusiasm for the role of popular majorities in the McKinley nomination is overstretched, it was true that "the 'favorite son' policy was a

days when regional bosses dictated presidential nominations without regard to party wishes or popular ideals were over."[128]

As with Whitney's role in the 1892 Cleveland campaign, Hanna's preconvention work for McKinley earned him his colleagues' admiration; for the first time in convention history, the victorious candidate's manager was called on to address the delegates. As Croly explained, "the delegates recognized that they were confronted by a new thing under the sun of politics, and behind the new thing was a new man." Yet unlike Whitney, Hanna (after declaring that McKinley's nomination was made "by the people") declared that he was "now ready to take my position in the ranks,"[129] and he was appointed to the national committee and elected chairman. As head of the national party organization, Hanna continued many of the organizational innovations of his predecessors and further consolidated many of them under the organizational umbrella of the Republican National Committee. He selected an advisory committee and directed its fundraising closely. He insisted that the National League of Republican Clubs "would have to make itself absolutely subservient to the National Committee" to receive funding and noted that it had not been "under the control of the committee so much as desired."[130] Detractors and defenders of Hanna alike have observed that he directed the party's "first major public relations campaign in modern American politics,"[131] but the negative connotations of this claim obscure the lineage of his methods: under Hanna's leadership, the Republican campaign of 1896 was oriented toward purposes that had been common to national campaigns for the previous decade at least. Hanna later recalled that "the work before us was a campaign of education of great magnitude."[132]

The Republican National Committee's novel role in the campaign is reflected in the greatly expanded scope and scale of the organization it built to contest it. Charles Dick later insisted that "the campaign was different from any we had ever had," largely because it "demanded a greater number of speakers to argue the question, greater quantities of literature for distribution and greater efforts to reach the educational influence of the press," and so "the national committee was compelled to create a larger organization."[133] Recognizing these conditions, Croly concluded that the new type of campaign required "certain departures from the customary methods of organization," and "the work [of the campaign] devolved to a much larger extent than usual upon the National

confession of weakness, which could offer no resistance to a candidacy like that of McKinley." Croly, *Marcus Alonzo Hanna*, 182.

[128] Morgan, *From Hayes to McKinley: National Party Politics*, 493.
[129] "Named their Napoleon," *Atlanta Constitution*, June 19, 1896, 3; Croly, *Marcus Alonzo Hanna*, 205.
[130] "Now in the Background," *New York Times*, September 26, 1896, 1.
[131] John Morton Blum, *Liberty, Justice, Order: Essays on Past Politics* (New York: W.W. Norton & Co., 1993), 93.
[132] Hanna, *Mark Hanna*, 54.
[133] Dick to Morrow, February 10, 1906, box 4, Hanna-McCormick Family Papers.

Committee." As Democrats had done in 1892, Hanna deemphasized the work of the traditional committee and centered independent power in an executive committee, thus "the National Committee, instead of being a kind of central agency of the State Committees, became the general staff of the whole army."[134] The committee hired a tremendous clerical staff. Dick remembered that there were two hundred national committee employees at the Chicago headquarters alone, responsible for "handling documents just as men would handle shoe boxes and other merchandise," in addition to 1,400 speakers. Documents "were printed in 21 different languages," and to control the language of the party press, "plate matter was also furnished to the newspapers throughout the country." Organizers formed associations of old soldiers, first voters, and other potential constituencies, completely bypassing the traditional Jacksonian organization's campaign clubs, as well as the new club leagues[135]; the party spent about 13 percent of its budget on these organizing efforts.[136] Both types of jobs differed markedly from the traditional party work of organizing rallies, making speeches, and canvassing voters – the sort that Dorsey had relied on in 1880 in Indiana.

To reassure donors of the probity and efficiency of the national organization, the party's fundraising efforts were similarly systematized. Hanna instructed Dawes to institute "a complete system of bookkeeping with as thorough a check upon expenditures as you would have in a bank" to showcase the campaign's honesty, and he brought in big donors for a tour of headquarters "to show them what he had been spending their money for."[137] Dawes prided himself on the businesslike quality of his bookkeeping, keeping precise records of all expenses, taking competitive bids for all services contracted by the committee, and requiring that all expenses be funneled through him.[138]

The state party organizations comparatively suffered from the inflation of the national organization. Having so effectively grounded his nomination fight in direct appeals to the people, the McKinley campaign saw no reason to turn the general election back over to the subnational organizations. The national committee took on work that had previously been left to state committees because "the State committees in 1896 could not... get together and develope [sic] sufficiently to supply all the ammunition to the orator and to the newspapers which was needed." Where state organizations were unfriendly or hostile, the national committee "had to send out some documents to individuals direct" and relied on the local McKinley clubs it had cultivated at the preconvention stage, reducing pressure to conciliate subnational leaders as

134 Croly, *Marcus Alonzo Hanna*, 213, 218.
135 Dictated statement of Senator Charles Dick to Morrow, February 10, 1906, box 4, Hanna-McCormick Family Papers.
136 Dawes, *Journal of the McKinley Years*, 106.
137 Dictated statement of Senator Charles Dick to Morrow, February 10, 1906, box 4, Hanna-McCormick Family Papers.
138 Dawes, *Journal of the McKinley Years*, 93–5.

Garfield had done.[139] It is for this organizational shift, as well as a braggadocio's claim about the appeal of Republican principles, that Hanna could state that "the results coming in indicated that the people were reading, thinking, and determining conclusions for themselves. They were beginning to see where their interests were at stake."[140] This was a campaign eminently capable of approaching voters directly, appealing to them along lines of self-interest.

McKinley's actions during the campaign mimicked those of Harrison in 1888: he campaigned to visiting delegations from his front porch, although under Hanna's guidance, the front porch campaign became a massive undertaking. It provided an ideal forum for rallying the McKinley-for-president clubs, the local affiliates of the National League of Republican Clubs, and a plethora of special-interest associations. The Republican National Committee rounded up visiting clubs and worked with railroads to provide cheap excursion rated to McKinley's home.[141] Most greeted the candidate with prepared remarks, previewed first by McKinley, who recommended revisions.[142] McKinley was also pressured to tour the country, but he defended the front porch campaign by suggesting that launching a tour to compete with Bryan would result only in a spectacular joust: "if I took a whole train," he mused, "Bryan would take a sleeper; if I took a sleeper, Bryan would take a chair car; if I took a chair car, he would ride a freight train."[143] McKinley gained an enormous audience simply by staying at home. Three-quarters of a million visitors flocked to Canton, and millions more read copies of the more than three hundred carefully prepared speeches that he gave there, as distributed to newspapers and as pamphlets by the national committee.[144] That McKinley refrained from a speechmaking tour has belied his campaign's novelty, as has the fact that he and Bryan, although operating with slightly different methods, were campaigning in substantially the same style.

In his letter of acceptance, McKinley was more attentive to his party's role than Cleveland had been, referring respectfully to the platform and contrasting past Republican administrations with past Democratic ones. Still, he insisted that his nomination relied on the people rather than the party apparatus; emphasizing his mastery of the new campaign style, he even questioned the traditional acceptance letter as outdated, apologizing that "perhaps this . . . might be considered unnecessary in view of my remarks . . . I have made to delegations that have visited me since the St. Louis Convention."[145] The new campaign,

[139] Dictated statement of Senator Charles Dick to Morrow, February 10, 1906, box 4, Hanna-McCormick Family Papers.
[140] Hanna, *Mark Hanna*, 55.
[141] Leech, *In the Days of McKinley*, 88.
[142] Dictated statement of Senator Charles Dick to Morrow, February 10, 1906, box 4, Hanna-McCormick Family Papers.
[143] Quoted in Troy, *See How They Ran*, 105.
[144] Louis Gould, *The Presidency of William McKinley* (Lawrence: Regents Press of Kansas, 1980), 11; Jensen, *Winning of the Midwest*, 287.
[145] William McKinley, "Letter of Acceptance," in "Mr. McKinley Accepts," *New York Times*, August 27, 1896, 1.

McKinley was acknowledging, had overtaken the formality of the traditional nominating convention; McKinley had already accepted the acclimation of the party-in-the-electorate, the convention had merely responded, and so the convention's notification agent was virtually superfluous. It would be incorrect to read this as the candidate abandoning his party in favor of a personalist campaign. Rather, it was a claim that particularly suited the new kind of campaign he had fought; it demonstrated the declining importance of the republican forms of deference and hierarchy embodied by the convention.

McKinley, like Cleveland, insisted that an educational campaign would break down traditional party loyalties. He explained that the campaign was not a campaign of traditional partisan loyalties, because the Democratic platform represented "a peril so grave that conservative men everywhere are breaking away from their old party associations, and uniting with other patriotic citizens in emphatic protest against the platform of the Democratic National Convention as an assault upon the faith and honesty of the Government and welfare of the people." This required a campaign of education; for voters, the decision called for "the most painstaking investigation, and, in the end, a sober and unprejudiced judgment at the polls." In a paraphrase of Cleveland's warning against ideological enthusiasm in his tariff address, McKinley insisted that in addressing the currency issue, "we must not be misled by phrases, nor deluded by false theories." Instead, he declared that "if the people are aroused to the true understanding and meaning of this silver and inflation movement they will avert the danger.... and we appeal to the intelligence, conscience, and patriotism of the people, irrespective of party or faction, for their earnest support."[146]

Bryan's nomination posed a problem for the McKinley campaign on this account – there were, after all, a good number of pro-silver Republicans – and in both rhetoric and method, he struggled to turn it to his advantage. McKinley was careful to declare unwavering support of the gold plank but to emphasize the Republican platform's clause recommending an international agreement on bimetallic currency, a measure that would prevent what gold standard supporters warned was the greatest danger: the rapid devaluation of American currency compared with European countries that maintained gold. Most eastern Republicans believed this to be unimportant, as they considered such an agreement improbable. Yet in McKinley's terms, the distinction between the two parties centered on the possibility of such an agreement, not the gold standard alone. In his acceptance letter, he described the Democratic position as supporting "free and unlimited coinage of silver by independent action on the part of the United States"; the Republican party, he said, had "declared in favor of an international agreement, and if elected President it will be my duty to employ all proper means to promote it."[147] This allowed McKinley to present himself as an independent executive who brought his own value to the ticket beyond the legitimacy of the party's nomination. International agreement implied

---

[146] "Mr. McKinley Accepts," *New York Times*, August 27, 1896, 1.
[147] "Mr. McKinley Accepts," *New York Times*, August 27, 1896, 1, emphasis added.

presidential action, and promoting it placed the full weight of the currency issue on presidential shoulders. Much as Cleveland had hoped that centering discretion on tariff rates in the executive would allow more assertive presidential leadership, McKinley held out the possibility of the presidential negotiating power as a compromise measure that allowed him to attract wavering Republicans "beyond the Mississippi," while assuring eastern Republicans of his adherence to the gold standard. As with Cleveland's tariff strategy, the success of McKinley's gold "straddle" depended a great deal on how he presented himself to the nation rather than on the deferential compromises that governed the party platform and thus provided expanded presidential coalition-building possibilities.

The McKinley Presidency

With McKinley in office, the Republicans' embrasure of the Whig model of executive power was fully abandoned; unlike Harrison, McKinley combined his manner of campaigning with a conception of the role of the president as party leader. An important indication of this came from his inaugural address. In it, McKinley sought to bind his fellow Republicans to the results of the election, as he defined them. Most striking, McKinley turned his attention not to the currency issue (generally understood to have been decisive in the 1896 campaign) but to the tariff. "Nothing has ever been made plainer at a general election," he insisted, "than that the controlling principle in the raising of revenue from duties on imports is zealous care for American interests and American labor."[148] Urging action on tariff revision, he declared that "to this policy we are all, of whatever party, firmly bound by the voice of the people – a power vastly more potential than the expression of any political platform." McKinley also gestured toward the novel nature of his election, maintaining that it was grounded on the vote of a whole people: "the triumph of the people whose verdict is carried into effect today is not the triumph of one section nor wholly of one party, but of all sections and all the people."[149] Just as Bryan had done, McKinley brandished his command of the new idea of party as a tool with which to effect his political will.

Without understanding the context of McKinley's election as following on the Cleveland revision of the notion of availability, this emphasis is puzzling. In McKinley's mind, however, the turn back to the tariff reflected the fact that he had built his candidacy as the clearest articulator of the party's tariff policy. Having selected him, the party had committed itself to his tariff politics. He did speak in detail about currency reform; recommended that Congress create a commission to consider reform of coinage, banking, and currency laws; suggested consolidation of the various forms of paper money then in

---

[148] Gould, *The Presidency of William McKinley*, 15, 6.
[149] William McKinley, "Inaugural Address," *Inaugural Addresses of the Presidents of the United States from George Washington, 1789, to George Bush, 1989*, 196, 201, 196.

circulation; and pledged to pursue international bimetallic agreements. But the centerpiece was the tariff.

Calling it his "public duty," McKinley used the inaugural address to announce that he was calling a special session of Congress later that month, claiming that "the people have only recently voted that this should be done."[150] Considering that Congress typically adjourned shortly after the presidential inauguration and new congressmen were not sworn in until the end of the year, such a move was considered by some to be a practical necessity, especially given cyclical currency contractions in the fall. Harrison and Cleveland had considered calling special sessions – although not in their inaugural addresses – to deal with financial crises brought about by the tariff, and both had been criticized for inaction.[151] By exercising this constitutional power, McKinley was emphasizing its renewed legitimacy growing out of a more popular campaign. This was no mere spectacle. McKinley had made his intentions clear through consultations with congressional Republicans, and his party responded, clearly taking seriously the aspects of the campaign that he had shaped personally. The House began drafting tariff legislation in December 1896, and Senator Edward Wolcott, a silver Republican who found McKinley's straddle on an international currency agreement credulous, left for Europe to begin negotiations with the French and British on an international agreement to monetize silver.[152]

McKinley matched rhetoric with action. Owing little to the state leaders whom he had bested for the nomination, he withheld patronage from congressmen until the tariff had been dealt with in the special session.[153] The resulting Dingley Tariff restored or increased tariff rates to roughly their 1890 McKinley Tariff levels, which was very much in line with McKinley's 1896 recommendations and also included the provisions for presidential negotiation of reciprocal trade agreements that McKinley had promoted and would evolve into McKinley's more nuanced view of American trade policy aimed at securing overseas markets for American goods, rather than protecting American workers exclusively. Although focusing on the tariff before currency had the advantage of holding his fractious party together – silver senators from the West cast enough votes to doom any tariff proposal – the fact that McKinley had created an image of himself as a tariff defender provided him with sufficient political cover to allow him to shift the agenda away from the focus on the currency, thus allowing him to maintain leadership of his party without forcing a fight on the gold standard.[154] In this he perhaps proved a more savvy party

[150] William McKinley, "Inaugural Address," 201. McKinley decided early on to call Congress into a special session; as early as May 9, 1896 – before he had received his party's nomination – he told campaign aide Charles Dawes that he intended to call a special session if elected. *Journal of the McKinley Years*, 82–3.
[151] Gould, *The Presidency of William McKinley*, 35.
[152] Gould, *The Presidency of William McKinley*, 13.
[153] Gould, *The Presidency of William McKinley*, 39.
[154] Leech, *In the Days of McKinley*, 140–1.

leader than Cleveland had, but the motivation to lead their respective parties was present in both cases.

It was not until his second year in office that McKinley took significant action in the area of currency reform, and the means in which he did so was closely modeled on Cleveland's 1895 letter to Chicago Democrats. Although his defense of gold in 1898 could be construed as a continuation of the 1896 campaign, conditions had changed substantially in the intervening year, and McKinley's recommendations had changed as well. Talks on international bimetallism had broken down early in his administration, the 1897 Yukon gold rush boosted confidence in American gold reserves, and economic recovery undercut the insurgent spirit that had animated the 1896 election. Yet now he was advocating legislation formally declaring the U.S. commitment to the gold standard – an achievement that his party had been unable to reach for the previous twenty years because of Western Republican support for silver.[155]

He used a speech delivered at the meeting of the National Association of Manufacturers to make his point. Like Cleveland's tariff address, McKinley's 1898 speech on the gold standard was meant for the public as much as its immediate audience; like Cleveland's 1884 civil service letter and his 1891 and 1895 silver letters, McKinley used an extra-partisan association to present his argument. Abandoning his vacillation on the currency question, he asserted that "nothing should ever tempt us – nothing ever will tempt us – to scale down the sacred debt of the nation through a legal technicality." This stance, he insisted, came not only from his conception of good policy, but from his interpretation of the mandate of 1896: "this is our plain duty to more than seven million voters who, fifteen months ago, won a great political battle on the issue . . . that is my interpretation of that victory." McKinley was unafraid to wield this mandate as a club with which to beat waverers within his own party, warning that "all those who represent, as you do, the great conservative but progressive business interests of the country, owe it not to themselves, but to the people to insist upon the settlement of this great question now, or else to face the alternative that it must be again submitted for arbitration at the polls" and that "for us to attempt nothing in the face of the prevalent fallacies and the constant effort to spread them is to lose valuable ground already won." Although this was ostensibly a call to arms for the association's membership, McKinley deftly sent a shot over the bow of congressional Republicans, lest his speech be interpreted as a general public appeal. Reading a copy of the currency plank of the 1896 platform, McKinley insisted "this is in reality a command from the people who gave the Administration to the party now in power and who are still anxiously waiting for the execution of their free and omnipotent will by those of us who hold commissions from that supreme tribunal."[156]

---

[155] See Bensel, *The Political Economy of American Industrialization*, chap. 6.

[156] William McKinley, "Speech at the Banquet of the National Association of Manufacturers of the United States," January 27, 1898, *Speeches and Addresses of William McKinley*, 63, 64, 65. See also "Manufacturers Dine," *New York Times*, January 28, 1898, 1.

The speech, like Cleveland's tariff message, was seen as a clarion call to the party, "a stirring appeal to his party to advance their standard in finance and make an aggressive movement."[157] Following Cleveland's lead, McKinley was establishing a role for the presidency in holding his party accountable to party commitments.

The outbreak of the war with Spain (the USS *Maine* was destroyed two weeks after this speech) deflected attention from McKinley's domestic leadership, so it is difficult to know exactly how far he would have gone with his strategy. Nevertheless, he had learned Cleveland's lesson well and was committed to taking the lead in defining party objectives. Events proved the power of the attempt. His 1900 letter of acceptance defined the course of the party in that year's campaign, and although the letter "was his only public attempt to influence the minds and action of the voters," it was authoritative, for it "it was the chief campaign appeal on the Republican side."[158] In this way, the parties discovered the advantages of what would come to be called a "rose garden campaign," in which the record and promise of the incumbent seeking reelection became the party's de facto platform.

McKinley's presidency was remarkable for the confidence with which he led his party and Congress by public appeals. Milkis and Nelson argue that "McKinley was the first post–Civil War president to take the political initiative without arousing the resentment of his party in Congress."[159] Even as events led him somewhat unwillingly into the Spanish-American War, he quickly used his authority as commander-in-chief to seize control of war operations – from his early request for executive discretion outside a declaration of war to his control of the peace process that ended it – and to control the public debate on the war. These actions "laid the foundations for the modern presidency," according to Lewis Gould.[160] He also launched significant speaking tours, campaigning for Republicans in congressional elections in 1898, promoting the Treaty of Paris in the South (where McKinley felt he could get the necessary votes for ratification from southern Democrats) in December 1898, defending the gold standard again in a nine-state tour in 1899, and promoting his pet idea of reciprocal trade agreements in the 1901 tour that led him to his fatal engagement at the Pan-American Exposition in Buffalo. In his 1900 acceptance speech, and his letter of acceptance, he proclaimed his support for policies that had been deliberately rejected from the Republican platform and took a tougher stand on the trusts than did the platform.[161] Like Cleveland before him, McKinley recognized that stepping outside the bounds of party dogma had become a vital prerogative of presidential party leadership.

---

157 "Mr. M'Kinley's First Year," *New York Times*, March 4, 1898, 6.
158 "President M'Kinley in the Campaign," *New York Times*, November 6, 1900, 6.
159 Milkis and Nelson, *The American Presidency*, 194.
160 Gould, *The Presidency of William McKinley*, 93.
161 Gould, *The Presidency of William McKinley*, 127, 143, 207, 244, 220, 225.

There was, given the tentative steps toward presidential dominance of the partisan agenda during the Cleveland years, little in McKinley's presidency that was surprising, other than the fact that Democratic-style presidential party leadership had been fully embraced by the Republican party. Republicans had been inching slowly toward the new idea of party that this style implied at least since the defeat of Grant's third-term aspirations in 1880, when the principle of the presidency's constituency in a national party-in-the-electorate was articulated and instituted in the convention rules. Blaine's nomination in 1884 and Harrison's campaign in 1888 both affirmed the implications for convention politics, but perhaps it was the intervening example of Cleveland's popular party leadership that pushed the Grand Old Party to McKinley's full embodiment of the modern president as party leader. As the party most committed to nationalization, it would have been difficult to maintain a style of leadership that was less national than their opponents' popular new efforts.

McKinley's assassination elevated Theodore Roosevelt to the presidency, and his example influenced later presidents – and later American publics. The expansion of presidential authority often highlighted in the administrations of Roosevelt and Woodrow Wilson, as well as the evolution of presidential power over the course of the twentieth century, was a continuation of this transformation from within the parties, not a sui generis assertion of the potentialities of presidential leadership. Roosevelt achieved greater popularity and a more lasting reputation among historians and political scientists than his predecessor, but McKinley's presidency showcased the mode of presidential party leadership that came to dominate the twentieth century.[162] To be sure, Roosevelt was a unique candidate, suited by personality to dominate such a campaign. At a meeting of his political allies, Speaker Joseph Cannon conceded TR's dominance, suggesting, "Mr. President, there are many things about you that I wish were different, but for better or for worse you are the platform."[163] It seems inconceivable for the same to have been said of any president before Cleveland, but after Roosevelt, such sentiment has often been assumed. Roosevelt got away with it not because of his personality but because party leaders had, by then, learned a lot about the value of presidential party leadership.

---

[162] TR's great admirer and intellectual muse, Herbert Croly, saw this, and his biography of Mark Hanna is a celebration of the nationalizing effects of the campaign that Hanna organized for McKinley. Croly, *Marcus Alonzo Hanna*.

[163] Unsigned memorandum, May 1, 1904, box 37, Cortelyou papers.

Conclusion

This narrative of the emergence of the late-nineteenth-century party mode is not intended to suggest that twentieth-century parties emerged full-fledged from the late nineteenth century. Post-1900 American parties were still structured in part by the Jacksonian organizational mode, and its organization continued to reflect elements of the republican orientation of its founders. However, party leaders – and reformers – thought differently about the appropriate role of the national party organizations, and this different way of thinking shaped much of twentieth-century party change. This is not to suggest that they had become good liberals but that they had come to accept the application of certain liberal operating principles to party politics.

Some elements of their conception of the role of the national party organizations were fleeting. Campaigns did not retain the public language of education or the thick instruction provided in late-nineteenth-century campaign documents (although in their insistence on articulating clear policies and reaching voters in a private capacity, these campaigns would be more familiar to voters today than the hurrah campaign or the still hunt). As explained in Chapter 4, the national party club networks failed to achieve a lasting place in the party system (although the conceptualization of a national party-in-the-electorate, responsible chiefly to the national party, is much closer to today's conception of party than is the nineteenth-century vision of local partisan communities bound together chiefly by geographic ties). Other elements of this transformation proved enduring, most notably, the increasingly prominent and independent role of presidential candidates in defining party principles, the notion of the presidency as the arbiter of competing interests within society, and the acceptability of the relationship between interest associations and the parties.

The influence of late-nineteenth-century political practice resonates through the early twentieth century, reminding scholars accustomed to viewing a sharp divide between nineteenth- and twentieth-century political practice – a divide that too often positions Progressives as the first stirrings of modern American politics – of the nineteenth-century roots of twentieth-century developments.

Theodore Roosevelt's aggressive embodiment of the presidential office looks much less revolutionary when it is recalled that TR rose with Grover Cleveland from New York politics into national prominence and served under the transformative leadership of William McKinley. Like William Jennings Bryan, TR dominated his party into the second decade of the twentieth century. Analyses of both men's influence necessitate understanding "their symbolic value as ego-ideals for ambitious young men," and their impact in shaping public views of proper party leadership,[1] and this understanding reminds scholars that Bryan, Roosevelt, even Woodrow Wilson, were links in a chain of influence that stretches beyond the relatively short period of time known as the Progressive era. The successor to Bryan and Wilson as leader of the Progressive element of the Democratic coalition, William Gibbs McAdoo, came to power as a national fundraiser for Wilson – much as the great national party leaders of the late nineteenth century had – and his proposed economic policies aimed to foster closer cooperation between organized interest associations and the federal government – carrying on the reformist ideal of interest associations fostering a purer form of politics than the parties offered. McAdoo also contemplated efforts to silence the two-thirds rule in the 1924 election, continuing the late-nineteenth-century effort to make the convention system more majoritarian and less protective of local factions.[2] In 1920, Democratic candidates James M. Cox and Franklin Delano Roosevelt made a campaign tour of the country that imitated Bryan's tours. In 1924, Franklin Roosevelt proposed reforms for the Democratic National Committee that echoed those proposed in the late nineteenth century, only to be rebuffed by former committee members who pointed out that his suggestions had long been a part of committee operations.[3] In 1920, Warren G. Harding launched a front porch campaign that was so consciously imitative of William McKinley that he had the flagpole that stood in McKinley's yard in 1896 moved to his own.[4] Despite his image as a dowdy, silent figure, Harding's successor, Calvin Coolidge, demonstrated a knack for generating the kind of national publicity that had enabled late-nineteenth-century presidents to gain leadership of their parties. One historian suggests that Coolidge reflected Republicans' recognition that their party "needed a bit of the common touch to combat the increasingly populist Democrats," making him a strange pairing to William Jennings Bryan.[5] Coolidge's 1924 vice presidential candidate was none other than Charles Dawes, who had served a pivotal role

[1] Arthur L. Stinchcombe, *Constructing Social Theories* (Chicago: University of Chicago Press, 1968), 109.

[2] James C. Prude, "William Gibbs McAdoo and the Democratic National Convention of 1924," *The Journal of Southern History* (November 1972), 621–8.

[3] Douglas B. Craig, *After Wilson: The Struggle for the Democratic Party, 1920–1934* (Chapel Hill: University of North Carolina Press, 1992), on McAdoo, 33, 40; on Roosevelt, 86–9.

[4] Robert K. Murray, *The Harding Era: Warren G. Harding and His Administration* (Minneapolis: University of Minnesota Press, 1969), 50.

[5] Buckley, "A President for the 'Great Silent Majority,'" 594.

in the McKinley campaign of 1896, and Dawes himself made a speechmaking tour of the country, bringing that form of presidential campaigning firmly into the GOP.[6] Coolidge effectively used the resources of the office to define his party's principles, in part by using the radio – the first president to do so – to reach voters directly. Herbert Hoover's time as secretary of commerce was marked by a sophisticated understanding of the campaign of education and by a thoughtful effort to make voluntary citizen associations an alternative to government expansion – a practice he influentially advocated in the Wilson, Harding, and Coolidge administrations.[7]

The most direct evidence of nineteenth-century impact on early-twentieth-century politicians is Woodrow Wilson's emulation of Grover Cleveland. Although this is rarely drawn out in studies that link Wilson with the theoretical basis of the modern presidency, Wilson was acutely aware of the intellectual debt he owed Cleveland.[8] In *Congressional Government* (published in the year Cleveland first took office), Wilson advocated strengthening ties between the executive and legislative branches, drawing on the experience of British parties, by picturing the emergence of leadership within Congress – as it had emerged in the British parliamentary system – as the best means of modernizing the American constitutional system. In this work, Wilson set the template for the "responsible party government" model that shaped political scientists' critique of party decline throughout the twentieth century.[9]

Wilson, however, came to adopt a very different vision of constitutional modernization in which presidents led Congress through popular leadership, rather than through closer executive-legislative relations. Although it is tempting to assume that Wilson's views only changed as his presidential ambitions emerged, it is important to notice that by the time he wrote *Constitutional Government* (published in the year that Cleveland died), the presidency was in a very different state than it was when he completed his first book – thanks in no small part to Cleveland (Wilson declared that between 1865 and 1896, "no President except Mr. Cleveland played a leading and decisive part in the quiet drama of our national life"[10]). Although Wilson's portrayal of party in this later work remained hopeful of the kind of centralizing leadership that England had undergone – recognizing "the extraordinary part political parties have played in making a national life which might otherwise have been loose

---

[6] Robert H. Ferrell, *The Presidency of Calvin Coolidge* (Lawrence: University Press of Kansas, 1998), 59.

[7] Ellis W. Hawley, "Herbert Hoover, The Commerce Secretariat, and the Vision of an 'Associative State,' 1921–1928," *Journal of American History* (June 1974), 130.

[8] An excellent study that provides a good sense of this change without considering Cleveland's role in it (by a scholar who has generously considered my argument) is Brian J. Cook, *Democracy and Administration: Woodrow Wilson's Ideas and the Challenges of Public Management* (Baltimore: The Johns Hopkins University Press, 2007).

[9] "Toward a More Responsible Two-Party System: A Report of the Committee on Political Parties," *American Political Science Review* (September 1950), 44:3, Part 2, Supplement.

[10] Wilson, *Constitutional Government in the United States*, 58–9.

and diverse almost to the point of being inorganic, a thing of definite coherence and common purpose" – his focus turned to the presidency, calling the president a potential "national boss."[11]

Wilson's change of tactics may stem from his involvement in the Democratic party, itself shaped by Cleveland's leadership. In this vein, Lewis Gould argues that Democrats saw the presidency as a negative force that could protect it from the GOP's postwar electoral growth.[12] Yet Wilson did not understand the Cleveland presidency as a chiefly negative force; Cleveland's experimentation with presidential leadership demonstrated for Wilson that the presidency was not only a necessary tool for Democrats but an alternative solution to the problems he had outlined in his first book.[13] In March 1897, as Cleveland was leaving the Executive Mansion, Wilson published an article in the *Atlantic Monthly*, praising Cleveland as "the sort of President the makers of the Constitution had vaguely in mind . . . hardly a colleague of the Houses so much as an individual servant of the people."[14] It was not only Cleveland's energetic inhabitation of the office that impressed Wilson, but also his ability to break down the barriers of the Jacksonian organization. "'Magnificent,'" he imagined "the trained politicians" declaring of Cleveland's leadership, "'but it is not politics.'" It was not, Wilson meant, party politics in the Jacksonian mode. He praised Cleveland for giving direction to a party that "was little more than an assemblage of factions, a more or less coherent association of the various groups and interests opposed to the Republicans," and declared that Cleveland "was too good a Democrat . . . to stand by and see the policy of the country hopelessly adrift without putting his own influence to the test to direct it. He could not keep to his rôle of simple executive." Indeed, in the face of his party's inability to achieve tariff reform, Wilson insisted that "no man of strong convictions could stand there, where all the country watched him, waiting for him to speak, the only representative of the nation as a whole in all

---

[11] Woodrow Wilson, *Constitutional Government in the United States* (New York: Columbia University Press, 1908), 222, 215.

[12] Gould, *The Modern American Presidency*, 2–3

[13] Cleveland, who moved to Princeton, New Jersey, after retiring from office, socialized with Wilson. Is it possible that the two men, both working on books on American constitutionalism at the time (Cleveland's *Presidential Problems* was published in 1904), shared thoughts about the nature of presidential power in the new party mode? See Grover Cleveland to Daniel S. Lamont, March 25, 1898, box 87, Daniel S. Lamont Papers, Manuscript Division, Library of Congress. It is clear from Cleveland to Lamont, August 8, 1904, box 87, Lamont Papers, that Cleveland saw himself as an advisor to later Democratic politicians, including 1904 presidential candidate Alton B. Parker, so he was willing to discuss his thoughts on presidential politics with aspiring Democrats at the time that he was friendly with Wilson. Wilson himself wrote to Cleveland that their association "has given me strength and knowledge of affairs." Quoted in James Kerney, *The Political Education of Woodrow Wilson* (New York: The Century Company, 1926), 7. As Allan Nevins explains, their relationship grew testy during Wilson's controversial presidency of Princeton: then serving as a Princeton trustee, Cleveland became a critic of Wilson's plans to reorganize the university. Yet Wilson and Cleveland socialized in a more relaxed environment before they clashed in this official capacity. See Nevins, *Grover Cleveland*, 732–4.

[14] Woodrow Wilson, "Mr. Cleveland as President," *Atlantic Monthly*, March 1897, 289.

the government, and let a great opportunity and a great duty go by default."
In issuing his pivotal State of the Union address of 1887, Cleveland "gave his
party a leader" and "settled the way the next campaign should go."¹⁵ Similarly, in a 1910 speech to the National Democratic Club of New York, Wilson
formulated his thoughts on Cleveland and the Democrats in a way that fully
explicated the new idea's rejection of the Jacksonian mode and simultaneous
embrasure of party for new national purposes:

> There is no way in which to determine opinion or to control opinion except through
> the action of men in bodies exercising a close concert of action. You cannot, among
> disputing and discordant individuals, accumulate force enough to conduct a govern-
> ment.... Mr. Cleveland recognized that ... and avowed his recognition of it in many a
> notable utterance.¹⁶

This was the promise of the new idea of party to the confident national liberals
of the twentieth century, the argument that enabled them to maintain partisan
cooperation despite the Progressive critique of it.

During his own term in office, Wilson chose strategies strikingly similar to
Cleveland's. He challenged the norms surrounding State of the Union addresses
in an effort to grab the attention of the public, turning the event into a public
speech rather than a written report for the first time since Jefferson's presidency.
As Cleveland took issues with which he was most closely identified – civil service
reform, tariff reform, and the gold standard – to the people, so Wilson put his
reputation on the line in a public appeal for the League of Nations. In this
sense, modern presidential practice grew out of the lessons and conditions of
the late nineteenth century rather than those of the early twentieth century; and
the broad temporal appeal of this form of presidential leadership suggests that
presidential party leadership is more deeply rooted in American constitutional
practice than a mere Progressive era innovation.

Although few scholarly commentators have emphasized the connection,
Cleveland's example was still fresh in some minds as Franklin Roosevelt was
elected in 1932; Allan Nevins's classic biography of Cleveland was published in
that year, and some newspaper columnists still looked to Cleveland for models
of leadership.¹⁷ Roosevelt drew directly from Cleveland's penchant for spectacle when he flew to Chicago to accept his nomination – the first time a major

---

¹⁵ Woodrow Wilson, "Mr. Cleveland as President," 291, 294, 295.
¹⁶ Woodrow Wilson, "An After-Dinner Speech on Grover Cleveland to the National Democratic
   Club of New York, March 18, 1910," Arthur S. Link, ed., *The Papers of Woodrow Wilson, v.*
   20 (Princeton, NJ: Princeton University Press, 1975), 259–60.
¹⁷ See "The President Acts," *New York Times,* April 19, 1933, 16; "Extraordinary Powers," *New
   York Times,* April 23, 1933, E4. Upon FDR's election, the *Times* evoked an anecdote (since
   picked up by numerous Roosevelt biographers) in which five-year-old Roosevelt is said to have
   visited Cleveland in the Executive Mansion; Cleveland supposedly said to the boy: "I wish
   for you that you may never be President of the United States"; "Roosevelt Started Fighting
   Tammany," *New York Times,* November 9, 1932, 9. Milkis's *The President and the Parties*
   draws out Wilson's influence on FDR's notions of presidential leadership.

party's nominee accepted the nomination in person during the nominating convention, a clear reference to Cleveland's dramatic Madison Square Garden acceptance ceremony in 1892. Cleveland had turned the acceptance ceremony into a public event; FDR simply linked its timing to the national convention. Yet without an electorate primed to recognize the legitimacy of independent presidential party leadership, Franklin Roosevelt's party leadership would have been unthinkable. Further, although the Democratic party had long held on to restrictive convention procedures that Republicans abandoned in the nineteenth century, the years of nationalization of the party apparatus by Cleveland and Bryan made the abolition of the two-thirds rule in the 1930s the whimper that it was rather than a full-fledged confrontation with an entrenched Jacksonian party mode. Roosevelt as party leader trod in the footsteps of Cleveland and Bryan, and the path was well worn.

Qualities of Party Change

It would, however, be a mistake to suggest that with Wilson – or with Theodore Roosevelt – the insititionalization of the new idea of party had come into its own. The process of late-nineteenth-century party change did not end neatly in 1896, or 1900, or even 1912. The period from 1896 to 1972 saw a number of steps fulfilling the change: the use of the direct primaries in the presidential selection process around the 1912 election, the end of the Democrats' two-thirds rule in 1936, the increasing personalization of the presidency. But there were also reversals. The party clubs on which late-nineteenth-century party leaders placed so much hope for reviving the parties' connections with voters faded away; in the early 1900s, direct primary reform emerged as a viable alternative serving the same purpose, but by the 1920s, it was displaced. Urban machines solidified and resurged in the early twentieth century, as did state party machines like that of Matthew Quay and Boies Penrose's Pennsylvania Republican party.[18] The New Deal momentarily breathed new life into urban machines, and the traditional party establishment continued to shape presidential nominations throughout the twentieth century. Instead of a clear transformation, what emerged was a "mixed" organizational mode featuring elements of the old Jacksonian mode coexisting uneasily with elements informed by the late-nineteenth-century mode. It was not until the implementation of the McGovern-Fraser Commission's recommendations for party reform that the Jacksonian mode was effectively scuttled.

This is not to say that twentieth-century party change was unusually tepid; "the process of change extended over many years and involved a series of

---

[18] Erie, *Rainbow's End*, 20–1; Peter McCaffery, "Style, Structure, and Institutionalization of Machine Politics: Philadelphia, 1867–1933," *Journal of Interdisciplinary History* (Winter 1992), 435–52.

adjustments and readjustments before equilibrium was finally achieved."[19] Further, party development has taken place amid contradictory counter trends, which have obscured broader patterns. The move from the caucus to the convention system took from 1816 to 1840, although the convention method of making party nominations emerged as early as 1801.[20] The full development of the presidential direct primary system took from 1908 to 1972, and although the popularization of the direct presidential primary around 1912 flowed out of the party transformations of the late nineteenth century,[21] the direct primary's influence peaked in the presidential elections of 1916 and then precipitously declined in significance over the next fifty years. The best explanation of this lag is that the subnational party organizations were firmly ensconced in American political life and within the party system. They did not depend on the national organizations for existence, nor could the national organizations change their behavior; instead, late-nineteenth-century national party leaders built an apparatus that bypassed them to reach the people directly. That left subnational organizations to compete for subnational offices and the loyalties of voters. As Richard L. McCormick explains, the "traditional system no longer formed the entire political order; next to it now stood a parallel system, having its own distinctive types of political expression and government policy." This is not meant to say that national and subnational party organizations were divorced from one another. To the contrary, state party organizations took advantage of the national organizations' increased lucidity on substantive matters. McCormick notes that New York State Republicans under Thomas Platt used national issues to gloss over divisive state issues.[22] This selective use of popular aspects of party identity to cover unpopular aspects had been part of the symbiotic relationship between state and national party organizations for some time, and it helps to clarify exactly why state politicians viewed the new idea of party as less than threatening.

What enabled this long time lag between the emergence of a new idea of party and its more thorough institutionalization? Why did the parties tolerate such marked confusion in the fundamental operating procedures of their national organizations for so long? Without disputing the value of the concept of path dependency to political science, it is important to delineate between types of political institutions that are more or less susceptible to self-reinforcing

[19] Ceaser, *Presidential Selection*, 3–6.
[20] James S. Chase, *Emergence of the Presidential Nominating Convention, 1789–1832* (Urbana: University of Illinois Press, 1973), 33. Chase notes that Delaware was the first to employ fully the convention model at the state level. The convention model was fully established at the local level between 1822 and 1832, even though it was not fully employed at the national level until the end of that time. Chase, "Jacksonian Democracy and the Rise of the Nominating Convention," 86.
[21] Reynolds, *The Demise of the American Convention System*, 198.
[22] McCormick, *From Realignment to Reform*, 270, 98–102.

developmental processes; failing to do so "masks underlying dissensus over policy and programs" and obscures the role of political conflict in instigating political change.[23] The long lag between the emergence of the idea of nationalized parties and its institutionalization suggests that parties are a good test case for understanding this claim. Indeed, much of what makes parties distinct from other political institutions should lead political scientists to expect quite different developmental processes in political parties. Party leaders come and go according to the relative strength of the faction with which they are affiliated; unlike bureaucracies (and despite the language of bureaucracy embedded in the concept of "party as organization"), there has always been a relative absence of a permanent staff, headquarters, or even consistent procedural rules in American parties. As John Aldrich argues, "the major political party is the creature of the politicians, the ambitious office seeker and officeholder."[24] Or, as a Massachusetts editor observed in 1876, politicians' appraisals of current strategic situations differ on the basis of the level of perceived crisis: "your genuine politician," he began, "always looks beyond the election," hoping to secure party nominees who would work with the regular party establishment, "unless frightened out of his wits and reduced to the 'Anybody, Lord' state of mind," at which point the politician tended to be surprisingly open to reform.[25] These actors, who recognize that party organization is but a means to particular ends, and a means that is useful only insofar as it can deliver measurable results in the short run, tend to be willing to try new methods when faced with challenges. Historical institutionalism presumes the greatest expectation of consistency in political behavior under very different conditions: when short-run pressures encourage economizing decision-making costs even at the cost of goal attainment, the pressure to rely on existing practices is intense (and thus, path dependency works better when explaining the politics of civil servants, for whom the latter conditions tend to predominate). Under the distinct conditions faced by party leaders, the "ability to overcome a dominant perception (frame) and to substitute an alternate construction of the reality being confronted" is more often rewarded than in bureaucracies.[26] New methods need not even be successful to be imitated; failures who enhance their performance with novel methods often highlight those methods for later candidates.

This is not to argue that party leaders are completely unrestrained in their organizational innovations but that, unlike the restraints that operate on other political institutions, much of the restraint that party leaders experience comes from their own perceptions of strategic necessities and the willingness of intraparty allies to cooperate with institutional transformation – hence,

---

[23] B. Guy Peters, Jon Pierre, and Desmond S. King, "The Politics of Path Dependency: Political Conflict in Historical Institutionalism," *Journal of Politics* (November 2005), 1275.

[24] Aldrich, *Why Parties?*, 4.

[25] "Available Men," *Springfield* (MA) *Republican*, February 6, 1876, 4.

[26] Peters, Pierre, and King, "The Politics of Path Dependency," 1284.

the central importance of ideas of acceptable behavior within parties and of self-presentation in understanding party leaders' actions. Party leaders face pressures for both consensus and dissensus vis-à-vis the dominant styles of political practice. Dominant candidates might be expected to act conservatively to maintain their leads, underdogs might be expected to shake up conventional wisdom to undermine the strengths of their opponents, and, in closely matched elections, both candidates might be confused as to the best path to maximizing their vote. In this sense, the "idea of party" might be thought of as a toolkit of accepted notions of what works, what is acceptable, and how to defend one's actions. Those politicians who can most confidently claim to understand effective methods might gain power despite overblown claims of the kind of change they represent. Understanding the means by which broad groups of elites come to hold complementary ideas about proper behavior thus is essential to understanding change in institutions like parties.

Other institutions – bureaucracies, policy regimes, and so forth – take off from moments of conflict resolution; negotiations between officeholders freeze circumstantial distributions of power and resources in place.[27] Institutionalization occurs as political actors come to see more value in maintaining stable arrangements than in reopening old conflicts. But the politics that parties make differs somewhat, as questions about power distributions are continually reopened – both between parties and within them. This kind of environment is fertile ground for intercurrent orders, because some candidates swear by old methods and others tout new ones; intercurrence actually benefits politicians by providing alternative ideas of how to legitimate their position. In 1896, for example, William Jennings Bryan, eager to give his party allies confidence in his candidacy, demonstrated his mastery of the new style of campaigning; William Whitney, who had triumphed in 1892 with those same methods, now emphasized Bryan's unorthodox conception of party loyalty and mouthed something like the Jacksonian ideal of party harmony. By 1896, both ideas of party were familiar enough that they could be presented to party members as a virtual choice, even as the mechanisms that made the Jacksonian idea work hampered the full institutionalization of the new, liberal idea of party.

This kind of political learning is particularly relevant to parties because relatively flexible rules govern their behavior – another feature of party organizations that tends to differentiate them from other political institutions. Although this changed significantly in the twentieth century because electoral reform limited some of the parties' freedom, much of what parties did throughout the nineteenth and twentieth centuries was either unregulated or only weakly regulated, in keeping with the parties's status as private entities. To the extent that parties became more tightly hemmed in by legal restraints, it should not be forgotten that these laws have been passed by party leaders who have just

---

[27] Samuel J. Eldersveld, *Political Parties: A Behavioral Analysis* (Chicago: Rand McNally, 1964), 7–12.

as often seen reform as a means of advantaging their parties as of achieving political purity.[28]

So in the dual-track system that persisted between 1900 and 1970, reforms that ultimately facilitated national party development occasionally took unexpected turns. For instance, the direct primary was more thoroughly institutionalized at the state and local levels than at the national level, and its local impact actually undermined its reform impulses. As Alan Ware's study of the American direct primary establishes, by 1915, all but three states had adopted some form of the direct primary in selecting state and local nominees, suggesting that the convention reforms of the late nineteenth century might have been quickly consolidated in the early twentieth century by the widespread adoption of the direct primary. However, the first two decades following the institution of this "popularizing reform" saw the consolidation of urban machine power; the direct primary, often assumed to provide a hostile environment for traditional party organizations by popularizing the nomination process, benefited the majority party organizations and incumbent officeholders. Primary laws imposed costs that minor parties – and especially third-party challengers – found difficult to bear. The increased costs to candidates – who now had to win two elections instead of one – benefited incumbents and weakened challengers, who had less experience, name recognition, free publicity, and access to major fundraisers, allowing incumbents opportunities to consolidate personal machines. Similarly, ballot reform enhanced the benefits of party regularity at the local and state levels by legalizing regular status and prohibiting fusion tickets.[29] Alternative explanations by E. E. Schattschneider and Walter Dean Burnham – identifying the roots of the decline of partisan competitiveness following the 1896 election – suggest that electoral politics played an aggravating role; just as the "Battle of the Standards" polarized the country, the effects of the reform and reorganization of the parties began to kick in, enabling majority parties to lock in their status.[30]

Having consolidated, the machines that had proved to be engines of immigrant assimilation since the 1840s closed off the spigot of both suffrage and patronage; "having already fashioned a minimal winning electoral coalition

---

[28] Reynolds and McCormick, "Outlawing 'Treachery'"; Ware, *The American Direct Primary*.

[29] See Reynolds, *The Demise of the American Convention System*, 145, 165, 229. On the spread of the direct primary, see Ware, *The American Direct Primary*, 97–100; on decreased competitiveness, see V. O. Key, *Politics, Parties, and Pressure Groups*, 386–7; on the growing trend toward incumbency in the U.S. House of Representatives, see Nelson W. Polsby, "The Institutionalization of the House of Representatives," *The American Political Science Review* (March 1968), 144–68; on ballot laws, see John F. Reynolds and Richard L. McCormick, "Outlawing 'Treachery': Split Tickets and Ballot Laws in New York and New Jersey, 1880–1910," *Journal of American History* (March 1986), 835–58, and Peter H. Argersinger, "A Place on the Ballot': Fusion Politics and Antifusion Laws," *The American Historical Review* (April 1980), 287–306.

[30] E. E. Schattschneider, *The Semisovereign People: A Realist's View of Democracy in America* (New York: Holt, Rinehart, and Winston, 1960), chap. 5; Burnham, "The Changing Shape of the American Political Universe."

among the earlier-arriving immigrants. . . . the second-generation party organizations did not naturalize, register, and vote" later immigrants "at anything
approaching the rate at which the Irish had been politically incorporated."
Established machines such as Tammany benefited the most, and even welcomed the expanded social and regulatory policies of the twentieth-century
administrative state, turning expanded government supervision of the private
sector into a source of corporate donations and private sector jobs.[31] Martin Shefter's analysis of the development of Tammany Hall suggests another
source of machine stability: centralized corporations benefited from political
consolidation because it limited the opportunities for multiple extortionate
demands from politicians, and political machines similarly benefited from corporate consolidation because it limited the number of business entities willing
to subsidize (or bribe) politicians, thus limiting the resources of challengers
to the established order.[32] Similar developments took place at the state level
as well.[33] In the years following the state and local institutionalization of the
primary, most states experienced a reformist reaction to them after 1919 as
reformers abandoned direct primaries as a panacea for the ills of the two-party
system and gave the shell of the traditional Jacksonian mode a renewed vitality
that obscured the extent to which its usual operations had been transformed.
The mixed period was thus a genuinely distinct phase of party development,
not merely a reversion to pre-Progressive "normalcy."[34]

---

[31] Erie, *Rainbow's End*, 69, 73, 87.

[32] Shefter, "The Emergence of the Political Machine: An Alternative View," 37–8. M. Craig
Brown and Charles N. Halaby have quantified the emergence of consolidated urban machines,
and the results lend support to this interpretation. They argue that "the heyday of boss rule –
measured in terms of the prevalence of citywide machines – ran from the late 1920s to the
early 1930s," but further that the emergence of the machine was different in each city and
the difference was to some extent rooted in trends in machine consolidation that extended
back to the last two decades of the nineteenth century. Thus, machines that began the process
of consolidation earlier (and before the effects of reform helped "lock in" a single dominant
machine) tended to consolidate more effectively. "Machine Politics in America, 1870–1945,"
Journal of Interdisciplinary History (Winter 1987), 587–612.

[33] McCaffery, "Style, Structure, and Institutionalization of Machine Politics," 435–52.

[34] Ware, *The American Direct Primary*, 227–8. The decline in turnout that has long concerned
political scientists thus is not only the result of party nationalization, although it probably
facilitated the concurrent increase in the salience of national politics to voters' political identities. Donald Stokes, "Parties and the Nationalization of Electoral Forces," in William Nesbit
Chambers and Walter Dean Burnham eds., *The American Party Systems: Stages of Political
Development* (New York: Oxford University Press, 1975), 182–202, 183. Reexamining Stokes's
data nearly twenty years later, William Claggett, William Flanigan, and Nancy Zingale con-
firm his conclusions of increased nationalization in determining turnout. They do contradict
Stokes's (weaker) conclusion that there is also an increased national effect on partisan voting.
In short, they argue, partisanship is no more nationalized today than in the nineteenth century,
even as turnout is more nationalized. William Claggett, William Flanigan, and Nancy Zingale,
"Nationalization of the American Electorate," *The American Political Science Review*, 78:1
(March 1984), 77–91. Two years later, a similar analysis by Laura L. Vertz, John P. Fren-
dreis, and James L. Gibson again confirmed the nationalizing trend and added that the trend is
greater for presidential than for Congressional races. "Nationalization of the Electorate in the

The Practice of Party Politics in the Mixed Mode

At the national level, the impact of presidential primaries, and the further erosion of the Jacksonian organizational mode, was stunted as the intercurring orders informed by the new and the old ideas of party interfered with one another, producing an otherwise confusing context in which neither idea alone fully explains the behavior of party elites. During this time, the number of states holding presidential primaries varied from year to year, as did the number of delegates apportioned by primaries and the number of voters participating in primaries. At the same time, an increasing number of presidential aspirants looked to the primary system as a pathway into office that either supplanted their weaknesses in traditional party politics or bypassed the traditional party establishment altogether. Traditional party leaders also learned how to manipulate primary rules and practices to maximize their control over the nominating process as a whole. For instance, until a majority of delegates (or, in the Democratic party, a super-majority of two-thirds of the delegates) were elected by direct primaries, the strategic environment of national conventions meant that the capacity of direct presidential primaries to confer popular legitimacy on candidates was limited. In the meantime, subnational party leaders found the new nominating procedures to be helpful in maintaining their traditional ability to shape outcomes. In short, it is incorrect to simply equate the advent or spread of primaries with increasing nationalization of party politics or with declining control by traditional party organizations.

Table 4 demonstrates the problem as it played out between 1912 and 1932. Between 1912 and 1932, the top primary vote-getter won the nomination only about half the time. Candidates typically only entered those primary contests in which they felt they were competitive, and relied on more traditional methods elsewhere. Except in situations in which popular incumbents competed in primaries (as in the Democratic party in 1916 and the Republican party in 1924), it was unusual for primary candidates to receive a majority of primary votes – much less enough to provide a majority or two-thirds super-majority. Finally, because such a relatively small number of states held primaries, even candidates who won a sizeable number of primary delegates were still far short of a convention victory. Thus, even when William Gibbs McAdoo received nearly 60 percent of all primary votes cast in 1924, only 35 percent of Democratic National Convention delegates were selected by primaries – for McAdoo, this translated into about 24 percent of votes on the first convention ballot (possibly

United States," *The American Political Science Review* 81:3 (1987), 961–966. More recently, Larry M. Bartels's comprehensive study of voting patterns between 1868 and 1996 confirms that a significant nationalizing trend began at the end of the nineteenth century and continued throughout the twentieth. Although he concludes that the magnitude of the effect of national forces on election returns of the 1868–1900 period does not come close to the large effect of national forces on the 1900–96 period, his evidence clearly shows that the trend toward nationalization began in the late nineteenth century. Larry M. Bartels, "Electoral Continuity and Change, 1868–1996," *Electoral Studies* 17:3 (1998), 301–26.

TABLE 4. *Top Primary Candidates, 1912–1932*

	Number of Republican Primary Candidates	Top Republican Candidate's Percentage of Primary Votes	Number of Democratic Primary Candidates	Top Democratic Candidate's Percentage of Primary Votes
1912	3	51.5	4	44.6*
1916	12	12.1	1	98.8*†
1920	7	30.3	5	16
1924	3	68.4*†	6	59.8
1928	9	49.2*	8	39.5*
1932	6	48.5	7	44.5*

* Top primary vote-getter received the nomination.
† Incumbent president was the top primary candidate.
Source: Devis, *Presidential Primaries*, 279–302.

as low as 17 percent of McAdoo's first ballot vote[35]). Similarly, although the top primary vote-getter in the 1932 Republican selection process (Joseph France) received more primary votes than the incumbent president (Hoover received only 33 percent of the primary votes), only 37.5 percent of Republican National Convention delegates were selected by primaries, rendering France's primary victory nugatory. Direct primary–elected delegates alone were not enough to change the strategic calculus.

State and local party leaders used primary rules to maximize their traditional position, and as state organizations consolidated, this became an easier task. Primaries enabled state party leaders to undermine the impact of district conventions because primaries allowed dominant state organizations to remove the nominating process from the hands of dissident district conventions. Primary-selected delegates could be unpledged, allowing party leaders greater control over their delegations (see Table 5); in 1916, unpledged delegates accounted for 23.6 percent of all primary-selected delegates – 14 percent of all primary voters cast their votes for unpledged delegates in that year – and in 1920, 28.9 percent of Democratic delegates were unpledged. Further, few states bound their pledged delegates to vote for their candidate after multiple inconclusive convention ballots; in some states, delegates were released from their primary obligations after a single ballot. Thus, the high numbers of ballots in the 1920 and 1924 conventions (forty-four in the Democratic party in 1920 and 103 in 1924 and ten in the GOP in 1920) can be best explained by the manipulations of state party leaders within the reformed environment, not the perpetuation of nineteenth-century convention politics-as-usual. It was harder

[35] Compare, for instance, James W. Davis, *Presidential Primaries: The Road to the White House* (Westport, CT: Greenwood Press, 1980), 286–90, with Richard C. Bain and Judith H. Parris, *Convention Decisions and Voting Records* (Washington, DC: The Brookings Institution, 1973), Appendix C. The estimated percentages that I cite are based on Davis's account of states in which McAdoo won votes and the votes those states gave McAdoo on the first ballot.

TABLE 5. *Unpledged Delegates in National Conventions, 1912–1932*

	Percent Republican Delegates selected by Primary	Percent of Republican Delegates Unpledged	Percent Democratic Delegates selected by Primary	Percent of Democratic Delegates Unpledged
1912	41.7	0	32.9	0
1916	58.9	23.6	53.5	0
1920	57.8	9.5	44.6	28.9
1924	45.3	0	35.5	7.5
1928	44.9	1.6	42.2	20.8
1932	37.7	3.5	40	5.1

Source: Davis, *Presidential Primaries*, 279–302.

for subnational party leaders to control their delegations in an age of popular presidential nomination campaigns, but primaries did promote new opportunities for procedural manipulation of convention outcomes. Subnational party leaders packed primary ballots with delegates who had strong second choices for a particular candidate and encouraged multiple candidates to enter primaries, knowing that the more candidates to enter the convention, the more chance of a stalemate that could quickly loosen the restraint of popular preferences. Thus, delegations that appeared pledged for one candidate might turn out, at a critical point in the balloting, to have strong preferences for another.

Operation of presidential direct primaries in the mixed system thus fell short of the expectations of their advocates. Further, the role of primaries varied over the course of sequential elections, maximizing both voter confusion and opportunities for manipulation. For instance, the numbers of pledged and unpledged delegates varied considerably over the years. There were no unpledged delegates selected by primaries in the 1916 DNC or the 1924 RNC (Table 5), evidently because in those years relatively popular incumbent presidents were seeking renomination. But in the 1916 RNC and the 1924 DNC, the numbers of unpledged delegates were quite high. With such volatility, the waning popular enthusiasm for primaries displayed in Table 6 might be expected. As Ware concludes, "given this record, it was impossible for [the direct primary's] supporters to put forward the kind of defense that could be made of the direct primary – namely, that it appeared to be a more democratic device than caucus-convention systems."[36]

There were clearly some exceptions. The 1912 primary season did not select the nominees, but the novelty of the device, together with the dramatic atmosphere of the contest and the prominence of primary advocates Theodore Roosevelt and Woodrow Wilson, drew voters to the primary polls. The results were important: Roosevelt's success in the primaries provided legitimacy to his quixotic third-party candidacy after his defeat at the Republican National Convention, and Wilson's success helped him demonstrate his popularity despite

[36] Ware, *The American Direct Primary*, 251.

TABLE 6. *Primary Participation as Percent of*
General Election Participation, 1912–1932

1912	22
1916	17
1920	12
1924	15
1928	15
1932	13

Source: Author's calculations based on William Crotty and
John S. Jackson III, *Presidential Primaries and Nominations*
(Washinton, DC: Congressional Quarterly Press, 1985), 16;
and U.S. Bureau of the Census, *The Statistical History of*
the United States: From Colonial Times to the Present (New
York: Basic Books, 1976), 1073.

his relatively unknown status in national politics. The primary contest of 1920
provides a more typical manifestation of the mixed system, however. That year
is often viewed as a return to what Republican nominee Harding referred to
as "normalcy," and a reassertion of old guard control of the political process.
On first glance, the 1920 election looks like just that: the nomination of two
dark horses (Harding and J. Cox) through the politics of the smoke-filled room.
Further, it seems a significant departure from the trends that appeared in the
late nineteenth century in which preconvention campaigns effectively shaped
public opinion ahead of the delegate-selection process.

A closer look at that election reveals something quite different, however; the
persistence of emergent nineteenth-century campaign styles combining with the
problematic operation of the primary system and contingent events to produce
the false appearance of a reversion to an older form. 1920 was the last election
in what James W. Davis calls "the early period" of direct primary development
and demonstrates the confusing effects of intercurrent party orders.[37] Sixteen
states held Democratic primaries, in which 971,671 voters participated, selecting 44.7 percent of the delegates to the Democratic National Convention;
twenty states held Republican primaries, in which more than 3 million people
participated, selecting 57.8 percent of the delegates to the Republican National
Convention. Not until 1964 for the Democrats and 1976 for the Republicans
would such a high percentage of delegates be selected by primaries.[38]

Still, factors unique to each party prevented primaries from proving decisive
in the outcome in 1920. For Democrats, there was an insufficient number
of primary-selected delegates to produce a two-thirds majority, and a plethora
of candidates prevented the emergence of a clear primary winner. Four major
candidates contested the nomination through to the convention, and until the
end, many thought that William Jennings Bryan might make a final grasp for
the nomination. Wilson's refusal to disavow a third term until the convention

[37] Davis, *Presidential Primaries*, 41.
[38] Davis, *Presidential Primaries*; Crotty and Jackson, *Presidential Primaries and Nominations*.

derailed the aspirations of the candidate who might have otherwise had the widest popular following (and the one who might have had the most to gain from a vigorous primary campaign), his son-in-law, McAdoo, who refused to compete openly until Wilson's intentions were clear. Cox, the eventual nominee, competed listlessly in the primaries; as the governor of a large state, he hoped to became the most logical choice in the likely event of a deadlock.

Republicans faced a similar dynamic. Sensing that the popular tide was turning their direction, "in many states organization leaders had agreed to work for an 'old fashioned' convention with nothing predetermined," maintaining uncommitted delegations and promoting favorite son candidacies to maximize their influence.[39] This expectation, which has been maintained in the popular imagination for years, was actually quickly uprooted by a flurry of candidates with national reputations who relied on the new national strategies. General Leonard Wood, for many months the front-runner, was blessed with coronation as Theodore Roosevelt's successor. He formed Leonard Wood Leagues in every state in the Union, claimed sixty thousand members nationally, and believed he had the most to gain from primaries. Yet although Wood inherited the Roosevelt mantle, he was no Progressive, and Hiram Johnson, the California governor who had helped form the Progressive party in 1912, entered the race to fight him for the Progressive vote. Mistrusted as a bolter by much of the regular party establishment, Johnson *had* to enter primaries to demonstrate sufficient popular support to force his name on the convention. Frank Lowden, Jr., of Illinois, who had the support of party regulars in a number of nonprimary states, entered a few primaries to bolster his popular credentials. Calvin Coolidge, governor of Massachusetts, had gained national prominence in putting down a police strike in Boston in 1919; his campaign managers conducted a savvy "educational campaign" that involved distribution of books of Coolidge's speeches, favorable coverage in the national press, and the conscious construction of a public image intended to contrast with Bryanite populism.[40]

Then there was Ohio Governor Warren G. Harding. Hardly a dark horse, Harding was encouraged to run both by party regulars who hoped to block Wood's popular campaign and by his own Hanna-figure, Harry Daugherty, who billed Harding as a McKinley-esque politician who was both popular with the people and willing to work with congressional Republicans. He expected to do well in Ohio's primary, but Wood picked up nine Ohio primary delegates, and party leaders began to question Harding's capacity to win his pivotal home state.[41] Harding's nomination cannot be attributed merely to traditional

---

[39] Wesley M. Bagby, "The 'Smoke Filled Room' and the Nomination of Warren G. Harding," *The Mississippi Valley Historical Review* (March 1955), 657.

[40] Kerry W. Buckley, "A President for the 'Great Silent Majority': Bruce Barton's Construction of Calvin Coolidge," *The New England Quarterly* (December 2003), 593–626.

[41] Wesley M. Bagby, *The Road to Normalcy: The Presidential Campaign and Election of 1920* (Baltimore: The Johns Hopkins Press, 1962), 36–42.

politics but to politics in the transformed party organizations. Wood and Lowden both funded their operations through funds donated by businessmen who were invested in their candidacies; Wood, in particular, expended significant sums building up his amateur league of supporters and contesting primaries across the country. This novel means of funding campaigns ended up derailing their campaigns; seeking to gain political capital for his Progressive ally Johnson, Senator William Borah launched a congressional investigation into campaign finance that irrevocably contaminated the candidacies of the two front-runners. Acknowledging the strategic importance of Ohio and Harding's base of popular support, and reluctant to turn the election over to another Progressive president, party leaders with influence in their delegations worked to throw the nomination to Harding. Harding was not simply chosen out of a hat, however; party leaders turned to him as the most desirable in a field of primary contestants. Had Harding *not* entered the primaries, he would likely not have been nominated.[42] Nearly every significant aspect of the campaign's strategic atmosphere thus bears the marks of the transformations that had reshaped party politics over the previous forty years. As one historian of the election concludes, "the chief result was to dramatize [the direct primary's] serious inadequacies as a route to the presidential nomination."[43] Primaries continued to shape the presidential nomination process, but the reform momentum behind their spread dissipated. Not until the 1950s – in a period of "reawakened interest" – did primaries expand again in importance. But even then they were mainly used by presidential aspirants to prove their national popularity as a part of a broader strategy that included appealing to state party leaders in a traditional Jacksonian mode style.[44]

The New Idea and Political Science

This new idea of party was not self-institutionalizing, and indeed, it would be somewhat simplistic to say that the late-nineteenth-century idea of party was absorbed completely by the party organizations through the adoption of the presidential direct primary in the 1970s (although the post-1970s party system is closer to the late-nineteenth-century idea than the Jacksonian idea of party). What the late-nineteenth-century idea of party did was carve out an image of national party institutionalization that informed Americans' understanding of the role of the national party in the two-party system and indeed the defense of the two-party system itself. The argument for a necessary boundedness between national and subnational party organizations, the specialization of the national party organization (especially as an aggregator of national interest

[42] Bagby, "The 'Smoke Filled Room' and the Nomination of Warren G. Harding," 657–674; see also Bagby, *The Road to Normalcy*, 88.
[43] Bagby, *The Road to Normalcy*, 49.
[44] Davis, *Presidential Primaries*, 41.

associations), and a universalistic conception of the party-in-the-electorate all shaped notions of acceptable party reform during the twentieth century.[45]

Most notably, these assumptions lie at the heart of the 1950 report of the American Political Science Association's Committee on Parties, "Toward a More Responsible Two-Party System," perhaps the most complete statement of mid-twentieth-century party reform aspirations. Although this report can be called neither a consensual statement of the political science profession nor the root source of subsequent party reform (although political scientist Barbara Sinclair recently suggested, without fanfare, that "political parties seem to meet the requirements of responsible parties as defined by these scholars to a greater extent today than at any time in the past half century"[46]), it is telling to note just how far this academic exercise in charting institutional reform draws on the language and concepts of late-nineteenth-century party leaders. To be sure, its presence is a reminder that the new idea had not, by 1950, been realized, but its embrasure of the central features of the late-nineteenth-century idea points to the influence of that idea on the aspirations of later reformers; as one committee member later recalled, "the position taken and the arguments presented were by no means new and, in fact, had a long and distinguished pedigree."[47] (Another had recognized earlier the popular-intellectual change necessary to effect such organizational change, observing "once a respectable section of the public understands the issue, ways of promoting party government through the Constitution can be found," which would "facilitate the solution of the greatest constitutional problems."[48])

Fundamentally, the report insisted on parties that "are able to bring forth programs to which they commit themselves" and promised that "the development of a more program-conscious party membership may attract into party activity many who formerly stayed away." It claimed that "more general and wholehearted support of the party program will follow wider participation in the program's development," creating a sense of "self-discipline which stems from free identification with aims one helps to define," drawing explicitly the same link that late-nineteenth-century party elites drew between better representation of voter interests and greater party loyalty within the electorate.[49] It attributed the independence of the different geographic layers of party organization as "the principle reason for the frequent difficulty, discord and confusion within the parties," particularly the fact that "the Republican party of

---

[45] See Polsby, "The Institutionalization of the House of Representatives."

[46] Barbara Sinclair, *Party Wars: Polarization and the Politics of National Policy Making* (Norman, OK: University of Oklahoma Press, 2006), 344.

[47] "Toward a More Responsible Two-Party System: A Report of the Committee on Political Parties," *American Political Science Review*, 44:3, Part 2, Supplement (September 1950); Evron M. Kirkpatrick, "'Toward a More Responsible Two-Party System': Political Science, Policy Science, or Pseudo-Science?" *American Political Science Review* (December 1971), 965.

[48] E. E. Schattschneider, *Party Government* (New York: Rinehart, 1942), 209–10.

[49] "Toward a More Responsible Two-Party System," 1, 70, 67.

California may take a position on public questions and even on party strategy very different from that of the Republican party of Iowa, and both may differ in these respects from the national organization," thus rejecting something very close to Croker's defense of the Jacksonian mode (as quoted in Chapter 1). Instead, party members were to be encouraged to "think in terms of national issues and a national program, rather than in terms of primarily local considerations."⁵⁰ It advocated "local party meetings, regularly and frequently held, perhaps monthly," groups that "should be different in composition and function from most of the existing local party committees," and suggested "local party leagues" as a means of calling such meetings. Just as late-nineteenth-century party leaders looked to their extra-partisan challengers as a model of democratic participation, the Committee on Parties pointed to "the ease with which labor groups and political leagues have moved into areas of activity in which local party communities once reigned supreme indicates the need for a new type of local organization."⁵¹ The report celebrated interest groups because they "counteract and offset local interests," "define their objectives on a national scale," and as such "are a nationalizing influence," and so advocated "the integration of the interest groups into the political system is a function of the parties."⁵²

The parties outlined in the report were very much in keeping with the late-nineteenth-century idea: clearly national, presidency-centered (Grover Cleveland began its list of exemplary party leaders⁵³), programmatic, responsible for interest aggregation, and responsive to the party-in-the-electorate to the point of bypassing subnational party organizations. Like Wilson, the Committee on Parties had abandoned the British parliamentary model for one that had emerged from the proving ground of practical party politics. The committee was composed of men and women who came of age with the campaign of education (the oldest member was born in 1890, the youngest in 1916); they had absorbed the parameters of appropriateness sketched out by the late-nineteenth-century idea of party. That they felt the need to articulate it does not deny its relevance to political practice in their day; as noted earlier, Franklin Roosevelt had recommended reforms along similar lines just under three decades before, only to be reminded that his suggestions had been tried. Thus, even as the new idea of party failed to institutionalize fully, it provided a ready-at-hand set of assumptions for reformers who wished to preserve the fundamental coherence of the two major parties, while infusing new legitimacy in them.

The committee did overreach the rules of appropriateness governing practical politics in some of its recommendations, and those moments of overreach clarify why the new idea was as weakly institutionalized as it was by 1950,

⁵⁰ Ibid., 66.
⁵¹ Ibid., 68.
⁵² Ibid., 20.
⁵³ Ibid., 40.

and thus why traditional forms of party politics resurged well into the twentieth century. The committee recommended that the parties form party councils (composed of presidents and vice presidents, or failed presidential and vice presidential candidates, members of Congress, governors, national committee members, and appointees by party leagues or associations), which were intended to provide national coherence and "to deliberate on matters touching the party welfare."[54] In spirit, the goal was similar to that of the Democrats' reorganization of their national committee in 1892 (and Cleveland's de facto alteration of that organization by actually attending national committee meetings) – namely, to provide greater national coordination for campaigns and maintain the party's interests throughout the years between elections. The ambition-serving nature of party organizations quickly tore this purpose apart, however; Bryan and his fellow silverites mounted their own competing shadow party organization to mobilize power from without the regular party apparatus, limiting the capacity of any one group to control party fortunes. The recommended party council envisioned a body composed of officials who traditionally formed the pool of presidential aspirants (failed nominees, governors, members of Congress) and institutionalized cooperation among them was unworkable. Supposing a role for the national associations of party clubs similarly missed the reasons for the original club leagues' dissolution: these entities quickly came to be seen as serving the interests of particular candidates and were thus deeply suspect. Indeed, as presidential candidates continued to utilize streamlined national party organizations, they tended to rebuild them to remove the supporters of their predecessors (as happened when Bryan was nominated in 1896, Wilson in 1912, Cox in 1920, Davis in 1924, and Smith in 1928), and then to emphasize their rebuilding of the national party apparatus as a means of highlighting their competence in party leadership. The political scientists who wrote the report were under different restraints and could afford to advocate ideal solutions. (As a reminder that ideas live beyond their initial utterance, the party council concept was partially enshrined in the addition of superdelegates to the body of nominating convention delegates in the early 1980s, although they have not played the role indicated in the 1950 report.)

Similar problems are evident with the Committee on Parties' recommendation for greater national party discipline of state and local party organizations.[55] Late-nineteenth-century national party leaders struggled with this problem but found discipline of subnational party organizations a task fraught with peril. Disciplining party franchisees risked an incomplete mobilization on the ground and coaxing locals to work for the ticket through side payments was usually a better option than discipline. Their solution was to bypass subnational organizations, reaching voters directly and allowing local organizations to continue operating as normal – hence preserving the federated party structure. Given the expanse of territory that the American constitutional

---

[54] Ibid., 41–2.
[55] Ibid., 44–8.

system requires for contesting national elections, it is difficult to imagine any arrangement in which a national party organization would not contain pockets of localized power capable of resisting centralized discipline. Again, the limits of late-nineteenth-century practice appear less a question of political will and more a question of ineradicable limitations of political possibility.

Finally, the committee claimed that "any tendency in the direction of a strengthened party system encourages the interest groups to align themselves with one or the other of the two major parties" and recommended that "the parties be held accountable to the public for the compromises [with interest groups] they accept." Again, the report echoes the efforts of late-nineteenth-century party leaders, here in their effort to manage "the phenomenal growth of interest organizations" with "a reinforced party system that can cope with the multiplied organized pressures" that followed it.[56] As national party leaders recognized half a century earlier, the proliferation of interest associations presented a threat to the traditional party organization by organizing citizens into national communities of interest that were not effectively addressed within the traditional party framework. These leaders did not go so far as to assume responsibility for the interest groups they courted, however; indeed, although compromise within the traditional party structure could be defended as a popular value in and of itself, the parties' relationships with interest groups have always been more complicated. This is probably because intraparty compromise allowed party leaders to insist on a fundamental community of party members (if everyone compromises, everyone wins), whereas interest group compromise tends to highlight harsher divisions (as the party appeals to one interest, it risks slighting others – hence, the wisdom of nineteenth-century party leaders in directing such appeals to voters in a private setting[57]). Proposing that parties accept responsibility for the positions of their interest group partners is, for this reason, problematic.

What is telling is the fact that the Committee on Parties considered compromise with interest groups to be acceptable, even desirable. In this vein, E. E. Schattschneider, an influential member of the Committee on Parties (who served on its drafting committee), looked to Madison as "the first American theorist to have a philosophy of pressure groups." In his classic text, *Party Government*, Schattschneider dismissed Madison's elaboration of the separation of powers, and drew on his account of faction in *Federalist* 10 to articulate a definition of party that rested on the assumption of parties' responsibility to aggregate interests. In the process, it should be noted, he stretched Madison's argument a bit to fit contemporary political experience. Probing the

---

56 Ibid., 19, 20.

57 Although recent studies of party change emphasize the evolving cooperation between extra-partisan interest group associations and the parties as ushering in a new phase of party development in the late twentieth and early twenty-first centuries. Steven Teles, *The Evolution of the Conservative Legal Movement* (Princeton, NJ: Princeton University Press, 20008); Gregory Koger, Seth Masket, and Hans Noel, "Partisan Webs: Information Exchange and Party Networks," *British Journal of Political Science* (July 2009), 633–53.

"unstated implications of Madison's hypothesis," Schattschneider concluded that "majorities can be produced only by compromise and accommodation among a variety of interests." Further, he interpreted *Federalist* 10 to imply that "the discussion of 'interests' becomes inevitably a discussion of associations" and that "organization is proof of the reality of an interest." He added the caveat that "there are common interests as well as special interests," suggesting that some interests possess an inherent assimilability (which parties could then use to their advantage).[58]

Perhaps recognizing the anachronistic quality of his reading, Schattschneider conceded that "Madison did not observe the consequences of his own theory." This view was also in considerable conflict with the Jacksonian notion of party, which held individual participation in the local party organization – and a willingness to compromise individual interests in the short term in exchange for long-term gain – the keystone to the party system. Schattschneider worked to counteract the residue of that notion, suggesting that "the concept of the party membership of the partisans is abandoned altogether," in favor of a view of the party-in-the-electorate with a relationship with the party organization that resembles "a concept such as that of the 'good will' relation of a merchant and his customers." This was hardly the notion that traditional partisan practice encouraged, but it was both the product of the new idea of party and a necessary step to understanding the parties as fundamentally aggregators of national communities of interest. Schattschneider concluded with a call for "party government," a term that was more than a euphemism for "responsible parties"; as Wilson had before him, Schattschneider had come to accept the fact that "presidential politics is the principal rallying point for the great public interests of the nation, the point at which the issues of public policy are discovered and exploited" and through which "the President of the United States today receives a mandate to govern the nation." "Party government" was not a responsible party government model in the tradition of *Congressional Government*; it was the distinctively "democratic and liberal solution of the problem of reconciling authority and liberty."[59]

The increasingly pluralistic nature of the associational universe, the parties' embrasure of their appeal to the diversity of national interests, the reordering of the boundaries of political conflict, the presumption of the national party as the best medium for intraparty democracy – these all helped to slowly remake the assumptions underlying party organizations over the course of the twentieth century. However, the broad parameters were effectively worked out in the late nineteenth. Indeed, the increased academic popularity of *Federalist* 10 at roughly this point in time (*Federalist* 51 having been more prominent

[58] E. E. Schattschneider, *Party Government* (New York: Rinehart, 1942), 19, 18, 21, 32. On separation of powers, Schattschneider insisted that "classical concepts, such as the idea of the tyranny of the majority and with it a large part of the theory of the separation of powers, must be discarded," 16.

[59] Schattschneider, *Party Government*, 18, 59, 60, 206, 209.

throughout the bulk of the nineteenth century) appears to have been part of a gradual mental adjustment among political scientists to a political environment that looked more like Schattschneider's description than the political environment of the mid-nineteenth century.[60] This is not to suggest that Madison's view of politics was inaccurate in the early or mid-nineteenth century, but that the operationalization of the new idea of party had made it salient in a new way, and its liberal view of politics more commonly accepted in practice, by the early twentieth century.

---

[60] See, for instance, Douglas Adair's work on *Federalist* 10 in *Fame and the Founding Fathers* (New York: Norton, 1974), chaps. 3 and 4.

Selected Bibliography

Manuscript Collections

Chester A. Arthur Papers, Library of Congress
Wharton Barker Papers, Library of Congress
William Jennings Bryan Papers, Library of Congress
Thomas Henry Carter Papers, Library of Congress
William Chandler Papers, Library of Congress
James S. Clarkson Papers, Library of Congress
Grover Cleveland Papers, Library of Congress
George B. Cortelyou Papers, Library of Congress
Joseph Benson Foraker Papers, Library of Congress
James A. Garfield Papers, Library of Congress
Elijah W. Halford Papers, Library of Congress
Hanna-McCormick Family Papers, Library of Congress
Benjamin Harrison Papers, Library of Congress
Daniel Scott Lamont Papers, Library of Congress
Manton Marble Papers, Library of Congress
Massachusetts Reform Club Papers, Massachusetts Historical Society
Louis T. Michener Papers, Library of Congress
J. Hampton Moore Papers, Historical Society of Pennsylvania
John Sherman Papers, Library of Congress
Matthew Stanley Quay Papers, Library of Congress
Moorefield Storey Papers, Massachusetts Historical Society
John Wanamaker Papers, Historical Society of Pennsylvania
Elihu B. Washburne Papers, Library of Congress
William C. Whitney Papers, Library of Congress
George Fred Williams Papers, Massachusetts Historical Society
Young Men's Democratic Club of Massachusetts Records, Massachusetts Historical Society
Young Men's Republican Committee Records, Massachusetts Historical Society

Newspapers and Journals

Arkansas Gazette
The (Red Wing, Minnesota) *Argus*
Ashland (Wisconsin) *Daily News*
Atlanta Constitution
Atlantic Monthly
Boston Globe
Centreville (MD) *Observer*
Century
Chicago Tribune
Cleveland Press
The (Topeka, KS) *Commonwealth*
(Nashville, TN) *Daily American*
Denver Daily Times
(Philadelphia) *Evening Bulletin*
The Forum
(Portland, OR) *Morning Oregonian*
Napa County (California) *Reporter*
The Nation
New York Times
North American Review
Oregon State Journal
The Outlook
San Francisco Examiner
Scribner's Monthly
Seattle Post-Intelligencer
Springfield (MA) *Republican*
Weekly Alta California

Published Convention Proceedings (selected)

Barr, John C., H.H. Cummin, Herman Kretz, and John O'Connor, *Proceedings of the Democratic State Convention of 1872, Nominating Governor and Auditor General, Judge of the Supreme Court and Congressman at Large, Selecting an Electoral Ticket, and Electing Delegates to National Convention, at Baltimore* (Pittsburgh: Barr & Myers, Printers, 1872), Library of Congress collection

Chairman of the (Pennsylvania) State Committee, *Proceedings of the Pennsylvania Democratic State Convention, at Lancaster, Wednesday, March 22, 1876* (Lancaster: Steinman & Hensel, Printers, 1876), Library of Congress collection

Journal of the Democratic Convention, Held in the City of Montgomery on the 14th and 15th of February, 1848 (Montgomery, AL: M'Cormick & Walshe, Printers, 1848), *Library of Congress collection*

New York Republican State Convention, Held at Syracuse, September 18 and 19, 1856, Library of Congress collection

Proceedings and Address, of the Democratic County Convention, Held at Galena, in the County of Jo Daviess, in the State of Illinois, on the 22nd February, 1839 (Galena, IL: Galena Democrat and Advertiser, 1839.), Library of Congress collection

Proceedings and Address, of the Democratic County Convention, Held at Galena, in the County of Jo Daviess, in the State of Illinois, on the 22nd February, 1839, (Galena: Galena Democrat and Advertiser, 1839), Library of Congress collection

Proceedings of the Democratic State Convention, Held in Albany, January 21, and February 1, 1861 (Albany, NY: Comstock and Cassidy, Printers, 1861), Library of Congress collection

Proceedings of the Democratic State Convention, Held at Charlottesville, VA, September 9 and 10, 1840, Library of Congress collection

Proceedings of a Meeting of the State Central Committee of The Union Republican Party of Georgia, Held at Atlanta, Wednesday, November 24, 1869 (Atlanta: New Era Job Office, 1869), Library of Congress collection

Proceedings of the Republican State Convention, Held at Sacramento, June 20, 1860, Library of Congress collection

Republican National Committee, *Official Proceedings of the Republican National Conventions, 1868, 1872, 1876, and 1880* (Minneapolis, MN: Charles W. Johnson, 1903)

Rules of the Union Republican Party, Adopted May 24, 1872 (Philadelphia: William White Smith, Publisher, 1872), Library of Congress collection

Index

Adams, John Q.; 151
Agricultural Wheel; 88, 89
Aldrich, John; 27, 31, 54, 242
Altgeld, John; 181–2, 188
Altschuler, Glen C.; 16, 44, 56
American Iron and Steel Association
    (AISA); 72, 79–81, 85, 87, 91, 97, 103,
    110, 138
American Political Science Association's
    Committee on Parties (1950); 252–5
Apgar, E.P.; 101
Argersinger, Peter H.; 95
Arthur, Chester A.; 199, 207, 211, 213,
    214–15
Associational Explosion; 66–8, 69–76, 89, 95,
    98, 99, 100–4, 107, 109, 110, 124, 126,
    133, 134, 154, 158–9, 186, 219
Australian (secret) Ballot; 72, 100, 108
"availability" (of candidates for nomination);
    26, 46, 52, 161
    revision of, under Cleveland; 161–2, 206,
    230

Bailey, Jeremy; 20
Balogh, Brian; 77, 132
Barker, Wharton; 102, 118, 209, 221
Bensel, Richard Franklin; 5, 17, 23, 50–1, 51n,
    65, 77, 167, 183, 185, 190
Benson, Lee; 23–4, 51
Berry, Jeffrey M.; 67
Black, Chauncey; 110, 128, 129, 133, 134,
    187
Blaine, James G.; 84, 85, 114, 126, 141, 150,
    160, 171, 175, 198–201, 207, 210, 211,
    215, 217, 219, 234

Blodgett, Geoffrey; 82n, 186
bloody shirt rhetoric; 72, 84, 103, 108, 114,
    207
Blumin, Stuart M.; 16, 44, 56
Brice, Calvin; 112, 125
Bridges, Amy; 34–5
Bryan, William Jennings; 154, 182–90, 236,
    240, 249
    Cleveland's influence on; 154–5, 168–9,
        181, 182, 186, 187, 189–90, 192–3
    1896 nomination; 87, 95–6, 140–1, 166,
        170, 172, 183–6, 229, 243
    and insurgent movements; 93, 101–2,
        183–7, 190, 254
    and national associations; 184–7
    and new campaign methods; 14, 17, 103,
        122–3, 230
    party leadership post-1896; 187–9
    speechmaking tour; 150, 187, 228
Bryce, James; 55, 85
Burnham, Walter Dean; 17–18, 122, 244
businessmen in politics; 81, 102, 118–23, 155,
    221–2, 251

Cameron, Donald; 48, 59, 75, 114
Cameron, Simon; 198–200
campaign fundraising; 63, 81, 221–2
campaign literature; 1, 70, 71–2, 98–9, 235
    and civic associations; 79–80, 84–5, 87
    and parties; 104, 105–6, 109, 112, 134,
        137–9, 189, 227
Carpenter, Daniel P.; 148–9
Carter, Thomas; 95, 115
Ceaser, James W.; 2n, 19
Chandler, William; 60, 133

263

Chandler, Zachariah; 113–14
civil service reform; 15, 60–4, 73, 83–5, 100, 154, 160–1
Clarkson, James S.; 13, 100, 105, 107, 109, 122, 207, 217, 225
    and National League of Republican Clubs; 126–7, 129, 131, 133, 134, 141–2, 156
    and Republican National Committee; 64, 98, 110, 115, 124, 126–7, 134
Clay, Henry; 152
Clemens, Elisabeth; 71, 76
Cleveland, Grover; 81*n*, 110, 154–82, 183, 189–90, 220, 230, 237–40
    on campaign of education; 158, 159, 166, 168–9, 171–2, 178, 181, 229
    early executive experiences of; 155–9
    1884 nomination; 101, 192
    1888 nomination; 171–3, 192
    1892 nomination; 114–15, 120, 173–7, 192
    executive messages and letters; 20, 22, 149, 159–70, 177–8, 219, 232
    and Mugwumps; 82, 85–7, 95, 101, 140, 156, 160, 165–6, 174–5, 189
    and new campaign methods; 14, 105, 108–9, 120–1, 132
    on party; 156–9, 161–3, 174–5, 180
    party leadership of; 144, 146–7, 149, 206, 217–18, 221, 228, 230, 233, 234, 253, 254
Conkling, Roscoe; 198–9, 208, 210, 211–14
Constitution (U.S.); 2, 5, 57
    conservative impact of; 4
    geographical divisions in; 8–9, 13, 254–5
    national scope of; 5, 140
    and the presidency; 18, 21, 19–20, 45, 63, 144–5, 148, 151–2, 167, 213, 239
convention system; 25–8, 29–30, 32, 33–4, 241
    abuse of; 38–9, 40–1, 42, 44, 51
    congressional district delegates' representation in; 48–9, 193, 201–6, 215–16, 225, 247
    continued role of; 3, 99, 183
    democratic form of; 6, 7, 26
    and national campaigns; 7, 45–9, 56–7, 110
    parochialism and; 10, 19
    and the presidency; 144–8, 152–3
    Republican party reforms; 1–2, 21, 148, 150, 191, 193–206, 215–16, 244
Coolidge, Calvin; 22, 236–7, 250

Cox, Gary W.; 99, 146
Cox, James M.; 236, 249–50, 254
Croker, Richard; 49–50, 253
Croly, Herbert; 122, 221, 223, 226, 234
Curtis, George William; 84, 160–1, 169, 171

dark horse candidates; 61, 201, 207, 209, 211, 249
Davis, James W.; 247–9, 254
Dawes, Charles; 117, 224, 227, 236–7
Democratic party; 122, 154, 163, 172, 182, 183, 238
    and adoption of convention system; 25, 27, 47, 193, 197, 199
    and national committee centralization; 112–13, 114–15, 135
    regional political base; 92, 94–5, 116, 165, 178–9, 191
Dick, Charles; 225, 226, 227
Dorsey, Stephen W.; 208, 210, 227
Dover, Elmer; 113
Duverger, Maurice; 32*n*

educational campaign; 103–4, 104–9, 143, 154, 235, 237
    civic associations and; 67, 70–1, 73–4, 79–80, 88, 90–3, 98, 184
    features of; 8, 73–4, 117–19
    parties adopt; 97, 98–100, 132, 166, 189, 206
    and party nationalization; 109–10, 111–12, 123, 124–8, 131, 134
    and presidents; 154, 156, 167–9, 171–2, 191, 221, 222
election of;
    1880; 207, 209
    1884; 82, 85–6, 111, 160
    1888; 111, 112, 171, 216–17
    1892; 92, 111, 178–9
    1896; 17–18, 122, 140–1, 144, 186, 189, 226–30, 244
    1920; 236, 247–51
Erie, Steven; 18, 43

Farmers' Alliance; 87–97, 101–2, 183, 222
    critique of parties; 75
    and educational campaign; 72, 74, 90, 92–3
    imitated by parties; 14, 17, 93, 124, 133, 138, 140
favorite son candidates; 49, 176, 215, 225, 250
The Federalist; 2, 13, 145, 255–7
Foster, James P.; 125–6

Fowler, Dorothy Ganfield; 58, 62–3
front porch campaign; 20, 144, 150, 209–10,
   216–17, 219, 228–9, 236
fusion; 72, 94–6, 97, 188–9

Garfield, James A.; 60, 84, 192, 221, 228
   1880 nomination; 114, 200–1
   and front porch campaign; 150, 175,
     209–10, 216–17
   presidency of; 211–14, 215
   role in 1880 campaign; 207–11, 219
geography; 51, 64, 144, 202
   and boundaries of party regularity; 1, 5–6,
     27, 35, 44, 45, 57, 69, 84
   erosion of traditional boundaries; 10–11,
     71–2, 84, 88, 99, 110, 124–5, 131, 129,
     143, 235
   the U.S. Constitution and; 8–9, 254–5
Gerring, John; 50, 172
Gilder, Richard Watson; 166–7
Gold Democrats; 140, 181, 185
gold standard; 10, 154, 174, 179, 181, 182,
   183, 190, 229, 231–2
Goodwyn, Lawrence; 69, 71, 91, 96, 129, 183
Gould, Lewis; 19, 151, 155, 233, 238
the Grange; 11, 88, 94
Grant, Ulysses S.; 60, 82, 84, 146, 192,
   197–201, 205
Greenback-Labor party; 88, 133, 215

Half-Breed faction; 60, 211–12
Halford, Elijah; 59, 61
Hancock, Winfield Scott; 175, 192, 209, 210
Hanna, Marcus A.; 17, 50, 75, 101, 107
   and campaign fundraising; 8, 118, 121–3
   management of McKinley campaign; 116,
     142, 221–8
Harding, Warren G.; 22, 236, 249–51
Harrison, Benjamin; 215–21
   1888 campaign; 216–19, 234
   and front porch campaign; 20, 150, 175,
     216–17, 219
   Garfield's influence on; 209–10, 215–17
   and new convention procedures; 192,
     215–16
   party leadership of; 144
   and patronage; 59, 61, 64
   rejection of Cleveland-style leadership;
     217–20, 230
   strained relationship with chairmen of
     Republican National Committee; 115–16,
     119–20, 142
Harrity, William; 114–15, 188

Hayes, Rutherford B.; 20, 60, 61–3, 207,
   211–12, 214
Hearst, William Randolph; 142–3, 188
Heclo, Hugh; 13, 23
Hicks, John D.; 92, 96
Hill, David B.; 172, 176, 177, 182
Hirshon, Stanley; 114
Hofstadter, Richard; 1, 2, 6, 106
Hoover, Herbert; 22, 237
hurrah campaign; 53–7, 81, 129, 130, 235

interest groups; 3, 8, 11–12, 76–81, 88, 105,
   251–3, 255

Jackson, Andrew; 19, 20, 146
James, Scott; 15, 29, 43
Jefferson, Thomas; 20
Jensen, Richard; 50*n*, 76, 106, 223
Johnson, Andrew; 149
Johnson, Hiram; 250–1
Johnson, Ronald M.; 15, 100, 117
Jones, James; 123, 186

Kehl, James; 38
Keller, Morton; 10, 69
Kelly, Robert; 155
Kleppner, Paul; 22, 25, 29, 51, 54, 109

labor associations; 72, 75, 76, 87, 89, 94, 101,
   102, 222, 253
Laracey, Melvin; 149, 192
Libecap, Gary D.; 15, 100, 117
liberalism; 4–9, 68, 73
   Founding version of; 2, 4, 67–8
   and national civic associations; 76
   new idea of party and; 3, 12, 13, 20, 124,
     172, 235, 256–7
   and self-interest; 65, 70, 74–5, 97, 124,
     131
Lincoln, Abraham; 19, 146
Logan, John; 198, 200, 208
Lowden, Frank; 250–1

McAdoo, William Gibbs; 236, 246–7, 250
McCormick, Richard L.; 3, 7, 28, 241
McCormick, Richard P.; 28, 31, 152
McFarland, Gerald W.; 66, 70
McGerr, Michael; 15–18, 127, 143
McGovern-Fraser Commission; 240
McKinley, William; 17, 20, 154, 190, 192,
   236
   and campaign of education; 221, 222, 229
   1896 nomination; 222–6

McKinley, William (*cont.*)
  first inaugural address of; 22, 230–1
  and front porch campaign; 150, 228–9, 236
  and new campaign methods; 14, 142–3, 221–30
  and new convention procedures; 225
  party leadership of; 144
  as president; 151, 230–4
McWilliams, Wilson Carey; 6
Macune, Charles; 89–91, 93, 94, 95, 101*n*
Macy, Jesse; 18, 49, 113, 116, 122
Mahone, William; 205, 214
Marcus, Robert; 53, 54, 81*n*, 92, 115, 189
Massachusetts Reform Club (MRC); 85–6, 100, 137, 138
Milkis, Sidney M.; 2, 5–6, 19*n*, 44, 146, 220, 233
Moe, Terry M.; 150
Monroe, J.P.; 15
Moore, J. Hampton; 132
Morgan, H. Wayne; 225–6
Mugwumps; 81–7, 87–8, 90, 91
  critique of Jacksonian mode; 73, 76, 84
  and Grover Cleveland; 82, 85–7, 95, 101, 140, 156, 160, 165–6, 174–5, 189
  imitated by parties; 14, 97, 99, 105, 107, 124, 125–6, 137–9
  national networks of; 72
  see also Reformist Account

National Association of Democratic Clubs (NADC); 124–37, 142, 187
national civic associations; 65, 66–8, 69–76, 98, 103
National Civil Service Reform League (NCSRL); 84–5, 160
national committees; 30, 103, 109–16, 194–5
  centralization of; 98–9, 101, 124, 126–7, 134, 142, 172–3, 189, 226–8
  and centralized fundraising; 1, 21, 99, 110, 112–13, 116–23, 189–90, 221–2, 227
  permanent headquarters; 112–13, 126, 128
  and presidential campaigns; 1, 109, 141, 146, 148, 176–7, 228
  weak under Jacksonian mode; 27, 49, 110
National League of Republican Clubs (NLRC); 124–5, 125–37, 142, 156, 228
Nelson, Michael; 220, 233
Nevins, Allan; 239
New Deal; 19, 151, 240
newly nationalized citizens; 32
  emergence of; 3, 9–13
  mobilization of; 8, 14, 65

and national civic associations; 66–8, 69, 70–1, 74–5, 76, 77, 98
and political parties; 57, 98, 103
Nichols, David; 20–1, 151
nominating caucuses; 7, 26, 29, 152–3
  congressional caucus; 25–6, 241

Orren, Karen; 3
Ostrogorski, Moisei; 2, 16, 27, 28, 32–3*n*, 38–9, 42, 52, 58, 63–4*n*, 68, 105, 189

Pangle, Thomas; 5, 8
Parker, Alton B.; 142–3, 155
party clubs; 1, 99, 110, 124–43, 195, 235, 240, 254
party decline argument; 3–4, 14–18, 206
party-as-organization; 29–32, 36–44, 193–5, 242
party-in-the-electorate; 30, 36, 97, 124, 193, 194–5, 202, 253, 256
  connection with nationalized party organizations; 57, 99, 110, 134, 143, 235
  disconnection from traditional party organizations; 35, 38, 42, 44–5, 47, 48–9, 57, 65, 111
  nationalization of; 1, 66, 110, 125, 130, 135, 137, 143, 188, 201, 205, 235, 252
  presidential appeals to; 21, 99, 156, 181, 191, 206, 215, 222, 229, 234
party-in-government; 30, 145, 178, 194–5
patronage;
  the presidency and; 15, 20, 57–64, 153, 197, 211–14, 220
  role in Jacksonian mode; 43–4, 100
Pendleton Act (1883); 81, 85, 118, 160–1
People's party; 72, 94–6, 178–9, 183, 188–9;
  see also Populists
platforms, party; 3, 23, 84, 154, 161, 171, 233
  and convention procedures; 26, 45
  flexibility of; 50–1, 56–7, 70, 75, 164
Platt, Thomas C.; 116, 120, 213, 215–16, 223, 225, 241
political learning; 12–13, 14, 75, 100–4, 210, 215, 243–4
Polk, James K.; 20, 61–3, 211
Polk, L.L.; 74, 91
Populists; 15, 72, 95–7, 118, 123, 172, 181–2, 186, 188–9; *see also* People's party
presidency; 23–4, 144–54, 165, 171, 182
  constitutional provisions for; 18, 144–5, 151, 167

focus of party competition; 3, 13, 18, 256
Jacksonian mode restraints on; 1, 18–20,
  21, 44, 45, 52, 57–64, 62, 144, 148, 151,
  153, 206
modern presidency; 18, 19–20, 21, 147–54,
  154–5, 221
and the new idea of party; 1, 12, 18–22, 99,
  141, 144, 146, 148, 187, 191–2, 206,
  209, 213, 218, 233
rhetorical presidency; 149–50, 175, 191,
  217, 218–20
presidential candidate speechmaking tours;
  150, 160, 175, 187, 210, 217, 222–3,
  228, 236–7
primaries; 29–30, 32–4, 39, 41–2, 46, 64,
  108
presidential direct primaries; 3, 16, 21–2,
  27, 100, 191, 206, 240–1, 244–5,
  246–51
Progressives; 15, 28, 82, 235, 236, 239, 250
prohibition; 67, 72, 76, 133

Quay, Matthew "Matt" Stanley;
  Republican National Committee chairman;
    64, 112–13, 114, 115, 119–20, 219
  state party leader; 59, 64, 116, 119–20,
    215–17, 223–5, 240
Question Clubs (AISA); 80, 138
Quincy, Josiah; 86, 121, 172

railroads; 9, 69, 149, 228
Randall, Samuel; 164, 169–70, 172
realignment; 25, 27–9
Reed, Thomas B.; 220, 225
Reformist Account; 14–18
regularity; 27, 32–44, 46–7, 198, 244
  undermined by new associations; 80, 84, 94,
    103
  undermined by new idea of party; 99, 124,
    129, 130, 133, 135, 137–8, 154
Reiter, Howard; 48n, 66–7n, 99
Remsen, David; 37, 38
Republican party; 58, 191–234, 218, 234
  and adoption of convention system; 25, 27,
    47, 199
  Liberal Republican faction of; 82–3, 212
  and national committee centralization;
    105–6, 112–13, 142
  and protectionism; 10, 77, 78–9, 218, 230
  and reform of nominating process; 1, 21,
    148, 150, 191, 193–206, 215–16
  regional political base; 58, 94–5, 116–17,
    165, 207, 214–15, 231, 232

republicanism; 4–9, 13, 56
  challenged by new idea of party; 76, 99,
    109, 122, 186, 191, 229
  Jacksonian ideology of; 2, 3
  and localism; 31, 35, 44, 45, 49, 65, 66–8,
    70, 104
  and mistrust of ambition; 48, 52, 70, 144,
    191
  preserved by Jacksonian mode; 25, 26,
    64–5, 73, 97, 235
  and unity; 45, 54–5, 104
Reynolds, John F.; 2, 6, 21–2, 38, 42, 46, 97,
  100, 117, 145, 206
Robertson, David Brian; 19–20
Roosevelt, Franklin D.; 22, 151, 236, 253
  Cleveland's influence on; 155, 159,
    239–40
Roosevelt, Theodore; 13, 248, 250
  on party; 33, 36, 74, 106
  presidency of; 149, 151, 234, 236, 240
Rusk, Jerrold; 108

Sanders, Elizabeth; 88, 89, 90
Schattschneider, E.E.; 244, 252, 255–7
Shefter, Martin; 28, 29, 245
Sherman, John; 102, 121, 201, 204, 207, 219,
  221
Silbey, Joel; 4–5, 12, 23, 26, 28, 32, 35, 45,
  49, 106, 110, 145
silver movement; 95, 181–7, 190, 214, 229
Silver Republicans; 123, 186, 188, 229, 232
Sinclair, Barbara; 252
single-term pledge; 61–3
Skowronek, Stephen; 3, 12, 21n, 57, 64, 149,
  153, 170
Smith, Rogers; 5, 7–8
Stalwart faction; 60, 208, 211–12
still hunt campaign; 56, 111, 235
Storey, Moorefield; 83–6, 88, 90, 99, 100,
  124, 137–8
Swank, James M.; 79
"System of 1896"; 27, 87, 96, 122

Tammany Hall; 56, 101, 121, 162–3, 187,
  245
tariff; 10, 111, 218, 222, 230
  Dingley Tariff Bill (1897); 231
  and interest associations; 77–81
  McKinley Tariff Bill (1890); 173, 177, 219,
    222
  Mills Tariff Bill (1888); 166, 170
  Morrison Tariff Bill (1886); 164
  tariff reform; 154, 163–70, 173, 179